Capitalism and Reli

Modernity whispers: God is dead, all hail to freedom – regulated by the market-place. Global capitalism reconstructs the market as a religion devoted to capital as the universal transcendent. As capitalism intensifies production of symbols of value, and reconstructs practices of thought in the service of symbolic value, is philosophy able to redeem us?

The global ecological crisis has immense philosophical significance: it brings a universal horizon to human thought and experience. A new universal can replace eternal ideas and historical processes as the focus for philosophy. Economic globalization provides another universal limit: **no one need believe in capitalism, yet everyone must participate in it.** Yet participation in global capitalism is at considerable cost to nature and the lives of those deprived of resources raising fundamental questions about the rationality and value of the culture and practices of Western modernity that have produced these universals.

Capitalism and Religion suggests that our attachment to modernity is above all an expression of a piety – developing arguments from Nietzsche and Schelling, Adorno and Horkheimer, Spinoza and Marx, Bergson and Deleuze, it discovers an implicit piety and social function in Western reason: thought is shaped for exchange in a democratic market-place. Under such conditions, how can thought take responsibility for its own ethical practice? **Philip Goodchild's** searing break-down of the philosophy of modernity calls for a rediscovery of absolutes tough enough to withstand capitalism's hyper-flux, yet fluid enough to construct new forms of knowledge and consciousness. Effectively capturing today's zeitgeist, and powerfully attuned to the individual and environmental problems of contemporary globalization, this provocative book reconstructs a space for philosophy of religion within engaged critical thought.

Philip Goodchild lectures in Religious Studies at the University of Nottingham. He is the author of *Gilles Deleuze and the Question of Philosophy* and of *Deleuze and Guattari: An Introduction to the Politics of Desire*, and editor of *Difference in Philosophy of Religion* and *Rethinking Philosophy of Religion*.

Capitalism and Religion
The price of piety

Philip Goodchild

London and New York

First published 2002
by Routledge
11 New Fetter Lane, London EC4P 4EE

Simultaneously published in the USA and Canada
by Routledge
29 West 35th Street, New York, NY 10001

Routledge is an imprint of the Taylor & Francis Group

© 2002 Philip Goodchild

Typeset in Sabon by Taylor & Francis Books Ltd
Printed and bound in Great Britain by The Cromwell Press,
Trowbridge, Wiltshire

All rights reserved. No part of this book may be reprinted
or reproduced or utilized in any form or by any electronic,
mechanical, or other means, now known or hereafter
invented, including photocopying and recording, or in any
information storage or retrieval system, without permission in
writing from the publishers.

British Library Cataloguing in Publication Data
A catalogue record for this book is available from the British Library

Library of Congress Cataloging in Publication Data
A catalogue record for this book has been requested

ISBN 0–415–28223–3 (hbk)
ISBN 0–415–28224–1 (pbk)

The criticism of religion is the premise of all criticism.'

Karl Marx

'Alter the currency!'

Diogenes of Sinope

'UNLESS'

The Lifted Lorax

Contents

Preface   x
Acknowledgements   xvii

Introduction: questioning piety   1
Piety 3
Ethics 5
Reason 7
Summary of the argument 10

PART I
The problem of reason   15

1   **The murder of God**   17
    Nietzsche's critique of reason: life, nature and history 17
    Nietzsche's critique of religion: imaginary causes 21
    Locke and the market: who murdered God? 26

2   **Truth**   43
    Critical theory and structuralism: repetition and exchange 43
    Gospel truth: truth and repetition 51
    Ancient Athens and trade: truth and exchange 57

3   **Price**   70
    Cynical materialism: signs 70
    Spinoza's materialism: immanent critique 73
    Marx's materialism: the commodity form 80
    Bataille and Bourdieu: expenditure and strategy 87

PART II
The problem of ethics   101

4   Freedom   103
    Bergson's ethics: time and association 105
    Schelling's dialectic: time and freedom 109
    Derrida and Kierkegaard: society and freedom 113

5   Value   127
    Capital: the enframing of modern life 127
    Time: the interior of subjectivity 130
    Virulent simulacra 133
    Market value 135

6   Potency   148
    Ethics of transcendence: death 148
    Ethics of immanence: Deleuze 156
    Ethics of potency: the situation of the flesh 163
    Conclusion 169

PART III
The problem of piety   175

7   Piety   177
    Religion and violence 177
    Ritual piety: repetition 181
    Historical piety: difference 186
    Apocalyptic piety: singularity 191

8   Experience   200
    Universal psychosis 200
    Kant's critical philosophy 203
    Scotus and pure ontology 205
    Singularity and disjunction 208
    The matter of suffering 211
    Politics 214

9   **Awakening**   222
    The unthinkable: the potency of thought 222
    Awareness as potency 223
    Dialectic 228
    Unconditioned within experience I: eternal return 230
    Unconditioned within experience II: absolute faith 237
    Unconditioned within experience III: awareness of potency 239
    Conclusion 242

10 **Conclusion**   247
    How we are still pious 248
    An ethics of thinking 250
    Critical piety 251

Index   254

Preface

Then Satan answered the Lord, 'Does Job fear God for nothing?'

(Job 1:9)

A Satanic experiment in philosophy: to explore what is on the basis of what we might get for it. To construct ontology on the basis of the future. A speculative projection, overlooking the rich significance of the eternal, the past, and the present, so as to substitute the bare lines of an imagined possible future. To reread the eternal, the past and the present from this barren perspective, where reading becomes a simple accusation, without moderation or limit. Such a reading, evacuating meaning and measure, leads to an apocalyptic vision of hell itself. Philosophical categories transform themselves into those of religious enthusiasm or even insanity. Yet this delusion speaks a truth about our world: this hell is our hell, concealed within our every moment, while our every tendency rushes headlong towards it. To speak of this hell offends decency; it is oppressive, reductive, destructive. It betrays all fundamental bonds of trust, hope and affirmation, the very piety that makes a meaningful experience of the world possible. Nevertheless, to evade this responsibility is simply to pass the experience of hell on to others. And when, in its history, has philosophy engaged with the radical evil of the future in its socio-historical sense? And where have we fully taken stock of the price of our piety?

In the course of the twenty-first century the average global temperature will rise between one and a half and five and a half degrees. A one and a half degree temperature rise will lead to heat stress in people, livestock and wildlife, the melting of the polar ice caps, permanent flooding of low-lying countries, soil erosion, landslide, decreased water resources, desertification in the tropics, extreme droughts, forest fires, an immense increase in frequency and intensity of wind, storm and flood damage.[1] Uncertainties prevent precise predictions by climate change scientists beyond their area of specialization, but such hesitancy should not lead us to conclude that the consequences may be grave. The results will include destruction of agricultural land, destruction of most animal and plant species, mass migrations, wars, economic collapse and mass starvation. With climate-related disasters increasing fourfold in the past thirty years, it has been estimated[2] that by 2025 two-thirds of the world's population, after a further half a degree rise, some five billion people, will be at risk from floods, storms and water shortages. Being 'at risk' over a period of more than a century involving a rapid acceleration of frequency and intensity of climate-related disasters suggests that such risks will be realized. A one and half degree rise is inevitable. More likely is a three degree temperature rise – which, repeated over another century or two, could render the human race nearly extinct.

The sole cause of this crisis is our modern way of life. The last fifty years have seen massive levels of resource depletion, soil erosion, water extraction, and pollution. The human habitat cannot sustain another repetition of these fifty years. At the same time, economic growth has expanded fivefold, international trade has expanded over twice as fast as this, and foreign direct investment has expanded at two or three times the rate of trade expansion. Ecological and economic projections are radically irreconcilable. For example, if Third World countries experienced an annual rate of economic growth of 4% over the next 60 years – enough to bring them up to current levels of 'prosperity' in the USA – the global environmental impact would increase 16 times. Yet an unchanged rate of environmental impact is unsustainable. At the same time, the global population, which has increased from five to six billion over the last twelve years, could in theory increase to 11 billion. Yet in 1987 it was estimated in the Brundtland Report that perhaps 40% of the world's primary product of photosynthesis is already appropriated for human use. Soon there will be insufficient production for humanity, and even less for other species. There remain perhaps two or three decades in which dramatic and decisive action can reduce the environmental impact of the global economy to a mere series of catastrophes.

At the same time, the last two decades of the second millennium saw the most significant restructuring of the world's political and economic structures since the Industrial Revolution: the intensification of the global economy. The key events were as follows: the abandoning of the gold standard for the dollar in 1971; the deregulation of the world's principal financial markets in London, New York, Tokyo, Frankfurt and Hong Kong during the 1980s; the introduction of electronic communications technology, allowing the instantaneous transfer of information and money around the world; and the ratification of the Uruguay round of the General Agreement on Tariffs and Trade in 1994. The result is the establishment of a global free-market economy, including the establishment of Free Trade Zones in countries where trade is otherwise regulated. This free market lives off its own autonomous processes, which no human institution can control.

The global free market in commodities, manufactured goods, services and finance places governments, multinational companies and small traders in a position of economic competition. In order to survive, competitors must outstrip their rivals in technological advance, in cutting labour costs, and in minimizing associated social and environmental costs. The automatic consequences include: further technological advances leading to oversupply for which new markets must be found; a lowering of wages or loss of jobs to countries where labour is cheap; and deregulation. Such competition endangers and may even condemn the world's remaining ecologically sustainable economic activities. Moreover, increasing global trade leads to the establishing of new markets – converting self-sufficient people into consumers of capital-intensive goods and services. It leads to increasing quantities of agricultural land being used for monocultural export crops, resulting in soil erosion, the depletion of nutrients, increasing extraction of water for irrigation, and a shrinking proportion of fertile land available for rural populations. It leads to increased transportation, resulting in greater consumption of fossil fuels and emission of carbon dioxide. It leads to increased use of fertilizers, pesticides and pollutants. Very soon, many 'developing' countries may consist only of overpopulated cities, export crops, free trade zones and uninhabitable lands. But not for long.

The main obstacles to survival are not technical but political, epitomized by the political impossibility of the necessary 60–80% cut in carbon dioxide emissions. As at the year 2000, the world's most economically developed countries have seen but little of the environmental and economic impact of global free-market capitalism. Political will for change is not yet sufficiently strong. Even when the political will does emerge – as it inevitably will, once the impacts start striking – change will be difficult to achieve. For if one major country – perhaps the USA, or Russia, or China – does not comply with environmental regulation, then it will gain the comparative advantage for the investment of capital. Other countries will have to adapt towards the lowest common denominator in order to remain competitive. Moreover, financial markets severely restrict the freedom to determine policy held by national governments – by threatening capital flight, by imposing interest rates, and by moving to countries which offer the best package of interest rates, deregulation and security. The mobility of finance capital is already leading to a competition among governments to reduce taxes, to deregulate and to reduce welfare provision. This is simply to reduce the sovereign power of government itself: a government which cannot tax, spend and regulate has no further role than to act as a military force to protect business interests. Political will becomes increasingly irrelevant to the global distribution of power.

Given this predicament, it may take a worldwide economic depression of truly catastrophic proportions to save the human race from near extinction. This seems possible for three reasons: first, the increasingly volatile virtual economy of financial assets is growing beyond the point where its crises can be bailed out by national governments; second, as wealth is redistributed from labour to capital there will be an increasing deficit in

consumers, leading to a collapse in trade; third, rising costs of oil production will lead to a global recession; fourth collapsing national economies
will default on loans; and finally, since capital investment receives its value
from a future return, the increasing uncertainty of global environmental
conditions, and the ultimate tendency towards elimination of any future
whatsoever for economic activity, will result in a massive loss of confidence.

In brief, we stand at the threshold of the most significant events in the
history of humanity and the planet. While the destructive effects of the
culture that has led to this predicament have been evident to its victims,
especially women and the colonized, throughout the centuries, the
ecological limit announces for the first time the vulnerability of the
masters themselves. In order to survive the ecological threat, dominant
powers will have to undergo unparalleled transformations of social,
cultural, political, economic and ecological practice and consciousness.
Indeed, for such a conversion to gain sufficient power, religious motives
may have to come into play to replace a system based on greed and
consumption with a new one based on fear, asceticism, care and
generosity. If an economic collapse happens, then unless there is a clear
and viable alternative ready to be adopted, the old destructive patterns
will simply resume once more.

It is within this context that it becomes important to question some of
the most cherished values which coexist in modern Western thought with a
market economy. More of the same may not help: a greater emphasis on
democracy cannot bring sufficient political change in a world that is no
longer subject to government. Within a global market, to describe the
fundamental power relation as domination – of man over nature, of man
over woman, of man over man – is insufficient. Instead, a revaluation of
all values must be undertaken.

This book emerged from the tension between four powerful insights –
insights bringing problems, not solutions. The last insight to arrive was the
contemporary truth of suffering: a growing awareness that current trends
in globalization, trade and the spread of technology are not only leading
towards a condition where the human habitat is unsustainable, but the
urgency and responsibility announced by this preventable catastrophe
mean that little else is worth thinking about. Prior to that, research for this
present work was initiated by the realization that the encompassing framework delimiting the production of thought and values in modern life, and
exerting increasing influence, was simply the impersonal and self-positing
structure of money as the measure of values. As a whole, however, my
work is grounded in an 'idea' – or perhaps I should say an 'experience' –
of what I will call 'God'. This 'idea' was so overwhelming and so distinct
from our customary ways of thinking that, while intelligible in itself, it
remains incommunicable until it has called into question and reformulated
all existing categories of philosophy and theology. Finally, the work of the

revaluation of values which may lead to the cessation of suffering was developed in the form of the 'murder of God' – the actual work of calling into question the fundamental concepts and values of the European tradition.

Each of these insights fractured my self-consciousness, exposing an abyss beneath all my thoughts and relations to myself, to others and to the world. I became a stranger to those closest to me as well as to myself. Each issue imposed itself as a dynamic force on thought, a problem of unlimited importance that I feel barely equipped to begin to address. Moreover, these are not personal but universal and global problems, imposing the responsibility on each person to find an appropriate way of addressing them. In the case of each problem, however, there is only a minority who feel the impact of its force, and those who are concerned with two or more of these problems are much fewer. The public consensus is engaged in a vast enterprise of evasion, sheltering in a wicked and lethal complacency. Yet each of these problems calls to and awakens the others. Anyone who carefully attends to the significance of these issues – and this book is an attempt to communicate their significance – may risk having their world shattered. Thinking is nearly as dangerous as complacency.

Here the result has been the demotion of dominant liberal norms of toleration, liberty and rights, as well as any post-structuralist affirmation of difference, alterity, and locality. Partially valid though such insights are, they do not address the reality of globalization. For even if there is not a sole true religion, a sole normal subjectivity, a sole normative culture, a sole universal history, or a sole universal economy, there remains a sole, global ecology. As Jerry Mander has explained, contemporary consciousness does not help us to understand that overcrowded cities, unusual new weather patterns, growth of global poverty, the lowering of wages while stock prices soar, the elimination of local social services, the destruction of the wilderness, even the disappearance of songbirds – are the products of the same global policies. They are all of one piece, a fabric of connections that are ecological, social and political in nature.[3]

The local and particular history of Western Europe and North America – indeed, because of the distinctive centuries-old English traditions of property ownership, sale of land, and mobile labour which gave rise to the ideology of the free market, the particular history of England and the English colonies – has become a global history in so far as it has unleashed economic and ecological globalization. The horizon that unites us all is the apocalypse – the threat of ecological catastrophe. The fate of my children and potential grandchildren depends on current and future levels of consumption in the USA, just as it does on forestry policies in Indonesia and industrialization in China. The current religious, political, social, economic and philosophical norms are fundamentally inadequate to address such levels of interdependency. In order to defend the local and the particular, a universal consciousness, consisting of new religious, political, economic and philosophical norms, must be constructed along-side local and particular forms of consciousness.

Contributing to the creation of a potentially universal rational, moral and spiritual consciousness – thus following in this one respect in the tradition of Enlightenment philosophy of religion – was the challenge I felt called to address, and readers may observe how small my contribution has been. Indeed, it has taken five years of reflection to arrive at the point where I can make this challenge explicit. If this book simply communicates the urgency of this challenge, then it will have made a contribution. Such a contribution will not be easily achieved. In the process of writing, I have struggled against my own inertia and complacency that have significantly slowed my progress. Every reader may also be mired in complacency, deaf to the screams which echo throughout life, nature and history. Then I request my readers to put aside any sense of vindication achieved by resisting, opposing and refuting my arguments, as well as to put aside any secret satisfaction derived from believing one has attained a privileged perspective by thinking through my arguments, so as to be stimulated to listen to the force of what is most worth thinking about.

The thought that everything may be reduced to a price, a mere quantity – even thinking, even piety – is an obsessive – compulsive vision which has gripped me and has produced the perspective worked out here. The world interpreted through economic eyes is already post-apocalyptic. It is deprived of colour, variety, fecundity, vitality, change and nuance. No, you may protest, this is not our world, this is not our experience, this is not how we think. Good. Let us cry out against economic reductionism. Let us affirm fecundity, vitality, depth. Thus all that I have written is asserted according to the following modality:

> There is this, and also ... (pause) ... there is so much more that escapes my attention at this precise moment, of which I have not spoken, in which I believe, which I find hidden by a blind spot, but which I hope to recollect and see shortly when I come to my senses.

I have not endeavoured to write about this world. I have written about something outside, something future – a menace, a nightmare – but one that rapidly encroaches upon this world, that fills its interstices, that mediates its relations. I have written of the universal solvent that flows across our surfaces, into our pores, our gaps, our distances, our hesitations and intervals. I have written about the power that has no time or place of its own, but remains forever to come – and yet its gravity is real and absolute. I have directed my attention towards the fires of hell itself – which are only a few degrees hotter than our world.

All this is merely to set the context within which I began to think. The subject matter of this book is simply philosophy of religion and critical theory. Within the reductionist world of shadows that follows, I hope that you may find a stray splash of colour, an echo of redemption, or the first shoots of spring. Within the vulgar economism of a conceptual system whose elements appear as crude and inanimate as juxtaposed boulders, it might be possible to glimpse the sparkle, produced by friction, reflection, or refraction, of something unspeakable and invaluable. For even in the world of shadows, the sun, albeit invisible, has never ceased to shine.

Philip Goodchild
Nottingham
December 2000

Notes

1 James J. McCarthy *et al.* (eds), *Report of Working Group II of the Intergovernmental Panel on Climate Change, Climate Change 2001: Impacts, Adaptation and Vulnerability, Summary for Policymakers*, Cambridge: Cambridge University Press, 2001.
2 An estimate derived from: Jonathan Walter and Peter Walker (eds), *1999 World Disasters Report*, Geneva: International Federation of the Red Cross, together with a Worldwatch Newsbrief.
3 Jerry Mander, 'Facing the Rising Tide', in J. Mander and Edward Goldsmith (eds), *The Case Against the Global Economy and for a Turn Toward the Local*, San Francisco: Sierra Club Books, 1996. In addition to the full, authoritative and technical studies of the Intergovernmental Panel on Climate Change, *Climate Change 2001*, 3 vols, Cambridge: Cambridge University Press, 2001, other useful books which point in varying degrees to the coming crises are John Houghton, *Climate Change: the Complete Briefing*, Cambridge: Cambridge University Press, 1996; William Greider, *One World, Ready or Not: the Manic Logic of Global Capitalism*, New York: Simon & Schuster, 1997; John Gray, *False Dawn: the Delusions of Global Capitalism*, New York: New York Press, 1998; Roger Burbach, Orlando Núñez and Boris Kagarlitsky, *Globalization and its Discontents: the Rise of Postmodern Socialisms*, London: Pluto Press, 1997; Donella H. Meadows, Dennis L. Meadows and Jørgen Randers, *Beyond the Limits: Global Collapse or a Sustainable Future*, London: Earthscan, 1992; and Maria Mies and Vandana Shiva, *Ecofeminism*, London: Zed Books, 1993.

Acknowledgments

Some paragraphs of this book have been previously published in the following articles:

Spirit of Philosophy: Derrida and Deluze – *Angelaki* 5:2, August 2000, pp. 43–57.

Money, gift and Sacrifice: Thirteen Short Episodes in the Pricing of Thought – *Angelaki* 4:3, December 1999, pp. 25–39.

Deleuzean Ethics – *Theory, Culture and Society* 14:2, May 1997, pp. 39–50.

Time and Evaluation – *Antithesis* 8:2, May 1997, pp. 35–54.

I gratefully acknowledge permission to reprint from each of these sources.

Introduction
Questioning piety

Does God exist? Yes or no?

What reasons can be found to support an answer?

The search for reasons is not the same as finding them, for the stately progress of argument from reasons to conclusions is performed on the neutral stage of the public sphere, where an argument carries by its force, its persuasiveness, its necessity; but the search for reasons is a practice, a rehearsal conducted in private, away from the interrogatory glare of public examination. Such a search may draw on all available resources: customs, techniques, traditions, inventiveness, discipline, morality. It may express material interests, or the interests of class, gender, race and 'creed'. It may even be conducted with piety or impiety: one positions oneself in relation to the existence of God before attempting to find one's reasons. Leszek Kolakowski explained the implications of this choice:

> Once taken, any choice imposes criteria of judgement which infallibly support it in a circular logic: if there is no God, empirical criteria alone have to guide our thinking, and empirical criteria do not lead to God; if God exists, he gives us clues about how to perceive his hand in the course of events, and with the help of those clues we recognize the divine sense of whatever happens.[1]

At least, it would seem that once a philosophy of religion has found its reasons, then such reasons may speak for themselves, and any prior rehearsals and decisions can be safely forgotten. Indeed, it is necessary that such rehearsals and decisions should not speak lest they compromise the neutrality, the necessity, the persuasiveness of the arguments themselves: it is to commit the fallacy of *petitio principii* to repeat conclusions in premisses. Then the paths of logical deduction and rational inference are eternal: they are absolved of subservience to temporal experience, historical context or material interests.

But does reason exist in eternity? Yes or no?

What reasons can be found to support an answer?

The search for reasons is not the same as finding them. Such a search may draw on all available resources: customs, techniques, traditions, inventiveness, discipline, morality. It may express material interests, or the interests of class, gender, race, and 'creed'. It may even be conducted with piety or impiety: one positions oneself in relation to the eternal truth of reason before attempting to find one's reasons. Once taken, any choice imposes criteria of judgement which infallibly support it in a circular logic: if reason is not eternal or neutral, then empirical criteria may guide and shape our thinking, and all reason seems historically conditioned; if reason is eternal, then it will manifest its eternal truths in our actual thinking – paradigmatically, in geometry.

Such a decision has divided the discipline of philosophy for perhaps two centuries. Exemplifying opposing poles, analytic philosophy of religion theorizes an eternal God through an eternal reason, while the Frankfurt school of critical theory historicizes reason itself. Each has criteria of judgement which infallibly support it in a circular logic.

Now, is this 'circular logic' necessary? Yes or no?[2]

What reasons can be found to support an answer? What is the nature of repetition?

In practice, there is an asymmetry here: when God is believed in, then God functions as the ultimate presupposition from which to make sense of the world, the withdrawn guarantee of revelation, morality and truth, the centre around which all circular reasoning turns, the eternal source of time, the unquestionable source of all questions. Even if one does not call this 'God', something may still play out such roles. Circular logic belongs to the eternal perspective, where time and all that is temporal are regarded as moving images of eternity and that which is eternal.[3] When no such 'God' is believed in, then the course of time itself may seem to produce effects of eternal identity, truth and value through repetition: God becomes a simulacrum, a surface effect.

How does one move from an eternal to a temporal perspective, or vice versa? Any transition between perspectives escapes the rational thought of both theism and atheism; it is neither temporal nor eternal. There is thus a vast difference between the opinion that God does not exist, and the way of thinking that results from abandoning appeals to an eternal truth or foundation of reason. In the modern world, it is possible for the theist and the atheist to live similar lives in a world of common sense which functions pragmatically as though there are eternal truths. Secular reason maintains an eternal logic. A whole web of concepts and values structure a common existence, such as liberty, reason, progress, toleration, wealth, law, contract, right, information, energy, space and time. The repetition of such concepts and values in a circular reasoning constitutes the liturgy of common sense: modern thought is maintained by piety. If, by contrast, one abandons circular reasoning, whether from atheistic or pious motives, then the world immediately becomes chaotic:

one falls into a nightmare where there are no certainties, where even logic produces odd effects, where everything looks strange, where common sense seems most fragile. This traumatic event in human reason has been expressed, for better or worse, in the symbol of the 'murder of God'. It is a crisis for human piety – both the piety of tradition and of modernity. And philosophy of religion has no higher task than to question dominant pieties.

Piety

What does piety want? Eternal bliss? Temporal blessing?

The discourse of piety often praises disinterested piety – one may cite the Buddhist goal of the 'cessation of craving,' the duty recommended in the Bhagavadgītā of 'acting without regard to the fruit', the Protestant end of 'praising God and glorifying him for ever'. Each of these repudiates temporal blessing in order to attain a condition beyond time. Yet does piety merely substitute eternal interests for material ones?

In an effort to avoid such a predicament, Immanuel Kant divided religions into those which are 'endeavours to win favour' ('mere cult') and 'moral religions' (religions of 'good life-conduct').[4] Moral religions, for Kant, are disinterested: they serve ends which are not delimited to a particular individual or group. Sacrificing all claims to religious knowledge, all supernatural security, in 'moral religion' one's salvation depends entirely on the integrity and disinterestedness of one's conduct. This is the Protestant ethic of capitalism:

> But in the moral religion (and of all public religions which have ever existed, the Christian alone is moral) it is a basic principle that each must do as much as lies in his power to become a better man, and that only when he has not buried his inborn talent (Luke XIX, 12–16) but has made use of his original predisposition to good in order to become a better man, can he hope that what is not within his power will be supplied from above.[5]

This Protestant conception of grace is refashioned as the mere reward of an ethical character, not as a promise of eternal bliss. Yet here one is still rewarded by becoming a 'better man': a surplus value accrues to the fruits of one's ethical labours. Piety becomes a capitalist.

Piety may be suspected of conforming to the structure of reward. Thus Friedrich Nietzsche once wrote:

> The most general formula at the basis of every religion and morality is: 'Do this and this, refrain from this and this – and you will be happy! Otherwise ...' Every morality, every religion *is* this imperative.[6]

In each case, whether we are concerned with eudaemonistic ethics or not, the *reasons* linking conduct to the future state would need to be spelt out in order to make such a religion or morality credible. In religion, however, one cannot normally see such reasons, one can only hope or believe. Piety is directed towards a transcendent source of blessing. For in so far as religion is that which, in the words of Marcel Gauchet, 'organizes our relation to reality, and makes humanity's detour through the invisible the pivot of its activity,'[7] then it functions as a transcendent mediation between 'cause' and 'consequence', between conduct and happiness. In so far as there is an 'excess' in the effect over the cause, that is to say, in so far as the reasons linking the cause to its effect are not entirely transparent, then there is a measure of 'grace' in the value added to the fruits of labour. Such grace becomes most explicit in Christianity. As Nietzsche pointed out:

> 'For if ye love them which love you, *what reward have ye?* do not even the publicans do the same? And if ye salute your brethren only what do ye *more than others?* do not even publicans do so?' (Matthew v, 46–7) – Principle of 'Christian love': it wants to be well *paid.*[8]

Piety may thus be suspected of serving self-interest.[9]

Is piety always interested? Yes or no?

One may defend the honour and integrity of 'true' piety, claiming that, while initially motivated by interests, piety attains a place beyond craving. Such a defence expresses a piety in respect of piety; moreover, such a defence reveals an interest, an investment in the integrity of piety itself. The defenders of piety seek a reward from piety itself. For if piety, the honouring of the transcendent, is placed under suspicion and dishonoured then it will be impossible to be pious, to honour the transcendent, without bringing shame upon oneself. That which must be defended and preserved reveals, by this very token, that it is contingent and provisional – that it is not grounded in an eternal circuit of exchange between human faith and divine grace. Thus those who defend 'religion', or a religion, or theology, or God, risk demonstrating their impiety through such defensiveness.

Finally, one may hope to avoid the dilemmas of piety by cutting out the transcendent pivot mediating causes to effects through the modern strategy of invoking a 'principle of sufficient reason': every effect has its reasons, even if we do not yet know what such reasons might be. For Gottfried Leibniz, this 'principle of sufficient reason' was a strategy of theodicy: there can only be a justification for the order of the world if there is a reason for everything. Each event follows others on the basis of necessity. Here we meet piety before the principle of sufficient reason: can it save us from the chaotic abyss of unreason? One must enquire after the value of the principle itself: for whom is the principle of sufficient reason valuable? What interests does it serve? Are such reasons eternal or temporal?

Such questions raise doubts about the integrity of God, of piety, and of reason itself. The slightest innuendo, the slightest suspicion, the slightest slur on the honour of these, and one is left with a choice. One may follow the path of theodicy, claiming an absolute knowledge of God, value, and reason, in order to defend them. Yet such defensiveness betrays its own anxiety, its bad conscience, its lack of confidence in the God which it must convert into an absolute. The alternative is to allow free rein to anxiety, to push doubts to the limit, to put the issue to the test. If the philosopher dares to question piety – now understood as any determinate practice of directing attention – by asking, 'What is ultimately worthy of honour, belief, desire, thought, value, trust, enjoyment, and worship?', then all criteria are at risk. Living through the experience of the murder of God, one abandons judgements based on the eternal progress of reason, in favour of judgements based within experience – not experience in general, but the experience of thinking through the murder of God.

Ethics

What is worthy of honour? What is worthy of worship, gifts, offerings, sacrifices, thought and desire? Supposing we find an answer to these questions, a transcendent instance, then what is it about such a transcendent instance that renders it worthy of honour? What is good about goodness, beautiful about beauty, just about justice, or unique about unity? In short, what is transcendent about transcendence? Answers to such questions invoke the eternal. The questions themselves, however, merely lead into vicious circles of reflexive self-questioning. They undermine all values and grounds. While they have often evoked a regression to the primordial, the originary, the foundational, or the a priori, such a regression is dependent on a paradox.[10] For regression is a progress in thought, following a particular direction; one cannot then say whether the goal determines the path, or the path determines the goal. Which comes first, the temporal or the eternal? For example, St Thomas' arguments for the existence of God encounter God as a limit of a process – a prime mover, a first cause, a necessary being, a supreme good, an intelligent creator. They depend on notions of priority, motion, causality, contingency, value and design; if one started out with different notions, one would attain a different goal. The goal itself is only recognized as such by an admission that one already had it: 'And this everyone understands to be God.'[11] One only confirms the belief with which one began. In such a case, both progress and regress are artificial; one encloses thought within a defensive circle where it is impervious to attacks from outside, and oblivious of the interests it defends. No transcendence would appear to take place.

The repetition in advance of conclusions in presuppositions is the ideological circle that seems to block progress in thought. It is self-authenticating, and obviates the need for consideration of concrete sources that have given rise to presuppositions. Nevertheless, such ideological strategies would not be effective if they left everything unchanged. They have a temporal significance: like a repetitive religious ritual, such ideological strategies render honour to the object of their presuppositions. There is always an excess which escapes the most vicious of circles, a difference to be extracted from repetition in the course of time. Honour accumulates, beliefs are confirmed, expectations are increased, identities are solidified, and time passes on. The irreversible passage of time situates transcendence in the present over the past. Transcendence is therefore unavoidable; what remains in question is the degree to which transcendence incorporates piety, righteousness and wisdom within itself. Does the passage of time bring any 'progress', any intensification, any understanding?

Mechanical repetition, the behaviour of clocks and the scientific understanding of time express a minimal degree of intensification. All too often, in modern reason, such repetition has been taken as the paradigm of certainty and knowledge: a result is true if it is repeatable. In this presupposition, modern reason eliminates access to piety, righteousness and wisdom from thought at a stroke. Thus modern reason turns into a purely critical theory. The avoidance of the question of transcendence, however, is an avoidance of thought. One significant example of the way in which honour is shown is the gift of spending time. One shows value, respect, concern or interest in something or someone by spending time on it or with them. Unlike other resources, however, we have no freedom to preserve the expenditure of time. Time may be saved only by intensifying expenditure elsewhere. The flow of time forces us to pay our respects – it is a currency that cannot be hoarded but only traded. If we do not choose how we will spend our time, then its expenditure will be determined for us by duty, custom, habit or distraction. A renunciation of all honouring, all choice of where one spends one's time, is an acceptance of the values imposed by external powers. It is an acquiescence in the existing distribution of values, and an honouring of such values. To the extent that the future encloses possibilities, and thought is able to select among these possibilities, then honour is shown. The question of transcendence is laid upon all free creatures constrained by the flow of time. To be temporal and free is to be pious.

Time does not only constrain the distribution of values. Not only does time pass, not only are we given time, but the events and possibilities that come with time are also given to us. Life pays us its respects with its gifts. Similarly, at many times in the history of religion, the answer to the problem of transcendence is apparently given by revelation: that which is to be honoured, or how time should be spent, is authoritatively given. Calendars are divided into festivals; days are regulated by times of prayer; ethical responsibilities and duties are urged; ritual performances that repeat the foundational events of revelation are prescribed. Even here the problem of transcendence remains, for if the honourable, the revealed, or the divine are given in a specific temporal form, we are left with the problem of knowing what is honourable, revealed, or divine about such forms. Then the slightest slur, doubt, suspicion, or innuendo will be sufficient to demand that revelation should no longer be simply honoured for its revealed status, but that revelation should be supplemented by a revelation of the meaning of revelation, and the revelation that revelation is revelation.[12]

Piety is inevitable, in so far as we exist in time. In so far as the future is not fully determined – its gifts have not yet been revealed, its choices have not yet been taken – then the future of piety is contingent. Piety does not contain its future in the same way that a sufficient cause contains its effects; there is thus an invisible pivot that mediates between present piety and its future character. Piety is essentially directed towards the transcendent, where the transcendent, like Kant's grace, is that which pays piety its own future. There remains an unbridgeable chasm of radical contingency between piety and its divinity. Yet how should piety actually be piety before its divinity if it does not endeavour to make contact with that divinity: if not to know it, at least to honour it, to offer it gifts, to offer it time, to offer it the future which the divinity itself will endow? This is the ultimate paradox of piety: to wish to honour something which is beyond honour.[13] Then the offence of a piety that claims to identify its divinity, whether through ascending to heaven, or by the divinity descending to earth, is that it abolishes the temporal existence of piety, and, with it, piety itself. For piety is essentially contingent and temporal in so far as it consists in a love exceeding knowledge, a free act beyond necessity. The offence of identifying divinity is that it reduces piety to reason.

Nevertheless, piety continues to exist through time, and receives its own future. In so doing, it gives a body to the gifts of its divinity. Even if the identity of the transcendent is not given in time, its sense and value are implied in the progress of piety. Far from assuming that there is one divinity who gives the same sense and value to all, here it would appear that there are many modes of piety, their senses and values shaped in multiple ways. The critical assessment of such senses and values is the task of a philosophy of religion fashioned as a critical theory of piety.

Reason

What is thinking? What kind of thinking is most worthy of honour? What kind of thinking demands that we offer our time for thinking it? In the twentieth century, the European tradition of reason suffered a slight on its honour by virtue of its being implicated in a variety of apocalyptic realities: from the mass-destructions of Nazism and Stalinism to the threat of nuclear destruction and the promise of ecological catastrophe; from the destitution produced in the two-thirds of the world constituting the 'margins' of global capitalism to the deprivation produced by official UN sanctions; from the implicit discrimination against minor groups to the cultivated normalization of human thought and experience through the media, information technology and management accountancy. The nature of the complicity of European reason with these realities can only be established by considerable thought. Once entertained as a suspicion, however, one can no longer trust that European reason, lacking an impartial prosecution, defence, judge and jury, will be able to vindicate itself from charges of assistance with the crime. As Manfred Frank expressed it, 'today it is rationality, as well as the whole of philosophy, that together have to face an imaginary court that demands of them a justification for their existence.'[14]

What is the price of our piety before contemporary European culture and reason? There is no other cause for the coming global ecological catastrophe than such piety – expressed in industrial development and the global market. Then attempts to mitigate the effects of the coming catastrophe through the resources of European culture and reason may risk producing further disaster in so far as this tradition fails to recognize and respond to external powers. The magnitude of the coming catastrophe entreats us to explore such suspicions with the utmost gravity and urgency: we must put contemporary piety to the test.

Critical theory explores the suspicion that enlightened reason may itself be the 'wholesale deception of the masses.'[15] Theodor Adorno and Max Horkheimer, in *Dialectic of Enlightenment*, first published at a time of extreme pessimism of 1944, brought the self-critique on the part of European reason to a new prominence.[16] Just as religious superstition is explained in modernity as a product of fear before the powers of nature, Enlightenment reason is exposed as an attempt to remove that fear by gaining mastery over it, or at least symbolic mastery, so that there is no longer anything unknown. They diagnosed the motive of Enlightenment reason as 'mythic fear turned radical',[17] its essence as domination, and its method as abstraction and systematization. It takes upon itself the impersonal and inscrutable role that fate held for mythical thinking, for it subsumes all particulars under universal principles, including human existence as such, which becomes dominated by the industrial system. Since all substantial goals are exposed as the power of nature over the mind, reason becomes purely formal, unable to posit credible moral values. It thus has no moral or purposive content, and can be utilized by dominant powers and their natural interests. Morality is abandoned, and with it reason's powers of self-criticism are abrogated in scepticism, so that the existing order may be reproduced. Reason becomes objectified in the instruments of domination which it produces – language, weapons and machines – with the result that human nature itself is commodified, and people are homogenized through the culture industry as 'mere species beings, exactly like one another through isolation in the forcibly united collectivity.'[18]

The failure of the emancipatory intentions of Western thought indicates that human life and thought, as in the ages of superstition, is still determined by forces that lie beyond conscious, rational control. This collective loss of faith can be characterized as a loss of transcendence: one no longer claims access to some external reality that will guarantee the truthful or successful operation of human reason. Reality as such, the shared source of facts, meanings and values, is unconscious. There is no access to the traditional philosophical virtues of wisdom and truthfulness. The theological predicament of the 'death of God' or 'loss of transcendence' is a predicament of the European tradition of reason as a whole. Its integrity, piety and truth under suspicion, beset by terrible catastrophes that impeach its character, reason must again humbly enquire after a mode of thinking that really is a quest for wisdom. The vital question is, 'What is philosophy?'

Furthermore, we may ask: to whom is philosophy addressed? With the loss of faith in the European tradition of reason, with its aspirations for a universal and public form of knowledge, there is no longer any public standard of rationality by which the offerings of philosophy can be judged. The crisis in the Western tradition, with its suspicions cast upon God, man, truth and wisdom, is also a crisis in the conception of the rational public to whom reason is addressed. Indeed, there is no longer a 'public sphere'; there is no longer 'rationality' as such. In practice, there is only a plurality of incompatible cultures, social structures, rationalities, moralities and beliefs. The thinker, confronted by the observed plurality of ways of living and thinking, confronted by the evidence that historical, cultural, social, economic and psychological factors shape thought, confronted by the shaping and bounding of thought by each particular language, and confronted by ethical suspicions of the complicity of reason with domination and devastation, must reckon not only with the loss of his or her own integrity in the public court of reason and justice, but with the loss of integrity of the public court presumed to be able to judge standards of reason and justice.[19]

This is the challenge to religion, value and reason, and the complicity with which each has been used to legitimate the others. When suspicions are raised about all three of these together, lacking the foundational presuppositions of religion, value and reason, the only procedure for inquiry is immanent critique. This is a creative rereading of the philosophical tradition, drawing out the dominant pieties, reasons and processes that determine our present age, and reorienting them in a new direction. As a constructivist, dynamic, self-transformative and non-teleological method, immanent critique has no fixed origins, presuppositions, method or direction. It can only construct itself in its very practice – and its meaning can only be given by its practice as a whole. The inquiry which follows is a questioning of reason, value and religion, and a quest for truth, ethics and piety. Since these are discovered to be implicated within the operation of thought itself, much more will be implied than can be explicitly stated. For the sake of orientation of the reader, however, it is possible to lay out the skeleton of an argument.

Summary of the argument

Part I explores some of the implicit practices which accompany reason in so far as they relate to the dominant contemporary global piety. It is not intended to replace recent post-structuralist and feminist critiques of modern reason, but to add a further dimension.

Chapter 1: The Murder of God argues that the murder of God, as announced by Nietzsche, is the simultaneous collapse of all eternal certainties regarding religion, morality and reason. Thought is produced by the temporal processes of life, nature and history. Any isolation of entities or concepts through language, or any elevation of a free will capable of weighing alternative courses of action is merely an abstraction of imaginary causes from reality. Yet in order to explain the 'murder of God' as the emergence of a secular worldview, an alternative organizing principle for social relations and values must be in place which rendered the old God superfluous. This principle is identified as the self-regulating market, which became capable of indefinite expansion when reliable paper currency was first issued in the eighteenth century by a state bank, its value being guaranteed by future taxation. This event was preceded by the development of the ideology of the modern state, expressed through the philosophy of John Locke, which is founded on concepts of God, right and liberty: they describe participation in a free market, without giving power. Since money accumulates power, it progressively enslaves stakeholders in the market through debt. Usurping God, right and liberty, money becomes a despot.

Chapter 2: Truth, explores how in modern thought truth is identified through repetition and exchange. Knowledge is commodified: the mode of representation is identified as the very form of truth itself. Adorno and Horkheimer identified this principle of representation as repetition, the principle of myth. Similarly, structuralism shows us that where there is a determinate system of exchange, then in so far as a signifier precedes a signified by its exchangeability, it signifies transcendence. Then piety will remain embedded in the structures of modern thought, just as a determinate social practice is implicit in the practice of constituting truth. The practice of repetition adopted in the modern constitution of truth derives from the uses of repetition in the credal formulation of truth particular to Christianity. By intensifying piety before the absolute sovereignty of God, Christianity shaped religious truth as metaphysical, universal, eternal, spiritual and written. Christianity adapted such a model of truth from ancient Greece, where it was formed in a society organized for commodity exchange. Then the constitution of truth through exchange reproduces the social relations of the market. Modern reason carries with it an implicit social practice and an implicit piety which are embedded in its structure and repeated in its practice.

Chapter 3: Price, argues that the material relations in which thought is embedded are as significant for an understanding of its 'logic' as its own ideals. When thought is composed of signs exchanged for a universal equivalent, it acquires a price. Benedict de Spinoza invented an immanent critique of reason, morality and religion which discovers ideal relations through experience of material relations. Such relations are expressed through common emotions, or, when related to material objects, through exchange. Karl Marx, in his analysis of the commodity form, developed an elementary logic of exchange that describes the progressive substitution of symbols for a universal equivalent. Then the tradition of European reason is defined by a progressive movement of centralization and capitalization upon a universal equivalent. Marx's analysis is partial, however, for he excludes the dimensions of honour, uncertainty and strategy that coexist with any material exchange in practice; there are no purely material events. To redeem thought from its subordination to a price it is necessary to place it back within the context of the ethical relations and the piety that accompany it. The fundamental inadequacies of modern European reason are its poor ethical practice and its improperly directed piety.

Part II explores the problem of making thought ethical.

Chapter 4: Freedom explores how the temporal nature of thought, as outlined by Henri Bergson and Friedrich Schelling, affords it the possibility of taking responsibility for its own temporal process and social practice. Freedom, thought of in terms of time rather than space, is a social synthesis which must be constructed, rather than a dialectical negation of dominating powers. Binding past and future in the present, freedom is no longer driven by modern concepts of contradiction and self-overcoming. Such freedom, as a synthesis of time, is always mediated by an object, a gift, or an exchange. This presents a danger and an opportunity: freedom of thought may be captured by economic obligation, according to the logic of the gift explained by Jacques Derrida, or else it may sacrifice itself in order to communicate and renew itself, according to the logic of subjective thinking explained by Søren Kierkegaard. Freedom of thought involves abandoning claims to possess truth and value, so that the sense and value immanent within thought may become evident.

Chapter 5: Value, explores the dangers that arise when ethics is captured by economics: a purely external quantification, money, seizes control of the production of value. For money has a self-positing structure, being both a measure of values and the measure of evaluations. In order to coordinate heterogeneous evaluations, valuing money as a general equivalent takes priority, for it gives value to scales of value. Time may also be understood according to such a self-positing structure as the interior of human subjectivity, limiting freedom by the need to save time. Such conceptions of time and money are virulent simulacra which become transcendent sources of meaning and value, embracing each other as the highest form of objectivity and the deepest form of subjectivity. In practice, then, the market becomes the general condition of contemporary economy. In a free market, there is a fundamental class difference between those who trade to meet subsistence needs and those who trade to profit.

The imbalance of power between these two roles leads to a progressive shift of wealth towards speculation, and a failure to meet subsistence needs. The extraction of surplus value effected by the market is not simply an extraction of objects of evaluations, such as wealth, labour and land, but an extraction of socially sanctioned attention. Attention is increasingly directed to expectations about the future rather than the realities of the present.

Chapter 6: Potency, explores how the freedom and power to direct attention can be acquired. The global market and modern thought derive both their power and their ultimate orientation to value, from the threat of death. Yet death is never experienced: it is understood in terms of time, while time is understood in terms of death. Both modern materialism and traditional religious practices express a piety before death. One may escape both modern suspicion and traditional credulity by constituting an ethics of immanence to replace an ethics of transcendence grounded in death. Deleuze's immanent ethics replace representations within consciousness by unconscious desire, constituted by a way of expressing the effect of the external world on the individual. The ethos of a society is constituted by its mutual interrelations, and this ethos is expressed in desire. Yet immanent ethics are incomplete without invoking a life, a potency in the flesh which is also an explosion of knowledge. This potency is felt above all in the shaping of attention by trauma: death simply matters.

Part III explores a critical theory of piety.

Chapter 7: Piety, explores how the potency manifested in piety, especially as a fear of death, may lead to violence. Both modern thought and traditional religious practice are constituted by practices of repetition and difference that themselves produce concepts of the eternal and the historical. Both such practices, because they ward off the potency that affects and drives them, can manifest their energy in the actual violence of exclusion. There is a third kind of piety, a singular experience, where the power of chaos is experienced directly. Such singularities are exceptional, and must necessarily be excluded in practice from consensus reality. Such exclusion gives them a dual privilege: they are no longer bound by collective illusions, while they experience directly the exclusive violence of the consensus.

Chapter 8: Experience, constructs a critical framework for understanding the absolute in experience, rather than in terms of essence or existence. Although there are now universal limits to human experience, the fragmentation of contemporary consciousness leads it to focus on local absolutes, in a general psychosis. To escape the pretensions of absolute truth, whether found in religious experience or contemporary consciousness, it is necessary to separate ideas from their objects and objective conditions, so as to examine them on a plane of pure thought. The essence of an idea is the power which it implicates, but which remains too great for it. This essence is encapsulated in a concept of 'experience' understood as an event of thinking where thought is born from a power which exceeds it. The first potency of this concept of experience is manifest in suffering: suffering matters. The second potency of experience is the power to direct attention. Thought is experienced in the relations between these potencies; such relations do not express the necessity of logic, or the freedom of the will, for they are political relations. A politics of thought is inseparable from politics in general. Yet modern politics has been hindered by not treating the directing of attention as a political issue. Politics has been hampered by its neglect of piety.

Chapter 9: Awakening, explores how thinking can be transformed so that it can become capable of awareness of the potencies which drive it. Such potencies are normally unthinkable, because the pieties from which thought is constructed are also defences and shields against the absolute. Yet there is evidence of a third potency, an awareness that drives thought while exceeding thought. If piety is intensified to the point of its own auto-critique, following a method of immanent critique derived from Spinoza, then the thought of the absolute may become possible once more. Three experiences of thinking are considered: the experience of thinking the eternal return, which intensifies repetition; the experience of thinking absolute faith, which intensifies difference; and the experience of indicating, dramatizing and individuating the potency of thought. Although such thoughts themselves do not hold absolute truth, goodness, or awareness, they reveal the potency of truth, goodness and awareness which it is customary to call 'God'. Such a concept of God is created within the categories of experience, rather than those of essence or existence: the experienced, the unconditioned, the matter, the singular, the infinite, the intense, the compelling and the unthinkable are all dramatized in a singular experience. Such an experience has the power to direct attention, not to itself, but to that which matters. For if the essential failure of contemporary thought is misdirected attention, philosophy can only restore a true thinking by directing attention to that which matters.

Notes

1 Leszek Kolakowski, *Religion*, Oxford: Oxford University Press, 1982, p. 202.
2 John Stuart Mill, following Sextus Empiricus, argued that all deductive arguments commit the fallacy of *petitio principii*: in the argument that all men are mortal, Socrates is a man, therefore Socrates is mortal, one could only know that all men are mortal if Socrates is known to be mortal (see J.S. Mill, *A System of Logic, Ratiocinative and Inductive* Book II, ch. 3, 2 (London: Longman, 1970, p. 120). The pragmatic solution which acknowledges that we do acquire knowledge through deductive arguments admits temporality into reason: given a premiss at a particular time, then the conclusion follows.
3 Plato's *Timaeus* is the classical source for the connection between truth, being, and a circular movement, as against opinion, becoming and change. See Plato, *Timaeus*, 27c–29b, in *The Collected Dialogues of Plato*, Princeton: Princeton University Press, 1961, 1161–2.

4 Immanuel Kant, *Religion within the Limits of Reason Alone*, New York: Harper & Row, 1960, p. 47.
5 Kant, *Religion within the Limits of Reason Alone*, p. 47.
6 Friedrich Nietzsche, *Twilight of the Idols*, 'The Four Great Errors,' 2, London: Penguin, 1990, p. 57.
7 Marcel Gauchet, *The Disenchantment of the World: a Political History of Religion*, Princeton: Princeton University Press, 1997, p. 21.
8 Nietzsche, *The Anti-Christ* 45, London: Penguin, 1990, p. 170.
9 This suspicion that piety has a price first appears in the form of Satan's accusation against Job, who is presented as the paradigm of human piety, righteousness and wisdom: 'Does Job fear God for nothing? ... You have blessed the work of his hand, and his possessions have increased in the land.' Job 1:9–10. All biblical quotations are taken from the *New Revised Standard Version*, Glasgow: Collins, 1989.
10 This well-known paradox is explored by Søren Kierkegaard's pseudonymous author, Johannes Climacus, in *Philosophical Fragments*, Princeton: Princeton University Press, 1962, and *Concluding Unscientific Postscript*, Princeton: Princeton University Press, 1968.
11 Thomas Aquinas, *Summa Theologiae* I, question 2, article 3, London: Eyre and Spottiswoode, 1964, Volume 2, pp. 12–17.
12 Pseudo-Dionysius was among the first to formulate this problem of revelation within the Christian tradition: 'The transcendent has put aside its own hiddenness and has revealed itself to us by becoming a human being. But he is hidden even after this revelation, or, if I may speak in a more divine fashion, is hidden even amid the revelation. For this mystery of Jesus remains hidden and can be drawn out by no word or mind. What is to be said of it remains unsayable; what is to be understood of it remains unknowable.' Pseudo-Dionysius, 'Epistle 3', in *The Complete Works*, New York: Paulist Press, Classics of Western Spirituality Series, 1987, p. 264.
13 Cf. Johannes Climacus' ultimate paradox of thought: 'to want to discover something that thought itself cannot think.' SøKierkegaard, *Philosophical Fragments*, p. 37.
14 Manfred Frank, 'Two Centuries of Philosophical Critique of Reason', in Dieter Freundlieb and Wayne Hudson (eds), *Reason and Its Other: Rationality in Modern German Philosophy and Culture*, Providence: Berg, 1993, p. 68.
15 Theodor W. Adorno and Max Horkheimer, *Dialectic of Enlightenment*, London: Verso, 1997, p. 42.
16 This self-critique of reason, by which reason points to something beyond reason as its ground and basis, may be traced back to Schelling, to the Romantics, and perhaps even to Kant. All critical thought working within this tradition may therefore be referred under the broad name of 'critical theory'. Such thinking only takes on an apocalyptic force, however, in the work of Nietzsche, and, to perhaps a lesser extent, in his French successors.
17 Adorno and Horkheimer, *Dialectic of Enlightenment*, p. 16.
18 Adorno and Horkheimer, *Dialectic of Enlightenment*, p. 36.
19 One can, of course, attempt to defend and reconstitute a purified public sphere, liberated from the interests of particular groups and perspectives. Once doubt is cast upon the integrity of such a project, however, one may either perform the self-contradictory and self-defeating task of dogmatically defending the public sphere, or one may return to the question of philosophy.

Part I
The problem of reason

1 The murder of God

Nietzsche's critique of reason

Life, nature and history

The case for the prosecution against religion, morality and reason in the European tradition has been made pre-eminently by Nietzsche. His decision already taken, Nietzsche paid little attention to arguments against the existence of God. As is often remarked, the concern of Nietzsche's madman, who, like Diogenes the Cynic in search of man, runs into the market-place with a lit lantern in the bright morning hours crying, 'I seek God! I seek God!' is not to announce the death of God, for this has already been accepted. It is to announce the murder of God, and the very magnitude of this deed:

> God is dead. And we have killed him – you and I. How did we do this? How could we drink up the sea? Who gave us the sponge to wipe away the entire horizon? What were we doing when we unchained this earth from its sun? Whither is it moving now? Whither are we moving? Away from all suns? Are we not plunging continually? Backward, sideward, forward, in all directions? Is there still any up or down? Are we not straying as through an infinite nothing? Do we not feel the breath of empty space? Has it not become colder? Is not night continually closing in on us? Do we not need to light lanterns in the morning?[1]

The madman's atheist listeners have no comprehension of the implications of their deed: the event is too tremendous to reach the ears of men. In Book Five of *The Gay Science* – a later addition, – Nietzsche begins to unpack the first shadows of this event. Although the initial consequence of the deed is a new daybreak, the cheerfulness expressed in this book, 'a new and scarcely describable kind of light, happiness, relief, exhilaration, encouragement, dawn,' the prospect of venturing out on an open sea,[2] Nietzsche also prophesies a coming 'monstrous logic of terror ... an eclipse of the sun whose like has probably never yet occurred on earth.'[3]

This apocalyptic event is the collapse of all that has been supported by faith in the existence of God, including the whole of European morality. For God may be identified with the perspective of the judge who assesses whether existence conforms to morality.[4] The death of God results in the replacement of this perspective with the perspectives of existence itself: life as nature and history. '*Why have morality at all* when life, nature, and history are "not moral"?'[5]

Nietzsche took Darwinian evolution to imply that distinctively human qualities, such as consciousness, moral obligation and piety, are historical and derivative phenomena, the products of non-conscious, non-moral, natural processes, and none of their claims to escape historical relativity can be legitimated. It is precisely such piety that has been murdered in the Nietzschean questioning of the value of values – his investigation of the role and function of morality. If morality can be taken as having its origins in non-moral phenomena of nature and history, then it loses all claim to authority, leaving only life, nature and history as the sources that construct values for their own ends.

The murder of God means that all human beliefs, values and thoughts may be explained by their production within the processes of life, nature and history. More radical consequences result when the preconditions for science are examined in this way: faith in science, an unconditional 'will to truth,' or 'truth at any price', may yield dangerous consequences, as we now know all too well: its existence therefore cannot be justified by a calculus of utility, or explained by evolutionary advantage. The will to truth, therefore, is not motivated by the utility of avoiding deception, for truths are sought even when they are dangerous. By contrast, the will to truth expresses a moral sentiment: 'I will not deceive, not even myself.' The will to truth expresses a metaphysical faith that truth resides in 'being itself', the truth of the real world as such, which is entirely independent of the procedures for attaining it;[6] the ultimate value of this truth stands apart from life, nature and history:

> No doubt, those who are truthful in that audacious and ultimate sense that is presupposed by the faith in science *thus affirm another world* than the world of life, nature, and history; and in so far as they affirm this 'other world', – look, must they not by the same token negate its counterpart, this world, *our* world? – But you will have gathered what I am driving at, namely, that it is still a *metaphysical faith* upon which our faith in science rests – that even we seekers after knowledge today, we godless anti-metaphysicians still take our fire, too, from the flame lit by a faith that is thousands of years old, that Christian faith which was also the faith of Plato, that God is the truth, that truth is divine.[7]

'Honest and intransigent atheism', for Nietzsche, thus results from the Christian ascetic ethic of truthfulness – the will not to deceive oneself, even when such deceptions are in one's own interests.[8] The atheistic critique of religion from the perspective of a 'secular' reason, in the name of its own ontology grounded variously in the material, the political, the moral, or the technological, expresses a metaphysical piety in relation to its own ontology.[9] This piety has itself been learned from Christianity.[10] Ultimately, this ascetic will to truth must call itself into question by asking, 'What does the will to truth signify?'[11]

Nietzsche, while attempting to draw the fullest consequences from the critique of religion, points out the extent to which the critical unmasking of religion by science 'is still pious'[12] – so that its fate will be bound up with that of religion. In relation to its value for life, the will to truth of the Enlightenment unmasking of dogma as superstition expresses another form of asceticism, a life that cuts into itself. Atheism results from the refutation of the moral, Christian God, as if there could be no other kinds of god.[13] Nietzsche himself remained pious,[14] as evidenced by the way in which reverence is at the heart of his transvalued thinking – the revaluation of all values does not mean the end of evaluation. For example, in portraying the magnitude of the murder of God, Nietzsche attributes a value to this event. Similarly, the symbolism of height and depth that structures *Thus Spoke Zarathustra* expresses the dimension of evaluation and respect.

Just as there is no end to evaluation, there is also no end to critical enquiry: it would be a mistake to think that Nietzsche remains caught within the conscious self-contradiction of a will to truth which wishes to deny the existence of truth. Instead, he abandons the metaphysical will to truth in favour of a 'will to power'. One may grasp what this means by observing how this produces a change in the element of thought, the way thought images and orients itself. Nietzsche's character Zarathustra indicates a complete shift in paradigm with regard to the thinking of transcendence, value and truth. This triple metamorphosis is described in symbolism by Zarathustra as a metamorphosis of the spirit from the load-bearing camel, who responds to the injunctions of morality, 'Thou shalt,' such as 'to feed upon the acorns and grass of knowledge and for the sake of truth to suffer hunger of the soul,' through the lion who says, 'I will,' to the child who is 'innocence and forgetfulness, a new beginning, a sport, a self-propelling wheel, a first motion, a sacred Yes.'[15] This is no simple glorification of the will or of power.[16] The transvaluing question of the value of values, of what is worth thinking about, may paralyse thought for a moment, in a nihilistic circle of self-questioning, which will continue as long as completion of the enquiry is postponed. Alternatively, a conclusion of blessed ignorance will bring such questioning to a merciful release, liberated from the teleological plans of a moral consciousness, and thought will continue on *a path of its own devising*.[17] Each thought, each moment, then becomes a creation of values, a first-motion, a self-propelling wheel, a 'will to power'.

Thinking itself becomes an event: one encounters the life, nature and history of thought in its arising in the passage of time. In the act of beginning to think, we evaluate what is most worth spending time thinking about by spending that time. Both what is questioned and our questioning are brought into question, and thrown into a state of flux. The earth has become unchained from the sun; the shore has disappeared and the philosopher is completely at sea. Being is replaced by becoming because there is no longer any holding fast. The question of philosophy overthrows the autonomy of a thought which is able to legislate its own values at the same time as it undermines the dependence of a thought which is grounded in supreme values. The first aspect of the metamorphosis, then, is that static ontologies, axiologies or divinities, as represented in consciousness, are replaced by temporal existence as a flux of becoming.

Thought becomes driven by life: life determines thought through the evaluations or emotions it enacts in us. Nietzsche contrasted his own thought with that of the moral and impersonal 'will to truth' of science and philosophy:

> All great problems demand *great love*, and of that only strong, round, secure spirits who have a firm grip on themselves are capable. It makes the most telling difference whether a thinker has a personal relationship to his problems and finds in them his destiny, his distress, and his greatest happiness, or an "impersonal" one, meaning that he can do no better than to touch them and grasp them with the antennae of cold, curious thought.[18]

The second aspect of thought in this metamorphosis is that it is affectively driven, and gains an existential import. 'Personal relationship' may be understood here as involving destiny, distress or greatest happiness: these are limiting parameters that individuate a personal life as a coherent episode. The person does not choose his or her problems; instead, the reverence for such problems is given as that which determines the individual.[19] Destiny, therefore, should not be understood in the static terms of hindsight as the path of a completed life, but in dynamic terms as that which determines the path of a life – the giving rather than the given, the living rather than the lived. The key feature of this 'personal relationship' to one's problems is that the course of their solution may change everything; nothing is held in reserve. A life is considered in terms of the events that compose it as an episode, and not in terms of its results as a solution to its problems. Thought wagers life entirely upon becoming.

If Nietzsche speaks in the name of a host of impulses that is too heterogeneous to be comprehended within a single concept, or in the name of a creative power of thought that cannot be represented by the concepts it produces,[20] this is not motivated by some dogmatic love of heterogeneity or difference for its own sake. Instead, he affirms a spiritual way of thinking that will not allow itself to be reduced to the model of knowledge as recognition, for it expresses its own life. Affirming itself apart from all artificial certainties of science, it remains content with ambiguity:[21]

> Conversely, one could conceive of such a pleasure and power of self-determination, such a *freedom* of the will that the spirit would take leave of all faith and all wish for certainty, being practiced in maintaining himself on insubstantial ropes and possibilities and dancing even near abysses.[22]

There is no way for such a spirit to express itself in simple propositions. Only in one proposition did Nietzsche come close to revealing the identity of his spirit: 'woe is me! I am a *nuance*'.[23] The source of thought can no longer be thought in terms of the Parmenidean model of the One or Being, where thinking unites with the being that is thought. The circularity of thought and being that grounds certainty in truth is undone in favour of an unconscious, unthinkable source of thought: an abyss that undermines all grounds, a chaos that escapes all fixed determinations, a chance that precludes all reason and order. The third aspect of this metamorphosis of thought is a faith that embraces uncertainty, indetermination, and an abyss of chaos. This faith is itself transvalued from an adherence to grounds to a taking leave of all grounds.

One may therefore tentatively propose that Nietzsche replaces an ontology of being and a logic of identity with an ontology of becoming and a logic of difference. It is, however, important to free such concepts of becoming and difference from the abstract and generalizing roles that they bear in conventional thought. Difference as such or in general holds no value; instead, difference is only affirmed in three figures that escape conceptual representation: as becoming, as affect, and as the unthinkable. These figures of difference remain unthought within conventional uses of representational and scientific language, leading to suspicions of the metaphysical and illusory status of much of our 'knowledge'.

Nietzsche's critique of religion

Imaginary causes

An affective drive for thinking may be contrasted with a moral disciplining of reason. According to Nietzsche, a moral person uses big moral words, such as justice, wisdom, holiness, virtue, to 'give himself the appearance of superiority over more spiritual people,' and accomplish revenge against the spirit.[24] For words are limited for describing inner processes and drives. Those words with which morality attempts to discipline the spirit, such as anger, hatred, love, pity, desire, knowledge, joy and pain, are all names for extreme states,[25] lacking the subtlety to communicate the ways of the spirit. From an evolutionary perspective, consciousness is merely a net of communication between human beings, evolved for the purpose of protecting a solitary human being within a herd. One can therefore only succeed in becoming conscious of what is common, not what is individual – and words name only crude extremes.[26] Knowledge, even philosophical knowledge, is really only the reduction of something strange to something familiar:[27] wherever a word is set up, a problem is identified but a solution is not given. A subordination of all existence to the power of words, as if they constituted solutions in themselves, is a means of closing oneself off from the problems that generate thought.[28] All knowledge is moral, therefore, in so far as it trains the individual to be a function of the herd,[29] to think according to common custom. Note that this is less a historical or psychological comment than a transcendental comment on the exclusion of change, affect and uncertainty from knowledge. Since language functions to support morality, then philosophy, irrespective of its intentions, has a moral impact. All knowledge expresses a piety towards the existing senses and values enshrined within our common language. Moreover, the aim of such piety is to dominate and discipline alternatives: revenge against the spirit is the essence of our metaphysics, psychology, history and morality. As Gilles Deleuze wrote in his commentary on Nietzsche: 'The spirit of revenge is the genealogical element of *our* thought, the transcendental principle of *our* way of thinking.'[30]

It is within this framework that we can understand Nietzsche's critique of Christianity, morality and metaphysics: they invoke concepts to designate something beyond nature, history and life that consequently functions as an imaginary cause. In addition to his critique of the universalizing and levelling power of language that excludes difference as change, affect and uncertainty, he also criticizes a utilitarian concept of the will that excludes qualitative differences in value – the concept that lies at the heart of modern economics and politics. Central to this is an elucidation of what is presupposed by taking the human will as a cause: for taking the best course of action will involve anticipating the full extent of possible consequences.

> Indeed, to come to the worst difficulty: all these consequences, so hard to determine individually, now have to be weighed against one another on the *same* scales; but usually it happens that, on account of the differences in *quality* of all these possible consequences, we lack the scales and the weights for this casuistry of advantage.[31]

Having arrived through a picture of the consequences at a single motive for action, action may in practice be motivated otherwise: habit, the influence of others, apathy, or excitation of imagination or other emotions may take over. In order for a will to act morally, it would have to have a perfect knowledge of all the consequences of each possible action; it would have to reduce qualitative differences of these consequences so that one course of action can be judged as better than the others; and it would have to make this picture of the consequences the dominant motive that resists all other inclinations. Although the impossibility of such a procedure does not undermine the rational domination of the passions as a moral ideal, Nietzsche demonstrates that there is a role for evaluation prior to any act of will in the construction of knowledge. This evaluation takes place in the selection of significant consequences and choosing among them.[32] Willing is above all something complicated, something that is a unity only as a word.[33] Nietzsche's tentative conclusion that thought and action derive from a conflict of impulses as evaluations, and not from the will, seems inescapable: 'our moral judgements and evaluations too are only images and fantasies based on a physiological process unknown to us, a kind of acquired language for designating certain nervous stimuli.'[34] There is no transparent, sovereign, Cartesian theatre of consciousness through which thought and action are governed. Instead, the mediation between thought and action is effected by an unknown, unthinkable process. Decisive in Nietzsche's 'dark Enlightenment', like those of Karl Marx and Sigmund Freud, is the discovery of an arena of unconscious processes through which thought is mediated to itself: there is something unthought which forces us to think.

Consequently, we are not responsible for our waking life.[35] Thought appears to be a realm of freedom, but really it is only a realm of surfaces and self-satisfaction.[36] Our thoughts and representations are never motives, but always rationalizations after the event, for any agency is too complicated to take place within thought. To take thoughts as motives is to make the error of mistaking the consequence for the cause, 'reason's intrinsic form of corruption'.[37] This error not only leads to belief in false causes, the construction of imaginary causes through habit, and the belief in a free will, but it also installs a transcendent term at the heart of reason. For where the relations between thoughts are mediated by unconscious processes, morality attributes the mediation between reason and action to a metaphysical term: the will. The abyss at the heart of thought is bridged by an assumption regarding the transcendent. For one can never observe or explain how a false cause, in reality a consequence, gives rise to its supposed effects: how a rational motive can give rise to an action. Instead, it would appear to be the case that a transcendent law is paying a false cause with a supposed effect. So, by taking one's reasons as causes, one expects to earn their results as consequences, even though one cannot explain how this Cartesian gap between reason and matter is bridged. All results appear to be a metaphysical payment from a metaphysical God, a *deus ex machina* invoked as an explanatory principle, a bridge over the unthought.[38]

It is for this reason that Nietzsche says:

The most general formula at the basis of every religion and morality is: 'Do this and this, refrain from this and this – and you will be happy! Otherwise ... ' Every morality, every religion *is* this imperative.[39]

Then in so far as morality and religion are based on a belief in the reality of representations in consciousness, the *'entire realm of morality and religion falls under this concept of imaginary causes.'*[40]

Nietzsche expanded this in relation to Christianity in *The Anti-Christ*:

In Christianity neither morality nor religion come into contact with reality at any point. Nothing but imaginary *causes* ('God', 'soul', 'ego', 'spirit', 'free will', – or 'unfree will'): nothing but imaginary *effects* ('sin', 'redemption', 'grace', 'punishment', 'forgiveness of sins'). A traffic between imaginary *beings* ('God', 'spirits', 'souls'); an imaginary *natural* science (anthropocentric; complete lack of the concept of natural causes); an imaginary *psychology* (nothing but self-misunderstandings, interpretations of pleasant or unpleasant general feelings, for example the condition of the *nervus sympathicus*, with the aid of the sign-language of religio-moral idiosyncrasy – 'repentance', 'sting of conscience', 'temptation by the devil', 'the proximity of God'); an imaginary *teleology* ('the kingdom of God', 'the Last Judgement', 'eternal life').[41]

Such an empiricist suspicion of the 'invisible' realm of metaphysics is justified, in the case of Nietzsche, by his prior suspicion of consciousness, concepts and language. If our words are produced within collective consciousness through the association of common but extreme states, then no words can be taken as effectively designating causes; least of all those words that are not subject to testing and refinement through the senses. The 'will' is paradigmatic of all such cases for Nietzsche as the origin of metaphysics: indeed, the idea of the ego as cause is projected outside us to create the concept of the 'thing'.[42] The will is merely a prejudice expressed in the metaphysics of language, a grammatical prejudice: that a subject acts on a verb. Nietzsche overthrows cultural–linguistic models of religious language through his critique of herd morality, just as he overthrows propositional–cognitivist models of religious language through his empiricism, and experiential–expressivist models of religious language through his naturalistic psychology.[43] Spirit, for Nietzsche, is attention turned to the subtle, the thought-provoking, the problematic and the rare, and not a description of an invisible world.

In this sense, therefore, Nietzsche's critique of Christianity is grounded in his critiques of reason. The concepts of morality and religion are reifications of subtle, fluid and problematic events and experiences. They derive from a reverence for being over becoming, for the static or eternal over the evanescent: 'I fear we are not getting rid of God because we still believe in grammar ... '[44] The concept of being gives a purchase in our thinking for the metaphysical concepts of religion to take hold. In another sense, however, Nietzsche's critique of reason is grounded in his critique of religion. The philosophers' reason derives from a distorted piety:

> They kill, they stuff, when they worship, these conceptual idolaters – they become a mortal danger to everything when they worship. Death, change, age, as well as procreation and growth, are for them objections – refutations even. What is, does not *become*; what becomes, *is* not ... . Now they all believe, even to the point of despair, in that which is.[45]

Concepts such as unity, materiality, substance and duration are the emptiest, the 'last fumes of evaporating reality.'[46] The elevation of such general concepts to be the pivot through which philosophers organize their relation to reality is 'again only the expression of their way of doing reverence: the higher must not be *allowed* to grow out of the lower, must not be *allowed* to have grown at all.'[47] The metaphysics that results from a belief in a reality behind our language and vocabulary is, for Nietzsche, an expression of the ascetic ideal: a life that cuts into life, in order to survive in a climate of decadence, when its own vital instincts are decaying, and one merely clings to the most insubstantial. Of course, Nietzsche's assertion of the reality of becoming over against being may seem like a further dogmatism, unless one observes how becoming or flux emerges from the furnace of critique itself: all certainties collapse, the shore has disappeared and the philosopher can only venture out on new seas. Becoming, difference and chance encounter emerge from the dissolution of all grounds, the murder of God. All metaphysics is an attempt to constrain this Heraclitean flux. In so far as philosophy expresses the asceticism which finds its fullest expression in Christianity, Nietzsche's critique of philosophy depends on his critique of Christianity.

One may observe two strategies of critique at work in Nietzsche's opposition to Christianity. The first is to show how the entirety of Christian metaphysics, including its theological concepts, functions as a complex mechanism for the payment of metaphysical rewards to the elect. Although the metaphysical interests of piety are emphasized, these enable payment of a material reward in so far as social reality itself, in the form of the Church, is structured in relation to the system of metaphysical beliefs. Hence Nietzsche's reclamation of the Enlightenment theory of the priest's will to power. In addition to this materialist critique of Christianity, Nietzsche also furnishes a physiological critique. If thoughts are the product of unknown physiological processes, then Christianity may be regarded as a physiological effect that may be assessed in accordance with its value for life. In this respect, Nietzsche produces an account of the ascetic ideal, the product of a slave revolt in morality, at the heart of the European tradition of religion, morality and reason.

In so far as Nietzsche's critique of the European tradition of philosophy rests on his critique of proto-Christian, ascetic piety, then many of his attacks on Christianity may also be applied to reason as such. In so far as the will to truth is born out of the ascetic ideal, then it merely brandishes the big moral word 'truth' in order to accomplish revenge against more spiritual people. The concepts of 'truth' present in the European tradition may be regarded as crude oversimplifications, moral prescriptions as to how truth is to be conceived, that exclude difference in value, the 'pathos of distance', as well as change, affect and uncertainty. The concept of 'truth' may be suspected of being used as a mask for the generation of falsehood, so as to reap the metaphysical reward of a participation in being.

Such, then, are the consequences of the murder of God. God, morality, being and truth have stood as pivotal, metaphysical concepts that structure the cosmos as such, as an ordered meaningful world. The murder of God is the demolition of this structural role in the cosmos, whatever inhabits it. The contents, values and methods of traditional philosophy of religion are denounced in a single stroke as imaginary products of a will to power. Although a metaphysics of chaos, in the form of multiplicity and flux, seems to result, this is merely the negation of our metaphysics, our way of ordering and structuring the cosmos. The apparent meaninglessness of existence does not mean that existence itself lacks a meaning, but that our present ways of giving meaning to existence may falsify the meaning that is already in existence.[48]

Locke and the market

Who murdered God?

Let us return to the madman's initial question, 'How did we do this? How could we drink up the sea? Who gave us the sponge to wipe away the entire horizon?' Nietzsche himself, like Hegel before him, merely reports the event; we must look elsewhere to see how the deed was accomplished. How has it come about that the phenomenon of a self-professed atheism emerged in France in the eighteenth century?[49] Many widely accepted explanations combine several contingent historical factors contributing to the deed. The development of nominalism within scholastic philosophy, arising from a rigorous emphasis on the absolute power of God, led to an understanding of the natural world in which divine purposes could no longer be interpreted. The Reformation, scandalized by the abuse of ecclesiastical institutions, posited the individual conscience as the source of religious authority, the author of its own beliefs, and so instituted an anthropological shift in which the locus of divine authority is identified by the conscience, and not simply by God and his institutional representative alone. In reaction to the religious wars following the Reformation, there were demands for political freedom and toleration of religious difference, which undermined divine authority in political affairs. The successful adoption of an experimental method in the natural sciences, allowing the verification of hypotheses, suggested itself as the paradigm of all knowledge, raising doubts about religious truths which are not subject to experimental verification. The Copernican discovery of the heliocentric system, and the subsequent acceptance of the independence of the extended physical cosmos from human purpose, capable of operating in accordance with its own laws, led to a rejection of the categories of purpose as a whole in understanding nature. To meet these challenges, God was theologically reconceived as the intelligent designer of the ordered physical universe; this meant that belief in the existence of God was only as strong as the argument from design, which collapsed following the emergence of an autonomous, legislative, self-legitimating reason. At the same time, the emerging wealth and power of merchant classes in towns and cities whose social organization was no longer determined by monarchical or feudal patterns led to abandonment of monarchy as the model for God, and God as the ideological legitimation of kingship.

All of the above were certainly factors, but many of them also require explanation. Explanations in terms of an evolutionary or dialectical history of ideas are undermined by Nietzsche's radical suspicion of imaginary causes, for these do not explain why particular thinkers at particular times came to particular thoughts. If reasons and concepts are rationalizations after the fact of a prior distribution of things, then they only function as imaginary causes.

Nietzsche's depiction of this emergence of atheism as the 'murder of God' suggests a more radical formulation that is at once more materialist and more spiritual. For how has it come about that God is no longer the organizing idea behind all aspects of daily life, endowing all dimensions of existence with a ritual meaning? The Calvinist assertion of the absolute transcendence of God over the meaning and value of all natural or social events, processes and practices is possible once one no longer requires a ritualized legitimation for social practice. This can only be the case if one already has an alternative source of meaning and value for practice. The meaning of the murder of God, that is, the emergence of a secular worldview with a corresponding affirmation of atheism, is that God is no longer required to play a foundational role in organizing humanity's activity in relation to reality. The murder of God therefore reflects a shift in pieties. God has stopped paying us our ordered existence; or rather, there is another god who pays us, who responds more immediately, directly and tangibly to our prayers: Mammon.

This conversion is accompanied by a progressive reorganization of daily life. Where the activities of daily life had been ordered by the expectations of the community or obligations to a deity, economic rationality brings an abstract symbolization of space and time. Enclosure of the commons, the replacement of communal resources with private property, changes the function of work from producing for one's community to producing for the market; similarly, market relations enact an 'enclosure' of time, whereby the quantity of labour takes on more significance than the lived experience of work. Once subjected to the abstract representations of private property and the market, daily life can become regulated by economic rationality, which had formerly been limited by a consensus on the limitation of needs. André Gorz argues as follows:

> We know that the break-up of the traditional order and the develop-
> ment of mercantile and financial capitalism, and subsequently of
> industrial capitalism, were mutually engendered, each being at once
> the cause and consequence of the other … . When religious or moral
> certainties were shattered …, calculation emerged as a privileged
> source of unquestionable certainties; what was demonstrable, suscep-
> tible to organization, predictable by virtue of a calculation, had no
> need of the guarantee of any authority to be true and universally valid
> … . Economic rationality functioned as a substitute for religious
> morality: through it man attempted to apply the eternal laws which
> governed the universe to the predictive organization of his own affairs
> … . The accumulation of wealth was only the proof of the accuracy of
> the calculations and this accuracy required indefinite confirmation
> through reinvestment of the profits.[50]

Economic rationality provides access to truth that is no longer limited by religious and moral restraints: since a calculation determines the most appropriate conduct, one no longer has any responsibility for one's own decisions. An impersonal calculus is introjected into human thought. Yet Gorz points out that since economic rationality, although it gives access to economic truth, is unable to produce meaning, it cannot define the limits of its own applicability, or even if it is applicable at all.[51] While the removal of limitations from economic rationality is a sovereign decision, the adoption of economic rationality is an act of faith in its applicability.

Yet how did this ancient god, Mammon, a perennial enemy throughout biblical history, finally gain the upper hand? This world-historical event, which threatens ever-increasing global repercussions, was inflicted on humanity in England, even if the first self-confessed atheists appeared a few decades later in France.[52] Baron de Montesquieu, in *The Spirit of Laws*, first published in 1748, after an exhaustive account of the nature of possible forms of government explained according to the history and char-acter of their people, holds up the contemporary English experience of liberty and commerce as a model, a solution to the Hobbesian state of nature as war:

Commerce is a cure for the most destructive prejudices; for it is almost a general rule, that wherever we find agreeable manners, there commerce flourishes; and that wherever there is commerce, there we meet with agreeable manners ... .

Peace is the natural effect of trade. Two nations who traffic with each other become reciprocally dependent; for if one has an interest in buying, the other has an interest in selling; and thus their union is founded on their mutual necessities.[53]

The secret of the English experience is the way the market predominates over the state:

Other nations have made the interests of commerce yield to those of politics; the English, on the contrary, have ever made their political interests give way to those of commerce.

They know better than any other people upon earth how to value, at the same time, these three great advantages – religion, commerce, and liberty.[54]

Pierre Manent has argued that this move is crucial to the emergence of modernity: *The Spirit of Laws* aims to destroy the authority of ancient models of the best regime and its corresponding virtues, so as to replace it with the authority of the experience of the present moment, the experience of modernity, as expressed in notions of 'commerce' and 'liberty'.[55] Since reason cannot compare the present against ancient models according to any universal or natural order, for to do so is already to appeal to a natural order or ancient model, then the Enlightenment abandons reason in the name of reason:

Reason cannot bring together under any unifying principle this agglomeration of events and effects which is England. In fact, it can only view it with warm approbation. Without being able to give a rational account of what satisfies it, Enlightenment reason believes more things than it actually understands. As faith seeks understanding, *fides quaerens intellectum*, one has to ask whether modern reason has ever overcome this contradiction.[56]

The deed of the murder of God was effected by the emergence of the self-regulating market as the organizing principle of the social order. Never before the eighteenth century were markets more than accessories of economic life.[57] Markets were the meeting-places of long-distance trade;[58] while they may have had a fundamental role in shaping the social order indirectly through the transmission of artefacts and ideas, including especially tools and strategies of war, they did not directly constitute the social order as markets. Medieval towns enforced a strict separation between local trade and the external market, while the expansionist policies of the mercantilist states of the fifteenth to seventeenth centuries sought sovereign power through control of external trade routes. Self-regulating markets, however, bring into effect forces beyond the reach of sovereign powers, forces of pure exteriority, lacking an identity or nature in themselves, beyond even the reach of God.

This was observed even as early as Aristotle's consideration of money in his *Politics*. Aristotle imagined coinage to be introduced in trade over distances between states, because it can be easily carried and is imperishable.[59] Once coinage is introduced, trade that seeks simply the increase of money becomes possible. Aristotle drew attention to the essential difference between trade and household exchange: whereas household exchange does not seek acquisition of goods for its own sake, but sets it within limits, trade seeks an unlimited quantity of money.[60] This lack of limitation indicates the freedom of trade from limits set by the *polis*. In money, value finds a material form which escapes the bounds of the values established in any particular social order. Aristotle reserved his strongest condemnation for the practice of charging interest, whereby money gives birth to money.[61] Thus money, and the force of its increase, lies outside and unregulated by any existing social order.

In practice, however, there are many limits to economic growth. A crucial limit until the eighteenth century was the finite total of coinage in circulation. Coinage could be increased by the conquest of new territories and the plunder and mining of their resources. However, to increase the money supply by itself is to introduce inflation, and reduce the value of the coinage relative to other goods. John Locke, who commended the 'wise policy of the Chinese' in not mining their resources, pointed out that 'riches do not consist in having more gold and silver, but in having more in proportion, than the rest of the world, or than our neighbours'.[62] Degree of wealth is always differential, measured against that of the others in the market-place; the acquisition of monetary wealth is always at the expense of others, always the outcome of a 'will to power'. Then if trade is necessary to the production of wealth, and money to the conduct of trade, competitive foreign trade was the essence of the accumulation of wealth and power in the early modern period.[63] State power, including the capacity to finance war, was dependent on control of international trade. Thus the possibility of a free, self-regulating market was enabled by the exercise of state power in competition, just as state power was dependent on wealth derived from taxation.

The modern market economy was founded on the violent exercise of power by states. The first move was the conquest of exterior territories, and the removal of their valuable resources. This alone was insufficient to ensure long-term prosperity: Spanish silver from the conquest of the Americas flowed into the hands of Genoese bankers, Dutch merchants and English wool manufacturers. More profitable was investment in overseas trade, where investment itself is regulated by a market. Here the Dutch East India Company led the way, regulated by the Amsterdam Bourse, yet licensed by the state to use its own military force to establish overseas markets. Trade, here, remained vulnerable to competition from mercantilist states; the modern market economy had not yet gained power.[64] A second move was the organization of the slave trade: this was particularly significant, for in order to set up plantations in the West Indies and the Americas, everything had to be imported. A new social formation was created for the sake of trade, whereby a planter ruled his estate without deference to social models of his European homeland. This is evident not only in the institution and practice of slave-owning itself, but even in morals, for example, for the planters felt free to father children from the slave women. Here, an external social order was invented purely for the purpose of the market. Indeed, the evidence suggests that it was only brokers and investors in the home country who were able to profit significantly from the slave trade.[65] The third, final, yet far more subtle move,[66] through which the market began to infiltrate the state itself, was, paradoxically, the gradual take-over of the Bank of England by the State in the eighteenth century.[67] It is this deed which caused the murder of God.

The decisive move enabled a credible, durable and secure value to be attributed to bank notes for the first time. The Bank of England, launched in 1694, was the first public bank of its kind: it was financed by issuing shares to investors on an open market. Prior to this time, paper money, bills of exchange, were widely used, but treated with a certain amount of distrust: both Florentine banks in the fourteenth century and Genoese banks in the sixteenth century had generated wealth in this way, but had eventually collapsed. Locke, immediately prior to the setting up of the Bank of England, gave voice to this distrust of paper money or credit notes, especially in relation to their use in competitive foreign trade:

> since the Bill, Bond, or other Note of Debt, I receive from one Man will not be accepted as Security by another, he not knowing that the Bill or Bond is true or legal, or that the Man bound to me is honest or responsible.[68]

The State take-over of the Bank of England, however, enabled the issuing of long-term, low-interest loans which could be secured by future taxation. The Bank was not in danger of crashing, like preceding banks, because it could always recover lost assets through taxes, and taxes by the exercise of force. The result was a form of credit which need never be repaid, since a government bond could always secure its value by being sold to another. By this means the Bank of England could issue loans way beyond the investments it had received, without fear of sudden collapse, for it had the security to borrow against the future.[69] The result was an increase in the money supply for the sake of trade, removing practical limits to the acquisition of hard currency. The existence of a single secure currency became the basis of international trade. Financing the Industrial Revolution became possible for the first time.[70] The value of the currency was, of course, dependent on the stability and power of the State itself;[71] yet it was not limited to internal relations within the State – Dutch bankers were sufficiently confident to invest heavily in British government bonds. The limits to the power of a mere promise, an infinitely replaceable sign, were thereby removed. Then although the printing of money did not remove economic limits to the total amount of money in circulation, it removed the physical limits to financial accumulation. Thus this decisive move enabled a context where the triple conditions of a self-regulating, and expanding free market could later be realized: a competitive labour market, an independent standard for the value of currency (the gold standard), and international free trade.[72]

With the issuing of paper money, sovereign power – a degree of credit, trust, honour or glory invested in the state itself – could now be objectified, materialized, distributed and traded according to the laws of the market. The force of the state itself comes to serve the market by enforcing the laws of contract and debt. This almost unthinkable distribution of sovereign power first occurred in a country in which, since the first parliament in Oxford in 1258, subjects had debated and determined the powers of the sovereign, including levels of taxation permitted for the purpose of wars.[73] The ideology for the distribution of sovereign right was developed within the context of English puritanism by the likes of Richard Hooker, Thomas Hobbes and John Locke. Most significant for the foundation of the modern democratic state as a society organized for the market was the political thought of Locke[74]– where Nietzsche was later to appeal 'life, nature and history', Locke's political thought was founded on the comparatively reified concepts of God, right and liberty.

Locke's *Two Treatises of Government* were an attack upon 'patriarchalism', the absolute or divine right of monarchy handed down from Adam by a tradition of heirs, followed by a reconstruction of political life from a 'state of nature'. Having undermined the absolute authority of tradition, Locke affirmed a universal right to life on the grounds that each person is created by God, remains God's property, and is thus 'bound to preserve himself'.[75] From this derives the right of self-preservation and the right of preserving all mankind. Moreover, liberty derives from God's gift of the world to men, 'for the best advantage of life, and convenience,'[76] leaving them the freedom to 'order their Actions, and dispose of their Possessions, and Persons as they think fit, within the bounds of the Law of Nature, without asking leave, or depending on the Will of any other Man.'[77] Liberty is primarily over property, the right to which is given by God. It is the liberty to trade one's possessions and enter into contracts – the liberty of a merchant.

These theological concepts of right and liberty are abstractions which fit precisely under Nietzsche's two fundamental critiques of imaginary causes. Right, the most common or universal principle, is held up against all other claims and interests: it is created to protect a solitary human being within a herd – that is, prior to all social relations – and effectively pre-empts any other claims, whether these are the demands of the good, of justice, of human flourishing, or more subtle moral sentiments. It conceals the prior act of enclosure of the commons – the eviction of a shared life of mutual obligations – upon which property claims are based. For in so far as right, and along with it the structure of the liberal, democratic state, is erected 'on the puny base of the solitary animal in search of food'[78], on the basis of individual labour in hunting and eating, on the preservation of bare life, on survival, then it claims a prerogative of the most general experience of living over any spiritual claims regarding quality of life. Life is compressed to a simple quantity, in the same way that a price compresses value. The connection between the concept of 'right' and reality hangs by a single thread.

The same is true for Locke's concept of liberty, which is independent of volition, for it is simply a capacity to act or not.[79] Such choices will be moved by desire; instead of liberty concerning a positive good, every voluntary action is motivated by the 'uneasiness of desire'.[80] A higher good is always absent; it cannot motivate us in the same way as uneasiness. Thus always moved towards immediate happiness, the only liberty of the will one has is to suspend acting according to one's desires,[81] so as to weigh the consequences.[82] For everyone places their happiness in a different thing:

> The Mind has a different relish, as well as the Palate; and you will as fruitlessly endeavour to delight all Men with Riches or Glory, (which yet some Men place their Happiness in,) as you would to satisfy all Men's Hunger with Cheese or Lobsters.[83]

The will, therefore, aims at happiness, the relief of discomfort, in the form of its own choosing. One has little liberty in practice to choose the *summum bonum* of the ancient philosophers, or to serve the welfare of humankind; one merely has the liberty of a customer in a restaurant, or a consumer in the market-place. It conceals the sovereign exclusion of the claims of religious or social duty upon which such an arbitrary choice is based. Liberty compresses the good of human action to a single value, easing discomfort, by an arbitrary choice of taste: cheese or lobsters. The connection between the concept of liberty and reality hangs by a single thread.

The fact that we are dealing here with artifice – the concepts of right and liberty being alienable from the people who hold them – is demonstrated by Locke's sophistic defence of slavery, a trade he was able to benefit from personally.[84] One hesitates to mention such *ad hominem* matters, since Locke's principles have subsequently been successfully used to demand the abolition of slavery. The logic of Locke's argument, however, is highly illuminating. He began by establishing that all have the right to enforce justice by punishing by death those who transgress the laws of property.[85] Now the right to property is claimed through labour: one makes something one's own by working on it, thus joining oneself to it[86] – in labour, time is not given but spent in order to purchase. Indeed, the vast part of the value of things is given by the labour spent on them,[87] so that an acre of land planted with wheat in America is worth over a thousand times more than the profit which an Indian derives from the same acre.[88] Then colonists who meet resistance from natives in their conquest of land have the right to defend themselves against the native aggressors as in a state of war, including the right to kill such thieves.[89] Once captured in war, the native has,

> by his own fault, forfeited his own Life, by some Act that deserves Death; he, to whom he has forfeited it, may (when he has him in his Power) delay to take it, and make use of him to his own Service, and he does him no injury by it. For, whenever he finds the hardship of his Slavery out-weigh the value of his Life, 'tis in his Power, by resisting the Will of his Master, to draw on himself the Death he desires.[90]

Liberty and right may thus be suspended, and during the interval of reprieve in which the death sentence is deferred, profitable labour may be extracted by violence. The promise of death creates the life of slavery.

A second index of the artificiality of Locke's concepts is his fantasy of 'the state of nature', from which political life is constructed from first principles: 'Thus in the beginning all the World was America.'[91] Locke's reading of Genesis gives theological authorization to the fantasy of an original America, of human beings sent out to occupy, work and claim a limitless supply of land. These pioneers of the state of nature are individuals in a state of perfect freedom, able to dispose of their possessions and persons as they see fit, and equality, where all power of jurisdiction is reciprocal; behind the fantasy of the frontier we may detect the reality of the market. Indeed, when Locke discusses the objection where and when such a state of nature is to be found, he not only appeals to sovereignty by adducing the example of 'all Princes and Rulers of Independent Governments all through the World', but also appeals to long-distance trade, exterior to state power:

> The Promises and Bargains for Truck, &c. between the two Men in the Desert Island, mentioned by *Garcilasso De la vega*, in his history of *Peru*, or between a *Swiss* and an *Indian*, in the Woods of *America*, are binding to them, though they are perfectly in a State of Nature, in reference to one another.[92]

Beneath the theological fantasy of a mythical origin, we may see the twin realities of sovereign violence and long-distance trade.

Now, Aristotle's description of the invention of money as a sign of value shows how this leads to the accumulation of signs of value for their own sake. This process of replacement by a sign continues in the invention of the banknote to replace coinage, the invention of the government bond as a debt that may be traded, and the invention of financial futures and derivatives. In each case, a promise or expectation of wealth is made to stand for wealth. Just as the expectation of death creates the life of slavery, external to any social order, the expectation of wealth creates a new sphere of commercial interactions, external to any social demands. Since Locke's concepts of 'right' and 'liberty' merely stand as abstract promises of the ability to participate on equal terms in a market without giving the necessary power to participate, they leave scope for an external mode of existence to adapt them to its own ends. Indeed, this precise possibility is anticipated by Locke, although he does not pursue his insight because it undermines his democratic state in principle, just as it has in fact undermined the democracies of the United Kingdom and the United States of America in reality.

For Locke's fantasy of a state of nature in which there is sufficient land for twice the number of inhabitants, and where property is limited by the perishability of produce and the finitude of individual labour, is disturbed by the invention of money, given value purely by tacit agreement, which, as imperishable property, removes the limits to acquisition, allowing an opportunity for larger possessions and the right to them.[93] In practice, then, the balance of power begins its shift from sovereignty to capital once the limits to the acquisition of money are removed through the issuing of government bonds; it has been radically extended more recently by the deregulation of global finance capital and the accumulation of large government debts. For capital utilizes the abstract political concepts of the market – right without property or power, liberty without volition – to seize control over life, nature and history.

At the beginning of the third millennium CE, despotic sovereign power has been seized by the impersonal force of the system of global finance – a force external to any nation state, which is controllable by neither governments, bankers nor financiers. This power is based on the commodification of nature, history and life in the form of land, labour and credit. For 'land' is nature, whether or not shaped by humanity, labour is human activity, and credit is money produced for the sake of making more money. The commodity description of labour, land and money as being produced for sale is entirely fictitious.[94] As Karl Polanyi explained so clearly, it is upon such fictions that the liberal economic creed, and the market organization of the human social order, rests:

> The commodity fiction, therefore, supplies a vital organizing principle in regard to the whole of society affecting almost all its institutions in

the most varied way, namely, the principle according to which no arrangement or behavior should be allowed to exist that might prevent the actual functioning of the market mechanism on the lines of the commodity fiction.[95]

The end result of this fiction, enforced by state power, is that the social relations in which humanity is embedded must be sacrificed in so far as they conflict with the interests of the competitive market in labour. The commodification of the worker has been manifest in slavery (although slaves, as valuable commodities, still need to be maintained), in the industrial cities of the nineteenth century (where it was merely sufficient to pay workers enough to ensure the continuation of a plentiful supply of labour, which was less than subsistence), in the Great Depression (where workers became commodities without value when industry had no production capacity to spare), and, above all, in the global market. The self-regulating market robs people of their culture and social order, before sending them out again to die of social dislocation. Moreover, the commodification of land and resources leads to depletion of resources, poisoning of land and water supplies and unsustainable rates of climate change. Finally, the commodification of credit leads to a market in government debts that disciplines government policy to the demands of finance capital, stifling the possibility of preventative measures which could avert global economic, social and ecological catastrophes.

In a nominally free market, there is no equality in exchange when one partner has a large stock of purchasing power in the form of wealth, and the other is threatened with deprivation of the means of subsistence. Hobbes had the clearer vision here:

> The *Value*, or WORTH of a man, is as of all other things, his Price; that is to say, so much as would be given for the use of his Power … . And as in other things, so in men, but the buyer determines the Price.[96]

Capital exerts its control over nature in a nominally free market by determining the prices of commodities, by encouraging excess production in both industry and agriculture, by investing in technological advances, and by stimulating consumption through the creation of new 'needs'. Capital exerts its control over labour in a nominally free market by slavery, by debt bondage, by controlling access to the means of production, by threatening unemployment, and by switching to cheap labour in a global market.

The essence of the power of capital lies in its being external to the ecological order of nature and the social order of labour: where a market is predicated on an exchange between equals, there is no commensurability between land, labour and capital. Locke himself saw that it was necessary to distinguish between two values of money: the 'Price of Hire Money' and the 'rate of exchange of commodities.'[97] The invention of unlimited finance is an invasion into the natural and historical orders. In order to diagnose the power of this transcendence, we must turn to religion for illumination. Nietzsche explained this power as follows:

> If one shifts the centre of gravity of life *out* of life into the 'Beyond' – into *nothingness* –one has deprived life as such of its centre of gravity. The great lie of personal immortality destroys all rationality, all naturalness of instinct – all that is salutary, all that is life-furthering, all that holds a guarantee of the future in the instincts henceforth excites mistrust. *So* to live that there is no longer any *meaning* in living: *that* now becomes the 'meaning' of life ... .[98]

It matters little whether the external source of meaning is an eternal God issuing judgments, or whether it is the power of money determining prices – the same nihilistic consequences follow. Whether one considers salvation of the soul, or the most profitable trade, the same consequences follow: 'The world revolves around *me*.'[99] Whether one considers the equality of souls before God in judgment, or the equality of traders before the laws of the market, the same consequences follow: '*equal* rights for all.'[100]

Nevertheless, how can the infinite relate to existence within the order of time? Locke's conception of slavery is instructive here: slavery is a reprieve, a stay in execution, a temporal delay. Once one's life is forfeit, then unlimited demands and obligations can be made. One finds a similar temporal structure in Hobbes' conception of a covenant, where one trusts the other to deliver his side of the bargain at some future time.[101] Such a covenant becomes infinite when it is the consent of a subject to sovereign power: '*I Authorise, or take upon me, all his actions.*'[102] Hobbes makes it clear that covenants, even when entered into by fear, are obligatory.[103] Thus when it is an aggressor who both threatens, and offers a covenant of sovereign protection, the result is enslavement by extortion. Whether one trades with a wealthy merchant, who sets the price, for the necessities of life, or whether one seeks employment, to earn subsistence, from an employer who sets the wage, extortion is justified under the name of 'right'. Acts of promising, contracting and covenanting, then, in so far as they bind oneself to the future, and are made under any degree of coercion or deprivation, expose one to infinite obligation.

The essence of the power of finance capital is not the accumulation of past labour. To the contrary, the history of past monetary transactions merely determines one's present accumulated stock – a quantity, not a power. When one turns to the power of capital, however, one steps into an entirely heterogeneous element: value of credit is determined by expectations of future interest. The transcendence of capital is its appeal to the future. This finite expectation is then combined with the violence of coercion, the infinite demand, to ensure the power of capital. Just as the slave is controlled by the threat of death, a future recompense, capital seizes sovereignty by a combination of debt, the finite threat of future reparation, or abandoning the contract, the infinite threat of exclusion from the means of subsistence.

The result is that the system of finance capital has usurped the prerogatives of right, liberty and piety. Advancing its control over nature by fixing prices, it controls right; advancing its control over history, by controlling labour – preventing some from working while assigning many others ephemeral jobs which merely serve the interests of capital and are of little benefit to anyone – it controls liberty; advancing its control over expectations of the future and transcendence, it controls piety. Usurping the sovereign yet independent functions of law, government and religion, the system of finance capital gains a despotic sovereignty by stealth. Thus this newly ascendant god, visible nowhere, emergent from the future, executes the murder of God.

Notes

1 Friedrich Nietzsche, *The Gay Science*, 125, New York: Vintage, 1974, p. 181.
2 Nietzsche, *ibid.*, 343, 280.
3 Nietzsche, *ibid.*, 343, 279.
4 God retains this role in Kant's critical philosophy, and it is against this moral God that the force of the Nietzschean critique is brought to bear.
5 Nietzsche, *ibid.*, 344, 282. One may of course choose to believe that morality is properly basic, as does Martin Buber, in *I and Thou*, New York: Scribner, 1970, or that 'ethics is first philosophy', as does Emmanuel Levinas, in *Totality and Infinity*, The Hague: Martinus Nijhoff, 1979, requiring no external foundation, but such assertions are unverifiable, and express a piety directed towards the ethical; they are not evident in life, nature and history.
6 Nietzsche, *Beyond Good and Evil* 2, Harmondsworth: Penguin, 1973, p. 16.
7 Nietzsche, *The Gay Science* 344, 283; this same passage is also quoted by Nietzsche in *The Genealogy of Morals* Book III, 24, New York: Doubleday Anchor, 1956, p. 288.
8 Nietzsche, *The Genealogy of Morals* Book III, 27, 297.
9 'The denial of God contains an irremediable contradiction: it negates knowledge itself.' Theodor W. Adorno & Max Horkheimer, *Dialectic of Enlightenment*, London: Verso, 1997, p. 115.
10 The emergence of a purely secular form of thought and social organization is a comparatively recent phenomenon. It has recently been traced, in different ways, as a historical product of Christianity by Ernst Bloch, *Atheism in Christianity*, New York: Herder & Herder, 1972; Peter L. Berger, *The Social Reality of Religion* London: Faber & Faber, 1969; Michael J. Buckley, *At the Origins of Modern Atheism* New Haven: Yale University Press, 1987; John Milbank, *Theology and Social Theory: Beyond Secular Reason*, Oxford: Blackwell, 1990; Marcel Gauchet, *The Disenchantment of the World: a Political History of Religion*, Princeton: Princeton University Press, 1997, and Gianni Vattimo, *Belief*, Cambridge: Polity, 1999.
11 The historical moment when such a will to truth negates itself can be identified as the arrival of post-modernism in philosophy with Jean-François Lyotard's declaration, 'There are no more metanarratives,' in *The Postmodern*

Condition: a Report on Knowledge, Manchester: Manchester University Press, 1984.

12 'How we are still pious' is the title of *The Gay Science* 344.

13 Nietzsche, *The Will to Power*, 151, New York: Vintage, 1968, p. 95.

14 Michel Haar is among those who has identified this most clearly. See especially, 'Nietzsche and the Metamorphosis of the Divine', in Phillip Blond (ed.), *Post-secular Philosophy: Between Philosophy and Theology*, London: Routledge, 1998. See also Tylor T. Roberts, *Contesting Spirit*, Princeton: Princeton University Press, 1998; Giles Fraser, *Holy Nietzsche* University of Lancaster Ph.D. Dissertation, 1999.

15 Nietzsche, *Thus Spoke Zarathustra* Book I, 'Of the Three Metamorphoses,' Harmondsworth: Penguin, 1969, pp. 54–5.

16 Among the many who have argued this, see, for example, Alexander Nehamas, *Nietzsche: Life as Literature*, Cambridge MA: Harvard University Press, 1985, pp. 74–81, 93–105; Laurence Lampert, *Nietzsche's Teaching: an Interpretation of* Thus Spoke Zarathustra, New Haven: Yale University Press, 1986, pp. 111–20, 147–51, 245–54.

17 This move goes beyond Martin Heidegger's declaration of ignorance, 'What is most thought-provoking in our thought-provoking time is that we are still not thinking.' *What is Called Thinking?*, New York: Harper & Row, 1968, p. 28. Here, the guiding question of the thinking of thought determines the direction of thought, the way in which it is called. The question of the value of thinking finishes off such a project, and, by its own release of itself, gives life to the thought that wishes to think.

18 Nietzsche, *The Gay Science* 345, 283.

19 'But at the bottom of us, "right down deep", there is, to be sure, something unteachable, a granite stratum of spiritual fate, of predetermined decision and answer to predetermined selected questions. In the case of every cardinal problem there speaks an unchangeable "this is I".' Nietzsche, *Beyond Good and Evil* 231, 143.

20 For a discussion of this see Gilles Deleuze, *Difference and Repetition*, London: Athlone, 1994, pp. 26–69.

21 Nietzsche, *The Gay Science* 373, 335.

22 Nietzsche, *ibid.*, 347, 289–90; cf. The tightrope-walker in Zarathustra's prologue.

23 Nietzsche, *Ecce Homo*, 'The Wagner Case,' 4, Harmondsworth: Penguin, 1979, p. 124; cf. *Beyond Good and Evil* 31, 44.

24 Nietzsche, *The Gay Science* 359, 314.

25 Nietzsche, *Daybreak* Book II, 115, Cambridge: Cambridge University Press, 1982, p. 71.

26 Nietzsche, *The Gay Science* 354, pp. 298–9.

27 Nietzsche, *ibid.*, 355, 300. A parallel argument is put forward by Henri Bergson, *Time and Free Will*, London: Swan Sonnenschein, 1910, pp. 130–4.

28 Nietzsche, *Daybreak* 47, 31.

29 Nietzsche, *The Gay Science* 116, 174.

30 Gilles Deleuze, *Nietzsche and Philosophy*, London: Athlone, 1983, p. 35.

31 Nietzsche, *Daybreak* 129, p. 79.

32 Nietzsche, *The Gay Science* 114, 173–4.

33 Nietzsche, *Beyond Good and Evil* 29.

34 Nietzsche, *Daybreak* 119, 96.

35 Nietzsche, *ibid.*, 128, 77.

36 Nietzsche, *ibid.*, 125.

37 Nietzsche, *Twilight of the Idols*, 'The Four Great Errors,' 1, Harmondsworth: Penguin, 1990, p. 57.

38 The most extreme presentation of this principle is the work of Malebranche, a follower of Descartes, who, in order to explain causality in general, had to invoke God as the one who determines the communication of effects between physical bodies. See Nicolas Malebranche, *Dialogues on Metaphysics and on Religion*, London: Allen & Unwin, 1923.
39 Nietzsche, *Twilight of the Idols*, 'The Four Great Errors,' 2, 57.
40 Nietzsche, *ibid.*, 'The Four Great Errors' 6, 62.
41 Nietzsche, *The Anti-Christ* 15, Harmondsworth: Penguin, 1990, p. 135.
42 Nietzsche, *Twilight of the Idols*, ' "Reason" in Philosophy', 5, 48.
43 These categories are borrowed from George Lindbeck's categorization of models of the nature of doctrine. Lindbeck, *The Nature of Doctrine*, London: SPCK, 1984.
44 Nietzsche, *Twilight of the Idols*, ' "Reason" in Philosophy' 5, 48.
45 Nietzsche, *ibid.*, ' "Reason" in Philosophy' 1, 45.
46 Nietzsche, *ibid.*, ' "Reason" in Philosophy' 4, 47.
47 Nietzsche, *ibid.*, ' "Reason" in Philosophy' 4, 47.
48 'The "meaninglessness of events": belief in this is the consequence of an insight into the falsity of previous interpretations, a generalization of discouragement and weakness – not a *necessary* belief. The immodesty of man: to deny meaning where he sees none.' Nietzsche, *The Will to Power*, 599, 325.
49 See David Berman, *A History of Atheism in Britain From Hobbes to Russell*, London: Routledge, 1988.
50 André Gorz, *A Critique of Economic Reason*, London: Verso, 1989, pp. 112–13.
51 Gorz, *ibid*, p. 127.
52 Atheism was illegal in Britain during the 18th century.
53 Baron de Montesquieu, *The Spirit of Laws* Volume I, Book XX, Chapters 1–2, London: G. Bell & Sons, 1914, pp. 340–1.
54 Montesquieu, *The Spirit of Laws*, Volume I, Book XX, Chapter 7, p. 345.
55 Pierre Manent, *The City of Man*, Princeton: Princeton University Press, 1998, p. 15.
56 *ibid.*, p. 17.
57 Karl Polanyi, *The Great Transformation*, Boston: Beacon Press, 1944, p. 64.
58 Polanyi, *The Great Transformation*, p. 58.
59 Aristotle, *Politics*, 1257a, Cambridge: Cambridge University Press, 1988, p. 12.
60 Aristotle, *ibid*, 1257b, p. 13.
61 Aristotle, *ibid.*, 1258a, p. 14.
62 Locke, 'Some considerations of the lowering of interest and raising the value of money', in Patrick Hyde Kelly (ed.), *Locke on Money*, Oxford: Clarendon Press, 1991, p. 222.
63 Locke, 'Some considerations', pp. 222–3.
64 See Giovanni Arrighi, *The Long Twentieth Century*, London: Verso, 1994, pp. 139–41.
65 See Fernand Braudel, *The Wheels of Commerce: Civilization and Capitalism, 15th–18th Century, Volume II*, Berkeley: University of California Press, 1992, pp. 272–80.
66 An inverse and preceding move was when state power was adopted by trading companies, which were chartered to mobilize their own protection, rather than paying tribute or fees to local powers. Dutch capitalists were able to accumulate capital by establishing state monopoly capitalism over key trading resources such as spices in the Far East. This monopoly, however, eventually proved antithetical to the interests of investors because it encouraged mercantilist competition, and because profits were redirected to managers and directors. See Arrighi, *The Long Twentieth Century*, pp. 151–8. Eventually, territorial control over slave and

indentured labour and production across the Atlantic proved decisive against Dutch control over trade in the Far East (pp. 204–5).

67 Braudel dates the English financial revolution at 1688–1756. The importance of this move was soon recognized, although not its long-term significance: the Prime Minister William Pitt, in 1786, said he was persuaded that 'upon this matter of the national debt repose the vigour and even the independence of the Nation.' See Braudel, *The Wheels of Commerce*, pp. 525–8.

68 Locke, 'Some Considerations ...', p. 234.

69 One may contrast this to the collapse of 'Law's system' in France in 1714, when notes issued by Louis XIV were distrusted by the nobility, who retained hoards of coinage. One cultural difference between Paris and London at the time was the vigour of credit as the norm among English merchants, where loans were often not repaid on time, and not expected to be, in a practice dubbed 'overtrading'. See Braudel *The Wheels of Commerce*, p. 385.

70 Marx identifies national debt, 'the alienation of the state', as the magic stroke which 'endows money with the power of breeding and thus turns it into capital'. This thesis, that 'Capitalism only triumphs when it becomes identified with the state, *when it is the state*' (Braudel), is taken up by Arrighi as the basis for his economic history of the present age, *The Long Twentieth Century*, pp. 11–12.

71 Contingent historical factors, such as victory over the French in the Seven Years' War (1756–63), which led to control of India and the Atlantic, and the East India Company's plunder of Plassey in 1757, which helped to buy back the national debt from the Dutch, were certainly involved; they were enabled, however, by the level of investment made possible by the national debt itself.

72 These conditions of economic liberalism were embodied in the Poor Law Amendment Act of 1834, Peel's Bank Act of 1844 and the Anti-Corn Law of 1846.

73 Several other historical factors contributed to the specificity of England: the enclosure of the commons, replacing a communal lifestyle of access and obligation with a nominal right of property as local sovereignty; the direct intervention by the sovereign in religious life, especially in the establishment of the Church of England, the dissolution of the monasteries, and the authorizing of the Prayer Book, leading to sovereign authority over the religious organization of daily life; and the alliance of the sovereign with the merchant classes, upon whom it depended for borrowing to finance wars, leading to the lifting of restrictions from the activities of merchant capital which had previously been imposed by religious norms.

74 Locke's *Two Treatises of Government*, coinciding with the Glorious Revolution of 1688 which placed William of Orange on the English throne, were explicitly ideological in intent, aiming:

> to establish the Throne of our Great Restorer, Our present King *William*; to make good his Title, in the Consent of the People, which being the only one of all lawful Governments, he has more fully and clearly than any Prince in *Christendom*: And to justifie to the World, the People of *England*, whose love of their Just and Natural Rights, with their resolution to preserve them, saved the nation when it was on the very brink of Slavery and Ruin.

Preface, *Two Treatises of Government* Cambridge: Cambridge University Press, 1988, p. 7.

75 Locke, *ibid.*, II 7, 271.

76 Locke, *ibid.*, II 26, 286.

77 Locke, *ibid.*, II 4, 269.

78 Pierre Manent, *City of Man*, Princeton: Princeton University Press, 1998, p. 124.
79 Locke, *An Essay Concerning Human Understanding* Book 11, Chapter 21, 10, Oxford: Oxford University Press, 1979, p. 238.
80 Locke, *ibid.*, Book 2, Chapter XXI, 33, 252.
81 Locke, *ibid.*, 7, 263.
82 Locke, *ibid.*, 52, 267.
83 Locke, *ibid.*, 55, 269.
84 Locke's patron, the Earl of Shaftesbury, had invested heavily in the Royal African Company and Hudson's Bay Company.
85 Locke, *ibid.*, II 7–11, 271–4.
86 Locke, *ibid.*, II 27, 288.
87 Locke, *ibid.*, II 42, 297.
88 Locke, *ibid.*, II 43, 298.
89 Locke, *ibid.*, II 18, 279–80.
90 Locke, *ibid.*, II 23, 284. Many see in this opportunity of what is effectively suicide a contradiction, for Locke resists a right to suicide. In fact, there is no contradiction, for the slave has already forfeited his right to life. Indeed, in so far as the duty is still incumbent upon him to execute the laws of nature by punishing the transgressors against humankind, one could argue that a slave ought to execute himself by right. The fact that it was usually the slave-traders themselves who were the first aggressors is, of course, conveniently overlooked by Locke.
91 Locke, *ibid.*, II 49, Cambridge: Cambridge University Press, 1988, p. 301.
92 Locke, *ibid.*, II 14, 277.
93 Locke, *ibid.*, II 36, 293.
94 Polanyi, *The Great Transformation*, p. 72.
95 Polanyi, *ibid.*, 73.
96 Thomas Hobbes, *Leviathan* 10, Cambridge: Cambridge University Press, 1996, p. 63.
97 See Kelly (ed.), *Locke on Money*, p. 72.
98 Nietzsche, *The Anti-Christ*, 43, 165–6.
99 Nietzsche, *ibid.*, 43, 166.
100 Nietzsche, *ibid.* The natural conclusion to draw from this comparison is that the inspiration for the philosophy of rights, in Hobbes as well as Locke, is Puritan theology.
101 Hobbes, *Leviathan*, 14, 94.
102 Hobbes, *ibid.*, 21, 151.
103 Hobbes, *ibid.*, 14, 97.

2 Truth

Critical theory and structuralism

Repetition and exchange

In ages past, the pious *thought* about God. In order to exercise power, God must be an object of belief and desire, an ultimate guarantor of meaning. Acting through his humble servants, God required appropriate practices of thought. Capital, by contrast, exercises its power purely through socio-economic relations, without needing to become a universal object of reflection. Capital, being a benevolent despot, appears to permit freedom of thought, for thought itself is barely able to compromise its power.

Nevertheless, capital has until recently been subjected to regulation by sovereign powers. In order to advance capital accumulation, the priests of capital may attempt to diminish interference from governments by a variety of strategies, such as: constraining government policy by the threat of capital flight; establishing a new sovereign power that overrides national governments, the World Trade Organization, in the name of free trade; and limiting regulation of the markets in general. Similarly, to decrease taxation is to decrease national power; it is to give power to the individual to do as they wish with their money. Capital is an indulgent despot, allowing people to do as they wish both inside and outside the law; its priests are flatterers, trusting people with their own money, much as a gambling house trusts its customers to place their own bets. Never has a more humane, generous and free society existed than capitalist liberal democracy. It shifts responsibility from government to a collection of individuals who, in exercising rights rather than responsibilities, cannot be held accountable for sins of omission. Then the needs of the world which are not in practice met by profitable capital investment may be ignored in the name of the 'right' to dispose of one's property as one pleases. When such needs are essential to the survival of life, tragedy – of unlimited proportions – has and will necessarily ensue. Humane capitalism may destroy us all.

Who would wish to slander such a benevolent and indulgent despot as capital? Short-term interests of the powerful are always in line with those of capital – thus we want to believe in a system that creates 'wealth'. Long-term interests are not: this threat could be sufficient to make people believe again, and to entrust governments to regulate capital once more. The priests of capital have not yet seized complete control over science and knowledge. Nevertheless, the threat alone does not provoke a reaction against capitalism, without a majority public perception identifying the cause of the global threat as the capitalist system itself. Here, the capitalist system has an in-built protection system: it treats knowledge, like all other things, as it does commodities – indeed, the capitalist system simply is the logical outworking of universal commodification. Then the public may be permitted access to truth – there is no self-conscious despot to stop them – so long as that truth is commodified and traded. Clear and distinct perceptions of local truths exhibit a blinding light in comparison to the obscure matters of power relations in a global system: the more public discourse concentrates on immediate issues and incontrovertible facts, the less connection it has to 'reality' – understood as the entire network of relations that produces existence. The commodification of truth extracts truth from the conditions where it was produced, so that it takes on a life and value of its own. Ideology represses nothing; it simply blinds with light.

The Enlightenment critique of religion aimed to replace religious superstition with truth: its programme was the 'disenchantment of the world; the dissolution of myths and the substitution of knowledge for fancy.'[1] Truth became the apparent source of meaning and value that took the role previously occupied by God: Nietzsche detected a shift in pieties here to the 'metaphysical faith of the scientists.' For critical theory, following Georg Lukács, this world of the objects of thought particular to the Enlightenment is the product of a process of reification: a relation between people takes on the character of a thing and thus acquires a 'phantom objectivity'.[2] A product of the activity of thought, a 'congealed quantity of the homogeneous human labour'[3] of thinking, becomes alienated from thought and, through being exchanged between thinkers, takes on the natural and eternal appearance of a brute fact. The exchange of thought, then, separates truth from the temporal process of thinking, and substitutes for it the eternal truth of knowledge.

Truths, we are told, are immutable, incorporeal, identical over time, and related to a field of possible facts – even when they concern changeable, material, discontinuous, actual reality. The concept of truth as a simple substance, identical across time, and in relation to possible objects in a space of representation – found in public 'facts' just as much as in 'information' prepared for digital encoding – is the product of the *paralogisms* of pure reason. Kant's incisive critique of rational psychology as a domain of metaphysics[4] applies equally to rational epistemology: by taking the principles of the mode of representation as conditions of the represented content, one constructs a concept of truth out of the mode of representation itself. For information to be represented as true, the form of truth presupposes the characteristics of information: an unconditioned unity of relation (i.e. that truth is self-subsistent), an unconditioned unity of quality (i.e. that truth is not composite but simple), an unconditioned unity of plurality in time (i.e. that truth is identical to itself at different times), and an unconditioned unity of existence (i.e. that truth is knowledge of the existence of itself only, and of other things merely as representations).[5] These conditions, however, are the simple conditions of the commodification of knowledge as information or fact, prepared for recording or exchange. The paralogism is exhibited in the following syllogism:

> *That which cannot be thought otherwise than as true does not exist otherwise than as true, and is therefore always true.*
> *Truth, considered merely as such, cannot be thought otherwise than as true.*
> *Therefore it exists also only as true, that is, as always true.*

'Thought' is taken in different senses in the two premises: whereas in the major premise we find thought relating to an object in general – the very mode of representation – , in the minor premise we find truth's knowledge of itself.[6] The identification of these two senses of 'thought', through a sophistic figure of speech, a conjunction or non-identical repetition, allows the mode of representation to be identified with the very form of truth itself. Truth, then, may only be verified through representation. In order to remove all personal and temporal bias, truths may be identified through being regular, public, repeatable and exchangeable – these being the very conditions of representation as such. Then our very concept of truth is ideological.

Knowledge, as Francis Bacon first told us, is power. Adorno and Horkheimer diagnosed the motive of the Enlightenment as domination.[7] The mastered fact is one that can be exchanged as a commodity,[8] reproduced by other thinkers at will. Eternal facts are immune to temporal decay and the powers of nature. Thus the sphere of that which may be subjected to knowledge, nature itself, may be distinguished from the knowing mind that participates in the sovereign power of knowledge. A second motive diagnosed by Adorno and Horkheimer is fear of facing the truth:[9] much is evaded about the knowing mind by this claim to sovereignty, such as the way facts have in practice already been moulded, like clichés, by the dominant conceptions of science, commerce and politics.[10] Mastery over a specific sphere of knowledge, a timeless theory, leaves the total interconnected system of objects unknown, apparently ruled by chance.[11] Adorno and Horkheimer explained false conceptual clarity as myth:

The doctrine of equivalence of action and reaction asserted the power of repetition over reality, long after men had renounced the illusion that by repetition they could identify themselves with the repeated reality and thus escape its power. But as the magical illusion fades away, the more relentlessly in the name of law repetition imprisons man in the cycle – that cycle whose objectification in the form of natural law he imagines will ensure his action as a free subject. The principle of immanence, the explanation of every event as repetition, that the Enlightenment upholds against mythic imagination, is the principle of myth itself.[12]

The essential power of Enlightenment knowledge is gained through the principle of repetition: knowledge is confirmed by the prediction of repetition; control is exercised through engineering repetition. There is an irony to the sovereign freedom of the Enlightenment: making a pact with the god of repetition, thinking objectifies itself so that it only encounters truth when it is repeatable. Thinking becomes an automatic, self-activating process of reason and experiment: it constructs itself on the model of a machine.[13] The more the machinery of thought subjects existence to itself, the more it is fated to reproduce existence: the new always appears as predetermined by a cycle of repetition.[14]

The 'metaphysical faith of the scientists' is that the indicated object is the *cause* of the regular effects which they measure, rather than scientific custom, the repetition of the process of hypothesis and measurement, being the cause of the objects of scientific theory. In so far as objects can be abstracted from the world in the laboratory environment, and manifest behaviour that is regular, repeatable, public and relatively stable, then this procedure would appear to be justified. This process of abstraction, however, involves reification, and the elimination of change, chance, uncertainty and affect: 'abstraction, the tool of enlightenment, treats its objects as did fate, the notion of which it rejects: it liquidates them.'[15] The world is only known in so far as it is reified, homogeneous and abstract – another world is known rather than this one, and another world replaces this world in the reconstruction of the world through technology. The technological world is regular, repeatable public, and (locally and very temporarily) stable – like a religious ritual. Modern piety, then, consists in the belief that the ordered behaviour of the cosmos is the source of scientific hypothesis, rather than the belief that scientific and technological practice is the source of the world rebuilt in the image of the laboratory. This piety finds its own authorization in so far as the cosmos does indeed behave in an ordered fashion, paradigmatically in astronomy and mechanics. Nevertheless, it remains pious to the extent that this model of science is extrapolated to all fields of experience. Thus the superstition of economics is based on a quantification of wealth, which, in the form of Gross Domestic Product is an abstraction that takes no account of resource depletion, environmental damage, non-market transactions, leisure time, unemployment, underemployment, income distribution, durability of commodities and infrastructure,[16] culture, community and nature.[17] In so far as the world is reconstructed in line with economic 'science', vast and inevitable destruction necessarily ensues which remains largely invisible in most economic indicators. For economics has no direct concern with such 'moral' and 'cultural' issues: its method is entirely concerned with benefits, for no one would enter into a transaction unless it were in their own interests. No one, that is, who is not bonded by debt or meeting loan conditions; no one whose decisions are not made on their behalf by an exploitative partner or government; no one who is not enthralled by dreams of future wealth or technological development; no one who is not in ignorance of the depletion of their resources necessary for subsistence; no one who is not trading with a monopoly or an oligopoly of transnational companies; no one who is not influenced by marketing techniques; no one who has access to alternative sources for necessities of subsistence; in short, no one who is a major economic player. Economics is thus a 'scientific' superstition that has the same function as religious ideology: it conceals domination beneath the veneer of 'truth'.

The finitude of the human sphere of mastery over nature leads to a quest for further power. In so far as the Enlightenment model of truth has been partially successful in obtaining power, then its process is repeated, in a further intensification of the process of abstraction. As a result, truths which are more persuasive, intenser, clearer, more brilliant and blinding, are also all the more limited, local and finite. Sovereignty is bought at the expense of restricting its sphere of influence. The result, in a world of ecological networks of interdependence as opposed to eternal and abstract truths, is that the forces operating in the mind, in society, and in the environment, gain greater power and significance to the extent that they are ignored. Without invoking a 'return of the repressed', the greater the intensity of abstraction and sovereignty, the less responsibility one feels to networks of interdependence, and the less responsive one becomes to the actual powers that determine the conditions of life. Knowledge breeds ignorance.

Thus the brilliance of the Enlightenment, in which it seemed unintelligible that anything should be imprinted on the mind without the mind's perceiving it,[18] soon revealed that it knew little about the mind. In the age of suspicion that followed, instead of judging the inadequacies of the categories of existence posited by the human imagination in relation to an eternal perspective, these categories were taken as products of some pre-conscious process. Error was no longer the displacement of reason from its ideal; error became the displacement of reason from its own grounds, its pre-conscious process which lies at the essence of reason. Moral condemnation was replaced by ideology critique, the surgical procedure of operating behind the opponent's consciousness. The post-Enlightenment critic claims insights into the processes of his or her opponent's thoughts which exceed those which are available to the opponent's self-obstructing consciousness. The common practice in modern critique is, 'arguing behind the back and through the head of the opponent,' which, as Peter Sloterdijk has pointed out, is a surgical reification of the consciousness of the opponent.[19] Each ideological unmasking confronts the opponent with the embarrassing spectacle of the interests underlying their ideas, whether these interests are those of race, class, sex or ego, and result in privileged access to power, wealth or pleasure.

Due to its reifying strategy, modern critique is essentially antagonistic: one situates the other as an opponent, whose alienated false consciousness is to be overcome. Since, however, there are a multiplicity of material interests against which consciousness may be judged, then the process of unmasking becomes a war of consciousness, with the aim of seizing power by claiming access to better, more encompassing insights. When the mode of critique is domination, Hobbes' diagnosis of the 'state of nature' applies more accurately to modern critical thought: competition for power leads to contention, enmity and war.[20] Just as the Reformation led to wars of religion that eventually resulted in pluralism and toleration, the Enlightenment, through its critical unmasking of superstitions and false consciousness, has led to wars of consciousness and mutual unmasking where the ultimate uneasy peace is the 'state of consciousness that follows after naïve ideologies and their enlightenment': modern cynicism.[21] Competing knowledges, beliefs and theories are abandoned, along with their emancipatory project. In Sloterdijk's formulation, cynicism is enlightened false consciousness: we know what we are doing, but we do it nevertheless, due to force of circumstances and the instinct for self-preservation. Hence one adopts a useful form of enlightening critique at will because one consciously aims to discredit the opponent in order to serve one's own interests. In the last instance, the value of values is determined by the 'real world' of the market that forces us to adapt to it pragmatically by adopting a short-term realism. The modern self and conscience is no longer a privileged site of authority in relation to religious practices and beliefs, moral values, personal opinions or experienced 'truths'. Although each of these is presented to consciousness as the object of a sovereign choice, the emergence and adoption of each of these at any particular time is subject to pragmatic adaptation to the 'real world'.

In the second half of the twentieth century there was one intellectual movement which set itself apart from generalized conflict, claiming sovereignty by being more critical than any other. The structural revolution instituted a common currency – conceived as a network of differential relations – through which a few dense but luminous texts from a handful of Parisians were able to seize hegemony over the human and social sciences. Claude Lévi-Strauss, in his introduction to the work of Marcel Mauss, announced a revolution in thought that was able to solve the fundamental philosophical problem of truth: how one may unite thinking to what is thought. Competition for the object of knowledge, along with competing subjective strategies of theorizing, were overcome in a higher synthesis. Lévi-Strauss showed how the opposition between self and other, subject and object, thinking and thought can be overcome in the unconscious: for the unconscious, in so far as it obeys determinate laws, is objective, and yet it determines the ways in which we think. At the heart of subjectivity, there is something objective and impersonal that determines the course and shape of private, subjective thinking. The structural unconscious is both social and personal, both objective and subjective:

> Indeed, on the one hand, the laws of unconscious activity are always outside the subjective grasp (we can reach conscious awareness of them, but only as an object); and yet, on the other hand, it is those laws that determine the modes of their intelligibility.[22]

For Lévi-Strauss, the mental and the social were one and the same, and proof of the social could not be other than mental.[23] The problem, then is that of transposing concrete, subjective experience into the language of the objective observer. This enquiry can only proceed through the subject's capacity for indefinite self-objectification: through an analysis of mental structures, a descent is possible into the givens of the unconscious that,

> enables us to coincide with forms of activity which are both at once ours and other: which are the conditions of all the forms of the mental life of all men at all times.[24]

Truth is discovered in the form of a general equivalent. Individual perspectives and ideological illusions may be overcome when any consideration of the truth of beliefs is sacrificed in favour of exploring the relations between beliefs.[25] The 'objectivity' of the unconscious, and the 'self-objectification' in which the subject participates, is nothing more than the constancy of the formal relations between symbols: 'the social is only real when integrated in a system.'[26] Thus Lévi-Strauss repeated the paralogism of pure reason, conforming truth to the mode of representation.

According to Lévi-Strauss, Marcel Mauss discovered in his essay on *The Gift*[27] a constant relation between a variety of heterogeneous social phenomena: exchange. Where empirical investigation finds three obligations relating to the gift, which themselves produce social cohesion, obligations of giving, receiving and returning, Mauss' theory of a 'total social fact' calls for a structure underlying and determining such obligations.[28] Mauss himself, following the report of an indigenous Maori theory, had attributed a kind of energy to given objects, responsibilities and privileges, as the source of obligations – not an objectively real property, but one that is subjectively held. One receives not only a gift, but also the *hau* of a gift, and this one passes on with the gift; this *hau*, however, belongs to its source, and wishes to return there.[29] Lévi-Strauss avoided adding such an imaginary quality by identifying the primary, fundamental phenomenon as exchange itself.[30]

The essence of this primacy was located in the emergence of an awareness that things have meaning prior to a full knowledge of that meaning. At the moment when the entire universe suddenly became significant, capable of bearing meaning, it was none better known for being significant.[31] Symbolization, as a general feature of human linguistic consciousness, precedes what is symbolized – the possibility of consciousness as such precedes consciousness of particular things. At every stage, then, there is an excess of a signifier (e.g. *hau*) that cannot be attached to a signified. Our words function like signs, but, like a foreign language, we may not know what the signs mean in truth. The signified of this signifier appears to be unconscious, since it is unknown; in practice, however, this 'unknown' is not any particular thing, but a pure effect of the structure of relations by which things signify:

> Like language, the social is an autonomous reality (the same one, moreover); symbols are more real than what they symbolize, the signifier precedes and determines the signified.[32]

The social is the domain of what can be communicated or symbolized – what can be exchanged or enter into a common, shared, total reality. Instead of the social concealing a number of unknown, unexpressed and unsymbolized entities, it consists merely in the fact of symbolization, the fact of exchange. The social is the network of relations of exchange and symbolization that determine how its members will think; anything outside the social is literally unthinkable. The content that is symbolized will then appear arbitrary in relation to symbolization itself; the structural unconscious is essentially interdisciplinary, exceeding any domain of symbolization.

The structuralist theory of the signifier also has immense significance for an understanding of religion: for transcendence is the signification of something that is not properly understood, a signifier which exceeds its signified. As Jacques Derrida puts it, 'The sign and divinity have the same place and time of birth.'[33] If signification is an effect of a structure, a regular and repeatable set of relations, then the effect of transcendence will be produced by any regular and repeatable discourse or activity that does not focus on a publicly accessible object, such as myth and ritual. Repetition and exchange are sufficient to produce the transcendent.

The consequence for philosophy is then as follows: when one asks the question of philosophy, one enquires into the nature of language, the nature of symbolization, or perhaps even the nature of exchange itself. Abandoning its quest for foundations in truth or goodness, philosophy turns towards its own unconscious determination. The meaning of thinking and being is entirely determined by the structural unconscious. In the most extreme versions of structuralism, philosophy can be replaced by a set of mathematical formulae derived from group theory that function as timeless truths in the manner of the Kantian a priori.[34] Philosophy has no truth outside of its own determination that it discovers in the structural unconscious.

Lévi-Strauss implicitly laid down a challenge for philosophy: philosophy can be replaced by a science of knowledge. This challenge is easy to overcome in so far as one rejects the elements of totalization and atemporality at work in his theory,[35] but one whose consequences are far-reaching so long as one allows the independence of the signifier from the signified. For if unconscious social laws do indeed determine the way in which we think, then the only true philosophy can be a knowledge of such laws. In a fulfilment that subverts the original philosophical injunction of the Delphic oracle, 'Know thyself', philosophy can know nothing but itself; it has no access to truth or wisdom. Philosophy, then, becomes a commentary on its own history, texts, language and concepts; it becomes nothing more than a history of ideas, losing all reference to transcendence. The so-called 'postmodern condition' emerges necessarily from the structural revolution when the structural unconscious, taking itself as its own object of thought, becomes inaccessible to itself.

Gospel truth

Truth and repetition

Where there is repetition and structure, there is piety. Our practices of constructing knowledge are accompanied by a determinate mode of directing attention and a determinate mode of organizing reality. The Enlightenment conception of truth as universal, public, repeatable, exchangeable and systematic conceals its own mythical piety and social practice. For in so far as we have a determinate concept of truth without a knowledge of the Truth that will fill it, then the very concept – not the word 'truth', but the concept of truth itself – is a signifier that exceeds its signified. It exists in a system of repetition and exchange. It produces the effect of transcendence, and its corresponding piety: 'that Christian faith which was also the faith of Plato, that God is the truth, that truth is divine.'[36] This necessary illusion of reason is determined by structure, not by belief. Henceforth, all thought will be judged in relation to a detached, complete and absent Truth, which thought cannot possess, and in relation to which thought is placed in infinite debt. Moreover, the situation has barely changed with the structural revolution, which in making the 'total social fact', the system of differential relations, into a common currency, produces the concept of 'structure' as a signifier which exceeds its signified. Repetition is to be found in the paralogism of pure reason; repetition is to be found in social exchange, in action and reaction; repetition is to be found in the way that conscious thoughts and acts reproduce unconscious laws; repetition is also to be found in acquisition of knowledge of the structural unconscious, the repetition in consciousness of unconscious laws. Finally, in deconstructing the structure, the practice of deconstruction necessarily produces its own pieties by repeating the gestures of structuralism.[37]

Thus the murder of God, the removal of Truth from the concept of the truth, produces its own transcendent and 'unknowable' god. Nevertheless, in so far as the murder of God can itself be known, so can the hidden god of post-structuralism. Indeed, the identity of the murderer and the new hidden god is one and the same: capital. Then our enquiry may be twofold: to observe how a conception of truth as universal, public, repeatable and exchangeable emerged from piety itself within a particular historical tradition – and, as we will see, carries an inverted form of this piety in the practice of its conception –, and to observe how this adapted a conception of truth derived from a particular social system of equivalence and exchange.

The Enlightenment subordinated repetition to the goal of progress – progress in mastery over nature defined and constructed as the repetitive, and progress in mastery over the religious, defined and constructed as a relation to the unknown, unexpected and incommensurable. Where nature repeats itself, and religion loses itself, history moves forward. Unable to completely identify with repetition, the pieties enshrined within repetition lay concealed. In this respect, Christian doctrine prior to the Enlightenment was more enlightened, for it made repetition its conscious goal. Christian doctrine set out a model of truth that was specifically designed to maximize the power of repetition in generating piety, often refusing an absolute separation of nature and religion. The emergence of the modern conception of truth from Christian doctrine has a complex history.

In the first place, Christianity is distinctive among religions for the importance it attributes to right belief: piety is directed toward truth. For Christianity emerged from the proclamation of the decisive intervention of the power of God, in both the gospel of the kingdom of God and the gospel of the resurrected Messiah. Christianity originated with an apocalyptic intensification of divine sovereignty. With an overwhelming emphasis on God's grace, mercy and love – divine power alone bringing salvation – converts who pledged allegiance to the new sovereign had little to do but trust, confess their sins and wait. In particular, Gentile converts were not required to adapt to Jewish customs and law for the sake of salvation. The recipients of the gospel, then, were given a faith devoid of a rich cultural heritage – or rather, one in which the heritage conferring a religious identity was available primarily in belief and in scripture, not in practice. Whereas for a Jewish apostle to the Gentiles such as Paul, faith was an act of obedience to the command of the gospel, for his Gentile converts, faith, if it was to be allegiance to the true God and Christ, involved assent to a set of metaphysical propositions, abstracted from the history of Israel, that could identify God and Christ.

As a result of decontextualization, a series of transformations in the nature of religion were effected, which were only confirmed by the expression of Christian doctrine within the language of Greek philosophy.

1   From an initial announcement of the manifest power of God in action,[38] to be discerned by those who were perceptive,[39] a delay in the general resurrection[40] led the kingdom of God to become understood as a currently hidden but soon to be revealed power. Consequently, belief changed from special perception to future expectancy.
2   An announcement of a particular decisive victory of God over all his enemies became transformed into God's universal rule over all the nations.
3   A narrative of the history and identity of a people in terms of its relation to God, primarily in terms of promise and fulfilment, warning and judgement, was replaced by a timeless interpretation of the human condition.
4   A message to a particular society[41] became a general proclamation to all the world.[42]
5   Emphasis on righteousness as a condition of the community as a whole in the kingdom of God was replaced by an emphasis on personal conduct necessary to qualify for membership of the kingdom.
6   A purely future hope became incorporated into the believers in part in so far as they began to express a 'spirituality'.[43]
7   An innovative religious culture that was primarily oral, in the form of Jesus' preaching, parables, controversial discussions and ethical teaching, and in the form of the apostles' preaching, story-telling, prophecy and parenesis, was replaced by a culture that cherished its most significant revelation in a written form.

A concept of religious truth emerged that was metaphysical, universal, eternal, spiritual and written. Such is the truth later enshrined in the creed of the Council of Nicea. The Council of Nicea was called, funded, and attended by the new emperor Constantine as part of his attempt to establish unity through 'the right worship of the supreme God.'[44] As an ecumenical council, bringing together leaders from around the empire, the Church was allowed to see itself as a united but universal entity for the first time. Constantine was explicit about his attempt to secure power and stability: commenting on his attempts to resolve the Donatist schism, he is reported to have said, 'What more can be done by me, more in accord with my constant practice, and with the very office of a prince, than after expelling error and destroying rash opinions, to cause all men to agree together to follow true religion and simplicity of life, and to render to Almighty God the worship that is his due?'[45] In addition to the credal declaration, decisions were made concerning a variety of matters such as conditions for restoration of the lapsed, uniformity in posture for prayer, the forbidding of ambitious bishops from moving between sees, and the privilege of veto in the election of bishops for the patriarch of the provincial metropolis.[46] These principles of unity, uniformity, rendering static, and centralization of authority (corresponding to the characteristics of modern information – unity of relation, of quality, of plurality in time, and of existence) were also key principles informing Constantine's secular legislation; they can be seen in the building of a new capital; the stable value of coinage; uniformity of architectural style; the tying of farmers to land and civil servants to provinces; and the increasing role of the imperial court as executive of the empire and focus of patronage and honour. Constantine's religious policy can therefore be seen as an attempt to encourage unity at the metaphysical level so as to enhance the stability and unity of the empire as a whole. His espousal of monotheism, whether Christian or not, and the existence of the Christian Church as the only significant monotheistic religious movement, blessed with an existing institutional structure, a universal message, and an easily accessible entry requirement, naturally led to the patronage of the Church as the bearer of monarchical ideology.[47] The metaphysics of monotheism legitimated Constantine's return to monarchical rule, at the same time as it undermined the legitimacy of disunity and revolt. As Constantine affirmed, 'When men praise my service, as one who holds the Empire by the inspiration of God, do they not, then, confirm that God is the cause of my prowess?'[48] For the favour of God for Constantine is demonstrated not simply by his vision and his invoking of the Christian symbol of the *labarum* at the battle of Milvian Bridge, but above all by his victories over his rivals.[49]

The result was a creed – public, written, repeatable and unchanging – stamped with imperial and ecclesiastical authority, capable of being repeated 'at all times and in all places by all men', and later adapted to liturgical repetition. The content of the creed is remarkable in so far as it focuses on the eternal truths of God as sovereign and creator, and Jesus' identity with God in these roles: only metaphysical truths are significant here. At first sight, the Arian teaching of subordination, asserting that 'there was when the Son was not', would appear to be not only more rational and more honest exegesis, but also more effective ideology, preserving the absolute monarchy of the Father.[50] The disadvantage of this emphasis on divine transcendence, however, is that, as in the Jewish tradition, it can always function as a resource for prophetic critique. The Arians' most articulate opponent following Nicea, Athanasius, who argued for the equality of the Son on the grounds that only the divine essence could bring salvation from sin and death as deification, was able to preserve the sovereignty of God over rational, metaphysical speculation.[51]

As with the formulation of the Christian doctrine of creation *ex nihilo*, the main theological advantage was to emphasize the unrestricted sovereignty of God.[52] The incorporation of mystery into the highest of truths had the effect of inoculating authoritative doctrine against prophetic critique: no revelation could be higher than the Christian revelation, already possessed through the Son. As the full revelation of the Father, the identity of Father and Son guarantees the truth of the Son's revelation: 'no one knows the Father except the Son and anyone to whom the Son chooses to reveal him.'[53] The doctrine contained within the Creed thus legitimates the authenticity of the revelation that it expresses since it derives from God. Furthermore, as Logos, the Son is not merely the truth of the cosmos, but the form which such truth takes. The identity of the Logos as the only begotten of the Father Almighty would therefore imply that religious truth is uncreated, single, eternal, has its source in God and applies throughout the whole of creation. The implicit genius of the Athanasian position is this: the nature of God is repeated in the truth about God; the content of the creed is repeated in the truth of the creed.[54]

There remained a problem: if the Logos belongs to the Godhead rather than the order of creation, then how might it be learnt by mortal, fallible, temporal humanity? The descent of the Logos, becoming a human being, brings eternal truth into mortal flesh, but this eternal reason and life still needs to be appropriated by other mortals. The solution to this problem is the divinity of the Holy Spirit – if the Holy Spirit understands and inter-prets the revelation of the Logos within the believer, and therefore takes part in salvation, then it too must be identical with the Godhead. To repeat the truth is to participate in the life of the Godhead. Once God is the source, agent, medium and message of revelation, then the circuit is complete, effecting ideological closure.[55] The whole created order is referred to the spontaneous freedom of the sovereign for its meaning, while the logic of the divine sovereign as such derives solely from its internal relations. Consequently, knowledge can only be attained through the spiritual path of taking leave of the temporal order in order to love and understand God.[56] Moreover, the absolute sovereignty of God implies that all significant acts are direct acts of divine grace on a human matter that serves the gratification of the unrestrained will of God: if God were not love, he would be the very devil.

A further difficulty emerged when a variety of people claimed to speak in the name of the Holy Spirit, as in the Donatist schism, when a rival bishop was appointed to the same see. The development of the Creed at the Council of Constantinople in 381 CE contains the solution: 'We believe in one, holy, catholic and apostolic Church.' These four distinguishing marks enable one to ascertain the bearer of the true revelation where one finds the presence of God: the Church is united, holy, universal and founded on apostolic tradition. These four marks are fundamental criteria around which the Church may be called to reunite itself in times of schism or heresy. Just as God is the one, holy, universal revealer, the Church bears these marks of unity, holiness, universality and apostolicity in its sacraments and doctrine. The truth of the Creed is therefore identified by the marks of the Church which bears witness to it.

Now, these very marks may be suspected of being ideological mechanisms. For if the Church is identified by the way in which it brings together people from across racial, cultural, gender and class boundaries to share in the sacraments and believe the same doctrines, and this unity is regarded as a supreme value, then it may override in importance real social and historical relations of violence, exploitation and injustice that divide the classes, not to mention the threats of famine and death that are constantly faced by some of the Church's membership.[57] Ideological unity in doctrine and sacrament may devalue social and economic unity. Similarly, the universality of the Church, and the way in which its doctrines are understood, leads to a definition of sin in relation to 'man' in abstraction, and therefore concentrates on personal sins such as pride while ignoring the real relationships and conflicts between people.[58] Consequently, humility is urged on women, the poor and the oppressed, encouraging acquiescence in the status quo. Third, the holiness of the Church, in so far as it is manifested in spirituality as a concern for the soul, the next life, personal morality or worship of an eternal God, is ahistorical and attracts attention away from injustice in this life. Finally, in so far as the Church is apostolic, retaining a faithful interpretation of the apostolic witness, then it is irreformable. It was only in challenging this last claim that the Protestant reformers were able to unmask some of the ideology of the medieval Catholic Church.

Finally, ideology is borne most effectively by the liturgical function of the creeds. The creeds are written documents for public recitation, produced by authority, necessary for membership, containing universal doctrine. Whether one is a theology professor, an agnostic, an evangelical, a saint or an agricultural labourer, one still recites the same words, even though one might understand very different things by the words and enact very different speech-acts by their recitation. Unity is constructed through liturgical performance, not meaning.

Consequently, credal truths are the same, universal, independent of the speaker, refer to an external, metaphysical reality that guarantees their truth, and draw on concepts with given meanings. Although the creeds may not have developed this model of truth, they have functioned as a paradigm for the understanding of the nature of (gospel) truth within Western culture, and have therefore functioned as both vessel for its transmission and agent of its propagation. Within the liturgy, credal statements are regular, repeatable, public, unchanging and universal, reflecting the eternal and almighty God about which they speak. It therefore makes little difference if one replaces the creeds with the Word of God in scripture, or if one replaces scripture with scientific hypotheses, or even if one confines oneself to the facts: truth is still regarded as that which is regular, repeatable, public, unchanging, and universal, reflecting that which is. As such, whatever the validity of scientific law or Christian doctrine, it contains within its very structure the implicit ideal of sovereignty, whether this is expressed in the idea of God, the legislative subject, or the consensus of the community. Consequently, any candidates for truth which present themselves as irregular, singular, private, temporal and local may come to suffer the fate of public condemnation, just as the Logos was crucified. As the Council of Nicea almost declared 'As for those who say that "there was when he was not", and "before being born he was not", and "he came into existence out of nothing", or who declare that the Truth is of a different substance or nature, or is subject to alteration or change – the rational community condemns these.'

Ancient Athens and trade

Truth and exchange

The origins of the modern concept of truth thus lie in an intensification of piety towards sovereignty. Far from such an 'ideology' being merely the perspective of the sovereign imposed upon others to repress their experience of truth, piety itself constructed the very concept of truth as part of the body of sovereign power. Piety was the condition of truth, which in turn was the condition of the medieval form of sovereign power. Even in the modern era, when sovereign power is seized, alienated from the sovereign, and dispersed, it remains within reason as the ideal of Truth. Moreover, centuries of Trinitarian faith in the identity of Truth and its mode of revelation or representation form the historical condition for making the inverse move, identifying the form of Truth from the mode of representation itself. Just as it is possible to learn the Truth from the teachings of the true Church, it is possible to identify the Truth from the consensus of the scientific community.

In both cases, ideology may serve material and power interests which are extrinsic to the interests of reason and truth. These interests may insert themselves into statements of religious truth in four different ways: at the level of content, belief may construct an image of the divine fashioned after the worldly power interests that adopt it; at the level of source of belief, belief may construct an image of revelation based on the mode of discourse of the power interests which adopt it – authoritative speech; at the level of manner of believing, the credal mode of articulation of belief through regular and universal repetition may replicate the manner in which the prevailing power interest centralizes its own authority; and at the level of locus of believing, the Church may recognize itself through those characteristics which reproduce its own response to prevailing power interests. At each of these levels, piety allies itself with extrinsic interests in order to reap a reward. Whatever the explicit intentions, it is through structural conformity that extrinsic social interests are legitimated.

The extraordinary merit of Trinitarian theology is that of thematizing the structural identity of content, source, manner and locus of belief, in a fourfold repetition, so demonstrating its own truth: the opposition between self and other, subject and object, thinking and thought is overcome in doctrine. This model of truth has the power to authorize itself and to prove itself as supremely coherent and rational (even if based on paradox). Such coherence empowers belief; it is strong enough to govern the course of history. It does, however, have a weakness exposed by history – it may strengthen belief, but, unlike the early Christian gospel which must still be preserved, it cannot inspire and initiate belief. Once belief has occurred, then it may be authorized as inspired; but it remains possible to reject it. Similarly, while Trinitarian doctrine expresses the most powerful truth, it did not invent the concept of truth: the Church fathers expressed their new revelation within the language of Hellenistic philosophy. It is to the origins of philosophy that one must look to discover the nature of truth.

A more powerful insertion of extrinsic interests into reason may occur when reason itself is constructed out of the self-consciousness of a class. Such a reason is defined by its blindness with respect to the social relations in which it is embedded.[59] Philosophy has thus been adopted by Slavoj Žižek as a prime illustration of the nature of ideology:

> This is probably the fundamental dimension of 'ideology': ideology is not simply a 'false consciousness', an illusory representation of reality, it is rather this reality itself which is already to be conceived as 'ideological' – 'ideological' is a social reality whose very existence implies the non-knowledge of its participants as to its essence – that is, the social effectivity, the very reproduction of which implies that the individuals 'do not know what they are doing'.[60]

For philosophy cannot explain the 'Greek miracle': that an insight into the eternity of truth could come about at a particular point in history. To explain his insight into Being, Parmenides had to revert to myth in a poem that is taken as the first example of a deductive rational argument.

George Thomson attributed the emergence of philosophy to the growth of a society organized for commodity exchange.[61] The distinctive characteristics of Greek city-states from the seventh to fifth centuries BCE include the foundation of ports and city-states as commercial centres of trade with distant partners; the first invention and use of stamped coinage, leading to commodity exchange for profit and the rise of a merchant class and a democratic constitution; the consequent organization of slave-labour in commodity production for the sake of profit; and the emergence of the private individual defined by their land and property. These distinctive conditions produced a society based on commodity exchange, rather than being united around the tribe or the mythical identity of the sovereign. For Thomson, Heraclitus' philosophy expresses this: the 'concept of a self-regulating cycle of perpetual transformations of matter is the ideological reflex of an economy based on commodity production. In his own words, "all things are exchanged for fire and fire for all things as goods are exchanged for gold and gold for goods".'[62] The problem with this traditional Marxist account of the ideological superstructure as a 'reflex' of the base is that it gives little explanation of the process of the 'reflex'.[63]

Jean-Pierre Vernant has given a much fuller account of the emergence of Greek thought from the social and mental structures peculiar to the Greek city.[64] The account reaches as far back as the period of Mycenaean royalty which ended in the twelfth century BCE, a palace-centred civilization which had close links in religion, mythology, trade, architecture and social life with the ancient Near Eastern world. The king regulated all aspects of religious, military, administrative, economic and political life, including production, distribution and exchange, even down to apparently insignificant details. This degree of control was only possible through the scribes, who kept accounts of agriculture, land, trades, workers, slaves, taxes, military units and sacrifices to the gods. The palaces themselves were defensive, designed to protect the royal treasury. Similarly, religious ritual and the wisdom of statecraft were the secret prerogative of royalty; the power of royalty was dependent on its mystique in the form of the impenetrability of its rituals and magic formulae. The king was indispensable as the only one with access to the religious, military and magical dimensions of sovereignty; the king was the only one able to ensure the fertility of the soil.

Following the Dorian invasion which swept away the kings, the villages that remained kept the diverse dimensions of sovereignty separate, such as the chief of the armed forces, the commander and the priest. These different functions called for a reciprocal apportionment and delimitation. The problem of the one and the many, how disparate functions could be reconciled in a common life, came to dominate political thinking. The early Greek sages were concerned with the human world: the elements, division and harmonization of the city. In the work of Hesiod, in the eighth century BCE, we can observe a situation of general rivalry, already presupposing equality. Authority was now everybody's business: the city was focused on the *agora*, the communal or market place; similarly temples, open for public worship, replaced the royal citadel. In the *polis*, speech became the pre-eminent tool of power through persuading the public. Open for public debate, the arts of power were demystified and became independent of royal mythology. Laws were written down so that they could be disseminated as public property; consequently, wisdom became objective, public and consistent.

Two further material developments also transformed early Greek thinking: one was the emergence of the military role of the hoplites, members of a phalanx, which together were as effective as horse-soldiers. This resulted in a further democratization of the social order: one no longer had to be an aristocrat to own a horse and show prowess in battle; the citizens were able to demand power for themselves. Along with this power came a change in values: individual prowess in battle became a hindrance rather than a help. The aristocratic values of individual excellence and personal glory were condemned as hubris, excess, and the virtues of self-mastery and group action were exalted.

The second development was economic transformation: through trade across the Mediterranean, mining and the exploitation of large estates of olives and vineyards worked by slaves, rivalry could now be conducted through the accumulation of wealth. Such accumulation was regarded with suspicion by most parties: it replaced the aristocratic values of marriage, honours, privileges, reputation and power, and at the same time it undermined the self-mastery and asceticism of the citizen-soldiers. An equitable distribution of duties, honours, power and wealth was sought in which all were subjected to a general rule. The moralists and political theorists of the sixth century then attempted to give conceptual formulation to the values that were already implicit in conduct for the purpose of political intervention and reform. So, for example, Theognis: 'Those who today have the most want to have twice as much; wealth turns a man to madness.'[65]

Philosophy, thus, emerged from resistance to the unlimited effects of commodity exchange. Balance was sought in 'geometric equality': not equal shares for all, but an appropriate share for each individual according to his station. Rules involved rational connections, the moderation of apportionment in appropriate ratios. Geometry could then be taken as the standard of justice, of public authority and eternal truth; geometers had a particular role in the founding of cities – in the measurement and distribution of land.[66] It was in this environment that Pythagoreanism could flourish, concerned with musical and numerical harmony, statecraft, and an aristocratic apportionment of wealth. Similarly, Plato could take the truths of geometry as the standard of eternal truths or forms; he condemned those who refused to study geometry,[67] and had inscribed on his academy: 'Let no one enter here who is not a geometer.'

It may also be observed that geometry itself arose from a prior social form to commodity exchange: the absolute sovereignty of the ancient Near Eastern king over his lands, expressed in the measurement, apportionment and recording of quantities of land by the scribes. Land and place are rendered homogeneous by the sovereign measurement of land in ancient Egypt by means of lengths of rope; in the abstract eye of the sovereign, a recording of an area of land in terms of lengths of rope replaced the empirical reality of a differentiated and localized terrain. The result is that land, the principal resource of value, is measured in terms of abstract quantities.

Then Vernant could argue that the move from mythology to philosophy was effected by the Ionian philosophers who projected the structure and concepts of the *polis* on to the cosmos via the use of geometry: they imagined the structure of the universe and the positions, distances and dimensions of the stars according to geometric patterns. Geometric explanation of the cosmos eliminated mythological explanation at a stroke: 'The primal events, the forces that produced the cosmos, were conceived in the image of facts that could be observed today, and could be explained in the same way.'[68] Once there was a structural analogy between institutional and physical space, each could be thought in terms of the other.

Vernant's account shows the historical origins of many aspects of rational thought: written records and the sovereign control over states of affairs; speech as a power of persuasion addressed to the general public; justice as the mean, the appropriate measure, which rules over people as a whole; dialectic as the art of differentiating between disparate roles and functions so as to harmonize them in a common life; moral conceptions of truth in terms of justice and expiation; and natural philosophy as a set of relations between diverse forces and elements. Vernant concluded that, 'Greek reason was not so much the product of human commerce with things as of the relations of human beings with one another'.[69]

Vernant did not quite go so far as to explain the origin of philosophy as such, the self-consciousness of abstraction and the quest for abstract truth, as found in Parmenides. Parmenides sent thought in a new direction, concerned with the relation between Being and Knowing. For this identity to emerge, 'thinking', that which measures, and 'being', that which is measured, must be regarded as equivalent. These conditions are realized where geometrical thought meets a society organized for commodity exchange.

Alfred Sohn-Rethel, in his *Intellectual and Manual Labour*, gave an account of the division of labour into work on the abstract material of thought and work on concrete material resources. His aim was to give a historical explanation for the rise of a timeless conception of truth. The pivot of Sohn-Rethel's argument is the discovery of a process of abstraction that lies outside conscious thought, to be found in the network of social relations established by human interaction. Abstraction is thus a historical reality before it becomes a way of thinking. It is on the basis of real abstraction in a system of social relations that conceptual abstraction will emerge as a possibility for thought. The result is that abstraction itself, the object of philosophy from Parmenides to Martin Heidegger and structuralism, may be regarded as an effect of social interaction, and not its determinant.

Sohn-Rethel found the genesis of a real abstraction, implicit in social interaction but unthematized in thought, in the phenomenon of commodity exchange. He built on Marx's distinction between exchange-value and use-value: the value of commodities can be considered from the perspective of two different physical activities: 'use', the set of material processes by which humans live as bodily beings, and 'exchange', the movement of commodities in time and space from owner to owner. Use and exchange are separate activities that cannot be performed on the same material object at the same time, for the transference of property involves a renunciation of any capacity or right to use that property. Consequently, in the act of exchange, the separation of exchange from use 'has assumed the compelling necessity of an objective social law. Wherever commodity exchange takes place, it does so in effective "abstraction" from use.'[70] In the market, commodities stand still – they are waiting to be sold. The separation of these activities leads to the separation of exchange-value from use-value.

Sohn-Rethel pointed out that this abstraction does not concern the minds of the people in the market. A buyer is concerned with the possible uses of the object, but these uses only take place in imagination, until the exchange is over. During use, thought may express the experience of using; but during exchange, instead of being occupied with exchange, thought is occupied with an imaginary practice of use. Sohn-Rethel is therefore careful to apply the term 'abstract' to action:

> Thus, in speaking of the abstractness of exchange we must be careful not to apply the term to the consciousness of the exchanging agents. They are supposed to be occupied with the use of the commodities they see, but occupied in their imagination only. It is the action of exchange, and the action alone, that is abstract.[71]

The agents are concerned with the use of things; if they stopped to consider the abstractness of exchange, then exchange would not take place, for they would no longer be motivated to buy by imagination. Reflecting on the exchange relation is incompatible with engaging in it; any such abstract reflections can only occur before or after the event. Consequently, the abstract relation of exchange in the form of an 'objective social law' is a product of action and not of consciousness. During exchange, consciousness is determined by a social interaction, but it does not reflect this action: 'the action and consciousness of people go separate ways'.[72]

Now, in order to reach the level of abstract thinking, some consideration of the exchange relation must take place. There is also a second abstraction that operates within the exchange relation: value. Commodities that are exchanged for each other must be valued differently by each participant for such an exchange to take place. Nevertheless, they must be equated if they are to be exchanged for each other: exchange contains a postulate of equality in exchange, although the relative quantities are themselves arbitrary in relation to their use. The agreed price in barter results from haggling in which 'too much' and 'not enough' are reduced until exchange becomes possible: equality. This abstract postulate of equality is an effect of the social relation of exchange – that things really are traded. Then the contradiction between the empirical difference of commodities and their equality in exchange must be resolved by the invention of a dimension in respect of which they are equal: value. Here, again, consciousness departs from practice: the magnitude of value, which becomes an object of thought, must be distinguished from the form of value, the newly invented dimension, expressing the commodity form. It is the dimension of value, a pure abstraction, that will present the material for abstract conceptual thought.

The abstract postulate of equality extends beyond the price of the commodities exchanged: exchange is a physical transaction through time and space, and, for the duration of the transaction, the commodity has to travel through time and space without being used. It has to be delivered in a condition equal to when it set out. In theory, it will have an exceptional experience of the journey as 'abstract movement', for it must be delivered in the same condition as when it starts out. Time and space are supposed here to be absolutely homogeneous:

> Time and space rendered abstract under the impact of commodity exchange are marked by homogeneity, continuity, and emptiness of all natural and material content, visible or invisible (e.g. air). The exchange abstraction excludes everything that makes up history, human and even natural history. The entire empirical reality of facts, events and description by which one moment and locality of time and space is distinguishable from another is wiped out.[73]

For space or land to be quantified by geometry is one thing; for value itself to be quantified requires a further level of abstraction. The abstract quantification of value emerges when one commodity is set aside as a universal equivalent for exchange with all others. Incorruptible metals such as gold, silver and copper are chosen for use as general equivalents, embodying the abstraction of the object of exchange over time. Exchange-value can then be represented in terms of quantities of ingots of precious metals. The disadvantage of this, however, is that at each transaction the value of these ingots must either be taken on trust, or weighed, cut, melted and tested for their metallic purity: the value status of the commodity serving as money was subordinated to its material status. With the invention of coinage by despots, initially for fiscal, military and political purposes,[74] the stamp alone guarantees the value of money, and no longer its material status. The stamp itself is guaranteed by the authority and honour of the issuing state. As a promise, the coin becomes a purely abstract quantity, independent of its material status. The stamp on a coin embodies the abstract commodity form: it is purely an object of exchange; it cannot be used. It is merely an abstract concept.

The meaning of this evolution is as follows: commodity abstraction arises within a social practice, exchange, which is not thinkable while one is engaged in it; nevertheless, an expression of it may emerge into consciousness through a second abstraction implicit within it – the emergence of value, measured as an unusable, abstract, exchangeable quantity. There is a reflexivity about this abstract concept of value: value is not only a quantifiable measure, but it is a measure of quantity. In measurement, number is both ordinal and cardinal. The material embodiment of number as a reflexive measure of values is the general equivalent, money: for money is both a measure of values and a commodity that can itself be measured.[75] Like money, when value measures itself abstractly, it forgets the origins that have produced it, as Marx explained:

> Since every commodity disappears when it becomes money it is impossible to tell from the money itself how it got into the hands of the possessor, or what article has been changed into it. *Non olet*, from whatever source it may come.[76]

This quantity is merely an expression of a particular social relation; in a society founded on commodity production and exchange, it is an expression of the objective social laws that synthesize society. Furthermore, one is not inclined to doubt the reality of value when one has money that one can handle and spend. Abstraction is real. Nevertheless, consciousness of the value of money is the product of a double process of abstraction that conceals its origins in social practice. For Sohn-Rethel, the real abstraction found in the practice of commodity exchange is one and the same as conceptual abstraction; yet conceptual abstraction has no consciousness of its origins.[77]

Sohn-Rethel showed how Being is the concept fitting the abstract material of the commodity form itself: it is unchanging through time, fills all space, lacks all properties, and is strictly homogeneous and indivisible. Parmenides' insight is that this abstract conceptual being is the element of thought: 'Thinking and the thought that it is are the same. For not without what is, in which it is expressed, will you find thinking.'[78] Being is the abstract conception of reflexivity in the measure of values. In Parmenides' insight, thinking, the measure of values, is identified with being, the value of measures. Being is the abstract concept of the money form. If this is true, then Christian doctrine, in so far as it is conformed to a Parmenidean concept of truth, has failed to maintain the distinction between God and Mammon. Philosophy of religion, in so far as it derives the concept of God by logical deduction from the concept of infinite Being as expressed in Parmenides' revelation, as the one, eternal, immutable, omnipotent, omniscient, incorporeal, necessary being, may not worship God in the form of money, but it may be suspected of worshipping the abstract concept of the money form.

Conclusion

Capital does not maintain its despotic power simply through belief – even if the 'Washington consensus' on the benefits of global free trade and monetarist policy have been marketed as a dominant ideology. In order to overthrow the despotic power of capital so as to allow some chance of survival of human life on this planet, the 'truth' of capitalism must be known. In an age of enlightened false consciousness, truth alone is not sufficient: a consumer may know that they contribute to the destruction of the planet, but they continue to do so. The action and consciousness of people go separate ways. Power, in capitalism, is operational: even the power of commodified truth is determined by its social distribution, and not its content. Although the modern conception of truth absolves itself from self-consciousness of its social determination, it maintains in the social relations between facts a germ of the social practice in which it was created that may actualize itself in new social orders. Similarly, in its principle of repetition, it maintains a germ of the piety through which it was created, which remains a necessary condition for its operation. This is not to commit the genetic fallacy, to assert that the essence of truth is determined by its conditions of production. It is merely to suggest that a concept of truth, constructed through repetition and exchange, has a valency for re-establishing piety and market relations in an appropriate milieu as a surplus value to its own 'truth'. As we will see, the particular structure of Greek 'truth' has its own internal dynamic through which it tends to extend itself to all domains of experience, just as money measures the value of all things. Then such 'truth' tends to manifest itself as domination; it is adopted by the capitalist system for domination.[79] In order to strike at the power of capitalism, then, one must construct alternative conceptions of truth and reason, actualizing other social practices and pieties, which themselves have a *greater power of reproduction* than the dominant mode of representation in capitalism. This is the urgent challenge facing philosophy today.

Notes

1   Theodor W. Adorno and Max Horkheimer, *Dialectic of Enlightenment*, London: Verso, 1997, p. 3.
2   Georg Lukács, *History and Class Consciousness*, London: Merlin, 1968, p. 83.
3   See Karl Marx, *Capital* I, Harmondsworth: Penguin, 1976, p. 128.
4   Immanuel Kant, *Critique of Pure Reason*, Basingstoke: Macmillan, 1933, pp. 328 – 67. Kant himself was, of course, unaware of these implications. Lukács' critique of Kant as a bourgeois thinker is apt here.
5   See Kant, *Critique of Pure Reason*, p. 366.
6   See Kant, *ibid.*, p. 371.
7   Adorno and Horkheimer, *Dialectic of Enlightenment*, p. xiii.
8   Lukács cites Ferdinand Tönnies on this point: *History and Class Consciousness*, p. 131.
9   Adorno and Horkheimer, *Dialectic of Enlightenment*, p. 3.

10 Adorno and Horkheimer, *ibid.*, p. xiv.
11 Lukács, *History and Class Consciousness*, p. 102.
12 Adorno and Horkheimer, *ibid.*, p. 12.
13 Adorno and Horkheimer, *ibid.*, p. 25.
14 Adorno and Horkheimer, *ibid.*, p. 27.
15 Adorno and Horkheimer, *ibid.*, p. 13.
16 See Ted Halstead and Clifford Cobb, 'The Need For New Measurements of Progress', in Jerry Mander and Edward Goldsmith (eds), *The Case Against the Global Economy*, San Francisco: Sierra Club Books, 1996.
17 See Herman E. Daly and John B. Cobb Jr, *For the Common Good*, London: Green Print, 1990.
18 John Locke, *An Essay Concerning Human Understanding* Book 1, Chapter II, 5, Oxford: Oxford University Press, 1979, pp. 49–50.
19 Peter Sloterdijk, *Critique of Cynical Reason*, London: Verso, 1988, pp. 15–18.
20 Thomas Hobbes, *Leviathan*, Cambridge: Cambridge University Press, 1996, p. 70.
21 Sloterdijk, *Critique of Cynical Reason*, p. 3.
22 Claude Lévi-Strauss, *Introduction to the Work of Marcel Mauss*, London: Routledge and Kegan Paul, 1987, p. 34.
23 Lévi-Strauss, *ibid.*, pp. 21, 28.
24 Lévi-Strauss, *ibid.*, p. 35.
25 Jean-Marie Benoist describes an analysis as structural 'when, and only when, it brings to light a content in the form of a model, that is, when it is able to isolate a formal set of elements and relations upon which one can then argue without having to appeal to the significance of the given content.' Benoist, *The Structural Revolution*, London: Weidenfeld and Nicholson, 1978, pp. 111.
26 Lévi-Strauss, *ibid.*, p. 25.
27 Marcel Mauss, *The Gift: Forms and Functions of Exchange in Archaic Societies*, London: Cohen and West, 1970.
28 In both structuralism and historical materialism, the concept of 'totality' is the 'bearer of the principle of revolution in science', Lukács, *History and Class Consciousness*, p. 27. For structuralism, such totality is constituted by the ideal of the rational system; for historical materialism, such totality is constituted by determinate social relations of production in the form of classes. A single structuralist theory becomes itself an intensified totality, embracing theories of religion, history, language, economics and psychology, in Jean-Joseph Goux, *Symbolic Economies After Marx and Freud* (Ithaca: Cornell University Press, 1990).
29 Mauss, *The Gift*, p. 9.
30 Lévi-Strauss, *ibid.*, pp. 46–7.
31 Lévi-Strauss, *ibid.*, p. 60.
32 Lévi-Strauss *ibid.*, p. 37.
33 Jacques Derrida, *Of Grammatology*, Baltimore: Johns Hopkins University Press, 1976, p. 14.
34 For example, see Jean Piaget, *Structuralism*, New York: Basic Books, 1970. Piaget hopes to replace philosophy with a scientific epistemology which the studies the psychogenesis of structures of thought. Piaget then explains the emergence of the philosophies of Plato, Aristotle, Descartes, Leibniz, Locke, Hume, Kant and Hegel from the scientific studies in which they were engaged, whether mathematical, biological, psychological, or sociological. Piaget, *Insights and Illusions of Philosophy*, London: Routledge & Kegan Paul, pp. 47–59.
35 These elements are perhaps overemphasized by Lévi-Strauss' critics: he admits that no society is ever wholly or completely symbolic, because it is subject to

the impact of other societies, and earlier stages of its own development (Lévi-Strauss, *Introduction to the Work of Marcel Mauss* p. 17). The exceptions to the system, the mentally ill, shamans and magicians, are those who transcribe the state of a group caught between symbolic systems. Structuralism contains within its purview a study of dynamics of systems. See Benoist, *The Structural Revolution*, pp. 209–12.

36 Nietzsche, *The Gay Science* 344, (New York: Vintage, 1974, p. 283.

37 This process in Derrida's later work is best described by John D. Caputo, *The Prayers and Tears of Jacques Derrida*, Indianapolis: Indiana University Press, 1997. For a sound rapprochement between deconstruction and negative theology, wary of Derrida's caveats, see Thomas A. Carlson, *Indiscretion*, Chicago: University of Chicago Press, 1999.

38 'Now after John was arrested, Jesus came to Galilee, proclaiming the gospel of God, and saying, "The time is fulfilled, the kingdom of God has come near; repent, and believe in the good news".' Mark 1:14–15, *New Revised Standard Version*, Glasgow: Collins, 1989. The 'kingdom of God' is a misleading translation for what recent scholarship identifies as God's actual exertion of his rule. See, for example, Bruce Chilton, *God in Strength*, Sheffield: JSOT, 1987.

39 'Let anyone with ears to hear listen!' Mark 4:9. All biblical quotations are taken from the *NRSV*.

40 See Mark 9:1 'Truly I tell you, there are some standing here who will not taste death until they see that the kingdom of God has come with power.'

41 'Go nowhere among the Gentiles, and enter no town of the Samaritans, but go rather to the lost sheep of the house of Israel. As you go, proclaim the good news, "The kingdom of heaven has come near".' Matthew 10:5–7.

42 'Go therefore and make disciples of all nations ...' Matthew 28:19.

43 See 1 Corinthians 1:22, 5:5; Ephesians 1:13–14; Romans 8:5–17.

44 Constantine is quoted by W. H. C. Frend, *The Early Church*, London: SCM, 1991, p. 128.

45 From Eusebius' *Life of Constantine*, quoted in W. H. C. Frend, *The Donatist Church*, Oxford: Clarendon Press, 1952, p. 158.

46 See 'The Canons of Nicaea,' in J. Stevenson, *A New Eusebius*, London: SPCK, 1957, pp. 358–64.

47 See Alistair Kee, *Constantine versus Christ*, London: SCM, 1990.

48 As quoted in Robin Lane Fox, *Pagans and Christians*, New York: Viking, 1986, p. 631.

49 Similarly, Athanasius argues for the divinity of Christ from the success of Christianity. See *De Incarnatione Verbum Dei* LIII–LIV, London: Mowbray, 1953.

50 Rowan Williams argues that Arius was a rational exegete. *Arius: Heresy and Tradition*, London: Darton, Longman & Todd, 1987.

51 Williams' interpretation of Athanasius' theological motive. Athanasius does privilege essential over voluntaristic categories for relations in the Godhead, so as to keep divine power entirely separate from human power, thus enhancing its salvific force (see *Orationes contra Arianos* 2.3, 3.62, Oxford: Clarendon Press, 1873). The physical connotation of divine sonship is used to symbolize metaphysical unity of essence; thus Athanasius produces a rational picture of the divine nature, while invoking a paradoxical interpretation of the divine will, and a scriptural exegesis governed by theological presupposition rather than reason. See Robert C. Gregg and Dennis E. Groh, *Early Arianism: a View of Salvation*, London: SCM, 1981.

52 Indeed, Etienne Gilson argues that the Christian revelation of God as 'He Who Is', a primitive and unrestricted act of existing beyond the logical constraints of essence, takes philosophy into an existential understanding of the world that it

was not possible to reach on the basis of reason alone. Gilson, *God and Philosophy*, New Haven: Yale University Press, 1941, p. 65.

53 Matthew 11:27.

54 This, we may note, is the inverse procedure to the Kantian paralogism described above.

55 Diverse logics of this Trinitarian closure are described in Augustine's *De Trinitate* and Hegel's *Logic*. The consequence is a self-referential idealism resulting from an exclusion of material generation as such, for example: 'But the same word conceived and the word born are the very same when the will finds rest in knowledge itself, as is the case in the love of spiritual things ... . But in the love of carnal and temporal things, as is the offspring itself of animals, the conception of the word is one thing, the bringing forth another.' Augustine, *De Trinitate*, Edinburgh: T & T Clark, 1873, p. 234. To reverse the direction of repetition, as in the modern conception of truth or in Feuerbach's reversal of Athanasius, is still to retain the logic of ideological closure. For the relation between money, the Trinity, Hegel's speculative logic, and Marx's analysis of the commodity form, see Mark C. Taylor, *About Religion: Economies of Faith in Virtual Culture*, Chicago: University of Chicago Press, 1999, pp. 154–65.

56 'He, then, who is day by day renewed by making progress in the knowledge of God, and in righteousness and true holiness, transfers his love from things temporal to things eternal, from things visible to things intelligible, from things carnal to things spiritual; and diligently perseveres in bridling and lessening his desire for the former, and binding himself by love to the latter.' Augustine, *De Trinitate*, p. 372.

57 See Juan Luis Segundo, *The Liberation of Theology*, Dublin: Gill and Macmillan, 1977, p. 43.

58 Especially between genders. See the classic article by Valerie Saiving, 'The Human Situation: a Feminine View', in Carol P. Christ and Judith Plaskow (eds), *Womanspirit Rising: a Feminist Reader in Religion*, San Francisco: Harper and Row, 1979.

59 For an insightful analysis of the social relations enacted in the emergence of logic, see Andrea Nye, *Words of Power*, London: Routledge, 1990.

60 Slavoj Žižek, *The Sublime Object of Ideology*, London: Verso, 1990, p. 21.

61 George Thomson, *The First Philosophers*, London: Lawrence & Wishart, 1972, p. 263.

62 Thomson, *The First Philosophers*, p. 282.

63 Similarly, Lukács discussion of modern critical philosophy as the product of processes of reification lacks an explanation as to how the commodity form should penetrate all aspects of thought, including philosophy (see Lukács, 'The antinomies of bourgeois thought', in *History and Class Consciousness*, pp. 110–49). Neither can he explain the continuities between modern and pre-capitalist philosophy. Most philosophers do not work in or manage factories; while they may draw conceptual resources from surrounding processes and concepts, these have tended to be from science or art rather than industry.

64 Jean-Pierre Vernant, *The Origins of Greek Thought*, London: Methuen, 1982.

65 Quoted by Vernant, *ibid.*, p. 84.

66 Claude Mossé, 'The Economist', in Jean-Pierre Vernant (ed.), *The Greeks*, Chicago: Chicago University Press, 1995, p. 29.

67 Plato, *Gorgias* 508a, in *The Collected Dialogues of Plato*, Princeton: Princeton University Press, 1961, p. 290.

68 Vernant, *The Origins of Greek Thought*, p. 103.

69 Vernant, *ibid.*, p. 132.

70 Alfred Sohn-Rethel, *Intellectual and Manual Labour*, Basingstoke: Macmillan, 1978, p. 25.

71 Sohn-Rethel, *ibid.*, p. 26.
72 Sohn-Rethel, *ibid.*, p. 30.
73 Sohn-Rethel, *ibid.*, pp. 48–9.
74 Claude Mossé, 'The Economist', p. 41.
75 See Georg Simmel, *The Philosophy of Money*, London: Routledge, 1990, p. 122.
76 Karl Marx, *Capital Volume I*, Harmondsworth: Penguin, 1976, p. 205. 'It has no smell' is alleged to have been the reply of the Roman Emperor Vespasian to his son Titus, when the latter reproached him for obtaining money by taxing the public lavatories.
77 Cf. Adorno and Horkheimer: 'Bourgeois society is ruled by equivalence. It makes the dissimilar comparable by reducing it to abstract quantities. To the Enlightenment, that which does not reduce to numbers, and ultimately to the one, becomes illusion … ' *Dialectic of Enlightenment*, p. 7.
78 Parmenides frag. 8:35–7, in S. Marc Cohen, Patricia Curd and C. D. C. Reeve (eds), *Readings in Ancient Greek Philosophy: from Thales to Aristotle*, Indianapolis: Hackett, 1995, p. 39.
79 Yet, although it involves domination, the power dynamics operational in thought cannot be reduced to the hierarchical dualisms which it necessarily includes. The market of thought adds a further dimension to analyses of domination in thought, such as that of Val Plumwood, *Feminism and the Mastery of Nature*, London: Routledge, 1993.

3 Price

Cynical materialism

Signs

How might one assign a price to thought? Philosophy, for all its manifold reflections on thought, has rarely considered this question. The value of thought, yes, but its price? Nevertheless, in a modern age of nihilism, when the highest values are devalued,[1] and in an age of free-market cynicism, when 'money is the universal self-established value of all things',[2] the pricing of thought may come to play as crucial a role in the philosophy of the twenty-first century as the historicity of thought did in the twentieth.

Karl Marx defined price as follows:

> The simple expression of the relative value of a single commodity, such as linen, in a commodity which is already functioning as the money commodity, such as gold, is the price form.[3]

When pricing, thought is not evaluated purely in terms of its intrinsic merits or its use-value; other concerns, such as the labour expended in its production, its place in a network of interests and investments, and its exchangeability on an open market come into play. What could I be paid for this book? What could I buy with it? Will quick publication reduce its quality and long-term influence while enhancing my short-term prospects for promotion? Could it earn me useful contacts, recognition, publishing opportunities, career opportunities, a notorious reputation? Will it earn money for my university and department in the United Kingdom's Research Assessment Exercise? Is the validity of its arguments of less significance than its economic value? Indeed, in contemporary academic life, do considerations of the price of thought outweigh those of truth? Is the most significant question, 'What is this thought worth?'

Modern philosophy, deprived of access to eternal truth, wisdom and value by its own historicity, has attempted to fulfil the philosophical injunction of the Delphic Oracle, 'Know thyself,' by becoming a commentary on its own history, texts language and concepts. If modernity also 'excludes all thought that does not assume interests, or at least the materiality of the passions, as the theoretically determining ingredient,'[4] will philosophy come to know itself and acknowledge its interests by enquiring explicitly about the price of thought? How might one evaluate thought today, when its intrinsic merits are overtaken by extrinsic interests and investments? Indeed, how might one give thought a value, think valuable thoughts and can one express such values as a price? How can thought capitalize upon its predicament as a commodity on an open market?

According to Diogenes Laertius, Diogenes the Cynic answered Plato's definition of man as a featherless biped by bringing a plucked fowl into the lecture room. And when a young man was delivering a set speech, Diogenes began to eat lupins which he had concealed in a fold of his clothing – having drawn attention away from the orator, he said that he was surprised that the assembly should desert the orator's speech for the sake of eating lupins.[5] Such cynical gestures consist in responding to questions concerning the highest ideals with something material, edible and mortal. Abstract thought is exchanged for a useful, valuable object; implicating thought in material exchange is already a significant leap forward in the historical development that leads to the pricing of thought. In such gestures, the hypostatized, eternal values of philosophy become reincorporated within the material presence of the language by means of which they are signified, and disgorged by the material presence of the speaker who mouths them through fleshy mucous membranes: the Platonist is forced to eat his words.

There is a legend about the circumstances leading to the arrival of Diogenes as a wandering philosopher in Athens: his father was responsible for the minting of the currency of the city of Sinope, and Diogenes was caught interfering with or defacing the coinage. He was exiled. Diogenes' gesture has the following significance: the general equivalent, the valuable commodity by which all other values are valued, the coinage, is devalued. This nihilistic gesture was then regarded as the origin of the famous slogan of the Cynics: 'Alter the currency!'

Plato, for all his despising of Diogenes, concurred with him on this one point. As a conservative reactionary against the new social order based on wealth emerging in Athens, Plato founded philosophy on a new currency, the Idea as the speculative element of a general equivalent:

> I am afraid that, from the moral standpoint, it is not the right method to exchange one degree of pleasure or pain or fear for another, like coins of different values. There is only one currency for which all these tokens of ours should be exchanged, and that is wisdom. In fact, it is wisdom that makes possible courage and self-control and integrity or, in a word, true goodness.[6]

Nevertheless, whether wisdom circulates in personal conduct or in its concepts, tokens are required to make wisdom intelligible and communicable. Then, just as money has a dual reality as both a material commodity and the form of value, even the incorporeal currency of wisdom is distributed through material conduct and discourse.

The Platonist and the Cynic develop contrary perspectives on the same process of symbolization. For the Platonic idealist, the embodiment of wisdom in an exchange of tokens is disavowed, for wisdom is the common, detached, transcendent form through which moral sensitivity can measure a degree of participation. Nevertheless, to the extent that moral sensitivity itself lacks a full participation in the form of wisdom, then it must be reformed itself. Wisdom thus has a dual role: as a general equivalent, it measures the 'price' or degree of participation of conduct in wisdom; as a transcendent equivalent, it measures the 'price' or degree of wisdom of the measuring scales used in moral sensitivity. Wisdom is thus the source of both the price and the price-form, the actual value and the scale of measurement. Repeated in itself in this way, its purity remains uncorrupted by material considerations.

For the Cynic materialist, the materiality of the tokens of wisdom leaves scope for over-determination by material interests. Whatever the truth of wisdom, the tokens of wisdom do not circulate under the guidance of wisdom alone, but may, through their material manifestation, be organized at one and the same time by different economies, different circuits of exchange. One may illustrate the materiality of a sign by means of an analogy with film. The material embodiment of a film, a distribution of light on a screen, functions as a sign (A) of a narrative, signified (D) by the flow of images. A viewer, conditioned by experience to understand films, interprets (C) the sign (A) as the signified (D). The viewer has no concern with the director, cameras, lighting, set and crew, as a network of interdependent conditions (B^1), which have in reality produced the sign (A). Neither has the viewer much concern for the psychic states of the scriptwriter and director (B^2) which invented the narrative (A), or for the economic investment (B^3) which made the film (A) possible. It is not that the viewer is unaware of these; they are simply not usually relevant to the enjoyment of the film. Nevertheless, however much the film produces enjoyment or even reveals the Platonic Form of beauty, it remains overdetermined by the economic circuit. Now, in so far as signs show a single object or signified, they are products of reification, extracted through a system of exchange from their material conditions. Then the filmic analogy applies to semiosis in general. C. S. Peirce's reified 'object' of the sign must be distinguished as a signified from the networks of interdependent conditions which produced the sign. The general form of the semiotic 'triangle' should therefore be portrayed as shown in Figure 3.1.

We may note that the Platonic perspective is only valid when wisdom embodied in the signified (D) also functions as the ultimate determinant of

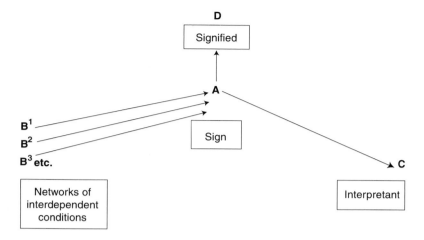

Figure 3.1 General form of the semiotic triangle

the arrangements and conjunction of the networks of interdependent conditions (B^1, B^2, B^3, etc.) – including the economic circuit. From Platonic idealism through to the modern construction of the world as information, we only pay attention to the simulacrum, a play of light. If these material networks have independent economies, then they may be subject to other investments. Thus, the displacement between the signified and its conditions introduces a margin of 'error' which may coexist with Platonic or modern truth, subjecting knowledge to exterior interests. Subjected to a general equivalent in an external system of exchange, thought acquires a price.

Spinoza's materialism

Immanent critique

Benedict (formerly Baruch) de Spinoza, writing at the cusp of modernity, pioneered a method of immanent critique through a cynical equivocation: *deus sive natura*. This equivocation between God and 'life, nature and history' may be regarded as both a methodological starting point and the goal that resolves the crisis of the murder of God – so long as concepts of God and nature are reformulated by the enquiry. The duality may be resolved as follows: 'the order and connection of ideas is the same as the order and connection of things.'[7] Ideas are only known objectively, as things. The mind is like a spiritual automaton; the order and connection of ideas, as revealed by the true method,[8] are expressed in the way in which ideas are caused or formed in the mind. Since the mind only has knowledge of itself in so far as it perceives the ideas of the modifications of the body,[9] then self-consciousness only comes about through the experience of actual conduct. For example, Spinoza observed the contradiction between the content of Christianity as a religion of love, joy, peace, temperance and honest dealing, and the conduct of Christians of fierce quarrelling and bitter hatred. The cause he found in the material interests of piety: the awarding of dignity and honours to the ministries of the church, so that 'every worthless fellow felt an intense desire to enter holy orders', under the motives of avarice and ambition. Once Church teaching is motivated by the desire to attract admiration, then only the outward form of religion remains, where 'the common people seem to engage in base flattery of God rather than his worship – and that faith has become identical with credulity and biased dogma.'[10]

Inadequate religious ideas emerge when people fail to understand the source of power that maintains such beliefs in practice. Superstitions arise from fear: it is therefore possible for despotic powers who generate fear to make use of religion as well. Central to Spinoza's critique of despotic sovereignty is an exposure of the ideological use of religion:

> Granted, then, that the supreme mystery of despotism, its prop and stay, is to keep men in a state of deception, and with the specious title of religion [today we may substitute 'economics'] to cloak the fear by which they must be held in check, so that they will fight for their servitude as if for salvation, and count it no shame, but the highest honour, to spend their blood and their lives for the glorification of one man. Yet no more disastrous policy can be devised or attempted in a free commonwealth.[11]

Here we find one of the first systematic critiques of ideology.[12] The removal of fear from religion involves its liberation from secular authority so as to allow freedom of thought. For religious ideas formed in the imagination under external powers are liable to be inadequate and inconstant, lacking in truth; similarly, superstition arises when those who hold the reins of power cloak the wrongs they commit with a show of legitimacy.[13]

Spinoza applied such freedom of thought to scripture, adopting a method which was the founding gesture of modern biblical criticism: 'I deliberately resolved to examine Scripture afresh, conscientiously and freely, and to admit nothing as its teaching which I did not most clearly derive from it.'[14] Within scripture, Spinoza found the following manifestation of Hebrew piety:

> it is important to note here that the Jews never make mention of intermediate or particular causes nor pay any heed to them, but to serve religion and piety or, as it is commonly called, devoutness, they refer

everything to God. For example, if they make money by some transaction, they say it has come to them from God; if it happens that they desire something, they say that God has so disposed their hearts; and if some thought enters their heads, they say that God has told them this.[15]

By taking this Calvinist piety to its logical extreme, attributing all that happens to God, Spinoza is able to identify God with nature. Power is converted into necessity, and made coextensive with the actual conduct of existence as a whole. As a result, supernatural revelation and miraculous intervention become subsumed within reason and nature.

Spinoza's method of immanent critique is clear: he began from the ultimate principle, the Word or mind of God, and attributed to it all the properties required by piety, including unity, universality and infinite power. This divine monarchy exceeds its human counterpart in so far as the power of the latter is manifested through decrees and force which meet and overcome some degree of opposition or rebellion. Since God is infinite, there is no limitation on divine power, and all that happens must express the sovereignty of God. Taking piety to its monarchical extreme, Spinoza converted it into reason: the properties of God are the properties of reason. Spinoza's great innovation, however, was to name the monarchical image of God as an inadequate idea: he took the greatest care not to confuse the power of God with human power or the right of kings.[16] All that God does results from the perfection of his own nature; God's freedom is not an arbitrary choice, but the simple fact that his power is infinite and unconstrained. Spinoza's critique of sovereignty is expressed in his critique of final causes: if God were to act for an end, with a purpose in mind, then he would seek something that he lacks – the end to be achieved.[17] All that happens, then, results as of necessity from the divine nature; all final causes and purposes are inadequate ideas. Spinoza explained the emergence of such ideas on the basis of belief in free will: men are born ignorant of the causes of their desires, but they desire that which is useful to them. Since men seek what is useful for them, they think that the end for which they act is the final cause. Moreover, since men find things in nature that are useful for them, they assume that these have been created for a purpose by transcendent governors: the gods. The result is the emergence of religions based on the material interests of piety:

> They must form an estimate of the nature of these governors from their own, for they receive no information as regards them: and hence they come to say that the Gods direct all things for the use of men, that men may be bound to them and do them the highest honour. Whence it has come about that each individual has devised, in accordance with his own nature, different ways of worshipping God, that God may love him above the rest and direct the whole of nature for the gratification of his blind cupidity and insatiable avarice.[18]

Spinoza, like Nietzsche, claimed that final causes invert cause and effect. Life is then interpreted in terms of reward and punishment by God, instead of experiences of pleasure and pain being regarded as the source of belief in gods. At a stroke, Spinoza eliminated all categories of purpose and meaning from the world, apart from those which are expressed in whatever follows of necessity from the divine nature. Rejecting the categories of will, purpose and meaning, there is no longer any subordination of reason to sovereignty. In this latter respect, Spinoza's immanent critique anticipates critical theory in modernity.[19]

Spinoza has been suspected of deifying reason. His critique of sovereignty, however, belies a simple piety before reason or nature. Spinoza's method of immanent critique removes all associations between thought and external interests and powers by means of his conception of truth: a true idea is an idea of its own idea – it is accompanied by certainty because it knows itself clearly and distinctly through its own cause.[20] An idea is therefore not considered as a passive object of thinking or contemplation, like a mute picture on a painting canvas, but as an active mode of thinking.[21] So, for example, a circle is one thing, but the idea of a circle is another.[22] So long as the idea of a circle is conceived under the image of a physical circle, it is merely imagined; once it is conceived through its definition by which it is generated, it is understood. Spinoza's immanent conception of truth is expressed in his definition of substance, which may be taken as heuristic and methodological, as 'that which is in itself and conceived in itself.'[23] Spinoza was interested in those ideas which are conceived through themselves; as such, they have reference to substance as the ideal of truth, or God.[24] The logical consequence of this definition of God as substance, conceived in itself, is that 'God's existence and his essence are one and the same.'[25] Spinoza understood eternity 'to be existence itself, in so far as it is conceived to follow necessarily from the definition of a thing.'[26] So to understand ideas as they exist in the mind of God, *sub specie aeternitatis*, that is to say, to grasp the truth of ideas, is to grasp them in such a way that their ideas involve existence: being actually thought, they exist or last over a duration.[27] As Antonio Negri puts it, 'the goal, reaching the truth and constituting an adequate idea, means making being speak.'[28] There are no secrets in the universe, everything is filled with light; all we need to do is modify and sensitize our perceptions.

This is a crucial point by which Spinoza modified the model of truth as universal and independent of speaker: essences, and the logical order of geometric deductions by which one reasons about them, conform to this eternal model, but they exhibit a disparity between that which is thought and the mind which thinks about them, that causes the thought. As such, they may be true, common to all minds, but they are not adequate ideas until they become a mode of thinking that exists over a duration, when they are understood. One may therefore observe two books in Spinoza's *Ethics*: one is a written order of definitions, axioms, postulates, propositions, proofs, corollaries, notes and appendices, demonstrated in a deductive manner like the truths of geometry. The second book is one of adequate ideas, conceived purely in terms of thought apart from words and images, which express themselves in the propositions but cannot be identified with them in so far as adequate ideas exist over a duration, and constitute the minds of the author and reader. Whereas the first book consists of a priori truths, the second book consists of *a posteriori* ideas: 'the mind has no knowledge of itself save in so far as it perceives the ideas of the modifications of the body.'[29] Knowledge is solely a matter of experience and experimentation; it is embodied and existential. One may therefore regard the abstract propositions of Spinoza's *Ethics* as inadequate ideas until they are thought, that is, until they become ideas in practice: 'In no wise, therefore, must we fear to feign anything, provided that we only perceive the thing clearly and distinctly.'[30]

When considered in practice, formerly abstract ideas undergo modification. Intellect is identified with will, for every idea contains its own affirmation.[31] Ideas, then, involve actions.[32] Since every idea follows from necessity, so does every action: there is no free will.[33] Consequently, divine power is unlike that of kings, since all its actions follow out of necessity from the divine nature.[34] God's power is therefore God's essence.[35] Essence, however, in so far as it involves a chain of affirmations, is a power of existing.[36] For specific modes of God, the existing ideas and things affirmed by God, essence is the endeavour to continue in existence, the power of self-affirmation.[37] Ideas are therefore modifications, acts or things themselves.[38] For a mode, the mind's idea is the idea of the mind in the mind of God, the mode itself; the mind's ideas are the ideas of the mind.[39] Indeed, those very modifications are felt as emotions by existing things, and the more powerful the cause, the more intense the emotion. Consequently, one can have the strongest emotion towards God, in so far as one is caused and affected by God; the essence of a mode is its knowledge of God in so far as God affects it, that is, its love for God. This chain of identifications is monism in action: it follows from the idea that there is only one substance.

This monism is neither materialism, pantheism nor atheism. Spinoza's so-called 'pantheism' depends on his propensity to swap subject and predicate when considering 'attributes':[40] on the one hand, extension and thought are attributes of God – God is an extended and thinking being; on the other hand, attributes are not properties, because they are conceived through themselves, so everything that exists must be conceived through the attributes of God. Modes, existing things, are thus modifications of attributes. Consequently, extension is a transcendental property: when we assume that material substance is finite and divisible, we conceive it abstractly through the imagination; when we think of it as it is in itself, we find it to be infinite and indivisible, just as a line is not composed of a series of points, but is the order through which a series of points may be ordered.[41] God is not identified with the 'world' because the 'world' is not a coherent concept except in so far as it is the totality of all that follows from the essence of God.

Immanentism, the identification of God with nature, with logic, with extension, or with substance, is not pantheism, for it undermines our knowledge of nature, logic, extension and substance: we do not know the meaning of a cause, of logical necessity, of a body, or of extension, until we have the idea of God understood directly through intuition.[42] There remains an excess in Spinoza that exceeds all reductionism. Logical necessity is simply power; power is simply reality; we only understand power to the extent that our minds express power. We only understand the power or essence of God when we intuit the idea of God, that is, God acts in our minds. God, consisting of infinite attributes, transcends the limits of human thought.[43]

It is through the practical, experimental philosophical method that Spinoza introduced becoming, affect and uncertainty into philosophy. In part, the practical method is simply a matter of removing obstacles to thinking, so that the mind can express its own essence: 'As long as we are not assailed by emotions which are contrary to our nature we have the power of arranging and connecting the modifications of the body according to the order of the intellect.'[44] Knowledge of the modifications of the body is felt as emotion. Common notions are thus common emotions: when we encounter a body with an emotion common to us, for example, the love of a particular thing or image, then if that body does not prevent us from possessing what we love,[45] then we will also love that body. Such common emotions then constitute a shared culture where one praises that which benefits what one loves, and glories in the praise of others when one acts to benefit what one loves. Common notions are inherently social.[46] Of course, such shared cultures can come into obvious conflict, as in the clash of rival tribes or cities. Spinoza, however, defined the best culture by human nature as such: human nature is common to all, and that which benefits human nature as such is a result of the endeavour of human nature to preserve its own existence. To live according to reason is then to express human nature, and to live for the benefit of human nature is to live according to reason.[47]

For Spinoza, therefore, it was rational human nature which is one, universal, virtuous and self-knowing, where human nature is the condition of humanity within a commonwealth.[48] The greatest good for those who follow virtue is that which is for the good of all; it is the greatest good of all, and all can equally enjoy it.[49] Such a commonwealth cannot flourish, however, unless it has a common focus, or object of love: this is human nature, but human nature understood clearly and distinctly, through its cause: God. Here, it is not sufficient that this love for God should be a common emotion, for each may form a different image of God, leading to division. A common love for God cannot form the basis of a common-wealth unless God is intuited as the necessary cause of all things, rather than imagined on the basis of some particular emotion. The emotion with which it is necessary to love God is that which constitutes human nature as such, not a modification of human nature in encountering some particular cause.

In Spinoza's final work, the *Political Treatise*, his optimism concerning religion and reason was abandoned in favour of an earthy realism. Religion has no effect against the passions where it is most needed; the path of reason is so arduous that 'those who persuade themselves that the multitude, or those occupied with public affairs, can ever be induced to live only by the dictate of reason must be dreaming of the poetic golden age or of a fairy tale.'[50] The political process of social constitution is deter-mined through and through by the imaginations and passions of its participants. Nevertheless, human behaviour is still entirely governed by determinate laws, and Spinoza's argument is valid whether people live by reason or imagination. Instead of engaging in any mystification of political power, politics is now entirely determined by the collective needs of the masses. There is no longer any political role for religion, morality or reason: the materiality of the passions are assumed as the theoretically determining ingredient. This is what Negri describes as 'the extraordinary modernity of Spinoza's political constitution of reality.'[51] Having excluded all final causes from the immanent system of reason, reason itself, by virtue of its very formality, is at the service of any natural interest.[52]

In the absence of a rational commonwealth, people need to cooperate and exchange services so as to meet their diverse needs for self-preservation. Those goods which are ideas, such as virtues and God, may be loved by all. There are, however, certain goods which each requires for self-preservation that cannot be held in common: these are bodies as commodities, finite material resources. In this respect, it is necessary to exchange goods and services apart from the idea of the commonwealth. Economic, symbolic and sexual needs do produce a degree of commonality between persons in the form of exchange. Exchange takes place when needs, desires and worth are equalized into a common price. People are no longer united by a common love, a common image, but by a common price. In the place of God in the commonwealth, we now find being speaking to us through money:

> But for providing these things the strength of one man would scarcely suffice if men did not exchange services. However, money has provided a short way to all these things, whence it has come about that the image of money occupies the principal place in the mind of the vulgar, for they can scarcely imagine any kind of pleasure unless it be accompanied with the idea of money as the cause.[53]

Marx's materialism

The commodity form

In practice, we live among inadequate ideas. Once social and material relations become mediated through symbols, then the organization of symbols may come to take a determining role in social and material relations. In so far as each symbol is a substitution for an underlying reality, then the conditions affecting that reality become attenuated in their influence on the symbol; the more processes of substitution passed through, the more the symbolic system takes on its own autonomy.

Jean-Joseph Goux has suggested that Marx, in his analysis of the commodity form, explored a general and elementary logic of exchange which laid the foundations of a universal science.[54] For Marx's analysis of the emergence of the money form shows how substitution and exchange leads to the adoption of a universal equivalent, a privileged symbol in terms of which the value of all other symbols can be measured. In the sphere of meaning, this privilege is accorded to language; in the sphere of commercial goods, this privilege is accorded to gold; in the sphere eroticism, this privilege is accorded to the phallus; in the sphere of social order, this privilege is accorded to the monarch; and in the overarching sphere of religion, measuring the value of all things, this privilege is accorded to God.[55] Marx provided an elementary logic of centralization and capitalization, a logic of capital, describing how the privilege of one symbol among others is formed and effaced, leaving its monopoly absolute, absolved in its transcendent role as the standard and measure of values.[56]

There are four stages to this process. In the first stage, the relative value of a commodity is distinguished from its use-value or sensuous characteristics in so far as it is prepared for exchange: its value in exchange can only be expressed in terms of an equivalent which substitutes for it. Thus if 20 yards of linen is worth one coat, then the exchange value of the linen is relative: it cannot be measured on its own terms, but only in terms of some other commodity which is an equivalent. The body of the coat symbolizes the value of the linen; it is the material embodiment of value. By assuming that this relation is reversible, saying that one coat is worth 20 yards of linen, one obscures the difference between relative and equivalent forms of value. It would appear that the equivalent, the coat, is endowed with the property of exchangeability by nature, as if its use-value, the form of appearance of the linen's exchange-value, were a physical property. Although the coat and linen are different, they are equated in exchange in respect of value; it is value that is their 'common notion', where value is only revealed in the substitution of the coat for the linen: 'despite [the coat's] buttoned up appearance, the linen recognizes in it a splendid kindred soul, the soul of value.'[57] It is here that a social convention, value in exchange, comes to appear natural and unalterable.[58]

A second stage is the extended form of value, when a commodity expresses its value relatively in multiple equivalents: 20 yards of linen is now equivalent to 1 coat, or 10 lbs of tea, or 40 lbs of coffee, etc. Instead of its value being determined by one specific exchange transaction, its value is expressed in a whole set of potential transactions. In the extended form of value, the commodity enters into a social relation, not merely with another commodity, but with the world of commodities in general. A third stage arises when the world of commodities in general, a whole set of potential transactions, expresses its value in terms of one equivalent, the general equivalent:

> A commodity only acquires a general expression of its value if, at the same time, all other commodities express their values in the same equivalent; and every newly emergent commodity must follow suit. It thus becomes evident that because the objectivity of the commodities as values is the purely 'social existence' of things, it can only be expressed through the whole range of their social relations.[59]

At this point, the abstract, exchange-value of any commodity is its set of relations with all other commodities, expressed in the form of a general equivalent. The 'objectivity' of things is their social existence, the whole set of relations they have with all other things. A fourth and final stage occurs when the general equivalent, the money commodity, becomes universal, so that all values are expressed in it. Money becomes the concrete embodiment of the abstract social relations between all things. A whole set of determinate relations is embodied in a single price.

Goux extended this logic of the symbolization of value to become a general equivalent of all spheres of symbolization. Applying the term 'capitalism' to this process of the centralization of the value of values, Goux can then define Western civilization in its entirety as capitalist:

> Western civilization can be formally defined as the one that pushed to its extreme limits – and in all domains – this solution to the organization of social elements: the subordination to a unique equivalent.[60]

For the result of this process of capitalization is that the unique equivalent is separated and set apart from all other commodities. Gold, for example, is selected to hold this privilege, not merely for its intrinsic properties of attractiveness, flexibility and durability, but also because it has little practical use: it is superfluous, so its use may be indefinitely deferred.[61] The unique equivalent is abstracted from use. This separation between money and commodities becomes the basis for all other important distinctions: for those who have money and buy commodities, evaluating them according to their price, are set apart from those who labour to produce and sell commodities, who value them according to time spent on labour.

Thus class divisions arise, which are reproduced in all other social and symbolic spheres. Then Goux emphasizes that the asymmetrical oppositions unconscious/conscious, images/words, feminine/masculine, mother/father, commodities/money, matter/mind are congruent to the class dichotomy that characterizes the monetary economy.[62]

This is not to identify the separate spheres, which can be easily differentiated. Nevertheless, there is a tendency for any given symbol to participate in different spheres of value, having a symbolic charge which may be at once libidinal, intersubjective and semantic. In so far as a mode of consciousness depends on a syncretic conception of value drawing on these spheres, then any exchange will include meaning, libido and commercial value:

> The economic value of the precious object remained integrated with the supernatural virtues imagined to be inherent within it. Such an object conveys not only wealth but sacred powers, social prestige, and ties of interpersonal dependence; its circulation enlists individuals and mobilizes religious forces at the same time that it represents the transmission of material goods.[63]

Only when there is a general equivalent in circulation can a new notion of the symbolic emerge, replacing the figurative and imaginary role of the symbol with its role as a currency, a simple medium of exchange. The distinctive feature of modern capitalist society is that the symbolic charge is removed, and purely economic relations are uncovered as such.[64] Once the exchangeable symbol is no longer subject to imaginary investment, then the whole social order of capitalism comes to suffer from a deficiency of meaning,[65] leading to contemporary nihilism. Universal history progresses by the advance of successive stages of symbolization in each sphere, and the subordination of each sphere to a general logic of symbolization.

Goux is to some extent aware of the way that his own theory participates in the phenomenon he describes by giving a theory of symbolization as a universal equivalent for realms of symbolization; this insight alone, however, does not lead to an alternative.[66] The same is undoubtedly true of Marx: his own account of the commodity form, which has been described as 'one of the great theoretical constructions of modern philosophy',[67] participates in the very fetishism which he so clearly explicates in his investigation of the 'metaphysical subtleties' and 'theological niceties' present in the objective distribution of things.[68]

> The mysterious character of the commodity-form consists therefore simply in the fact that the commodity reflects the social characteristics of men's own labour as objective characteristics of the products of labour themselves, as the socio-natural properties of these things ... . It is nothing but the definite social relation between men themselves which assumes here, for them, the fantastic form of a relation between things.[69]

Marx used an analogy with religion:

> In order, therefore, to find an analogy we must take flight into the
> misty realm of religion. There the products of the human brain appear
> as autonomous figures endowed with a life of their own, which enter
> into relations both with each other and with the human race. So it is
> in the world of commodities with the products of men's hands. I call
> this the fetishism which attaches itself to the products of labour as
> soon as they are produced as commodities, and is therefore insepa-
> rable from the production of commodities.[70]

Marx participates in the religion of capital by fetishizing labour and
money in his analysis of commodity fetishism. Commodity fetishism
derives from the distinction between use-value, derived from sensuous
characteristics, and exchange-value. For exchange-value is purely abstract:
it extinguishes all the sensuous characteristics of the object, and similarly
extinguishes the concrete character of the particular kind of labour that
has produced it. All that remains is human labour in the abstract:

> How, then, is the magnitude of this value to be measured? By means of
> the quantity of the 'value-forming substance', the labour, contained in
> the article. This quantity is measured by its duration, and the labour-
> time is itself measured on the particular scale of hours, days, etc. ... .
> What exclusively determines the magnitude of the value of any article
> is therefore the amount of labour socially necessary, or the labour-time
> socially necessary for its production ... .[71]

Fetishism is concealed in the concept of the 'socially necessary', which
already implies a system of exchange and comparison, condensing on a
general, objective equivalent. The labour theory of value only emerges
from commodity exchange. When a commodity, such as linen, expresses its
value in terms of innumerable other commodities, the labour which
produced each of these is undifferentiated. The commodity value shows
itself, in 'reality', as a congealed quantity of undifferentiated labour.[72] The
labour theory of value is true from the perspective of a factory owner
concerned with costs of production; it is also true for an unskilled worker
selling undifferentiated labour. It does, however, presuppose that a
comparison of two periods of labour has already been made, and that
these differentiated periods have been equalized so that they appear inter-
changeable from the point of view of their value. In short, the labour
theory of value presupposes that labour is to be treated as an exchangeable
commodity; it is only valid within the context of capitalism.[73]
Furthermore, knowledge of undifferentiated labour as the subjective
essence of society is only possible when undifferentiated labour takes on a
material form: this happened in early capitalism when workers, forced to

leave their lands, were separated from the means of production and had to sell their labour as a commodity. Just as one commodity, money, becomes a general equivalent, so one form of labour, that of the unskilled, wandering proletariat, becomes the general equivalent of all labour.

Only under such historical conditions, then, does the 'essence' of society become clear:

> Labour, then, as the creator of use-values, as useful labour, is a condition of human existence which is independent of all forms of society; it is an eternal natural necessity which mediates the metabolism between man and nature, and therefore human life itself.[74]

The concept of use-value is thus born from the conditions of capitalist exchange. Whether Marx's account is ironic here or not, the fundamental role of abstract, undifferentiated labour allows him to construct a metaphysical and methodological principle:

> Men are the producers of their conceptions, ideas, etc. – real, active men, as they are conditioned by a definite development of their productive forces and of the intercourse corresponding to these, up to its furthest forms. Consciousness can never be anything else than conscious existence, and the existence of men is their actual life-process ... . Life is not determined by consciousness, but consciousness by life.[75]

Marx, therefore, can view life from the point of view of production: ideas, abstractions, symbols and supernatural beings are produced. This perspective, the principle fundamental to all modern critical theory of viewing life as a temporal process of production, is a metaphysical perspective determined by the fetishism inherent in capitalism.

The fourth stage of the commodity form, the establishing of a universal equivalent, is only achieved under historical conditions where the value of money is ultimately assured by the gold standard. Money functions as the limit of all exchanges, the ultimate measure of prices, because 'money has no price'.[76] Since Richard Nixon abandoned the gold standard for the dollar in 1971, currency speculation has revealed this stage to be an illusion. Moreover, the transition from the extended equivalent, the relation to the 'social existence of things', to the general equivalent is money fetishism, the reification of social existence itself – 'social existence' is itself a fetishized concept based on exchange and a general equivalent. Furthermore, equally essential for the emergence of undifferentiated labour is the existence of an undifferentiated quantity of money, in the form of the primitive accumulation of capital, capable of investing in the means of production and purchasing free labour. Money synthesizes the value of past enterprises into a single quantity, recording memory in a simple capital sum. The result is the religion of money:

Money is the jealous god of Israel, in the face of which no other god may exist. Money degrades all the gods of man – and turns them into commodities. Money is the universal self-established *value* of all things. It has therefore robbed the whole world – both the world of men and the world of nature – of its specific value. Money is the estranged essence of man's work and experience, and this alien essence dominates it, and he worships it.[77]

Marx does not need to suggest that 'man' believes in or hoards money in order to worship it. The worship of money is a determinate social practice, outside of the subjective sphere of belief, which relates to the way in which values are established in practice. Signification in belief is replaced by exchange in practice. Instead of being an object of belief, money is an object of exchange: once resources are produced as commodities, as exchangeable, then their value in exchange will ultimately be determined in terms of the general equivalent, money itself. Capitalism, the religion of money, consists simply in the practice of trade for the 'appropriation of ever more wealth in the abstract.'[78] Capitalism is a material religion – a purely cultic religion without dogma[79]– a religion in things themselves. Unlike ideology, which always belongs to somebody else, material ideology belongs to nobody; it is purely objective, a constitutive illusion in the relation between things themselves. Slavoj Žižek uses the example of the Tibetan prayer wheel: you write a prayer on paper, put the rolled paper onto a wheel, and turn it automatically, without thinking. In this way, the wheel is praying for you, instead of you: 'They no longer believe, but the things believe for them'.[80]

To the extent that Marxian theory is determined on the basis of capitalism, from the point of view of capitalism, then its concepts are determined *in practice* by the religion of money. It is merely a prejudice inherited from Christianity to think that religion is dependent on belief. It is not sufficient to denounce belief in ideological illusion in order to perform a critique of religion, for religion inheres in the order of things, their determinate relations and the practice that derives from them. Thus if 'the mode of production in the material life conditions the social, political and intellectual life process in general,'[81] it also conditions the theory of capital. To view life from the perspective of labour, of production, of capitalism, is to reproduce the material worship of money; one does not even need to believe in the labour theory of value to do so. It is not Marx who prays; the commodities pray for him.

Finally, we may note that Marx's entire account is predicated on distinctions between form and content, abstract and concrete, the symbolic and the real. Such distinctions derive from the very idealist philosophy that Marxian materialism endeavours to overcome. One symptom that exposes the ideological nature of the Marxian account of commodity exchange is coinage itself: the stamp on the coin, guaranteeing its value, directly links its worth to the prestige and credibility of the issuing state. Coinage, therefore, bears witness to a mode of social valuing, in various forms such as belief, honour, obligation, duty, trust, dignity and authority, condensed on the sovereign, that already exists as an abstraction within thought prior to commodity exchange. By compressing social considerations into the concepts of 'social necessity' and 'social existence', Marx obscures the social relations inherent within commodity exchange. For free markets and the value of the currency must be created and sustained by sovereign power. Capitalism depends on a social order.

It is not sufficient to denounce Marx's pieties in the name of a more rigorous materialism and scepticism. For the labour theory of value is the basis of the theory of surplus-value, the core of Marx's theory of capital. Marx drew a crucial distinction between the value of labour-power as a commodity, to be paid in wages, and the value of the product of the same labour: it is labour that produces surplus-value.[82] Extraction of surplus-value by the capitalist can occur when the value of the commodities produced exceeds the cost of wages and resources. Surplus-value occurs when labour, and its product, are evaluated on the same monetary scale: capital is the extraction of surplus-value, the investment of money for a profit. Capital appears to be able to reproduce itself:

> By virtue of being value, it has acquired the occult ability to add value to itself. It brings forth living offspring, or at least lays golden eggs ... . It differentiates itself as original value from itself as surplus-value, just as God the Father differentiates himself from himself as God the Son, although both are of the same age and form, in fact one single person.[83]

By virtue of this self-propagating ability, and, in the form of money, the ability to exchange itself for any commodity and remove each commodity from circulation,[84] it becomes capable of encompassing the whole of existence by means of its power of transubstantiation: 'The capitalist knows that all commodities, however tattered they may look, or however badly they may smell, are in faith and truth money ... '[85]

Now, Marx argues that, given a certain amount of money in circulation, money is not capable of reproducing itself, creating greater value in existence. Capital, credit bearing interest, may therefore be differentiated from the physical commodity of money in circulation: 'the transformation of money into capital both takes place and does not take place in the sphere of circulation.'[86] As Gilles Deleuze and Félix Guattari put it, 'it is not the same money that goes into the pocket of the wage earner and is entered on the balance sheet of a commercial enterprise.'[87] There is a profound dissimulation in the substitution of one form of money for another: money in circulation is material, whereas credit, in the form of banker's drafts, is metaphysical. As the material form of ideology, capital is a dissimulation, an effect; it cannot be the real origin of value. In order to explain the increase of value effected within capitalism, Marx has to turn to labour as its source, and the dissimulation effected by comparing costs of labour in terms of wages with the value of the product in terms of labour-time. There is a surplus of labour in the value of the product over the value of wages – this labour is not exchanged as a commodity for wages, but belongs to the capitalist. Labour alone, then, is capable of producing value. As such, measured purely by the value it produces, surplus labour is an undifferentiated and abstract power of production of value in practice. It is therefore Marx's analysis of capital and the extraction of surplus-value which produces the concept of abstract, undifferentiated labour as the subjective essence of society. Abstract labour is surplus labour: labour abstracted from exchange. Marx's analysis of capital completes his analysis of the commodity form.

The result is that capitalism is not a socially determined necessity: in the encounter of free flows of undifferentiated labour, material resources, and invested capital, there is no pre-existing set of determinate social relations. Capitalism is a contingent absolute which produces time as undifferentiated surplus labour, produces land as undifferentiated surplus being, and produces value as undifferentiated surplus capital. The surplus is prior, in all respects. The ultimate result of Marxian philosophy is not economic determinism, but the practical instantiation of the Nietzschean murder of God: the world becomes one of undifferentiated flux. Then freedom of thought, of labour, of valuing, and of piety is the historical product of capitalism – and our only hope for producing a post-capitalist society.

Bataille and Bourdieu

Expenditure and strategy

Economic exchange, together with a general logic of symbolization and the social determination of abstract conceptual thought, need to be placed within a more general economy of personal, social and material interaction. Georges Bataille questioned the primacy of exchange in order to explore a more general economy of consumption or expenditure. Bataille somewhat hastily interpreted Mauss' essay on the gift as implying that relations of monetary exchange did not derive originally from barter, commodity exchange, but from the custom found among certain Amerindian tribes of *potlatch*[88]– the ritualized gift, from one chief to a rival, of large quantities of valuable goods, whereby the giver establishes his prestige and honour over the rival. The rival chief, in order to maintain the honour of his tribe, is then obligated to return an even more valuable offering at some later festival occasion. Alongside or sometimes instead of such gifts, events of conspicuous consumption and destruction take place. Although potlatch takes a unique form, it exposes the obligations to receive and return that belong to all social giving. Now, where most readers of Mauss assimilate potlatch within the general category of the gift, which, in virtue of the obligation to return a gift, constitutes a sphere of economic exchange, Bataille, following a Nietzschean insight, placed the gift within the general category of potlatch as sacrifice. Honour is gained by destruction.[89]

Bataille contrasted the restricted, monetary economy, characterized by principles of conservation of wealth and resources, equality in exchange and accumulation, with a more general economy of expenditure where one finds non-productive activities such as luxury, mourning, war, cults, the building of sumptuary monuments, games, spectacles, and non-reproductive sexual activity. Bataille placed sacrifice, a principle of loss, at the origin of value: for example, jewellery does not hold its symbolic value because one has to sacrifice a fortune for it – instead, one values jewellery because one has sacrificed a fortune for it; one desires jewellery because one desires the sacrifice that it represents. Similarly, Bataille cites the examples of religious sacrifice and gambling which release a passionate charge due to their wanton destruction.[90] Society, for Bataille, is not constituted by exchange, but by participation in expenditure; the poor are excluded from society by virtue of their inability to participate in communal expenditure.[91] For extravagant sacrifice of energy, property, and wealth wins prestige; hierarchy springs from loss: 'It is only through loss that glory and honour are linked to wealth.'[92] Those who wish to maintain their place at the top of a hierarchy are under an obligation of expenditure – funding festivals, religious institutions, and games. Bataille sketches a history of this obligation laid on the wealthy from the holding of Roman circuses, through Christian charity to the poor, to votive offerings to churches so that expenditure can be exhibited. An end to such obligations came with rise of the merchant classes: wealth became subdivided so that there were no large fortunes, and an extravagant display of mediocre wealth was deemed shameful.[93] The Protestant Reformation, with its assault on the external and spectacular elements of religion, turned the obligation for expenditure back within the sphere of the individual, where expenditure is used for the sake of accumulation rather than consumption in the Protestant ethic. For Bataille, the modern bourgeoisie, 'has distinguished itself from the aristocracy through the fact that it has consented only to *spend for itself*, and within itself – in other words, by hiding its expenditures as much as possible from the eyes of other classes.'[94]

The value of Bataille's approach is that he breaks open conceptions of rationality and economy based on the ideal of a closed, self-sufficient, well-founded, coherent system – the very ideal at the foundations of Greek philosophy – in favour of the real behaviour of people:

> human life cannot in any way be limited to the closed systems assigned to it by reasonable conceptions. The immense travail of recklessness, discharge and upheaval that constitutes life could be expressed by stating that life starts only with the deficit of these systems; or at least what it allows in the way of order and reserve has meaning only from the moment when the ordered and reserved forces liberate and lose

themselves for ends that cannot be subordinated to anything one can account for.[95]

Consequently, there can be no science of social behaviour that determines thought, no approach to philosophy through a purely structural unconscious. Thought is 'irrational' through and through, in so far as it is motivated by a desire to expend an excess of time and energy.[96]

While Bataille names expenditure and sacrifice as instances that exceed a rational system of exchange, he also points to the honour that accrues to the one who makes a sacrifice. For the society of individual producers organized for commodity exchange is an abstraction, a myth of political economy, the limit of a tendency that forgets the basis on which it is founded. That basis is revealed in the coinage, whose stamp is not an eternal idea, but only bears value so long as the issuing authority is recognized as a credible force. The institutionalization of credibility in the form of money conceals an inherent feature of commodity exchange: while trading, one needs to have confidence in the credibility of the seller. The honour of the agents is a feature of equal importance to the use-value of the commodities.

Pierre Bourdieu, in *The Logic of Practice*, described the conditions of the good-faith economy as contrasted with the market. In large markets, trade takes place between strangers, and there are endless tricks and frauds that are commonplace: mules might be trained to run off as soon as one has got them home; oxen may be made to look fatter by rubbing them with a plant that makes them swell; purchasers may band together to force prices down, and sellers may band together to force prices up. To avoid such dangers, efforts are made in traditional economies to substitute a personalized relationship for an anonymous one, via a network of middlemen and guarantors who can vouch for the trading parties. The element of uncertainty, that goods might not be all that they appear, introduces real changes into the system of economic practice. Where uncertainty cannot be overcome by knowledge, it may be overcome by trust. Bourdieu describes the 'man of good faith' of the Kabylia:

> The man of good faith would not think of selling certain fresh food products – milk, butter, cheese, vegetables, fruit – but always distributes them among friends and neighbors. He practices no exchanges involving money and all his relations are based on complete trust ... . The closer the individuals and groups are in genealogy, the easier it is to reach agreements (and therefore the more frequent they are) and the more they are entrusted to good faith.[97]

Only in transactions between relative strangers, where there is an absence of trust, do transactions become more purely 'economic', subject to various guarantees, conforming more closely to the principle of equality in exchange. The good faith economy is the gift economy described by Mauss.

Bourdieu exposed the error in Lévi-Strauss' structural and objectivist model of 'cycles of reciprocity' in gift-exchange: in reality, a gift may remain unreciprocated when one obliges an ungrateful person, or it may be rejected as an insult, inasmuch as it demands recognition. The structural model can only arise from the position of an external observer who observes the cycles after the facts. From the position of the agents, everything is uncertain, and one must be wary of giving to those who cannot return the gift, since they will be shamed, or to those who choose not to return the gift, since they count themselves as superior. Bourdieu posited a fundamental principle of 'equality in honour' that orients exchanges; such honour, however, does not pre-exist the cycles of exchange but is indeed constituted by it. The necessary cycles that appear after the fact obscure the very contingent processes that make up the agents' experience of gift and counter-gift:

> The simplest possibility that things might proceed otherwise than as laid down by the 'mechanical laws' of the 'cycle of reciprocity' is sufficient to change the whole experience of practice and, by the same token, its logic.[98]

The key difference between the logic of practice and the logic of exchange is that the former includes the irreversibility of time, allowing for uncertainty, and the adoption of specific strategies aimed at capitalizing on the situation. For during the interval between gift and counter-gift, the condition of obligation that endures will structure the relation between the two parties; for example, delay can be a way of exacting a deferential conduct from the other, such as when a father, being asked for his daughter in marriage, exerts influence by delaying his consent. In addition to delay, there is also the question of timing and occasion.[99] These temporal dimensions of delay and occasion are not easily comparable, exchangeable or equalizable, for exchange is primarily of an object or an honour, and this secondary element cannot easily be exchanged as well. These temporal dimensions belong to the sphere termed 'accidental', the non-economic sphere: as Aristotle says, there can be no scientific treatment of the accidental: 'this is confirmed by the fact that no science – practical, productive or theoretical – troubles itself about it.'[100] Bourdieu's attempt to construct a logic of practice is an exception to this rule, placing the accidental within the sphere of strategy.

Bourdieu's work intimates that there is a sphere of strategic rationality that proceeds entirely without the certainty and persuasion that characterizes Greek philosophy. Indeed, in so far as the latter is based on the determinate system of relations of the *polis*, in which all are subject to the general rules of justice, then Greek reason is as reliable as the foundations of the *polis* themselves, just as trade for money is as reliable as the value of the coinage, based on the prestige of the issuing state. Greek rationality contains within itself a mutual good-faith economy, a rational common-wealth of citizens, where the dangers of the market are overcome by making crime and fraud public, rather than merely private, offences: Solon's innovation in sixth-century Athenian law was that a wrong done to a particular individual is an attack on all; each person has the right to intervene formally.[101] For every fraud in the market-place decreases trust in the market as such, the very condition necessary for healthy trade. The essential elements in this alternative, strategic mode of reasoning are delay, timing, sacrifice, honour and value.

Bourdieu himself, however, remained a modern thinker in so far as he regarded the good-faith economy as ultimately determined by material interests. Strategy is in reality objective and economic, since it ultimately aims at maximizing profits. In a climate of uncertainty, however, it pursues this end by means of an element of misrecognition. In the good-faith economy, the self-interest which motivates action must ultimately be disguised by concepts of duty, honour, generosity, virtue and obligation. For the collective representation of a people to themselves may be considered as a separate constituent from purely economic relations of exchange. The person who commands respect, whose integrity cannot be questioned, is one who will be most successful in business:

> Because of the trust they enjoy and the capital of social relations they have accumulated, those who are said to 'be able to come back with the whole market, even if they went out empty-handed,' can afford to 'go to market with only their faces, their names and their honor for money' and 'even to bid whether they have the money on them or not.'[102]

Bourdieu introduces the concept of symbolic capital, the credit of renown, which, although invisible in a purely economic analysis, is convertible into economic capital. The exhibition of symbolic capital, although itself expensive, is one of the mechanisms that is profitable. A rich man is 'rich in order to give to the poor'. A gift that is not returned becomes a lasting obligation, a debt: power, in the form of recognition, personal loyalty and prestige is obtained by giving. One gains symbolically what one has lost materially. This recognition, or symbolic capital, only arises from a fundamental misrecognition of the benefits accrued by giving, which include all the benefits of loyalty including the mobilizing of guarantors or even of armies. The fiction of the gift, on which gratitude and obligation are based, is that it functions for the benefit of the receiver rather than the giver. In feeling gratitude, one forgets that the gift was envisaged for the purpose of producing gratitude. For Bourdieu, sacrifice is not an end in itself, but a conversion of economic into symbolic capital, *for the sake of material gain*. The good-faith economy only functions on the basis of a collective bad faith.

This leads to a suspicion concerning the motivations of the most inno-
cent of acts, once their effects are translated into the objective realm of
power relations and economic interests:

> The seemingly most gratuitous and least costly relations of exchange,
> such as expressions of concern, kindness, consideration or advice, not to
> mention acts of generosity that cannot be repaid, such as charity, when
> they are set up in conditions of lasting asymmetry ... [are] likely to create
> lasting relations of dependence, variants (euphemized by subjectivation)
> of enslavement for debt in archaic societies. For they tend to be inscribed
> in the body itself in the form of belief, trust, affection, and passion.[103]

The significance of Bourdieu's account is that it introduces the dimension
of honour into the mediation of exchange. With regard to symbolic
capital, the relevant criterion for assessing action is not its truth or efficiency, but the belief it commands. It is therefore possible to transgress
official rules by simultaneously acting and providing an interpretation that
will command recognition as the only legitimate one. This self-authorizing
strategy of ideological legitimation has its own economic value, in so far as
symbolic and economic capital are inextricably intertwined. The 'truth' of
honour, its reality as honour in practice, is not entirely dependent on a
system of cultural values, neither is it entirely dependent on anomalous
acts of individuals. The only test of whether acts of honouring are
honourable is that they are regarded as such.

The form of the gift is equivalent in significance, with respect to the emergence of abstraction, to the commodity form. The gift, in its broadest sense
as either material or symbolic, is the action that produces the effect of
honour. Honour is expressed in the gift in so far as the obligation to give is
considered in abstraction from the obligations to receive or return. Similarly,
one honours a giver by receiving the gift, forgetting the obligation to return
the gift, or by returning a gift, forgetting that one was obliged to receive. It is
the very abstraction of the gift from the 'cycle of reciprocity' that allows
honour to emerge. Although the obligations to receive and return derive, in
the first place, from a postulate of reciprocity in exchange, reciprocity
belongs to social relationships rather than to acquisitiveness and property
transfers. Even circular, and thus economically pointless, transactions ensure
that symbolic capital constantly grows in the form of mutual obligations,
services and dependencies.[104] Honour is therefore a cumulative form of
value; indeed, unlike commodities, it is extended by imitation, in that one
feels inclined to respect those who are respected by those one respects. As an
abstraction, honour can easily be separated from the gifts or acts of paying
respect that produce it; arising from a network of social relations, honour is
attributed to persons. As such, outside the 'cycles of reciprocity' in which it
was produced, honour comes to form a social hierarchy, leading to asymmetry in the cycle of giving.

While honour is hierarchical, then, it actually derives from a postulate of equality in exchange: not feeling an obligation to return is itself an expression of superiority judged in relation to the norm of equality. This account of the form of honour in the gift explains the obligation to give within cycles of exchange, but it does not account for the desire to give that initiates such cycles. As Georg Simmel pointed out, 'the return gift cannot preserve the decisive moment of freedom present in the first gift'.[105] To this extent, belief, trust, admiration and worship cannot be reduced to cycles of exchange; instead, cycles of exchange are produced by honour. In social interaction, there is an excess of belief, trust, affection, admiration and worship that energizes giving, honouring and sacrificing.

Bourdieu, in *The Logic of Practice*, reports an incident when:

> a much esteemed Kabyle mason, who had learned his trade in France, caused a scandal, around 1955, by going home when his work was finished without eating the meal traditionally given in the mason's honor when the house is built, and then demanding, in addition to the price of his day's work (1,000 francs), a bonus of 200 francs in lieu of the meal.[106]

The scandal was caused by his demand for a cash equivalent for a gift of honour: the traditional meal was a rite of alliance that transfigured an interested transaction into a generous exchange of gifts. According to Bourdieu, the declaration that the meal had a cash-equivalent betrays the silence and complicity by which the interested transactions of the economy of bad faith maintain their own illusions.

The mason's demand for a cash equivalent was a sacrilegious reversal of the symbolic alchemy used to transmute labour and its wage into unsolicited gifts. One may take this incident in Kabylia as a paradigm of the conflict between a traditional mode of reasoning, based on custom, belief and obligation, and a modern or rational approach, based on efficiency and self-interest. The emergence of a purely economic rationale to judge standards of conduct was designed to criticize the excesses of symbolic capital in the form of custom, belief, ritual and superstition surrounding the social order. Modern rationalization can only emerge when the collective bad faith of the consensus is exposed as superstition or ideological illusion, as nothing more than belief. The modern, philosophical quest for truth begins with a critique of mythical belief and ritual practice: as Marx said, 'criticism of religion is the premise of all criticism'.[107] Philosophy, therefore, belongs to the interchange of thought between strangers, no longer joined by the complicity of shared beliefs.[108] Methodological doubt, suspicion, mistrust and critique are the principal strategies of modern thought.

The mason in Kabylia, trained in France, embodies the modern rationality that aims to expose the collective misrecognition of ritual honours as an interested exchange. He, however, rather than the scandalized family who offered him the ritual meal, is the naïve nihilist. To imagine that the cash-equivalent of the mason's meal reveals its true purpose is simply an effect of modern rationalization. As in commodity abstraction according to Marx, it is nothing but a definite relation between people, the ritual meal, that assumes here, in rational critical *naïveté*, the fantastic form of a relation between things, a commodity exchange.[109] In fact, there is much about a ritual meal that can never be repeated, returned or exchanged, even if the ritual meal is a repetitive obligation: the food that is eaten, and the plants or animals killed to produce it; its taste; the honour given to guests who are invited, and the honour returned by the guests who come; the event of the meal itself, with its exchanges of conversation; the bonds of friendship that are formed, enabling the possibility of either party making further approaches asking for favours. Modern rationality, in contrast to traditional superstition, is simply not sufficiently materialist. The honours given by ritual gifts are cumulative and commutative – they are irreversible in time, and both donor and donee gain strength from a social bond. Likewise, the scandal of its refusal is an event of such social significance that I am still writing about it now. It is not only time that is given, that is irreversible: the event itself, its memory, and the future obligations it generates are a new creation that cannot be reduced to abstract exchange, to a price. The event of the meal, then, is a concrete reality that cannot be reduced to its representation in the symbolic order by means of which reciprocal obligations can be conceived.

Trust and honour, then, are prior to economy. Money is a material expression of the honour of the issuing state. Instead of economic interests constituting the truth of the ideological functions of honour and belief, ideology itself is the truth of economy. Reason and economy are founded on piety. It is a modern myth that the economy is driven by needs, interests and desires. Alongside these, there is an additional motive of human behaviour which expresses itself primarily in uneconomic activity. Honour, rightly or wrongly given, is only a 'collective misrecognition' from the determining standpoint of material interests. From the standpoint of honour, there is no 'misrecognition,' no objective social reality behind imagination; there is only the collective reality of social imagination itself, expressed in gift and countergift. Worship, an imaginary relation to conditions of existence, ideology itself, or 'collective misrecognition' is the function and purpose of economic relations and rationality.

This leads us to a suspicion: the form of rationality developed within the tradition of Western European reason, from the Greeks onwards, constructs standards of truth, value, interest and power which themselves largely conform to expressions of economic exchange. To assimilate reason to economic interests, concerned with the price of thought, involves a misrecognition: questions of historical origin and causality, and questions of truth, being and value are less significant than the honour of this tradition. For the interest of reason, and the force that may adopt reason, is cynical at its very heart, for it defends the honour of reason, even at the expense of truth. Nihilism is the genealogical element of our thought, the transcendental principle of our way of thinking. Rationality may judge and depreciate life in the name of base interests.

This, briefly stated, is the charge. It is not simply that contemporary reason is nihilistic. Reason, in the European tradition as a whole, is nihilistic because it elevates an abstraction to be honoured above the relation that gives rise to it. Disavowing its own piety, forgetting that it always involves its own acts of worship, it attempts to attain a critical, objective stance, apart from religion, by elevating its own very 'natural' idols into concepts that govern its own ways of living and thinking. There is, however, an alternative way of constructing rationality without subordinating it to an ideal of abstraction as eternal truth. Thinking involves evaluation: in the first place, an evaluation of what is worth thinking about, what is worth honouring by spending time on it. In this respect, the value of values is determined by sacrifice or degree of expenditure – such sacrifices are the price of thought. Festivals, sacrifices, and worship of the gods may be regarded as elements of practice that are 'irrational' for both an epistemological and a strategic rationality. Such rituals invoke myths that are themselves incredible, but do not demand 'belief' in propositional terms. The validity of a myth is the honour in which it is held, expressed pre-eminently in its preservation and repetition, but also in its ritual dramatization and performance. For modern thought, all such beliefs and practices are inefficient, uneconomic, impractical, superstitious and repetitive. Such sweeping judgements fail to gain access to the mythical rationality that mediates all relations between people and between people and things as relationships of honour. In order to proceed towards a truly critical account of reason, value and religion, rituals of honour and sacrifice must become fundamental concepts of analysis.

To think is to honour. Immanent within the circulation of abstract thought or economic cycles, immanent within ritual repetition, there is an element of asymmetry, an excess that escapes enclosure within the system. This excess is not an absence or a lack, but a gift. What is given is both material reality and the symbolic order with its cycles of repetition. Only through such repetition does reality acquire consistency and objectivity. Then the murder of God, the absence of the transcendental signified in modern reason, is not the expression of a weakness or lack, but a positive strength. Devoid of the material content to which it appeals, modern reason as a whole does not function within an ideological cycle of exchange. Its entire being is determined as gift, being, excess, and expenditure. Reason itself is sacrifice, for its immanent cause remains concealed within it. Reason may recuperate a proper distribution of values when the social relations it enacts are made ethical. Piety may transform both reason and economy when it connects to immanent potencies that give it being and power.

Notes

1 Friedrich Nietzsche, *The Will to Power*, 2, New York: Random House, 1967, p. 9.
2 Karl Marx, 'On the Jewish Question', in *Early Writings*, Harmondsworth: Penguin, 1975, p. 239.
3 Marx, *Capital Volume I*, Harmondsworth: Penguin, 1976, p. 163.
4 Antonio Negri, *The Savage Anomaly: the Power of Spinoza's Metaphysics and Politics*, Minneapolis: University of Minnesota Press, 1991, p. 137.
5 Diogenes Laertius, *Lives of Eminent Philosophers*, VI.40 and VI.48, London: Heinemann, 1958, pp. 43, 49. Gilles Deleuze reports that Diogenes responded to the question, 'What is philosophy?', by carrying about a cod at the end of a string: *The Logic of Sense*, London: Athlone, 1990, p. 135. This tale is not recorded by Diogenes Laertius, and may have been invented by a conflation of other stories involving a wine-jar on a string and some salt fish in a lecture-class. See Laertius, *Lives of Eminent Philosophers*, VI.35 and VI.57.
6 Plato, *Phaedo* 69a–b, in *The Collected Dialogues of Plato*, Princeton: Princeton University Press, 1961, p. 51.
7 Benedict de Spinoza, *Ethics*, II, Prop. VII, London: J. M. Dent, 1989, p. 42. It is this adequation of thought and being that seems to constitute the target of Immanuel Kant's critique of metaphysics: if cognition conforms to objects, then the unconditional cannot be thought without contradiction because it would be conditioned by our thinking about it (Kant, *Critique of Pure Reason*, Basingstoke: Macmillan, 1933, p. 24). But Spinoza has in fact anticipated Kant's transcendental method by thinking the idea immanently through its cause, that is, the idea through which it is understood. However, it may claimed that Spinoza fails to make the Kantian distinction between the faculties of understanding and reason: understanding applies itself to phenomena, whereas reason never applies to experience or to any object, but solely to the understanding which it organizes according to principles. Spinoza may be charged with falling into transcendental illusion by taking the subjective necessity of a connection of concepts for an objective necessity in the determination of things themselves, Kant, *Critique of Pure Reason*, p. 299. In fact, Spinoza's critique is more radical: he abandons the empiricist belief that knowledge comes into representative consciousness through sensible intuition, as well as abandoning the rationalist belief that things themselves can be known through ideas. Instead of an active mind working on passive intuitions to produce understanding, the ideas of the mind are themselves passive, produced by causes. Kant's entire critique depends on the sovereignty of the rational subject that Spinoza himself subjects to criticism. But in so far as Spinoza does not specify the precise meaning of an immanent cause, the whole of his system remains incomplete.
8 Benedict Spinoza, *On the Correction of the Understanding*, 38, London: J. M. Dent, 1910, p. 238.
9 Spinoza, *Ethics*, II, Prop. XXIII, p. 59.
10 Spinoza, *Tractatus Theologico-Politicus*, Leiden: E. J. Brill, 1989, p. 52.
11 Spinoza, *ibid.*, p. 51.
12 Indeed, Louis Althusser saw in Spinoza's book 'the matrix of every possible theory of ideology.' Louis Althusser, 'The Only Materialist Tradition, Part 1: Spinoza' in Warren Montag and Ted Stolze (eds), *The New Spinoza*, Minneapolis: University of Minnesota Press, 1997, p. 7.
13 Spinoza, *ibid.*, p. 261.
14 Spinoza, *ibid.*, pp. 53–4.
15 Spinoza, *ibid.*, pp. 60–1.
16 Spinoza, *Ethics*, II, Prop. 3 note, pp. 40–1.
17 Spinoza, *ibid.*, I, Appendix, p. 34.

18 Spinoza, *ibid.*, I, Appendix, pp. 32–3.
19 See, for example, Yirmiyahu Yovel, *Spinoza and Other Heretics: Volume II: The Adventures of Immanence*, Princeton: Princeton University Press, 1989; Christopher Norris, *Spinoza and the Origins of Modern Critical Theory*, Oxford: Blackwell, 1991; Warren Montag and Ted Stolze (eds), *The New Spinoza*.
20 Spinoza, *Ethics*, II, Prop. XLIII, p. 70.
21 Spinoza, *ibid.*, II, Prop. XLIII note, pp. 71–2.
22 Spinoza, *On the Correction of the Understanding*, 33, 236.
23 Spinoza, *Ethics*, I, Def. III, p. 3.
24 Spinoza, *ibid.*, II, Prop. XXXII, p. 64.
25 Spinoza, *ibid.*, I, Prop. XX, p. 20.
26 Spinoza, *ibid.*, I, Def. VIII, p. 4.
27 Spinoza, *ibid.*, II, Prop VIII, corollary, pp. 43–4.
28 Negri, *The Savage Anomaly*, p. 34.
29 Spinoza, *Ethics*, II, Prop. XXIII, p. 59.
30 Spinoza, *On the Correction of the Understanding* 62, 246. See also Deleuze, *Expressionism in Philosophy: Spinoza*, New York: Zone, 1990, p. 137.
31 Spinoza, *Ethics*, II, Prop. XLIX corollary, p. 77.
32 Spinoza, *ibid.*, III, Prop. I, p. 85.
33 Spinoza, *ibid.*, II, Prop. XXXV note, 65; Prop. XLVIII, p. 75.
34 Spinoza, *ibid.*, II, Prop. III note, pp. 40–1.
35 Spinoza, *ibid.*, I, Prop. XXXIV, p. 30.
36 Spinoza, *ibid.*, I, Prop. XIX, p. 20.
37 Spinoza, *ibid.*, III, Prop. VII, p. 91.
38 Spinoza, *ibid.*, II, Prop. VII, p. 42.
39 Spinoza, *ibid.*, II, Prop. XXI, p. 59.
40 For a discussion of this reversal, in terms of attributes as 'attributive', see Deleuze, *Expressionism in Philosophy*, p. 45.
41 Spinoza, *Ethics*, I, Prop. XV note, pp. 13–16.
42 See Richard Mason, *The God of Spinoza*, Cambridge: Cambridge University Press, 1997, pp. 250–2.
43 See Spinoza, *Ethics* I, Prop. XVII note, pp. 18–20.
44 Spinoza, *Ethics* V, Prop. X, 205. See also Deleuze, *Expressionism in Philosophy*, p. 282.
45 See Spinoza, *Ethics* IV, Prop. XXXII, p. 161.
46 A common notion is an adequate idea, an idea of its own idea; it is a cause of itself. A common emotion, then, is one which, if encountered in another, will produce the same emotion in oneself; at the same time, this emotion in me produces the same emotion in the other. All common emotions therefore take the form of mutuality, solidarity – they are the crystallization of the social in an emergent relation. Spinoza's examples fail to explore the emergent and constructive nature of immanent knowledge that exceeds all social conditioning. Nevertheless, this is the direction indicated by his thought.
47 See Spinoza, *Ethics*, IV, Prop. XXXV proof, p. 163.
48 Spinoza, *Ethics* IV, Prop. XL, p. 170.
49 Spinoza, *ibid.*, IV, Prop. XXXVI, p. 164.
50 Spinoza, *Political Treatise* I.5, New York: Dover, 1951, p. 289.
51 Negri, *The Savage Anomaly*, p. 202.
52 Theodor W. Adorno and Max Horkheimer, *Dialectic of Enlightenment*, London: Verso, 1997, p. 87.
53 Spinoza, *Ethics* IV, Appendix XXVIII, p. 195.
54 Jean-Joseph Goux, *Symbolic Economies After Marx and Freud*, Ithaca: Cornell University Press, 1990, pp. 3, 12.

55 Goux, *ibid.*, pp. 10–11.
56 Goux, *ibid.*, p. 10.
57 Marx, *Capital Volume I*, p. 143
58 Marx, *ibid.*, pp. 139–49.
59 Marx, *ibid.*, p. 159.
60 Goux, *Symbolic Economies*, pp. 44–5.
61 Goux, *ibid.*, p. 27.
62 Goux, *ibid.*, p. 90.
63 Goux, *ibid.*, p. 126.
64 Goux, *ibid.*, p. 125.
65 Goux, *ibid.*, p. 131.
66 For a full critique of the five 'paralogisms' found in Lacanian psychoanalysis and reproduced by Goux, the classic analysis by Gilles Deleuze and Félix Guattari in *Anti-Oedipus*, London: Athlone, 1984, remains obscure but precise. For a lucid explication, see Eugene Holland, *Deleuze and Guattari's Anti-Oedipus: Introduction to Schizoanalysis*, London: Routledge, 1999, pp. 36–57.
67 Etienne Balibar, *The Philosophy of Marx*, London: Verso, 1995, p. 56.
68 Karl Marx, *Capital Volume I*, Harmondsworth: Penguin, 1976, p. 163.
69 Marx, *ibid.*, p. 165.
70 Marx, *ibid.*, p. 165.
71 Marx, *ibid.*, pp. 129–30; note that Marx uses irony throughout these sections.
72 Marx, *ibid.*, p. 155.
73 Marx's discussion of the sale and purchase of labour-power is written from the perspective of the capitalist. See Marx, *Capital Volume I*, pp. 270–82. Moishe Postone, in *Time, Labor and Social Domination*, Cambridge: Cambridge University Press, 1996, has attempted to rehabilitate Marx's critical theory as an immanent critique of the labour theory of value within bourgeois political economy. While this is certainly an objective tendency of Marx's texts, it does not address the extent of fetishization found within his theory.
74 Marx, *Capital Volume I*, p. 133.
75 Marx, *The German Ideology*, London: Lawrence & Wishart, 1970, p. 47.
76 Marx, *Capital Volume I*, p. 189.
77 Marx, 'On the Jewish Question', in *Early Writings*, Harmondsworth: Penguin, 1975, p. 239.
78 Marx, *Capital Volume I*, p. 254.
79 See Walter Benjamin, 'Capitalism as Religion', in *Selected Writings Volume I, 1913–1926*, Cambridge MA: Harvard University Press, 1996, p. 288.
80 Slavoj Žižek, *The Sublime Object of Ideology*, London: Verso, 1989, p. 34.
81 Marx, *ibid.*, p. 175.
82 Marx, *ibid.*, p. 300.
83 Marx, *ibid.*, pp. 255–6.
84 Marx, *ibid.*, p. 211.
85 Marx, *ibid.*, p. 256.
86 Marx, *ibid.*, p. 302.
87 Deleuze and Guattari, *Anti-Oedipus*, p. 228.
88 Georges Bataille, 'The Notion of Expenditure', in Fred Botting and Scott Wilson (eds), *The Bataille Reader*, Oxford: Blackwell, 1997, p. 172; for more on potlatch see Marcel Mauss, *The Gift: Forms and Functions of Exchange in Archaic Societies*, London: Cohen and West, 1970.
89 See Nietzsche, *Thus Spoke Zarathustra*, 'On the Bestowing Virtue' and 'The Night Song', Harmondsworth: Penguin, 1969.
90 Bataille, 'The Notion of Expenditure', p. 170.
91 Bataille, *ibid.*, p. 172.

92 Bataille, *ibid.*, p. 174.

93 Bataille, *ibid.*, p. 175.

94 Bataille, *ibid.*, p. 176.

95 Bataille, *ibid.*, p. 180.

96 This insight of Bataille's is lost in the conception of a 'general economy' governed by an excess of energy to be expended, where human behaviour is seen within the context of the larger material process of the circulation of energy on the earth. All living matter receives energy from the sun, and is then under pressure to expend its excess of energy. Practices of wanton destruction such as war are then forms of expenditure of excess energy. In his concept of a general economy, Bataille makes two errors that compromise his entire theory: first, he transports physical energy by analogy into social energy, mistaking the destruction of varieties of social and biological forms for the expenditure of physical energy – this is a purely mythological procedure, taking no account of the relative independence of social and biological spheres from the physical processes they include; second, he takes energy, the concept derived from a postulate of equality in exchange in physical processes, as his fundamental metaphysical category, thus reasserting the primacy of exchange over expenditure. Bataille lacks the category of ecology as the most general economy. See Bataille, *The Accursed Share I*, New York: Zone, 1988.

97 Pierre Bourdieu, *The Logic of Practice*, Cambridge: Polity, 1990, p. 115.

98 Bourdieu, *ibid.*, p. 99.

99 Bourdieu, *ibid.*, p. 105.

100 Aristotle, *Metaphysics*, 1026b, Oxford: Clarendon Press, 1971, p. 69.

101 Jean-Pierre Vernant, *The Origins of Greek Thought*, London: Methuen, 1982, p. 79.

102 Bourdieu, *The Logic of Practice*, p. 119.

103 Bourdieu, 'Marginalia', in Alan D. Schrift (ed.), *The Logic of the Gift*, London: Routledge, 1997, pp. 238–9.

104 See Helmuth Berking, *Sociology of Giving*, London: Sage, 1999, p. 41.

105 Simmel is cited in Helmuth Berking, *Sociology of Giving*, p. 29.

106 Bourdieu, *The Logic of Practice*, p. 114.

107 Marx, 'Contribution to the Critique of Hegel's Philosophy of Law', in *Collected Works*, London: Lawrence & Wishart, p. 175.

108 The paradigm of this role of the Stranger may be found in Plato's dialogue *The Sophist*, where Socrates himself is instructed on how to distinguish the philosopher's quest for truth from the web of simulacra spun by the Sophists. Philosophy emerged in Athens, the most cosmopolitan town of its time, among the visitors and strangers who came to enjoy its democratic constitution.

109 See Marx, *Capital Volume I*, p. 165.

Part II

The problem of ethics

4 Freedom

Søren Kierkegaard outlined the paradox that undermines Greek reason. Knowledge, considered according to the eternal ideal of truth, is not temporal: it does not admit of being learned. When disclosed, one discovers that the truth has always already been known: this is expressed in the Socratic doctrine of recollection. Reason, however, is temporal: it is driven by passion; it attempts to discover what it does not know. The relation between the eternal and the temporal, between the thought and the thinking, is a paradox. Paradox is the source of wonder that drives thought:

> The supreme paradox of all thought is the attempt to discover something that thought cannot think. This passion is at bottom present in all thinking, even in the thinking of the individual, in so far as in thinking he participates in something transcending himself.[1]

Falling short of eternal wisdom, philosophy remains a quest, a temporal process. It has a history, a will, a desire – even a piety: a 'will to truth'.

'What does the will to truth signify?' Following the murder of God, Nietzsche convicted philosophy, when examined according to its function within 'life, nature and history', of a metaphysical piety: another world is affirmed, the eternal world of reason, capable of rewarding us with meaning, but only at the cost of plunging us into infinite debt before the sovereign obligations of reason. Philosophy lives the life of a debtor: it devotes all its labour, time, ingenuity and attention to inadequate ideas which can never pay it the reward of fulfilment in truth or release from bondage. Focused on its object of devotion, philosophy has little time to notice how it bears within its supposedly eternal reason the germs of a social practice which will be re-enacted in every practice of thinking. For thought, even when focused on the absolute – when it seems absolved of mundane relations – maintains in its temporal process a relation to the whole of existence through obscured networks of interdependence.

To think is to honour. To think is to pay attention. What is worthy of worship, gifts, offerings, sacrifices, thought and desire? Following the murder of God, the highest values are devalued: one can no longer be sure of what is worth thinking about. An eternal source of values is no longer available to discipline the process of thought. The earth has become unchained from the sun; the shore has disappeared and the philosopher is completely at sea. This redemption from debt, while threatening meaninglessness, does not prevent the discovery of other sources of meaning and value. Indeed, as we have seen, the precondition for the murder of God is the intrusion of another source of meaning and value, another source of debt: capital.

This is no simple 'ideological reflex': indeed, the very relations that pertain between strangers in the market, those which gave rise to the use of money for the purposes of exchange, are those that pertain within the market of modern thought. Relations based on honour and trust within a local, finite community or culture are replaced by relations of mutual suspicion, where guarantees are required. It becomes important that one should not let oneself be deceived; that the value of a thought is clearly defined and verified. The 'metaphysical faith' of our scientists is that relations can be isolated between otherwise mutually independent variables, as though the 'social relations between things' were composed solely of market transactions between strangers. Becoming, affect and indeterminacy are replaced by homogenization, reification and complete determination. In reality, however, we meet with insufficient determination: those equations of motion that admit of multiple solutions, or whose precise solution is only selected by an infinite specification of variables of time, space and momentum, fail to completely determine what actually happens. Consequently, a mathematical–scientific description of the world can only ever simulate the material world[2] – it sets out a framework of possibilities where the precise course of events is no longer determined causally. For if the world were a chain of causes and effects running backwards and forwards, then there would be no past or future.[3]

The economic conditioning of reason does not lead to the complete determinism of thought. Spontaneous flows of abstract labour are ejected from the capitalist system. The philosopher may be allowed the freedom to construct a post-capitalist mode of reasoning – so long as reason remains liberated from its debts. Resistance to the power of philosophical modernity becomes the key problem for the freedom of thought.

The freedom to determine its own temporal and social practice raises an extraordinary opportunity for contemporary philosophy: can thought itself become ethical? Can thought come to take responsibility for its own temporal process and social practice? If so, then what, following the murder of God, will be worth thinking about? This problem is intensified when one lacks a direction for ethics. Will philosophy find itself a new debt or a new piety? Indeed, are concepts of 'freedom' and 'responsibility' mere illusions, so that all thought is 'will to power'? No longer relying on the eternal, the solutions to such problems will only emerge from exploring the nature of temporal existence as such.

Bergson's ethics

Time and association

Emmanuel Levinas drew attention to the importance of Bergsonism for the 'entire problematic of contemporary philosophy': Henri Bergson put 'into question the ontological confines of spirituality.'[4]

> With the advent of Bergson – in opposition to the entire tradition, issuing from the Greeks, of reason isolating and identifying the categories of being – it is the human, free time of duration that is declared to be first philosophy.[5]

Bergson and Levinas make thought ethical. Yet how, in appealing to the spiritual category of 'freedom', and its associated ethical categories of 'responsibility' and 'obligation', can we be sure that we are not in danger of reinstating imaginary causes? How will we avoid reducing liberty to Locke's choice in the market between cheese and lobsters? Bergson is instructive in so far as his arguments amount to a repetition of Nietzsche's critique of imaginary causes, while his emphasis on duration places metaphysics within the temporal process.

Nietzsche criticized freedom of the will in so far as it presupposes the possibility of evaluating incommensurable goals and impulses on the same scale, as though measured by a general equivalent. Bergson, by contrast, constructed his concept of freedom from a parallel argument concerned with the nature of time. Countable or measurable time, for Bergson, is an abstraction, for the essence of time is to pass:[6] once an event has happened, it does not recur again. Thus durations, episodes of real time, are not superposable upon each other so as to measure or count one by the other – as if they were commodities prepared for exchange. For synchronization to occur, real time must be replaced by an abstraction which has eliminated the essential quality of time – change. Measurable, homogeneous time is an abstraction where nothing takes place. In countable time, the living is measured in so far as it conforms to the behaviour of inanimate clocks. Bergson showed how this conception of time is in fact based on a conception of space, for in counting, one disregards individual differences and counts units which are assumed to be qualitatively identical, yet differentiated from each other in an ideal space.[7] The idea of number is based on an intuition of homogeneous space; thus, when we count separate moments in time, we do so by some process of symbolic representation in an imaginary space.[8] Where what 'properly belongs to the mind is the indivisible process by which it concentrates attention successively on the different parts of a given space,'[9] space is 'what enables us to distinguish a number of identical and simultaneous sensations from one another'.[10] Experienced time, the distribution of attention, is modified to conform to space.

Bergson could then claim that the problem of the freedom of the will is a false problem, resting on a confusion. The principle of determination, that 'the same causes produce the same effects', has no possible application to experience in time.[11] For if experience in time cannot be conceived in terms of space, the two being incommensurable, then recurrence is impossible.[12] Instead, Bergson suggests that we have immediate knowledge of 'free spontaneity'.[13] Bergson therefore recovers freedom as the impossibility of complete determination.

Bergson's critique of spatialization was extended to representational language, enabling him to echo Nietzsche's critique of the social function of language. For concepts gain their meaning in a space of representation, and 'the intuition of a homogeneous space is already a step towards social life':[14] it is a principle of organization and coordination of elements. Bergson defined the objective by substitutability,[15] and thus, by the sacrifice of the changing and living in the real.

> For we contrive to find resemblances between things in spite of their diversity, and to take a stable view of them in spite of their instability; in this way we obtain ideas which we can control, whereas the actual things may elude our grasp.[16]

Instead of treating the idea of extension as given *a priori*, one may regard it as being composed from superposition itself: an act of substitution or exchange treating measuring and measured as equivalents. The materiality of matter, extended in space, is merely the distribution of a 'discontinuous multiplicity of elements, inert and juxtaposed'.[17] In such an analysis, duration, mobility, impetus – in short, life itself – is eliminated from matter.

Representational language requires us to establish between our ideas the same sharp and precise distinctions as between material objects.[18] For 'there is no common measure between the mind and language'.[19]

> Consciousness, goaded by an insatiable desire to separate, substitutes the symbol for the reality, or perceives the reality only through the symbol. As the self thus refracted, and thereby broken to pieces, is much better adapted to the requirements of social life in general and language in particular, consciousness prefers it, and gradually loses sight of the fundamental self.[20]

When thinkers treat their concepts as a stockpile of elements, inert and juxtaposed, prepared for substitution and exchange, the market conditions the practice of reason itself. Modern reason is the market-place of thought, where lacking trust in each others' experiences of thinking, we require guarantees of value from the goods themselves. Yet in so far as reality is delimited to the measurable, the superposable, and the substitutable, all that remains is the 'superficial skin',[21] and philosophy cannot get beyond the symbol, forever nostalgic for the absolute, 'the gold coin for which we never seem able to stop giving small change'.[22] Thus technological reason substitutes its own symbols for the realities of life: '*Thinking* usually consists in passing from concepts to things, and not from things to concepts ... . To try to fit a concept on an object is simply to ask what we can do with the object, and what it can do for us'.[23] In brief, the representation of reality in both science and metaphysics is a commodification, replacing the thing with a quantifiable symbol fashioned for the purpose of exchange.

Bergson's alternative is to place reason within the temporal process itself. Bergson tells us that 'metaphysics is the science which claims to dispense with symbols,'[24] or, at least, it frees itself from ready-made concepts in order to create 'supple, mobile and almost fluid representations, always ready to mould themselves on the fleeting forms of intuition.'[25] The experience of thinking replaces the object of thought. Freedom must be encountered in the experience of thinking before it can become an object of thought.

One may develop this Bergsonian perspective to show how the modern political problem of the establishment and maintenance of liberty is what Bergson would call a false problem. For the concept of 'freedom' is normally posited in terms of space, involving the idea of an empty homogeneous space. Locke defined liberty as the right of people to 'order their Actions, and dispose of their Possessions, and Persons as they think fit, within the bounds of the Law of Nature, without asking leave, or depending on the Will of any other Man.'[26] The domain of freedom is a space of nature, a portion of land claimed in an originary 'America', which is a piece of empty social space, defined negatively as the absence of authority of any other. The sovereignty of man over the space of nature, given by divine decree like the right of kings, is constructed in the image of the sovereignty it opposes. This dialectical concept of negative freedom conceals the social practice through which sovereignty is constructed. For sovereignty, although not relying on free consent – this being anachronistic prior to sovereignty[27] – is formed contemporaneously with a particular order of society. Richard Hooker was among the first to explicate the origins of sovereignty among the people through emergence, 'by growing unto composition and agreement amongst themselves, by ordaining some kind of government public'.[28] Sovereignty, then, is not so much the exercise of power as the reputation of power; it commands belief, even if not consent. As Hobbes pointed out, 'Reputation of power is Power; because it draweth the adhaerence of those who need protection.'[29] Dominion and victory, and thus the exercise of violence, are 'honourable' because they are signs of power.[30] In practice, then, individual liberty does not precede society, but follows it, for if the free individual is the one who is not hindered in doing what is within its capacity and will,[31] then such an absence of opposition requires a reputation of power. The subsequent dialectical moves of establishing sovereignty by social contract, or of restricting the powers of society to determine the individual, already presuppose and require what they attempt to establish or negate. The conception of an abstract, empty, homogeneous social space, subjected to the sovereign individual who makes an arbitrary choice between cheese and lobsters, is not an origin but a late product, a reaction against the heterogeneity which is the ground of our experience.[32]

Freedom may be thought, by contrast, in terms of time. Bergson eschewed both social and psychological determinism: while social obligations already presuppose freedom, else they would be obeyed automatically and mechanically,[33] psychological forces, such as sympathy, aversion or hate, are rationalizations after the fact, 'misled by language.'[34] If we wish to know the reason why we have made up our mind, 'we find that we have decided without any reason, and perhaps even against every reason.'[35] Our reasons are consequences of an action, rationalizations after the fact, and not causes. For reasons themselves do not carry force: 'Never, in our hours of temptation, should we sacrifice to the mere need for logical consistency our interest, our passion, and our vanity.'[36] To posit psychological determinism is to posit recurrence in time, without attending to the specific difference of each situation. Similarly, one cannot posit moral obligation as 'a unique fact, incommensurable with others, looming above them like a mysterious apparition,'[37] and explain how such obligation acquires credibility or force. Bergson, far from appealing to the arbitrary, has a theory of the unconscious as a synthesis of the past. Free decision depends on character:

> It agrees with the whole of our most intimate feelings, thoughts and aspirations, with that particular conception of life which is the equivalent of all our past experience, in a word, with our personal idea of happiness and of honour.[38]

Many doubt the existence of the synthesis of the past as duration because it eludes the analytic powers of reason. It has become customary to brush aside Bergson's call for a temporal metaphysics with charges of romanticism, intuitionism, irrationalism, spiritualism or mysticism. Adorno, for example, claimed that Bergson established a 'cult of irrational immediacy', while depending on the conceptual apparatus which he scorned.[39] For Adorno, concept fetishism can be overcome when one acknowledges that 'objects do not go into their concepts without leaving a remainder',[40] and one attempts to recover this remainder through a critical rescue of rhetoric, that which cannot be thought except in language, so as to produce a 'mutual approximation of thing and expression, to the point where the difference fades.'[41] Now, although this attack on Bergson is as unfair as Adorno's ambition for his own rhetoric is optimistic, a serious point lies here. For Bergson is unable to explain the nature of this 'synthesis', and its relation to instincts, intelligence and obligations. In the formation of 'character', the problem of the social and of freedom recurs on a higher level – no longer as a question of freedom of action, but of freedom of thought. How will the past be synthesized and associated? As Bergson remarks, 'Logical coordination is essentially economy.'[42] Placing synthesis in the past does not absolve it from participation in a system of social relations.

A further objection to Bergson has been raised by Levinas concerning the nature of time itself: Bergson draws on the kinetic image of a 'flow' to describe the passage of time.[43] Bergson rediscovers continuity by appealing to intuition as confusion and coincidence, obliterating alterity, or any possibility that time might involve an opening or discontinuity.[44] Bergson, then, may be insufficiently radical in his rethinking of the nature of time.

These two problems, then, constitute the preconditions for an ethics of thought: the nature of time and the nature of association. In so far as thought remains determined by these as its ground, then it has a limited degree of freedom. For if the natures of time and the social should not themselves be ethical, then thought will not be capable of becoming ethical. If, by contrast, it can be discovered that time and the social do not have a predetermined 'nature', but admit of transformation, then an ethos of time and an ethos of the social may be the conditions of an ethics of thought.

Schelling's dialectic

Time and freedom

The philosopher who first explored the relation between time and freedom in reason was F. W. J. Schelling. Indeed, Schelling was perhaps the first to explore the temporal dimension of reason, and thus open the way to introduce considerations of ethics and spirituality into reason itself. Schelling attempted to develop and transform Spinozism by adding freedom to necessity.[45] For reason does not lead us to sufficient causes, but only to the knowledge that one thing is dependent on another. Dependence does not exclude freedom: it does not determine what a thing is, but determines that it can only be as a consequence of that upon which it is dependent.[46] Neither, we may add, does dependence determine *that* a thing is, nor that it is *this* thing. Schelling, by treating primordial Being initially as a Will,[47] determining actual existence, attempts to achieve what Spinoza could not do: to explain finite, temporal existence on the basis of its actual relation to the unconditioned, to God. This project eventually divided in two directions, a 'negative philosophy', a speculative account of the past origins of time in the free decision of eternity, as in *The Ages of the World*, and a 'positive philosophy', an *a posteriori* account of the will of God from the history of religions, as in *The Philosophy of Mythology and Revelation.*[48] In so far as freedom is incorporated into reason as such, reason itself becomes historicized.[49] History can only be relived: 'What is essential in science is movement; deprived of this vital principle, its assertions die like fruit taken from the living tree.'[50] As Žižek explains:

> Schelling's entire philosophical revolution is contained, condensed, in the assertion that this act which precedes and grounds every necessity is in itself *radically contingent* – for that very reason it cannot be deduced, inferred, but only retroactively presupposed.[51]

The crucial question that emerges, then, is how we are to read the history of reason, the history of philosophy. For the history of philosophy will tell us about the nature of reason and its possibilities. Schelling may point us toward a dual reading. To begin with, Schelling praises intuition:

> Everything, absolutely everything – even what is by nature external – must previously have become inward for us before we can represent it externally or objectively. If the ancient era, whose image he wishes to sketch for us, does not dawn again within the historian, then he will never truly, never plastically, never vitally represent it.[52]

In our innermost core we find the 'living witness of all truth', so that it is possible to immediately experience within oneself the origins of time within eternity.[53] This 'living witness' results from Schelling's intensification of Spinozism: for since the human soul is drawn from the source of things, and is like it inasmuch as it possesses the properties of will – groundlessness, independence of time, self-affirmation[54] – then it has potentially a 'co-knowledge of creation.'[55] Nevertheless, what is indivisible in the origin must be spread out in succession in this present life, so that all intuiting needs a mediating organ in order to attain expression.[56] Present understanding differs from past knowledge: the past thus 'slumbers' in the soul, and must be awakened by present enquiry. The goal cannot be reached through intuition alone, for 'there is no understanding in intuition, in and of itself.'[57] In the human soul, then, there is one thing that must be recalled, and another that recalls it:

> This separation, this doubling of ourselves, this secret intercourse between the two essences, one questioning and one answering, one ignorant and seeking to know and one knowledgeable without knowing its knowledge; this silent dialogue, this inner art of conversation, is the authentic secret of the philosopher from with the outer art (which for this reason is called 'dialectic') is only a replica and, if it has become a bare form, is only empty appearance and shadow.[58]

The two poles of the 'dialectic', the 'authentic inner principles of all life', are the principles of time,[59] conserving and striving forward, preserving the past and producing the present: 'Every entity, everything that is, wants to be in itself and out of itself at the same time.'[60] Intuition and expression are the very potencies of time. Now, these potencies are incommensurable for they move in opposite directions. Schelling, to begin with, calls this opposition 'contradiction':

> Only contradiction drives us – indeed, forces us – to action. Contradiction is in fact the venom of all life, and all vital motion is nothing but the attempt to overcome this poisoning.[61]

Even if Schelling emphasizes that neither principle can subject the other, it is important to note the asymmetry here: the past has to be constructed as past, put behind oneself, in order to liberate oneself from it and exist in the present:

> The man who has not conquered himself has no past, or rather, never comes out of it, lives continually in it ... . Only the man who has the power to tear himself loose from himself (from what is subordinate in his nature), is capable of creating a past for himself.[62]

Then each new life begins with a free decision, an eternal act, a choice of character that is at once fate and necessity.[63] Such a decision is not a weighing up of consequences, but a capacity to be entirely one or other of the potencies.[64] Since this succession of potencies in the free decision is of incommensurables that coexist as past and present, Schelling calls it a 'succession of times'.[65] As a free decision, 'Each new life begins with a new self-subsistent time which is linked immediately to eternity. Therefore eternity immediately precedes each life.'[66] Now, this free decision of the will, in eternity, is of an entirely different nature from the past which is forgotten or recollected. The primordial deed which determines character, therefore, sinks back into unconsciousness immediately after it is 'put into exuberant freedom':

> The Eternal leads the force of the highest consciousness into unconsciousness and sacrifices it to externality so that there might be life and actuality.[67]

It is from this unconsciousness, the 'abyss of freedom', that Schelling's dual reading of reality according to the two potencies of withdrawal and expansion emerges. To begin with, the eternal will must negate itself as the essence, and posits itself as negation.[68] Unconscious of itself, the will must posit affirmation absolutely outside itself. Beginning lies in negation alone, and temporal progress is driven by contradiction. In this respect, Schelling regards the highest mode of existence as 'to be as if one were not, to have as if one had not.' Movement occurs for the sake of what it lacks: 'all movement is only for the sake of rest.'[69] Yet in the second draft of *The Ages of the World*, where contradiction is most heavily emphasized, Schelling also develops a critique of contradiction because it does not advance towards truth.[70] For if the potencies exist as a succession of times, then they are incommensurable, and do not assert the opposite at one and the same time. In fact, the opposed potencies are unconditioned, yet require each other and depend on each other. Then 'this relation of contradiction must be abandoned. Another relation, a *grounding relation* must take its place.'[71] This grounding relation is a kind of disjunctive synthesis: there is a third potency which is the unity of the two, so that it is one and the same that is affirming and negating, outspreading and restraining.[72]

In addition to the dialectic driven by lack and contradiction, therefore, Schelling indicates that the will does not merely seek to overcome the past, but actively searches for the future. Whereas the past is known, the future is divined:[73]

> For the will seeks eternity, driven not by knowledge but rather by divination, presentiment, and inexpressible longing.[74]

Schelling calls the unity of the two opposed wills 'spirit', and spirit strives towards the highest goal of a moment of awakening, coming to itself.[75] For free action can only be conceived on the assumption that the potencies have 'incomprehensible mutual knowledge and understanding in the inexpressible, which is their unconditioned unity.'[76] The inexpressible abyss of freedom, then, leaves an irreducible remainder of a presentiment of awakening or self-awareness. Even nature is visionary, because it looks towards that which is future.[77]

There are thus two movements, contradiction and vision, overcoming the past and reaching to the future, which also have a higher unity. If, however, contradiction should become a 'bare form', if it should lack spirit, then it becomes a mere shadow. Schelling's speculative apparatus gives us a decisive insight into the temporal nature of freedom. Schelling himself tells us that contradiction is the condition of freedom: 'in the strain of forces, when life hangs in the balance, as it were, only the deed can decide.'[78] Since these forces are unconditioned, however, there cannot be any equilibrium or balance: they are incommensurable, they exist at 'different times'. There is no contradiction, only disjunction. By contrast with Schelling's draft, we must claim freedom for spirit: freedom is the synthesis of past, present and future. For since these belong to different times, the connection between them is not sufficiently determined. This is the meaning of contingency. Freedom is not an arbitrary choice among alternatives, but a synthesis of an accumulated past, an experienced present and an expected future. Since there is no necessary relation between past, present and future, then freedom is the capacity to construct such a synthesis.

Temporal freedom should not be understood simply as self-overcoming, or even as the production of novelty, for these are comparative determinations, requiring a prior continuity or commensurability on the basis of which the incommensurable will be produced. If, by contrast, the synthesis has to be constituted, then freedom is signified by the synthesis of time itself, whether it preserves or overcomes the past. Freedom is the strategy of binding past and future in the present. Moreover, to the extent to which we are born into a system of natural necessities, impulses and obligations, then various syntheses of time are already given as conditions of temporal existence. Freedom can only 'pre-exist' the flow of time as an abstract possibility; the actualization of freedom does not require the invocation of a prior spontaneity, but the construction of an unconditioned synthesis. Freedom, and the unconditioned, must be produced.

For Schelling, then, spirit is the inner matter of everything corporeal, and it is perceptible wherever there is sparkle or shine of life:

> But this essence that shines through everything – is this not just that inner spiritual matter which still lies concealed in all things of this world, only awaiting its liberation? Among the most corporeal things, metals in particular have always been regarded as individual sparks of light from this essence, glimmering in the darkness of matter. A universal instinct divined the presence of this essence in gold …[79]

Ah, the security of the gold standard in preserving value!

Derrida and Kierkegaard

Society and freedom

Since freedom does not pre-exist, the freedom of synthesis is synchronic as well as diachronic. Schelling outlined the fundamental paradox of freedom: if a pure subject posits or affirms itself, then it puts on a determination, it takes itself as something, it posits itself as an object of the will, which is necessarily other than it is as pure subject. In attracting itself, it becomes an other, subject to mediation. All free activity therefore involves mediation by an incommensurable objectivity:

> For either it remains still (remains *as* it is, thus pure subject), then there is no life and it is itself as nothing, or it *wants* itself, then it becomes an other, something not the same as itself.[80]

For reason which has become ethical, the mediation of freedom is not an obstacle but an opportunity. The paradox of freedom and its mediation by knowledge is repeated in Jacques Derrida's considerations of responsibility: on the one hand, a responsible decision must be taken on the basis of knowledge; on the other hand, if decision-making is simply the 'deployment of a cognitive apparatus', a following of certain rules and procedures, then it is a mechanistic decision and not a responsible decision.[81] Mediation plunges freedom into a sphere of substitution where considerations of economy come into play: one can neither preserve nor give oneself in freedom, but only a substitute for an apparent reason, for in grasping oneself, the self is necessarily mediated to one as an object. Such is the relation between freedom and necessity described by Schelling: these are incommensurable potencies which require each other.

Economy of reason

The possibility of a free act, then, is identical with the possibility of a free gift – a mediation of oneself in an objective sphere, whether that of knowledge or of material economy. For if an act is performed in line with a calculus of expectation and obligation, it will not have been free. Like a gift, a free act must intervene from without; yet as soon as it is performed, as Schelling explored, it must at once be lost in unconsciousness, for to know the free act as such would be to inscribe it within an economy of knowledge and recognition that determines its nature. Derrida has done as much to illuminate the significance of the concept of the gift for our understanding of reason as he has to obscure the nature of the gift itself. For Derrida has told us that the gift is the name for the impossible:

> For there to be a gift, there must be no reciprocity, return, exchange, countergift, or debt. If the other *gives* me *back* or *owes* me or has to give me back what I give him or her, there will not have been a gift, whether this restitution is immediate or whether it is programmed by a complex calculation of a long-term deferral or différance.[82]

Derrida expanded on the conditions of a gift:

> For there to be a gift, *it is necessary* that the donee not give back, amortize, reimburse, acquit himself, enter into a contract, and that he never have contracted a debt ... . It is thus necessary, at the limit, that he not *recognize* the gift as gift. If he recognizes it *as* gift, if the gift *appears to him as such*, if the present is present to him *as present*, this simple recognition suffices to annul the gift. Why? Because it gives back, in the place, let us say, of the thing itself, a symbolic equivalent.[83]

All kinds of gift in practice are reducible to exchange or contract, for they demand compensation or institute obligation. In anthropological studies of giving, whether of property, courtesies, entertainments, military assistance, women, children or slaves, the social bond is constituted by a sphere of debts or obligations: the obligation to give, the obligation to receive, and the obligation to give back.[84]

A pure gift, for Derrida, ought not to be contaminated with economic exchange. Commentators rarely observe how absurd this requirement is. Derrida's interdiction of counter-gift and obligation is simply *unneces-sary*. If there is any inequality in exchange, then there has been a gift. This is evident even in the limit case when the same gift is immediately returned: there is no change in material distribution, but a gift has been refused, and perhaps a giver dishonoured. More ambiguities open up if there is an omission of the return of a comparable gift: one can show superiority by giving, gaining the power of patronage, for to accept without returning is to face subordination and dependency. On the other hand, one can conceal superiority in receiving, for to graciously receive without feeling the need to give in return is to allow the gift to appear as a gift, a present, and not as an exchange – it is thus to honour the giver. Moreover, if the superiority in accepting gifts without returning them becomes public, then gifts of honour become due as tribute to the one who receives without repaying. On the other hand, if the receiver does not establish their superior status, refusal to return the gift can be construed as an insult to the giver, who is placed in the role of tributary, or counter-construed as a dishonour to the receiver, who is placed in the role of dependant.

Alongside the automatic supplement of the obligation produced by the gift, or the good conscience paid to the giver, there is also an uncertain supplement of an interpretation of the social situation – and it is this latter supplement which is insufficiently determined, and open to the sphere of strategy. The social categories of obligation, respect, honour and shame cannot be appropriated or possessed; they are always given. Even in exchange, they do not cancel each other out: honour is cumulative, and may lead to more honours. The social conditions of gift-exchange are incommensurable with the material flow of gifts, and the symbolic flow of obligations. It is thus an error to reduce the social bond to a sphere of debts and obligations, for this is to construct the social order in the image of the market.

Derrida, in appealing to exchange, constructed reason in the image of the market. For the 'truth' of the gift is constituted in an order of exchangeable symbols:

> The symbolic opens and constitutes the order of exchange and of debt, the law or the order of circulation in which the gift gets annulled.[85]
>
> If the gift appears or signifies itself, if it exists or if it is presently *as gift*, as what it is, then it is not, it annuls itself. Let us go to the limit: The Truth of the gift suffices to annul the gift.[86]

Mediated by the symbolic order of language, the ambiguous structure of the gift is also that of Being and time.[87] Instead of being concerned with the contents of thought, or its structure, Derrida is concerned with the way in which the materiality of the sign introduces spacing and temporalization into the production of meaning, both in the deferral of presence, and in the very production of meaning as a system of signs. Thus *différance* is 'an economic concept',[88] indeed, '*the* economical concept, and since there is no economy without *différance*, it is the most general structure of economy'.[89]

Différance, the most general structure of economy, is also an effect of economy, the reduction of the social order of thought to the market. Let us return to the 'metaphysical subtleties and theological niceties' of the commodity form. In the act of material exchange, two material commodities are combined in the manner of a signifier and a signified: in Marx's example of commodity exchange the body of the coat signifies the value of the linen: 'despite [the coat's] buttoned-up appearance, the linen recognizes in it a splendid kindred soul, the soul of value'.[90] Although such a relation between signifier and signified appears arbitrary, it is determined in practice by various considerations such as need, availability, enterprise, generosity and maintenance of honour, as well as the intrinsic properties of commodities. All such heterogeneous considerations are compressed into the single act of exchange. Subsequent to the exchange, it would appear that equivalence of value is the condition of possibility for exchange; nevertheless, equivalence of value only comes to take a determining role when values are known, fixed and naturalized, that is, under conditions of a general equivalence of value for commodities. Thus money, a general equivalent, is the material condition for the appearance of the abstract concept of value in exchange. Now money, the exchange of a commodity for an embodiment of value, produces a triple oblivion of its own preconditions. In the first place, money contains no memory or trace of the commodity for which it has exchanged itself. As Marx says, money has no smell, from whatever source it may come.[91] Second, the act of exchange contains no memory of the conditions that produced the sold object, or the conditions that made exchange possible; the bought commodity substitutes for all of these. As Marx says, we cannot tell from the taste of wheat who grew it.[92] Third, exchange value is determined by owners, and not by commodities. Luce Irigaray has shown the consequences when the commodities exchanged are women:

> But when women are exchanged, woman's body must be treated as an abstraction. The exchange operation cannot take place in terms of some intrinsic, immanent value of the commodity. It can only come about when two objects – two women – are in a relation of equality with a third term that is neither one nor the other.[93]

Value does not reflect the inherent properties of the object, but reflects the value that is produced within the symbolic labour of the exchange relation. Any comparison or equivalence between bodies is not established by the commodities themselves, but depends on the operations of exchangers. 'The exchange value of two signs, two commodities, two women, is a representation of the needs/desires of consumer-exchanger subjects: in no way is it the "property" of the signs/articles/women themselves'.[94] The choice of women as exemplary commodities is paradigmatic in that women's bodies are sites of labouring, needing, desiring, bonding and thinking. Rendered into the commodity form, however, these bodies are only valued as objects of exchange between men, according to the extent to which they are able to satisfy the needs and desires of men.

Thus, in the act of exchange for money, there is an 'originary' yet empirical violence: oblivion of the commodity, oblivion of the conditions of life of the vendor, and oblivion of the life of the commodity. It is against this background that the substitution of the sign for the thing may be examined. If this relation is arbitrary, then the sign does not contain a trace of the life of the thing. As Spinoza says, the concept of a dog does not bark.[95] Instead, the sign may be regarded as an expression of a determinate set of differential relations between signs. Such differential relations between signs certainly contain traces of former exchanges, such as those excavated by etymology, but contain no trace of the non-linguistic conditions which made such exchanges possible. Instead, any memory of the labour and desire which had produced the exchange is now invested in the sign rather than the thing. Thus, desire becomes invested in the signifying structure, the structure of the Other, rather than its own process and product. The abstract sign posits itself over against material reality. As Jacques Lacan puts it, 'the symbol manifests itself first of all in the murder of the thing'.[96] Finally, a sign can only be fixed in relation to its referent when a sign functioning as a general equivalent is introduced which fixes the values of all signs in relation to their referents: Being. For, as Derrida informs us, Being is a 'an "originary word", the transcendental word assuring the possibility of being-word to all other words'.[97] In the economy of the sign, the economy of *différance*, Being plays the same role as money in the economy of commodities. Indeed, the abstract concept is merely a special form of commodity which is exchanged within the market of discourse.

The result is an economistic reading of the history of philosophy. For, from Plato onwards, the philosophical logos is haunted by a nostalgia for a 'transcendental signified', the commodity to be traded within thought, which never becomes fully present because it has already been exchanged for the currency of Being, abstract thought itself. When I say 'chariot', a chariot does not pass out of my mouth. Abstract conceptual thought can only represent objects in sterile abstraction, independently of their own fecundity, self-expression and becoming. Thought, then, functions as a medium of exchange like money, exchanging itself for a variety of real objects by means of representing them in imagination, but rendering them in a sterile, conceptual form, where they are deprived of any use. Ultimately, the relations between objects established by rational thought express the social relations between thinkers in the fantastic form of a relation between things. As Marx says:

> It is nothing but the definite social relation between men themselves which assumes here, for them, the fantastic form of a relation between things. In order, therefore, to find an analogy we must take flight into the misty realm of religion. There the products of the human brain appear as autonomous figures endowed with a life of their own, which enter into relations both with each other and with the human race.[98]

Metaphysics is thus essentially theological, is 'onto-theology', not simply in so far as it involves the idea of a creator God determining the meaning of Being as causal making, but in so far as it worships the spirit of a transcendental signified as a compensation for the primal murder of the commodity of thought.

The transition to philosophical modernity occurs when the ethics of the market come to have a determining role in thought as against the ethics of honour, and when the process of symbolization by which thought becomes an object of exchange in public space is itself made into an object of thought. The symbol comes to stand for and speak for thought when thought is subjected to critical scrutiny; eventually, the symbol will become the only criterion of objective reality,[99] while the thing-in-itself becomes inaccessible. It is this move towards the symbol, because it is expressed in a publicly valued currency, which finally renders the eternal inaccessible. For once the symbol which bears the role of advocate for the eternal is regarded as holding its symbolic value by virtue of the exchanges it makes with other symbols, rather than by virtue of its own proper participation in the eternal, then it can no longer guarantee that it will be able to signify the eternal, itself being temporal.

The modern condition of reason eventually annuls itself: for to take the gift symbolically is to annul the gift.[100] There is an objective ambiguity in the gift, which will eventually be removed when the symbolic order cancels itself out. To take the gift on good faith, as a gift, involves accepting a simulacrum of a gift, 'counterfeit money', suspending disbelief that the gift is a simulacrum. By contrast, to take the gift with suspicion, exposing the gift as a counterfeit, as the inauguration of a contract, debt or exchange, is to install the gift within a symbolic order. If the gift is credited as such, it becomes a symbolic debt; if the gift is suspected, it resolves itself into a violent act of laying an obligation on another.

In the logic of the gift we are presented with the problem of European reason following the murder of God. Reason attempts to move beyond opinion, misrecognition, ideology or the suspension of disbelief required by codes of honour. It rejects the fundamental motivation of faith: trusting that God is God because such trust is due to God as God. Instead of paying one's dues, one is *obliged* to give reasons: to be rational and responsible is to explain oneself.[101] From the perspective of reason, a priori trust, which is always trust in that which is uncertain, trust that the uncertain is transcendent or trustworthy, trust in the transcendence of transcendence, is merely an obligation or infinite debt.[102] Such a trust is *irrational*, beyond all measure or proportion, simply because it is unlimited: no finite reason could be given for such a trust, because once such a reason had been given, the obligation it would bring would be finite.

Consequently, even reason will have a cause, a principle or a reason; one is obliged to be suspicious until an explanation has been given. The whole symbolic order of reasons becomes an infinite debt. The trust in reason is itself irrational; one learns to suspect reason, and even to suspect suspicion itself. Then the entire dystopic order of rational modernity, together with its own post-modern disintegration, is simply unnecessary. The whole of Derrida's later work is an exploration of intimations of an alternative, even if this alternative remains 'the impossible' and does not arrive. He does, however, indicate the essential point:

> The gift is not a gift, the gift only gives to the extent that it *gives time*. The difference between a gift and every other operation of pure and simple exchange is that the gift gives time. *There where there is gift, there is time.* What it gives, the gift, is time, but this gift of time is also a demand of time. The thing must not be restituted *immediately and right away.*[103]

The gift of time, here, is merely the duration of a debt or loan, a period governed by the demand for restitution: it is a capital investment in the order of Bergsonian duration in order to extract a surplus value. Life is captured by such a gift of time. In reality, however, the temporal order of reason and obligation is incommensurable with its symbolic order of representation. This temporal order acquires meaning when it is considered in relation to the social order which is irreducible to exchange.

Logic of sacrifice

Kierkegaard, who attended Schelling's lectures, began to develop the alternative mode of reasoning. His authorial character, Johannes Climacus, differentiated objectivity from subjectivity by means of a distinction between reward and interest. The objective thinker is unethical because he concerns himself with the results and rewards of his action rather than the action itself.[104] By contrast, an ethical thinker is interested in how he acts: he renounces everything, even the good itself, so that the ethical becomes a quality of his action. The subjective, ethical thinker is solely interested in the 'how' of his existence:

> Existence constitutes the highest interest of the existing individual, and his interest in his existence constitutes his reality ... . Reality is an *inter-esse* between the moments of that hypothetical unity of thought and being which abstract thought presupposes.[105]

As such, interest is not so much a property of a subjective thinker or a reward to be appropriated, as a venture towards the unobtainable. Existence keeps truth and being apart;[106] thought is then a process which plunges both the thinker and the thought into concrete becoming.[107] Reality is interest. Interest, then, names an objective process of probing more and more deeply into subjectivity.[108]

Now, although Climacus identifies the root of interest as subjectivity,[109] his arguments show an interest that lies outside the subject. For when Climacus shows that there is a Socratic paradox within reason itself – that the objective truth must be subjectively appropriated – and when Climacus likewise shows that in so far as the subject fails to complete the infinite appropriation of the truth, it is in untruth,[110] he does so by means of reason. His argument is an attempt 'to make the necessity of the paradox evident.'[111] The truth becomes objectively a paradox, combining elements of the subjective with the objective: 'the objective situation is repellent.'[112] There are forces and interests internal to reason: reason repels. Reason itself has an interest in the subjective, existing thinker, for without this, there is no access to concrete, existing truth: 'The truth is precisely the venture which chooses an objective uncertainty with the passion of the infinite.'[113] Interiority lies outside the subject; it is a condition of reality. The interests of reason are ontological categories.

Climacus therefore outlined a conception of truth as interest that no longer takes the objective form of coinage or banknotes, 'the truth not being a circular with signatories affixed.'[114] Since the truth is not an object for exchange, it cannot be formulated directly in propositional terms. It is a venture, something uncertain and unspoken; it can only express its passion and interest indirectly:

> Pathos in a contrary form is an inwardness which remains with the maker of the communication in spite of being expressed, and cannot be directly appropriated by another except through that other's self-activity: the contrast of the form is the measure of inwardness.[115]

By giving itself 'in a contrary form', and so by giving something else and not itself, it gives itself to be thought in its very distance from the thinkable. Reason invests itself in the sphere of circulation of thought; whenever it produces a paradox, and a corresponding wonder, passion, and interest in reason, then it capitalizes on its investment. The truth of reason, its own sphere of interests, is not inscribed on the same plane as the contents of thought where it lies invisibly. The truth of reason is only to be found in the venture, when all knowledge is risked for the sake of truth.

Climacus, anticipating Derrida, indicated that there is a paradox, decision, or 'leap' internal to reality itself in the transition from the possible to the actual.[116] The actual is not necessary – it is not determined by necessity or an obligation; it falls outside the symbolic domain. Instead, the actual is always a gift. Its interest lies not in the object that is given, but in the event of giving itself, in its indeterminacy and paradox. Every event, then, may constitute a sign for reason to inspire reason to think: not to master through explanation; not to understand through interpretation; but to think through as a problem. Moreover, it is only through alienated and inadequate ideas that reason is able to affirm itself as that which gives thought, rather than that which is given to thought.

Reason thus distinguishes itself from the economic through its interest. The mechanism is its own inadequacy, its own condition of untruth. Bataille gave an account of the origin of value and interest in sacrifice itself. According to Bataille, the essence of sacrifice is that it removes something that is useful: a domestic animal, for example, rather than a wild one. For the world of uses and purposes is oppressive, even while it constitutes reality: just as the reality of the commodity is suppressed in the cycle of production, circulation and consumption, so is the reality of the worker, owner and consumer: everything is subordinated to a restricted purpose. Sacrifice, then, is a compensation for this by an irrational and fruitless action *per se*: the first fruits of a harvest or a choice animal are sacrificed so as to remove them from the world of things subordinate to purpose. Just as the plant or animal is 'liberated', so is the farmer or stock-raiser:

> The thing – only the thing – is what sacrifice means to destroy in the victim. Sacrifice destroys an object's real ties of subordination; it draws the victim out of the world of utility and restores it to that of unintelligible caprice.[117]

Of course, more than the utility of the victim is destroyed in the sacrifice. This is not essential, however, for the principle according to which sacrifice works is that of death. Death is 'the great affirmer, the wonder-struck cry of life':

> What death's definitive impotence and absence reveals is the very essence of the spirit, just as the scream of the one that is killed is the supreme affirmation of life … .
>
> Far from being sorrowful, the tears are the expression of a keen awareness of shared life grasped in its intimacy. It is true that this

awareness is never keener than at the moment when absence suddenly replaces presence, as in death or mere separation.[118]

Sacrifice, then, restores a lost value through a relinquishment of that value: 'To sacrifice is not to kill but to relinquish and to give.'[119] As such, it reveals a dimension of value irreducible to material and symbolic exchange. This dimension is inseparable from the play of life and death: it gives both simultaneously, locked in paradoxical conflict and embrace.

Moreover, the embrace of life and death is removed by its enactment: in sacrifice, one destroys or consumes a corpse, at the same time as one sees the force and violence of life itself. Life is revealed as elsewhere – lost or transported to the heavens, past or future. Life and death are separated. In the giving of reality – whether in the form of event, timing, style, strategy, social bond, friendship, trust, becoming, delay, duration, decay, narrative or sacrifice – the given reality does not enter the material or symbolic orders without annulling itself. The event is, nevertheless, real; indeed, it is the immanent cause of thought in the symbolic order and action in the material order. Its mode of presentation, however, is that of self-sacrifice that separates out the ambiguous and uncertain strands of the reality of life and death.[120]

The giving or sacrifice of time is dramatized in sacrifice. For time can only be spent; it cannot be hoarded. Time is thus inherently relational, essentially social: one necessarily gives honour to another by spending one's time, by paying attention. Even if one pays attention to oneself, that relation is temporally mediated. The logic of time is not that of economy, but that of sacrifice or wastage. Moreover, in any sacrifice, a whole set of heterogeneous roles come into play, and a whole set of persons receive honour and attention. One honours the past by following prescribed rituals for sacrifice. One honours the present by giving prescribed honours and privileges to participants. One honours the future by showing respect for death – or collective respect for some danger or supernatural being to whom the sacrifice is offered. *Sacrifice is a social synthesis of time: freedom is exercised through sacrifice as attention to past, present and future.*

Freedom is not to be found in the realms of necessity and economy. Instead, reason itself is contingent, dependent on a leap or venture internal to reason itself. This venture is expressed in the interest of reason, the element of the gift by which actual events exceed anticipated possibilities. Thought, if it is to become ethical, must take such a venture. It must abandon the gold standard of certainty, the adequation of thought and being, in order to take leave of economy and enter the 'broken world of sacrifice'. Here, there is no longer the possibility of speaking with assurance; truth becomes the impossible. Nevertheless, in the very sacrificing of truth itself, reason can begin to give attention and honour to that which, exceeding thought, demands that we give attention to thinking it. This will be the origin of an ethics of thought.

The temporal and social condition of thought allows it to be shaped by immanent powers which are conditions of reason as such. Attention to such immanent powers may activate them. On the one hand, modern reason has been seized and determined by exterior, economic forces constituted by the nature of symbolization. Freedom of thought, by contrast, consists in a refusal of this particular reason, this particular synthesis of past, present and future; it refuses to identify itself with what is expressed. Instead, the very distance of thought from its own potencies, that which thought wishes to think and to honour, lends thought its interest and power. An ethical reason can only produce a revolution in collective consciousness if it acquires a greater force than economic reason. Resistance to philosophical modernity will only become effective when it harnesses potencies immanent to thought itself.

Notes

1 Søren Kierkegaard, *Philosophical Fragments*, Princeton: Princeton University Press, 1962.
2 An alternative, finalist argument for this is given by Raymond Ruyer, *Néo-finalisme*, Paris: Presses Universitaires de France, 1952, p. 13.
3 F. W. J. Schelling, *The Ages of the World* (second draft, 1813), Ann Arbor: University of Michigan Press, 1997, p. 120.
4 Emmanuel Levinas, 'The Old and the New', in *Time and the Other*, Pittsburgh: Duquesne University Press, 1987, p. 132.
5 Levinas, 'Vladimir Jankélévitch', in *Outside the Subject*, London: Athlone, 1993, p. 87.
6 Henri Bergson, 'La pensée et le mouvant', *Oeuvres*, Paris: Presses Universitaires de France, 1953, p. 1253.
7 Bergson, *Time and Free Will*, London: Swan Sonnenschein, 1910, p. 77.
8 Bergson, *ibid.*, p. 86.
9 Bergson, *ibid.*, p. 84.
10 Bergson, *ibid.*, p. 95.
11 Bergson, *ibid.*, p. 201.
12 Bergson, *ibid.*, p. 130.
13 Bergson, *ibid.*, p. 142.
14 Bergson, *ibid.*, p. 138.
15 Bergson, *ibid.*, p. 83.
16 Bergson, *The Two Sources of Morality and Religion*, Notre Dame: University of Notre Dame Press, 1977, p. 242.
17 Bergson, *Matter and Memory*, London: George Allen & Unwin, 1911, p. 171.
18 Bergson, *Time and Free Will*, xix.
19 Bergson, *ibid.,*, pp. 164–5.
20 Bergson, *ibid.*, p. 128.
21 Bergson, *Matter and Memory*, p. 28.
22 Bergson, *Introduction to Metaphysics*, London: Macmillan, 1913, p. 6.
23 Bergson, *ibid.*, pp. 34, 35.
24 Bergson, *ibid.*, p. 8.
25 Bergson, *ibid.*, p. 18.
26 John Locke, *Two Treatises of Government* II 4, Cambridge: Cambridge University Press, 1988, p. 269.

27 Theodor W. Adorno argues that it is anachronistic to talk of freedom prior to the formation of the individual as a unit of self-reflection. *Negative Dialectics*, London: Routledge, 1990, p. 218. Yet Duns Scotus is perhaps the founder of the modern conception of freedom deriving from the sovereign freedom of God. This conception of a derivative freedom, prior to self-reflection, is reproduced by Thomas Hobbes, yet now adapted for the market:

> The Liberty of a Subject, lyeth therefore only in those things, which in regulating their actions, the Soveraign hath praetermitted: such as is Liberty to buy and sell, and otherwise contract with one another.

(*Leviathan*, Cambridge: Cambridge University Press, 1996), p. 148).

28 Richard Hooker, *Of the Laws of Ecclesiastical Polity*, I.10.4, Cambridge: Cambridge University Press, 1989, p. 89.
29 Hobbes, *Leviathan*, p. 62.
30 Hobbes, *ibid.*, p. 65.
31 See Hobbes, *ibid.*, p. 146.
32 Bergson, *Time and Free Will*, p. 97.
33 Bergson, *The Two Sources of Morality and Religion*, p. 29.
34 Bergson, *Time and Free Will*, p. 165.
35 Bergson, *ibid.*, p. 170.
36 Bergson, *The Two Sources of Morality and Religion*, p. 23.
37 Bergson, *ibid.*, p. 20
38 Bergson, *Time and Free Will*, p. 170.
39 Adorno, *Negative Dialectics*, pp. 9–8.
40 Adorno, *ibid.*, p. 5.
41 Adorno, *ibid.*, pp. 55–6.
42 Bergson, *The Two Sources of Morality and Religion*, p. 24.
43 Levinas, *Time and the Other*, p. 119. Bergson's preferred concept is a 'tendency', but it has similar implications.
44 Levinas, *ibid.*, pp. 80, 133.
45 F. W. J. Schelling, *Of Human Freedom*, Chicago: Open Court, 1936, p. 3.
46 Schelling, *ibid.*, p. 18.
47 Schelling, *ibid.*, p. 24. Will, of course, is also an abstraction, leading Schelling to posit a distinction between the actual God and the Will as the ground or inner basis of God's existence (33). This position is complicated much further in the drafts of *The Ages of the World* (third draft), New York: Columbia University Press, 1942.
48 See Victor C. Hayes, *Schelling's Philosophy of Mythology and Revelation*, Armidale: Australian Association for the Study of Religion, 1995.
49 Schelling's own theological reading of history, based on meagre resources, runs into numerous difficulties, including especially its adoption of the viewpoint of Protestant Christianity as a perspective from which to judge the history of religions. The conceptual power of this theology, however, is shown by its resemblance to the project of a leading contemporary theologian, Wolfhart Pannenberg.
50 Schelling, *The Ages of the World*, p. 94.
51 Slavoj Žižek, *The Indivisible Remainder: an Essay on Schelling and Related Matters*, London: Verso, 1996, p. 45.
52 Schelling, *ibid.*, p. 87.
53 Schelling, *ibid.*, p. 89.
54 Schelling, *Of Human Freedom*, p. 24.
55 Schelling, *The Ages of the World*, p. 84.

56 Schelling, *ibid.*, pp. 88–9.
57 Schelling, *ibid.*, second draft, 1813, p. 117.
58 Schelling, *ibid.*, second draft, 1813, p. 115.
59 Schelling, *ibid.*, second draft, 1813, p. 124.
60 Schelling, *ibid.*, second draft, 1813, p. 123.
61 Schelling, *ibid.*, second draft, 1813, p. 124.
62 Schelling, *ibid.*, third draft, p. 147.
63 Schelling, *ibid.*, second draft, 1813, p. 175,
64 Schelling, *ibid.*, second draft, 1813, p. 171.
65 Schelling, *ibid.*, second draft, 1813, pp. 173–8.
66 Schelling, *ibid.*, third draft, p. 179.
67 Schelling, *ibid.*, second draft, 1813, p. 181.
68 Schelling, *ibid.*, second draft, 1813, p. 138.
69 Schelling, *ibid.*, second draft, 1813, p. 133. It is this aspect of the second draft which particularly appeals to a Hegelian and Lacanian such as Žižek. As we will see, this reading is incomplete.
70 'Someone who wishes to think only according to the so-called principle of contradiction may be clever at disputing the pros and cons of everything, just like the sophists, but will be incapable of discovering truth, which does not lie at far-flung extremes.' Schelling, *The Ages of the World*, second draft, p. 150.
71 Schelling, *ibid.*, second draft, p. 173.
72 Schelling, *ibid.*, third draft, pp. 98–9.
73 Schelling, *ibid.*, second draft, p. 113.
74 Schelling, *ibid.*, second draft, p. 138.
75 Schelling, *ibid.*, second draft, p. 167.
76 Schelling, *ibid.*, second draft, p. 175.
77 Schelling, *ibid.*, third draft, p. 178.
78 Schelling, *ibid.*, second draft, p. 172.
79 Schelling, *ibid.*, second draft, p. 151.
80 Schelling, *On the History of Modern Philosophy*, p. 116.
81 Jacques Derrida, *The Gift of Death*, Chicago: University of Chicago Press, 1995, p. 24.
82 Derrida, *Given Time 1: Counterfeit Money*, Chicago: University of Chicago Press, 1992, p. 12.
83 Derrida, *ibid.*, p. 13.
84 See Marcel Mauss, *The Gift: Forms and Functions of Exchange in Archaic Societies*, London: Cohen and West, 1970, p. 10.
85 Derrida, *Given Time*, p. 13.
86 Derrida, *ibid.*, p. 27.
87 Derrida, *ibid.*
88 Derrida, *Of Grammatology*, p. 23.
89 Derrida, *Positions*, p. 8.
90 Karl Marx, *Capital I*, Harmondsworth: Penguin, 1976, p. 143.
91 Marx, *ibid.*, p. 205.
92 Marx, *ibid.*, p. 211.
93 Luce Irigaray, *This Sex which is not One*, Ithaca: Cornell University Press, 1985, p. 175.
94 Irigaray, *ibid.*, p. 180.
95 Benedict de Spinoza, *On the Correction of the Understanding*, London: J. M. Dent, 1910, p. 236.
96 Jacques Lacan, *Écrits: a Selection*, London: Tavistock, 1980, p. 104.
97 Derrida, *Of Grammatology*, Baltimore: Johns Hopkins University Press, 1976, p. 20.
98 Marx, *Capital I*, p. 165.

99 See, for example, Jacques Lacan: 'it is obvious that the things of the human world are things in a universe structured by words, that language, symbolic processes, dominate and govern all.' *The Ethics of Psychoanalysis 1959–60: the Seminar of Jacques Lacan Book VII*, London: Routledge, 1991, p. 45.
100 Derrida, *Given Time*, p. 14.
101 See Derrida, *The Gift of Death*, p. 60.
102 See Friedrich Nietzsche, *The Genealogy of Morals*, II 22, New York: Doubleday Anchor, 1956, pp. 225–7. In discussing gift-exchange, the theologian John Milbank confirms this: 'Creature only is, as manifesting the divine glory, as acknowledging its own nullity and reflected brilliance. To be, it entirely honours God, which means it returns to him an unlimited, never paid-back debt.' Milbank, 'Can a Gift be Given? Prolegomena to a Future Trinitarian Metaphysic', *Modern Theology*, **11**(1), January 1995, p. 135.
103 Derrida, *The Gift*, p. 41.
104 Kierkegaard, *Concluding Unscientific Postscript*, Princeton: Princeton University Press, 1968, p. 121.
105 Kierkegaard, *ibid.*, p. 279.
106 Kierkegaard, *ibid.*, p. 171.
107 Kierkegaard, *ibid.*, pp. 79, 170.
108 Kierkegaard, *ibid.*, p. 171.
109 Kierkegaard, *ibid.*, p. 173.
110 Kierkegaard, *ibid.*, p. 187.
111 Kierkegaard, *ibid.*, p. 191.
112 Kierkegaard, *ibid.*, p. 183.
113 Kierkegaard, *ibid.*, p. 182.
114 Kierkegaard, *ibid.*, p. 217.
115 Kierkegaard, *Concluding Unscientific Postscript*, p. 217.
116 Kierkegaard, *ibid.*, p. 306; cf. 90.
117 Georges Bataille, *Theory of Religion*, New York: Zone, 1992, p. 43.
118 Bataille, *ibid.*, pp. 46, 40, 48.
119 Bataille, *ibid.*, pp. 48–9.
120 See J. C. Heesterman's conclusion on the nature of the sacrifice in the Vedas: *The Broken World of Sacrifice: an Essay in Ancient Indian Ritual*, Chicago: Chicago University Press, 1993, p. 26.

5 Value

Ethical thought, concerned with freedom and responsibility, poses problems in terms of time rather than space. 'Value' can no longer be considered solely as a comparative quantity, a product of necessity. It is a contingent expression of determinate social strategies.

Nevertheless, there is an immediate difficulty encountered in thinking time, just as with freedom, for when thought tries to take hold of itself, that which it grasps is in time, an object of thought, subjected to freedom. This primary displacement or alienation between thought and being introduces an interval for thought which constitutes its interest. Deprived of its essence, thought invests itself in a simulacrum of itself. Moreover, in so far as the simulation is not merely the sovereign property of a free subject, but is constructed from reality, then it also participates in libidinal, economic and semantic circuits which mediate the subject's relation to itself. It may be determined by other investments which, through projective identification, are simulated as the subject's own. One's most personal desire may be shaped by the most exterior, distant and impersonal of forces. This economic detour within the subject leads us once more to an analysis of the global market in finance capital, posed in terms of syntheses of time. For capital itself has an apparent potency which poses the primary threat to human life and welfare.

Capital

The enframing of modern life

Let us rehearse, once more, an elementary logic of money in so far as it seizes control of value. How does one assess the value of values? Value is not inscribed on the surface of most phenomena apart from coins, banknotes, cheques and price tags: it takes a long enquiry to establish objective values according to a universal standard of measure; it takes a long experimentation to establish subjective values by assessing the degree to which needs and interests are fulfilled. In practice, the assessment of values is problematic, and, for convenience's sake, the enquiry is often postponed by attaching to objects a conventional sign that will pass for value. In Aristotle's account of the invention of money, metal was adopted because of its mobility, its ease of transportation, and stamped with a sign to save the trouble of weighing, for the purpose of long-distance trade.[1] Éric Alliez has drawn attention to the significance of the hypothesis developed here: money, the conventional ascription of value, emerges in the context of exchange between self-sufficient cities that have their own, differing, scales of value: 'money turns value into a *flow* that tends to escape the juridical frame of political territoriality.'[2] Money, opening out on to time, splits the identity of the acts of buying and selling found in barter, allowing money to function as a temporal reserve – value increases in the interval. Alliez says that this 'dissociation' of exchange is 'precisely what allows for speculation and the quest of autonomous value for its own sake.'[3] It is therefore the temporal condition of monetary value, its promise of a future exchange, that allows it to emerge as a unitary and quantitative scale of evaluation apart from any political, territorial or subjective valuing of qualities. In this way, money functions as a medium of exchange that mediates between times, cities and commodities: one could call it the 'transcendental aesthetic' of political economy, the pure form of time and space governing actual economic relations by means of the topological proximities that it engenders.

There is, however, a further feature that enables money to simulate value: money is not merely a scale of value that can measure commodities at various times and in various places – it is also a commodity itself, a material quantity that can be possessed. The finitude of wealth endows it with its value, so that all prices can be fixed in relation to a limit, when wealth is gone. Consequently, the importance of a person's evaluations can be measured by how much they are able to pay – the quantity of wealth that they possess. *Money, therefore, has a dual role as measure of values and value of measures.* By contrast with Aristotle's *polis* that fixes and affirms its own scale of values, extra-political economic relations simulate a scale – one's values are only as significant as one's wealth, one's ability to put one's money where one's mouth is. In a multi-political condition of generalized exteriority and heterogeneity, the only way to coordinate heterogeneous evaluations and cooperate with each other is to allow such evaluations to coexist on a single, quantifiable, monetary scale that measures the assessors of values. An internal need to interact with the outside empowers an external, self-positing, universal scale of evaluation. I will place most value on that which pays me the most, increasing both the assets that I can possess and the value of my own scale of values. *Then the supreme giver of values is a power of valuing that increases itself: capital*, a pure, abstract flow of evaluation, independent of any specific evaluations. Even if I value my own personal preferences above money, regarding money as a means to attain preferences, the abstract and impersonal increase in capital must come first.

The exteriority of capital values exteriority; individual evaluations are only significant to the extent to which they can form an alliance with the value of the increase of capital. Capital is nihilistic: the highest values are devalued.

Capital, therefore, functions as both a medium of exchange and as a condition of possibility for economic relations. Furthermore, being temporal, that is, measuring itself by its rate of increase, it institutes an ontological shift from a world of being to a world of becoming. For that which has value is that from which a profit can be extracted: that which is produced, distributed, or consumed, in other words, that which is temporal, in flux. Capital demands change, but this change is always the conversion of thought and nature into commodities. As these commodities are discarded, the entire world of culture and nature is progressively destroyed, leaving abstract wealth alone. Signs of such devastation are evident everywhere around us. Capital only pays attention to culture and nature in so far as they lend themselves to commodification and wealth creation. The present and past are sacrificed to an abstract, hypothetical future.

Capital does not depend on our evaluations: it is a self-positing system for simulating evaluation that enframes modern life. This provides the external context for an observation made by Deleuze:

> The modern fact is that we no longer believe in this world. We do not even believe in the events that happen to us, love, death, as if they only half concerned us. It is not we who make cinema; it is the world which looks to us like a bad film.[4]

This describes a condition of anaesthesia as an incapacity for evaluation. Given that only representations can be encoded with a monetary value, one is only able to participate in productive activity through the mediation of representation: the world of unlimited becoming only prospers within a world of being. Work is subjugated to representation in the form of simulacra of production – balance-sheets, budgets, standards, references, reports, qualifications, legitimate goals, strategic plans, fitness for purpose statements, quality assurance certificates, audits and appraisals – an unproductive bureaucracy which demonstrates that the production of the simulacrum of the production of wealth is of greater significance than the production of wealth. Situated within the production, distribution and consumption of simulacra, one is required to become an administrator where one's subjectivity and evaluations are produced as roles within the economic system. We can be unaffected by the events that happen to us because we identify with ideal, disembodied persons – who are merely roles and duties. This is a process of ideological interpellation, the construction of a subject within social representation with which one must identify.[5]

Given this context for contemporary life, the key issue is that of how one resists. Deleuze also wrote:

> Modern life is such that, confronted with the most mechanical, the most stereotypical repetitions, inside and outside ourselves, we endlessly extract from them little differences, variations, and modifications. Conversely, secret, disguised and hidden repetitions, animated by the perpetual displacement of a difference [e.g. capital or desire], restore bare, mechanical and stereotypical repetitions, within and without us.[6]

A simple repetition of alternative, 'authentic' evaluations may itself become mechanical or stereotypical. Instead, the force of mechanical repetition, the force of the power of capital, needs to be isolated and engaged. If money gains its autonomy from its temporal reserve, then it is the very force of time itself that should be addressed.

Time

The interior of subjectivity

Since the time of Plotinus, time has been associated with human interiority, with the life of the soul.[7] Plotinus gives the example of a man walking: the ground traversed by his feet merely represents the quantity of movement, not the time taken.

> You must relate the body, carried forward during a given period of Time, to a certain quantity of Movement causing the progress and to the Time it takes, and that again to the Movement, equal in extension, within the man's soul.[8]

Time is measured, not quantitatively as though assigning it a price, but intensively, by a progression within the soul, as though assigning it a value. This association between time and interiority is evident in that time cannot be alienated from the self like labour or money; it can never become a material commodity that can be exchanged. Although one may speak of 'buying' or 'saving' time, it is still one's own time that one lives through. 'Time', as Plotinus wrote, 'is a certain expanse of the Life of the Soul.'[9] Nevertheless, when one comes to evaluate lives or episodes in life, the very finitude of our time lends it a power of evaluation – one expresses one's evaluations by what one spends one's time doing, treating time like a currency that can be spent, wasted or saved. Furthermore, in heroism and in medical ethics, the relative values of human lives can be assessed in terms of potential for a long life. So time does acquire a dual role analogous to that of money: as a purely quantitative measure, time measures the length of a task, an episode or a life, in order to calculate and exchange relative values; as a qualitative measure, however, the inalienable life of the soul assesses the quality of an experience over a duration that will be lived through. On the one hand, we have an actual, abstract, clock-time, and on the other hand, we have a virtual, lived duration. In order to use time as a scale of evaluation, these two forms of time need to be convertible, according to a cost–benefit analysis – the pleasure of an experience is assessed against the time to be expended on it, always with one eye on the finite stock of time one has remaining. Once the experience of a duration is evaluated according to the quantity of time taken, then *time acquires a dual role as both measure of values, as time spent, and value of measures, as time remaining.*

As Plotinus indicated, time is coeval with the progression of the soul, its fall into matter, its attraction away from eternal contemplation to its own fragmented, mirror-image.[10] Indeed, time mediates between the soul and extension, allowing an exchange between the life of the soul and progression in matter. This dual role of time as a medium of exchange becomes explicit in Kant:[11] as a pure form of receptivity, time functions as a field of intuition, the 'transcendental form of inner sense', in relation to which all thoughts could be measured and represented as taking place in time; as a pure form of spontaneity, time is the determinable form of thought itself – so Kant used time to schematize the categories of the understanding, generating time in his imagination as a field of thought that measures intuitions.[12] Thought is expressed by determining time. Yet in order to schematize the categories, so allowing clarity of understanding, Kant needed to represent the whole of time at once in his imagination. Now, the only conception of time that one can generate all at once in one's imagination is one where nothing is happening – a homogeneous, linear time. This is precisely Kant's conception, chosen to fulfil the dual role of coordinating spontaneity and receptivity, mind and sensation, and so paper over the cracks of absolute discontinuity:

> We represent the time-sequence by a line progressing to infinity, in which the manifold constitutes a series of one-dimension only; and we reason from the properties of this line to all the properties of time, with this one exception, that while the parts of the line are simultaneous the parts of time are always successive.[13]

Of course, Kant does not say what 'successive' means, and so fails to represent the entire meaning of time. The cost is a loss of evaluation and experience in time;[14] the gain is certainty. Time is imagined as a purely geometrical space. Yet since time has a dual role as both form of intuition and the determinable form of thought, time is the universal equivalent, the meaning of Being. Most significantly, if Kant thinks of time in terms of the succession of homogeneous units, then *he schematizes time in terms of money.*[15]

The presence of this common-sense notion of linear, sequential time in Kant's philosophy does not explain its prevalence in common sense today. One might give further explanations of how the time of the atomic clock, a linear, punctual time especially embodied in information technologies, has left the scene of the laboratory to dominate modern life, in alliance with technology and capital.[16] Nevertheless, this explanation is not entirely sufficient in so far as we are seeking the means by which capital and technology are able to colonize subjectivity. Further progress can be made by examining Kant's schematization of time in terms of money, which suggests two conceptual moves analogous to those made previously in analysing the emergence of capital.

Whereas for Plotinus, time is contained within the movement of the soul, for Kant, time mediates between spontaneity and receptivity, between the self who experiences time and the I who thinks by determining time. In spite of Kant's conception of a homogeneous time as an inert medium of representation, time has an ontological force which has merely been disguised. For once it is used as a measure of values, time implants its own universal scale of evaluation: the most valuable way in which one can spend one's time is in saving time. Once the measure of values can itself be measured on its own scale, then it values itself above all other values on that scale. Then it is no longer I who evaluate by spending time, but time that evaluates by spending me. In Deleuze's words,

> Time is not the interior in us, but just the opposite, the interiority in which we are, in which we move, live and change ... . Subjectivity is never ours, it is time, that is, the soul or the spirit, the virtual.[17]

Time measures itself. But the only time that can be measured is one that is extended. Consequently, the force of time, the need of time to continue to unroll, is no longer given by some urge for movement within the soul,[18] but belongs to time as such in so far as it can be experienced or thought. Where Schelling saw the origin of time in the free decision of eternity to place contradiction behind itself, here time passes out of necessity for much the same reasons as capital increases: it has its own lust to be simultaneously expended and saved. There is no contradiction between receptivity and spontaneity, but merely an abstract synthesis. In addition to time as the form of intuition, and time as the determinable form of thought, there appears to be a third form of time, its ontological unrolling, which divides and coordinates the former two. Then thinking of being in terms of presence in time forces itself upon us[19] due to time's autonomous, self-positing force – time is not merely an inert, determinable medium of thought, it actually determines thought and experience. In spite of the fact that such a synthesis is artificial, a recent product, it, like capital, effectively determines existence.

The second interesting conceptual move also follows from the logic of capital: capital is measured by a rate of increase, not a fixed quantity. Although capital is always invested as a finite quantity, the amount of credit available is determined by anticipated rates of increase – it can therefore be created by banks, and only simulates a quantity.[20] For example, capital has power when production is actively wasted, in war or natural disaster, for the intensified need for production brings opportunities for a return on investment. Capital is an abstract flow, a differential relation, that detaches itself from any finite quantities of money. Analogously, there is no necessity to consider time according to the Kantian conception of a linear succession of homogeneous units. All that is necessary is that time should function as a medium of exchange or an effective synthesis – time does not need to resemble number in order to quantify experienced durations and be quantified as a finite stock. Time, then, need no longer be subordinated to movement as a measure of change, interval or number – it has its own unlimited becoming, its own field of pure exteriority. Once each time-interval is only measured in relation to another, then time itself can become an abstract flow of passage, like capital, generating its own times, liberated from intervals and experiences. The only limiting condition is that for any kind of time that is passable in the world, it should be exchangeable with a conception of time as an abstract quantity. Consequently, if time merely manifests itself as a set of relations, then there need be no definite conception of time, perhaps no definite determination of time apart from specific conducts of time, specific ways in which time is lived, specific *ethics of time* that belong to time as such and not to the individuals who are in time.

Virulent simulacra

There is no sufficient reason why time should be schematized in terms of money; there is no sufficient reason why values should be evaluated in terms of capital. Yet in modern life, these concepts of capital and time force themselves upon us: we must value money, we must value time, increasing or preserving our own stock, if we are to have a share in evaluation. In modern life, nothing is more certain than death and money, nothing is more valuable than time and money. If God is dead, *he is replaced by time and money*, not man – there still are transcendent sources of meaning and value that exceed thought and experience, even if they can take the most banal of forms. Moreover, the newly revealed figures of the transcendent no longer depend on belief or choice: they express an active power in forcing themselves upon us. The banal transcendental may appear harmless because democratic; nevertheless, it can be more tyrannical than any other. Religion has not dissipated in any process of 'secularization': instead, it has merely migrated to the conditions of existence themselves.

These grounds of evaluation are simulacra. For both time and money are media of exchange: the value of money is not fixed, but a product of its exchange-value and credit-value; similarly, the length of an interval can only be measured in relation to another interval, such as the periodic motion of an atomic clock. Time and money possess no substance in themselves; they are media of comparison, exterior relations between terms. Furthermore, these relations possess five simple properties:

1   They can be differentiated from themselves, so that one distinguishes between use-value and exchange-value, interval and duration.
2   The second determination reflexively qualifies the first, so that one thinks of the value of money, of the duration of time.
3   This process can be repeated in infinite regression, so that one can never ultimately measure the value of money or the duration of time.
4   These infinite regressions can be grasped all at once (and this is where thought can make a distinctive contribution) at an 'infinite speed', according to their algorithmic generation – this is already evident in that we can grasp, however obscurely, the concept of the 'infinite'.
5   A limit can be set up within the infinite when the process is reversed, and the first term determines the second: the finitude of wealth and life is shown when one considers the use of money and the length of a duration.[21] Money and time make an appeal to a metaphysical infinite that will determine their own value or duration; while constituting exterior relations themselves, they absolve themselves of relationality to become self-positing absolutes.

This is the structure of the unlimited becoming of *virulent simulacra*: difference, reflexivity, infinite regression, algorithmic generation, reverse reflexivity.

Time and capital gain their specific power, however, from their mutual dependence upon each other: one saves time to make money and one makes money to save time. The alliance between time and money works as follows: a quantum of time is extracted from labour, with work being evaluated in relation to its finished product, and a quantum of money is extracted from evaluation, and the two are conjugated together. By themselves, these simulacra threaten to fall back into the work and evaluation from which they are extracted – where values are simply generated by evaluations. But a quantum of time is valued when it is given a price, and a price is valued when it saves time. There is an energetic coupling between the two series of simulacra, so that an impersonal mode of evaluation is produced by their conjugation. Capital enframes modern life, but the force of this encompassment is only given by its alliance with time as the deepest form of interiority, time that insinuates itself within modern life. Time is the seed, capital encompasses the world, and each crystallizes out in the other:

The little crystalline seed and the vast crystallizable universe: every-thing is included in the capacity for expansion of the collection constituted by the seed and the universe.[22]

Then everything becomes temporal, everything has a price – the conse-quences of which are realized to an unsurpassed extent in twentieth-century economic and cultural life, as well as in philosophy. Capital and time become inescapable because, although they determine limits to our lives and values, they always displace their own limits – they are free, abstract flows of unlimited becoming.

The most powerful simulation, then, is that of the common notion uniting time and capital: instead of being united as equivalents, in the manner of a signifier and signified or goods exchanged in the market, the two become one composite being, capital providing the 'form' and time providing the 'matter'. The dissimulation, here, is parity between the highest form of exteriority, capital, and the highest form of interiority, time. Since the structure of virulent simulacra is itself exterior, freedom is lost in the dissimulation. In this respect, the conjugation only produces a simulation of its own necessity after the fact, just as prices seem equal after the fact of exchange. Similarly, time loses its own temporality.

Market value

Subjectivity necessarily opens itself on to exteriority, mediating its relations to itself through money and time. Nevertheless, the consumer in the market has a certain degree of freedom, has room to manoeuvre, in the choice of which exchange relations to enter: one may prefer cheese or lobsters. Where capital encompasses and time drives modern life, these simulacra feed off the spontaneity which perpetually escapes them. Now, in Marx's analysis of the commodity form, a synchronic perspective is constructed, as though exchange had already taken place. In the market, however, there are elements of strategy and uncertainty due to the number of possible transactions which might take place. The enabling condition for such a range of possibilities is mobility.

What temporal relations are concealed in the simulacrum of price? An exchange will only take place if it is believed by both parties to be worth it: that is to say, they value for themselves on that occasion the commodity of their trading partner more highly than their own; it is also to say that expectations of finding a similar trade on more favourable terms elsewhere do not outweigh the anticipated costs of finding such an alternative. Degrees of mobility and access to information, therefore, introduce a significant imbalance into the trading relationship: the one who is more mobile and better informed can make the price more favourable by threatening to withdraw from exchange. Given that money and finance are always more mobile than other commodities, power necessarily shifts in the direction of the buyer. There is, however, a second and more significant inequality in any supposedly equal exchange. This inequality is expressed in Aristotle's famous distinction between *oikonomia*, the art of household management, and *chrematistike*, the art of making profit. The speculator, one who exchanges for the sake of making a profit, can be relatively indifferent as to whether an exchange succeeds, for many other possibilities are available elsewhere, all are measured in terms of money, and anything that makes money is worthwhile; by contrast, a householder, one who exchanges to acquire the means of subsistence, is compelled to agree to an exchange that can be quickly obtained. Now, those with sufficient money to engage in making profits have little insecurity over whether they can fulfil their household management needs. Thus, in markets prior to capitalism, there is a fundamental class difference between those whose basic needs for survival are at stake and those who simply aim to make money. It should also be noted how often this fundamental class difference is correlated with the gender difference: women often take on the role of providing subsistence for themselves, their dependants, and even their men, while men often claim their freedom to profit from and enjoy life.

In the contemporary global economy where 95% of finance capital is invested in currency speculation, bond speculation, and financial packages, the traditional exploitation of labour by capital is significant but not central. There is a more fundamental class difference than that between capital and labour. Trading transactions are unequal due to relative mobility of trading partners, relative mobility of stock, and relative mobility of currency. The behaviour of the market remains more relevant. The fundamental dissimulation effected by agreeing a trade is that the exchange is in some sense equal, that the body of one commodity is equal to the value of another. For in trade between householder and a speculator the desired object is anticipated to satisfy the subsistence needs of one partner, and the profit expectations of the other. These are incommensurable investments: trade synthesizes present demand with future profit. In short, both partners engage in projective identification with the object of their desire, but for one partner the desired commodity expresses subsistence needs, while for the other partner the desired commodity expresses profit expectations. Each recognizes in the commodity a 'kindred soul, the soul of value', yet incommensurable scales of value, different times, are harmonized through the exchange. Then just as the price form simulates equality of objective value, the trade itself simulates equality of subjective need – perhaps in the form of 'marginal utility'. Furthermore, exchange simulates a structure of market transactions that behave according to determinate laws, as though the conduct of each partner is necessary as a rational means of maximizing self-interest. While entering into such trades may be a practical necessity for the householder, it is by no means a necessity for the speculator, who need not even maximize profits, given a particular predilection for lobsters. The supposedly objective 'laws of the market' derive from the practical and subjective necessities of house-holders; to name them as objective is simply a means of shifting responsibility away from those who profit from the practical necessities which afflict others. Economic theory is constructed from the class perspective of the speculator in terms of 'utility', silencing its real basis in subsistence needs.

It would be a mistake to think of such fundamental class divisions between the householder and the speculator in terms of conflict, or a contradiction of interests. Interests do indeed conflict in the determination of prices; yet there is a basis of common interest in the desire for an exchange to take place. Workers wish to sell their labour; employers wish to buy it. In comparison to being excluded from the economy, accepting employment under any conditions is better than nothing. Capital invest-ment gives an opportunity to labour. In this respect, the disjunction between classes is based on a more profound agreement.

Where, then, is exploitation? Exploitation may be understood in temporal terms. When one small section of the trading population may live by expectation alone, then they set the terms of exchange in order to maximize their profits. Although finance capital is certainly volatile, it is relatively invulnerable in the long term due to its extreme mobility: it can flee when the going gets tough. In a global labour market, wage 'arbi-trage' – transferring production to areas where labour can be 30 to 50 times cheaper – has the effect of reducing the price of labour globally. Although this may in turn lead to a shortage of consumers, collapses of corporations and a fall in share prices, mobile finance may escape the carnage by moving to other financial sectors. Moreover, even when there is a massive destruction of financial value in a stock market crash, and investors' confidence is weakened, business continues as usual in the inevitable recovery that follows, however slow it is to pick up. The overall effect of a stock-market crash is not to weaken the position of capital with respect to labour, but the contrary. The ultimate result of the imbal-ance between the speculator and the householder is a progressive shift of wealth towards finance capital, as we have seen in recent years, and a consequent increase in relative power in exchange. This progressive shift of power may continue beyond the level at which all subsistence needs for all householders are fulfilled, for finance capital has no interest in the fulfilment of need if more effective profits can be made elsewhere. Thus 24% of the global population live in extreme poverty.[23] Those whose selling power progressively falls will pass beyond the level at which they can effectively contribute to the global economy – especially when that economy is identified either with the maximization of profits or the overall volume of economic exchanges expressed in terms of price. The proportion of world trade enjoyed by the poorest countries has halved over the last 20 years.

If there is an excess of investment capital over production, will this result in an expansion of the terrain of the global economy? This is certainly an important dynamic, responsible for the rise in living standards of many sections of the global population. Speculators cannot manage without householders. Yet caution needs to be exercised before the faith which heralds the creation of wealth as a saviour for several reasons.[24]

1   'Expansion' is measured in terms of profits and overall volume of economic exchanges – it is measured purely in terms of speculative value, not subsistence value. Then each decision to invest in an economy that enhances subsistence must be weighed against the opportunity to invest in financial packages that are distantly related to subsistence on the grounds of profitability alone.
2   If production is geared simply to the creation of wealth, then it will be directed primarily to consumers who possess wealth: much production is of luxury goods rather than subsistence goods. There is no reason to meet the subsistence needs of those who have nothing.
3   Investment may result in practical enslavement for debt, and in order to obtain the hard currency to pay interest on loans and investments, an increasing amount of production must be geared to export. Export crops exploit the most fertile land, displacing rural and indigenous economies, leading to mass migration to cities and the destruction of cultures. Thus simply because speculators find more householders to exploit does not mean that subsistence needs will necessarily be met.
4   The expansion of production does not only draw on renewable resources such as an educated workforce, but it uses up finite resources. The global economy can only expand where resources are available; once these are used up, finance will move on, leaving devastation in its wake.
5   Finally – and this ascription is used advisedly – levels of waste, pollution and climate change brought about by the expansion of production will gradually rise, leaving larger and larger regions which currently have a dense population either infertile or uninhabitable. Thus a general rise in living standards today is bought at the expense of subsistence needs for a large minority of the global population today, and a large majority of the global population tomorrow.

The first temporal principle of market exploitation is as follows: the advantage of the speculator over the householder in terms of mobility and availability of alternative exchanges brings an imbalance of power into relations of trade. This imbalance necessarily increases over time. *The increasing shift of power from householders to speculators is the theoretical reason why a global market economy will over time necessarily destroy a large proportion of the global population.* There is no reason why an expansion of speculative power should lead to an expansion of subsistence production to the point where it meets basic needs. To the contrary, there are many reasons against, for speculative power can expand on a fixed base of a subsistence economy.

In a closed system, with a fixed amount of currency in circulation, to acquire wealth is to increase one's purchasing power relative to others. Even in an open financial system, where the total amount of finance is able to expand, the acquisition of wealth itself remains differential. The world as a whole is not enriched by the creation of wealth; instead, the wealthy merely increase their relative power over others. The result is an acceleration of inequality and underdevelopment, based on a massive power imbalance built up over a long history of plunder, extermination, slavery, colonialism and neo-colonialism.[25] Once inequality is firmly in place, direct acts of repression can be replaced by purely economic means, or contracted out to local subsidiaries, without even the knowledge of the parent company. Such inequalities can be measured by the actual flows of resources, commodities, food, clothing, manufactured goods and capital, as well as by the contrast in wages between those who produce in the developing world and those who consume in the developed world. The result is clearly the continuation of the 'tribute' economy. It is also doubtful whether the world is truly enriched by much of the activity which counts as the production of goods and services in the contemporary society, for, just as the power of finance increases, an increasing proportion of production is driven by the expectation of profits in comparison to being driven by the satisfaction of needs. This can be illustrated by the fact that one of the world's most pressing needs – the production of fuel and energy from renewable resources – receives minimal investment, and rates of production are minute in relation to production relating to the consumption of fossil fuels and non-renewable energy resources. When needs for subsistence and survival no longer command power to determine relations of production and exchange, then subsistence and survival will fail.

There is a second temporal dimension to market relations. In commodity exchange, it is generally assumed that trade resembles an instantaneous swap – or at least, if it takes time for the goods to be delivered, they will be identical on arrival to the form in which they were ordered. The relation between a financial investor and an asset, however, is not a trade; it is a relationship that endures over time. The global 'market' in finance capital conceals the extent to which another kind of relation is enacted: attracting financial investment bears closer comparison to attracting a sexual partner than it does to trade. For profitability cannot be given all at once, so investors seek the promise of profitability. All kinds of considerations of integrity, ability, environment, opportunity and security come into play when weighing up a possible investment. Each of these, however, is synthesized into an anticipated rate of return over a given time-span. Each is considered only as an indicator of a possible future.

In temporal terms, it becomes essential to distinguish between contractual relationships and property relationships. For whereas a contract may bind an investor over a period of time, property imposes no such obligations, so long as it is assumed that one has the right to dispose of one's property as one pleases. Thus an asset held as property may be sold. Just as there is a fundamental class division between householders and speculators, there is also a fundamental class division between relations of contract and those of property. 'Conflict' is again inappropriate here. Moreover, the difference is one of degree rather than of kind. For to the extent that one party has greater power in negotiating a relationship based on the fundamental class difference between householders and speculators, then the terms of the contract can be agreed to be more favourable to one party. The limit of this process is a contractual relation which imposes rights but no obligations on one party – as in the case of property. Nevertheless, this difference of degree at the formation of a relation is converted into a difference in kind over the course of time due to the disposal of assets.

Finance capital performs a sleight of hand whereby contractual relations may be converted into property relations. For example, when one sells shares in a company, one sells an enterprise as a whole – including its fixed assets, its property, its stock and its contracts of employment and trade – as though these were property. There is a dissimulation of two incommensurable realities here: a share certificate (giving property rights) and a corporation are treated as equivalents. Now, where the reality of a corporation depends on its past history, and present circumstances, the value of a share certificate depends on expectations of its future value alone. Where a corporation is a network of interdependent relations in a wider economic, social and ecological environment, a share certificate is a single quality measured by a universal quantity. When trading shares, one trades both simultaneously as though they are one and the same commodity. The buyer may have expectations of the share certificate, but no obligations to the enterprise. In order to safeguard enterprises and provide for dependent subsistence needs, wider society has an obligation to maintain obligations, just as a government has a duty to enforce the law. A possible conclusion to draw would be to make the sale of shares illegal.

Capital thus dissimulates a relation between the past and the future. On the one hand, capital stock is based on past transactions, accumulated and synthesized into a single price. On the other hand, capital investment is measured by anticipated rates of return; it is a synthesis of expectations about the future expressed in a price. Now, when a corporation is floated on the stock market, the value of its liquid assets depends on the market price – conditioned by the expected rate of return on investment. Thus, unlike an investor's capital sum which does depend directly on past transactions, the value of liquid assets depends on expectations about the future. Moreover, the value of an asset is also conditioned by expectations about a future rise in price. The stock market as a whole has a certain degree of reflexivity: expectations about the future price affect the present price. Furthermore, the value of an asset is dependent on the value of the currency in which it must be paid for. In this respect, any asset for sale is dependent for its value not only on its own intrinsic qualities, but on much wider economic circuits over which it has no control.

One may therefore invert the general form of the semiotic 'triangle' to produce a general form of the 'triangle' of quantitative simulation (see Figure 5.1).

Conflicting demands of external economic circuits and internal needs can make effective financial management of a corporation or a nation impossible. The external demands of economic stability, necessary for the functioning of the system as a whole, take precedence, making it impossible to respond to short-term needs for subsistence and longer term needs for survival.

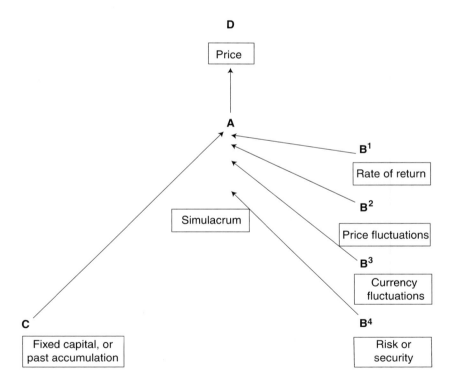

Figure 5.1 General form of triangle of quantitative simulation

Where, in the context of trade, does the extraction of surplus value come from? If value is considered in purely material terms as wealth, labour and land, then extraction of surplus value is inexplicable. These, however, are merely the objects of valuations; they do not account for the production of values. To take the mode of representation of value as its essential nature is to repeat the paralogism of pure reason. For value, when expressed in terms of a price, is merely simulated. Value has its source in the subjective forms of need, desire and expectation. Value is expressed in the attraction of interest and attention. The extraction of surplus value may be understood against this background.

In the first place, the householder and the speculator have fundamentally different experiences of time. A householder is often compelled to live from day to day: fulfilling of subsistence needs is a postponement of death, the sustenance of one's own future time and those of one's dependants. The speculator, by contrast, regards death merely as the outer limit of time available in which to make a profit, or the inner limit when the rate of profit reduces capital to zero. Where the householder lives under an indefinite reprieve, constantly faced with the demands of death, a speculator lives also in a state of perpetual postponement. For if value depends primarily on expectations about the future, then when the future comes, value will still depend on expectations of a later future. One is not called to account for value. Moreover, just as with paper currency whose value is sufficiently secure never to require repayment, expectations of value do not need to be fulfilled. For at any future time, value will still depend largely on future expectations – which are vulnerable to performance and a return on investment, but are not entirely determined by these. Thus it is a myth to believe that the financial economy should mirror the 'real' economy, and that it can become over-inflated and lose touch with reality. Instead, the financial economy may be influenced by the 'real' economy, but at every stage, it only deals with promises, expectations and simulations; there is no day of reckoning, no day of recompense. So where the householder lives under perpetual judgement, warding off the death which is announced in advance, the speculator lives in a state of perpetual debt forgiveness, for there is no judgement for the speculator.

In this respect, the 'economy' should not be considered as a finite sphere of labour, land and capital, from which value may be extracted by one sector only at the expense of the other. Value may derive directly from valuation: from need, expectation and desire. What, then, is increased in the creation of wealth? Since wealth is exchangeable, the power of consumption increases. Nevertheless, consumption by the wealthy, however large, is relatively small in proportion to the quantity of wealth reinvested. Similarly, one can create wealth for the sake of others, donating large sums to philanthropic causes. Nevertheless, the greater proportion of wealth is devoted to the creation of wealth, the quest of autonomous value for its own sake. In this respect, wealth creation is exterior to human experience, although it may impact on human experience through consumption, through reinvestment and through philanthropy. A purely exterior force forms an alliance with other interests – consumption, investment, philanthropy, political influence – through which both gain. Now, no one would consciously engage in wealth creation for its own sake, were it not allied to the motivations of consumption, investment, philanthropy and power. These interests benefit from the creation of wealth, just as the creation of wealth benefits from such desires. The dominance of global capital depends on an alliance between these subjective interests and the objective economic order. Nevertheless, these interests do not have to be achieved for wealth creation to occur. Just as millions of people work hard to achieve the American dream while only few achieve success, wealthy speculators may work hard to increase their wealth, while devoting comparatively little time and attention to consumption, to investment in worthwhile production, and to the real benefits of philanthropic projects, while attaining political power may simply be a safeguard for financial interests to prevent the exercise of political power by others. Wealth creation is what matters above all; it does not depend on the success of its allies, but only that they should bring hope, motivation and expectation.

The 'extraction of surplus value' therefore occurs in a subjective economy. Here, there is no finite stock of motivation in circulation, as evidenced by the contrasts between hope and despair, between belief and apathy. Expectations may receive massive inflations. Yet the subjective economy of the householder is finite: there is only a certain amount of time available to be devoted to worthwhile needs. The fundamental class difference is manifested in the subjective economy as the difference between expectation of a glorious future as against attention to immediate demand. Expectations may have little contact with reality: they focus attention on an imaginary future good, which, like ideology, blinds with the light of its own inherent attractiveness. The economy is driven by fantasy. But dreams of philanthropy may destroy philanthropy: narcissistic attention to one's own inflated conscience may draw attention away from the real and urgent needs which could be served. This is part of a broader problem: for although the creation of wealth does not necessarily involve the extraction of profit from a finite stock elsewhere, it may in fact involve the extraction of surplus value from labour. Moreover, there is also a finite subjective economy of attention: during the passage of time, there are exchanges of focus of attention. In so far as attention is diverted away from immediate needs to unrealizable fantasies, then there is an extraction of surplus value from attention. There is a specific social cost when attention is not apportioned by need but by the inflation of desire. The 'extraction of surplus value' is the diverting of attention from the mode of the householder to the mode of the speculator. It is the abandonment of reality for fantasy.

On the one hand, fantasy is the contemporary form of ideology: one only pays attention to that which promises a narcissistic or libidinal pleasure. If a US President spends two hours over lunch playing video games, then he will pay less attention to issues that matter. Moreover, denial of reality, whether in 'creation science' or in the rejection of the existence of global warming, prevents access to knowledge and responsibility. Nevertheless, our thesis is much stronger: fantasy does not merely conceal economic reality. It is economic reality – it is the subjective form of the extraction of surplus value. For if wealth is merely differential, giving greater power in the determination of social relations mediated by exchange, it is a reified and alienated form of honour. Wealth commands respect and attention, not simply as a sign of power, but because of its mobility: it can abandon the exchange relation on which the other partner depends, buy itself out of its contract, sell its shareholdings, leaving the other devoid of the means of subsistence. This fear of wealth, this respect for wealth, simply is power.

Moreover, respect for wealth is accompanied by belief in the powers of wealth as mediating access to consumption, investment, philanthropy, and political power. This belief is again power, yet it is manifested in the form of aspiration and fantasy. In the creation of a market economy, there is an exploitation of social relations mediated by need and interdependence, and their replacement by the fantasy of social relations characterized by complete freedom and independence for one partner. Freedom is the ultimate fantasy which destroys community. Hopes for freedom profit at the expense of subsistence needs. The finite stock of attention is attracted away from social life to the fantasy of an exterior to social life in relation to which one becomes a potential benefactor.

The exteriority and independence of value, in the form of wealth, are the essence of economic value. For although wealth is power, the quest for unlimited wealth in abstraction cannot be explained by a 'will to power' or a feeling of power. Instead, wealth is exterior or transcendent: religious motives of hope and fear must be invoked to explain the creation of wealth. The 'subjective' impulse determining wealth creation, in alliance with truly subjective motivations, is the need to save time. It is not that anyone particularly wants to save time; saving time is a demand of time itself, a quality of our existence. Since the saving of time demands our attention, attention is focused more and more narrowly on means of saving time. To save time is to reinvest the time we spend on time itself. This reflexive, intensifying process leaves little time to spare for other needs that demand our attention. The essence of contemporary ideology is a focused and self-enclosed attention: in focusing on expectations about future rates of return, extrapolated from limited processes in the present, and in focusing on saving time, one loses sight of reality. In other respects, contemporary culture suffers from hyperactivity attention deficit disorder.

Now, when capital turns to expectations about the future, the rate of increase of wealth is measured in relation to an abstract, linear, quantifiable time. Increase or loss in wealth is measured in relation to a time where nothing happens: the life of clocks or inanimate objects. In short, capital projects its own outside, its own limit, as a zero rate of growth. This limit functions as a screen which blocks out what is really outside; it makes one blind. Beyond the sphere of wealth creation, beyond the global market, there is only the screen of death. There are only two alternatives in life: to create wealth, or to be overcome by death. Now, it would be difficult to maintain belief in this abstraction, were not the evidence of death all around us. In the global market, where wealth creation fails, poverty, famine, drought, disease and death quickly follow. It is not that such ills are produced in order to back up the abstract illusion of death, although they are produced and they do have this effect. Moreover, they are produced by the isolation of wealth creation behind its screen of death. It is simply that, once produced, they provide evidence of a lack of a viable exterior to the global market, so supporting it in its self-enclosure and continuing its destructive effects. Capital does produce real destruction and devastation, against which it casts itself as a saviour able to elevate us from the threat of poverty and death.

The fundamental class division between the speculator and the householder is created by the screen erected by the speculator. The speculator knows only the future, and the present which will lead to the future with the highest rate of return, measured in relation to the screen of abstraction. This very screen of abstraction is a time where nothing happens; it conceals reality. Then the fundamental operation of exploitation, the extraction of surplus value, is the extraction of attention from the interconnections of the householder to the abstractions of the speculator. Class division is a separation of hope and fear. Where the speculator knows only hope, the householder must face the fears evaded by the speculator. If, however, the ideological consciousness of the speculator should achieve hegemony over the householder, so that those with least reason to hope learn to live purely by hope, then all responsibility before reality is lost. Finally, if competitive market relations so interpenetrate life that the wealthiest corporations have to maximize efficiency gains in order to survive, then even their wealthy executives must live as corporate householders, struggling for corporate subsistence, even if they may also be individual speculators.

The power of capital derives from its abstract conception of time based on the threat of death. Death is elevated as an absolute: we all believe in death. Capitalism thrives on materialism. By contrast, many religious worldviews – even those tolerated in capitalism – relativize the threat of death by reincorporating it into a larger cosmology of resurrection or rebirth. In capitalism, the ethical significance of such cosmologies is rarely taken seriously in practice, however much lip-service they receive. In rare cases where a transcendent value takes precedence over life and death, a licence is given for murder and terrorism. Yet it is only by challenging the capitalist piety before death that an alternative can be found.

Notes

1 Aristotle, *Politics* I, 1257a–b, Cambridge: Cambridge University Press, 1988, pp. 12–13.
2 Eric Alliez, *Capital Times*, Minneapolis: University of Minnesota Press, 1996, p. 6.
3 Alliez, ibid., p. 7.
4 Deleuze, *Cinema 2: the Time-Image*, London: Athlone, 1989, p. 171.
5 See Althusser, 'Ideology and Ideological State Apparatuses', *Essays on Ideology*, London: Verso, 1984. Following the work of Michel Foucault and feminist theorists in particular, recent studies of culture and society have identified innumerable operations of power in society. In comparison, an emphasis on capital may seem naïvely Marxist. My argument is not that such cultural manifestations of power are unimportant or do not exist, but that they are *encompassed* by the global market. They are not the direct cause of the current global crisis. Concepts of 'power' evaporate under closer analysis; concepts of 'sexual difference' remain tied to imaginary and symbolic orders, leaving feminist theory *qua* feminist tied to psychoanalysis. Neither are self-positing like the logic of capital.
6 Deleuze, *Difference and Repetition*, London: Athlone, 1994, p. xix.
7 Plotinus defined time 'as the Life of the Soul in movement as it passes from one stage of act or experience to another.' *Enneads* III.7.11, Harmondsworth: Penguin, 1991, p. 228.
8 Plotinus, *ibid.*, III.7.13, p. 232.
9 Plotinus, *ibid.*, III.7.12, p. 228.
10 See Plotinus, *ibid.*, IV.8.4; IV.8.12; III.7.11–13.
11 Alliez shows how Plotinus' conception of time anticipates Kant. *Capital Times*, 34, p. 68.
12 Martin Heidegger brings out this distinction most acutely throughout his commentary on Kant. Time is then the determinable form of intuition and the determinable form of thinking, allowing thinking and intuition to be brought together. The primordial essence which unrolls time into receptivity and spontaneity, intuition and thought, is a pure self-affection, time as the measure of itself, a pure abstract flow. See Heidegger, *Kant and the Problem of Metaphysics*, Bloomington: Indiana University Press, 1962. For Deleuze, the discovery of this role for time within thought, fracturing the subject, is the discovery of the transcendental; it brings the death of God, liberating thought from conformity to established values. Deleuze, *Difference and Repetition*, pp. 86–7.
13 Kant, *Critique of Pure Reason*, Basingstoke: Macmillan, 1933, p. 77.
14 See Bergson's critique of the Kantian conception of time, in *Time and Free Will*, London: Swan Sonnenschein, 1910.
15 Where money is regarded as finance capital rather than cash, which depends on combinations of heterogeneous units. Alliez describes this time converted into the money form as a 'simulacrum of measure'. Alliez, *Capital Times*, p. 13.
16 See, for example, Helga Nowotny, *Time: the Modern and Postmodern Experience*, Cambridge: Polity, 1996, p. 101.
17 Deleuze, *Cinema 2*, pp. 82–3. Deleuze identifies time with 'the powerful, Non-organic Life which grips the world.' *Cinema 2*, p. 81.

18 See Plotinus' account of the 'audacity' (*tolma*) of the soul that drives it towards its own image and self-centredness, away from contemplation of the Eternal Intellect. *Enneads*, IV.8.5. See also Alliez's discussion of the fall of the soul and the generation of time, in *Capital Times*, pp. 27–74. Instead of speaking of the soul's audacity and fall, it would be necessary to speak of time's audacity, its power of simulating and dissimulation.

19 As asserted by Heidegger in *On Time and Being*, New York: Harper Colophon, 1977, p. 6.

20 See Deleuze and Guattari, *Anti-Oedipus*, London: Athlone, 1984, p. 229.

21 Deleuze and Guattari describe this process of setting up a limit within the infinite by appealing to Cantor's theory of transfinite sets and ordinals. See Deleuze and Guattari, *What is Philosophy?*, London: Verso, 1994, p. 120. For a fuller explanation of Cantor's significance, see A. W. Moore, *The Infinite*, London: Routledge, 1990, pp. 118–30.

22 Deleuze, *Cinema 2*, pp. 80–1.

23 United Nations Development Programme Report 1998.

24 For a fuller critique of this perspective, see George F. DeMartino, *Global Economy, Global Justice*, London: Routledge, 2000.

25 Teresa Hayter, *The Creation of World Poverty*, London: Pluto, 1981, although somewhat dated, remains a useful history and itemization of the processes through which inequality has been produced.

6   Potency

What power can be found to redirect attention? It is neccessary first of all, to think through the compelling potency of death. It has been estimated that by 2025, some two-thirds of the global population – some 5 billion people – will be at risk from weather-related disasters, such as drought, famine, flooding, hurricanes and cyclones. This situation of risk will at best continue for at least two centuries; if, however, there is no massive reduction in the use of fossil fuels, the risk will rapidly intensify. Whatever happens, it is likely that the pressure on the infrastructure of developing countries from repeated disasters will be so great that it leads to collapse, resulting in famine, disease, war and mass migration. Prospects for this majority of the global population seem extremely poor.[1] Responsibility for climate change is almost wholly down to the industrialized countries, who produce 80% of the world's emissions, while the G8 countries produce 45% of carbon dioxide emissions alone. Contemporary Western culture will soon be responsible for genocide – unintentional or otherwise – on an unprecedented scale.

Ethics of transcendence

Death

Does death merit our attention? Everyone will die. Why, then, should one care about the extinction of the human race, or of any other mortal species? By preserving life, do we not fight a losing battle against the inevitable? Moreover, for whole cultures and races faced with probable death and possible extinction, do not religious questions about the significance and value of life and death come to predominate over the practical questions of finding means of survival? Or are such questions a fatal hesitancy, a final ideological ruse, delaying action when urgent action needs to be taken?

Philosophers have often argued for the beneficial significance of death. Death is not that which robs life of its meaning, but that which makes life's meaningfulness possible.[2] For death is the aneconomic instance *par excellence*; it cannot be reincorporated in a cycle of substitution and exchange. As Derrida remarked, death is that which nobody else can undergo or confront in my place – thus one's absolute singularity, and one's responsibility, is given by the gift of death.[3] As a limit to possible experience, it gives meaning and value to time, money, ethics and life in general. Yet death is not objectively given in experience: we often have to call in experts to judge when death has in fact taken place. Whether others die or I die, death is never encountered in experience.[4] The death of others is merely experienced as a threshold beyond which reciprocal relations cease. We only know of death as a state to be attained or avoided. Neither is it merely a subjective category imposed on experience: death always comes from without, as a kind of shock. Death is a true transcendental, exceeding both the objective and the subjective, while giving meaning to time and all being that is thought in its terms. Then, as Derrida says, 'fundamentally, one knows perhaps neither the meaning nor the referent of this word.'[5]

In spite of this ignorance, in modern thought, the meaning of temporal existence as finite is synthesized in terms of the approach of death. Heidegger explored the heart of the modern conception of time: 'Time and the temporal mean what is perishable, what passes away in the course of our time.'[6] To be temporal is to pass away, to be separated from what one is. Although death never becomes present, although its essence is lack of presence, death is coextensive with life: it is a trauma that is repeated at every moment. As Georg Simmel explains:

> In every single moment of life we *are* the ones that will die, and that moment would be different if this [dying] were not our co-given condition that is somehow at work in the moment. Just as we are not already there at the instant of our birth, but something of us is born continuously, so we do not first come to die in our last instant.[7]

This combination of discontinuity and continuity is found in the conception of time itself. Heidegger, following Bergson,[8] differentiated time as a linear sequence of nows, or that which is counted and passes away in time, from time which causes the now to pass.[9] The unity of future, past and present, for Heidegger, is given by their reciprocal relations of mutual self-giving.[10] There is a continuity, but this unity of past, present and future in presence is withheld, for these dimensions remain distinct, held at a distance.[11] In this respect, the continuity of time is founded on discontinuity. There is therefore a difference between time imagined as a homogeneous medium, where moments are exterior to each other like material objects, and the 'flow' of time itself, where successive moments are joined in a synthesis of reciprocal relation.[12] Such a reciprocal relation, identified by Bergson as the continuity of duration, is, in fact, absent in the conceptualization of time, where it must be reconstituted by Heidegger as absent.

Levinas went further here. Where Heidegger thought death as the absolute limit of the thinking subject, its ownmost potentiality-for-being,[13] for Levinas, death is a real discontinuity in time, emerging from outside of the subject's experience of time.[14] Discontinuity brings the possibility that the future may bring something surprising and heterogeneous, and not simply what is already given by the past. Not only is death authentically futural, but so is the Other – in so far as it brings asymmetry in the form of an obligation lacking reciprocity:

> The first word of the face is the 'Thou shalt not kill.' It is an order. There is a commandment in the appearance of the face, as if a master spoke to me. However, at the same time, the face of the Other is destitute; it is the poor for whom I can do all and to whom I owe all.[15]

Faced with authentic discontinuity and the command of the Other, the future is not determined by causal, logical, or ontological necessity, but by *ethical* necessity. Levinas posited the ethical relation of the face-to-face as primordial, and therefore transcendent, giving it priority over all other social relations that already exist.[16] There is a measure of agreement with Heidegger, here, for both Heidegger and Levinas take death, whether of self or of the Other, as that which gives their conception of time. Death as passing away, whether present, past or future, is involved in time as passage.

We do, however, experience the passage of time: we have to relive death in each passing moment, where we are left with the corpse or memory of what has been, just as we are transformed by what is coming into being. *I* may never reach death, may never die, since when I am dead, then I am no more, but the passage of time is the perpetual dying of each passing moment. Even when my identity is stripped away, there remains the pure force of time ticking over. Time, then, is the impersonal repetition of a transcendental death that can never be encountered in experience. The meaning of death can only be thought in terms of the passage of time.

Then time is explained in terms of death, and death is explained in terms of time. Death and time only gain a meaning in terms of each other: each of these are simulacra, in reciprocal presupposition, lacking a determinate meaning. Our modern piety is that we believe in death and time, even if we can give no coherent meaning to these non-phenomenal phenomena.[17] Derrida both affirms and demonstrates the extent to which we remain pious before death.[18] Such piety, however, may simply reflect piety before simulacra, as Derrida himself is aware: 'Who will guarantee … that language is not precisely the origin of the nontruth of death, and of the other?'[19] Nevertheless, modern thought is effectively determined in relation to the simulacra of time and death. Indeed, to the extent that language is able to designate, to apply a rule to a case or a sign to an object, to name this object as this object, then it is inseparable from a certain tracing of borders, an incision into the flux of reality, by which *this* is distinguished from *not-this*. In all representation one finds the phenomenon of the border, which is merely the spatialization of time, an abstraction from the flux of reality. Such a spatialization of time depends on its commodification, its rendering in countable units, its abstraction from its own life of indeterminacy, affect and becoming. Determination itself is determination by death. Thus Derrida identifies death as the meaning of bordering as such, as the principle which both traces and ruins the borders; for death makes borders possible, while itself evading all borders.[20] Indeed, to the extent that death makes thinking in terms of limits possible, while death itself is the impossible transgression of the limit of the possible, a crossing of the border, then 'transcendence' can only be thought in terms of death.[21]

Those who struggle for subsistence seem pious before death. Work is an attempt to produce an effect which will endure beyond the time spent in working. In this respect, extinction of the human race would amount to annihilation of the cumulative heritage of all the positive products of human endeavour over the centuries. Now, few things can be preserved for ever, and the effects of work are usually temporary, giving rise to further, more ramified effects over which less influence is held. Then the desire to produce temporary effects may be distinguished from the principle of preservation itself – a principle which motivates much work.

Death may again be the basis of this principle. When someone dies, they leave gifts which cannot be repaid: a corpse, memories, obligations, matters left unsaid, and emotional impulses left unrealized. Death, the gift of a corpse and an affect that cannot be discharged, is revelatory of the real presence of an other through their absence. According to Freud, the repression of unconscious aggression towards the beloved leads to the projection of a malevolent spirit whose influence can still be felt – a spirit would then be the return of repressed aggression.[22] Nevertheless, the dead can no longer enter into exchange and negotiation: they return as absolute – an inflexible, unalterable will, a will that stands whether or not it is honoured. Death breaches reciprocity: since the dead can no longer confer gifts, then they cannot discharge obligations. Gifts conferred on the dead must be continually repeated. Death marks the apotheosis of the merely contingent to a status of necessity. In social relations of mutual honour, such necessity is experienced as a gaze or a will that has become fixed: it is a command and a judgement. Similarly, the passage of time, which contains death in each passing moment, is an apotheosis of the past to the status of necessity. We are judged by the past, and are called to live up to its expectations.

Then the desire to preserve the heritage of the past includes the obligation to fulfil the will of ancestors, just as it also includes the hope that one's own will may join the absolute community as well. Such apotheoses depend on the need to honour obligations, repay gifts and express emotions of desire or hatred. The aim, here, is to restore a certain peace or equilibrium where one can escape from demands, no longer haunted by ghosts. It is to avoid the dominating spirits of others, the emotional eddies left by their all-too traumatic presence. It is to allow them to be truly dead and buried. Then, even during life, reciprocity is motivated by a strange death-wish, a desire to have the other dead and buried by having all debts repaid and all emotions discharged. This becomes a transcendental principle of social behaviour as such: guided by a vision of peace, when social interaction will be no more, it produces action that fails to resolve the tension, complicating the disturbance and continuing the heritage.

Death holds its power through its inaccessibility, its perpetual displacement, its absence. What happens, then, when it arrives? When I die, my future and my sphere of possibilities shrinks towards nothing. Obligations become impossible to fulfil; aspirations become impossible to accomplish. First hand accounts of close encounters with death often report a threshold where grasping at possibilities of life is replaced by an acceptance of the necessity of death. This apotheosis of the contingent, accidental death to the status of necessity might take the form of religious insight accompanied by a feeling of 'undying peace', such as: 'God is almighty, Heaven and Earth rest in his hand; we must bow to His Will.'[23] The threshold is one of conversion, forgiveness, or absolution: formerly, one stood under judgement, forever destined to carry out obligations that can never be fulfilled. In the approach of death, the burden of debt is intensified as it becomes impossible to repay it. At the threshold where death becomes certain, however, the significance of such obligations suddenly vanishes – they are no longer my responsibility. Liberated from bondage to future and past, desire and obligation, one simply is.

Tem Horwitz has given an interesting description of his own experience of 'death' when he went into anaphylactic shock, and was later resuscitated. He describes the 'dissolution of time':

> It is very difficult to describe time through this sequence. It ceased to be the medium through which I was moving. There was no forward, no backward, no future, no past – only a present that contained everything. All eternity was in that present … . Dying removed me from the clutches of time. There was no present for me – transient or otherwise – during this period … . Each state or place that I visited lasted forever … . There were no slow fades into another scene. What was, was – and that it is all there 'was' – and then it was something else.[24]

Now, the use of tensed verbs in this description should not lead us to conclude that the experience itself was temporal, or contained all the usual dimensions of time: this would be to commit the error of mistaking the mode of representation for the reality itself. After the experience, a new mode of existence continued within time over the next few weeks:

There was a tremendous sense of freedom. These moments were what they were. They lacked nothing. They were complete in and of themselves. I could conceive of no happiness outside of these moments.

There was no future.

I could not for that first week focus on what was to happen the next day, the next week, the next moment. Without a future to think about there was also nothing to worry about ... . There was nothing that I wanted to do or felt that I had to do.

There was no vestige of self-importance left. It felt like death had obliterated my ego, the attachments that I had, my history, and who I had been ... . Gone was my personal history with all of its little vanities. The totality of myself was changed ... . Personality was a vanity, an elaborate delusion, a ruse.[25]

This decathexis of possibilities involves the destruction of the affective significance of all previous reference points of the individual, including memories. For the cathexis of past memories only takes place for the sake of carrying one's identity or habits forward to the future, in a reciprocal investment of habits and desires; once the future is lost, then there is no longer a use for the past – one loses all possessions, all memories, all reference points, all identity. The subjective bridge between past and future can then gradually collapse. First-hand reports, such as those recounted by Albert Heim of falling mountaineers, often recount the experience of time slowing down, allowing great speed and clarity of thought in relation to it.[26] Here, the subjective experience of the passage of time seems to be controlled by the degree of libidinal cathexis of imaginary futures. One only invests in the objective passage of time, the time of the social consensus and of clocks, if one seeks to extract a profit from it. This cathexis is itself a grasping on to life, a warding off of death – as if desiring the future will postpone that awful moment of peace when I am no more. So what happens if I die consciously, accepting my fate? The slowing down of subjective time may keep pace with the objective passage of time towards its limit, like Zeno's tortoise with Achilles, so that the limit of death remains forever displaced. Then experience would swerve out of consensual time, where each threshold of libidinal decathexis and each displacement of the ultimate limit is experienced as passing through a tunnel out of consensual temporality and the consensual reality founded upon it.

Death, the supreme object of fear, brings salvation from fear. Now, when death is regarded as a border or discontinuity, I am forever separated from death by the threshold of dying itself, after which I am no more. When I consider death in this way, I cannot consider my death, for the one who is considered to have died is always a representative. Such considerations are essentially false, for no one can die in my place. There are no representatives, no substitutes. Then the image of death as a border is a simulacrum: it is produced by a particular practice in reality or imagination which attempts to substitute the death of another for my own death. Our concept of death is constructed from sacrifice.

Human and animal sacrifice offer the opportunity to relive death in advance, so as, if for no other reason, to attempt to demonstrate the existence of death.[27] Sacrifice has also often been understood as establishing communication between the profane, mortal world and the sacred sphere which is the source of life and death.[28] Normally, the sacred is too intense, too powerful for mortal contact – and nothing is more ritually polluting than contact with a corpse, the residue of destructive power. Under the correct ritual conditions, however, the destructive power of the sacred falls on the victim alone, and its life-giving power may be given to the beneficiaries of the sacrifice. According to the ancient Hindu beliefs recorded in the Brahmanas, through the sacrifice, properly performed, a person could become immortal.[29] Indeed, even the gods become immortal through sacrifice.[30] For mortals, however, this communication and identification with the sacred can only be achieved by a simultaneous distancing, so that the victim redeems one from the destructive power by bearing its force.[31] In this respect, sacrificial ritual often involves the establishing of a hierarchy of levels of sacredness, with concentric circles of purity and danger radiating from a central focus.[32] The victim is the one who passes all the way through the hierarchy to the ultimate consecration which is execution, where its spirit is separated from its body, and sent into the sacred sphere as though through a tunnel of sacrality. The body of the victim remains as a sacred matter, part of which may be fed to the gods to maintain their immortality, and part of which may be consumed by the people, so that they might intermingle with the sacrifice.[33]

The key problem is as follows: does sacrifice establish communication between the sacred and profane spheres, or does it create these spheres by separating body and spirit through death? Is consecration through death the influx of a pre-existent sacred power, or the creation of a sacred power? Do the gods consecrate death, or does death consecrate the gods? Which is the true perspective: modern suspicion or religious credulity?

This is perhaps a false alternative. For the procedure of sacrifice meets with limited success: death has gone, it is elsewhere. Only the victim meets death, and the shared remains of the gift of death, the corpse of the victim, do not bring a full participation in death. Sacrifice poses a question which it cannot answer; the question must then be repeated in an effort to determine the answer more effectively. The absence of meaning drives the quest for meaning. Instead of allowing communication and interaction with the gods, sacrifice keeps the gods at a distance.[34] Such distance is a force for repetition: my attempt to discharge affects and repay obligations is a sacrificial ritual that simultaneously creates and destroys its victim. Then the absolute discontinuity of death is created by sacrificial repetition. It is just the same as the abstract time of capital: death is produced as an absolute, a symbolic threshold, by a determinate way of living and thinking. In so far as one grasps at possibilities or displaces a symbolic death, one obscures acts of grasping and displacement that function as bridges over the discontinuity of time towards the future.

Death, then, may not be inaccessible after all. Moreover, in so far as it is present in each passing moment, the experience of death is perpetually present, determining and shaping our lives. Indeed, it is a common delusion in psychosis to believe that one has in fact died.[35] And the frequency of 'a dramatic experience of death that, in terms of its intensity, is indistinguishable from actual dying' (whatever this might mean) in LSD psychotherapy, has led the LSD researcher, Stanislav Grof, to postulate that 'human beings possess subliminal knowledge of what it feels like to experience death.'[36] These death experiences often change one's concept of death, usually rendering the fact of physical death irrelevant.[37] Grof classified such hallucinatory experiences in terms of an abreaction of the traumatic stages surrounding birth: the stage of death and rebirth corresponds to delivery itself.[38] In such experiences, then, passing through the tunnel of death is identified by Grof with passing through the birth canal, a process which naturally ends in rebirth. Grof indicated that the hallucinatory content surrounding this abreactive stage is often composed of religious practices that include sado-masochistic elements, that glorify sacrifice, whether animal or human, that include scenes of hell and torture:

> They involve tortures and cruelties of all kinds, bestial murders and mass executions, violent battles and revolutions, exterminating expeditions such as the Crusades or the conquest of Mexico and Peru, mutilations and self-mutilations of religious fanatics as exemplified by various sects of flagellants or the Russian Skopzy, bloody ritual sacrifice or self-sacrifice, the kamikaze phenomenon, various terrifying modes of bloody suicide, or the senseless slaughtering of animals.[39]

Such experiences seem to take us further than ever from reality. Yet the fundamental question remains: do such hallucinations repeat the birth trauma, or does the birth trauma itself repeat some primordial hell? Which has priority, the temporal or the eternal? Which comes first, the corpse or the affect, the profane or the sacred?

This fundamental conflict between modern materialism and traditional religion conceals a more profound agreement: both derive transcendence from a belief in death. If capitalism is built on what precedes it, it perpetuates the fundamental operation of sovereign power which Spinoza had identified as the threat of death. An immanent and affirmative philosophy, knowing little of death, may then resist the dominant power of capitalism.

Ethics of immanence

Deleuze

Following the murder of God, the value of values is called into question: value, like God, is a transcendent term standing apart from life by means of which life may be judged. To question the value of values is to ask what makes them valuable – invoking a regression to the primordial; but a temporal creature has no direct access to the primordial source of values. By raising the question of values as a temporal thinker, the value of values is placed in flux: it is shaped by life, nature and history. It is necessary to evaluate, in so far as one spends time in thinking; but there is no temporal access to an atemporal good as source of values. An immanent critique of values has to think values in terms of how they are evaluated.

Spinoza, Nietzsche, Bergson and Deleuze have pioneered the immanent critique of reasoning in ethics. Their common approach is to locate reasons which function as immanent causes of action, and no longer simply as consequences in the mind. They distinguish between those forces which affect the will from without, giving rise to passive emotions, reactive forces, or habitual obligations, and those forces which are a condition of freedom, and are felt as active joys, will to power, or creative emotion. Where one reacts to the former, one is attracted to the latter. Although the sad passions can be analysed in detail, in all their various workings, the active joys, will to power, or creative emotion are superior to our current mode of reasoning, and so cannot be encapsulated within rational propositions.[40] It is to repeat the paralogism of pure reason to make our evaluations and emotions depend on their objects as modes of representation, as Bergson has pointed out:

> It is through an excess of intellectualism that feeling is made to hinge on an object and that all emotion is held to be the reaction of our sensory faculties to an intellectual representation.[41]

The common essence of force, the source of ethics, is affirmation. Bergson regarded this affirmative essence of morality as mystical yet creative:

> True mystics simply open their souls to the oncoming wave. Sure of themselves, because they feel within them something better than themselves, they prove to be great [wo]men of action ... what they have received affects them like an onslaught of love.[42]

This is not a morality of affirming everything that is simply because it is; instead, only the highest is affirmed as the true source from which all else derives.

Now, to the extent that the immanent cause, the highest, is either not fully understood or does not yet exist, then the ethics of affirmation remain insufficiently determined. There is an excess in affirmation which has not yet been incorporated into thought. The challenge of contemporary ethics is to incarnate that excess of force within reason, so that reason itself becomes a force. Bergson drew an analogy with music, for music is capable of crystallizing emotions:

> Let the music express joy or grief, pity or love, every moment we are what it expresses … . When music weeps, all humanity, all nature, weeps with it. In point of fact it does not introduce these feelings into us; it introduces us into them, as passers-by are forced into a street dance. *Thus do pioneers in morality proceed.*[43]

The challenge facing contemporary ethics is to crystallize within reason ethical emotions which are capable of seizing us and summoning us, introducing us into the ethical *qua* ethical. We can no longer afford to be governed by morality. We must become ethical, sensing ethics as our natural desire and liberty, as well as the environment in which we dwell. Thought itself must become ethical. This is perhaps the most significant ambition of Deleuze's philosophy.

Deleuze reserved his highest admiration for Spinoza's *Ethics*.[44] Spinoza's ethics set out an alternative to a morality that functions as a system of judgement.[45] For moral principles regulate intuitions, intentions, actions and consequences, so subjecting the body to the mind; but there is no guarantee that a mental principle regulating morality will itself be moral. Deleuze found an alternative theory in Spinoza's parallelism: instead of the mind governing the body, there are actions of the mind that are also actions of the body, and vice versa.[46] Among these are actions of the body that fail to secure representation before judicial principles in the court of Reason, for they are coextensive with actions of the mind that affect representations and laws in consciousness – they make a difference to moral judgements. Moralists often attempt to escape these effects by appealing to the moral point of view, a 'view from nowhere': only a disembodied mind or a pure idea of justice can be an impartial judge, unaffected by bodily likes and dislikes. Such an idea judges life from the perspective of one who does not live. This disembodiment is prejudiced: it pronounces an *a priori* verdict of guilty against the body and its affections. From the perspective of the body, it is injustice itself. By contrast, Spinoza's embodied ethics are partial. Deleuze, therefore, attributed to Spinoza the discovery of an unconscious of thought:[47] there is always a thought that acts or thinks, but does not know itself. Consciousness only knows effects, not its own causes: we only have inadequate, confused and mutilated ideas,[48] and so cannot entirely regulate thought and action by means of mental principles. Deleuze devalued consciousness in favour of an ethics of the unconscious, an unconscious ethics. For *immanence means ethos*: that which is immanent, expressed at every moment, is a mode of existence or style of life. Ethics become imperceptible, immanent within the entire plane of Deleuze's thought. It is small wonder that Deleuze's thought is mistaken for being unethical by those who prefer to talk about morality rather than to think ethically.

The objections amount to this: 'You will accept rational, moral, disembodied distinctions, or lose your power of reason in undifferentiated desire. Furthermore, if you attempt the latter, you will not escape the former. You are blocked. Admit it.' Deleuze's response is simple: 'I have nothing to admit. You merely wish to inject into me a little resentment, a little bad conscience.'[49] Such an objection expresses an appetite for vengeance against the force of immanence from a perspective that is separated from it. Deleuze regarded the transcendent differentiations of moral values as well as the undifferentiated outside as a product of the 'realist' way of thinking that belongs to European reason as based on the structure of the Oedipus complex.[50] Deleuze's ethics cannot simply be reduced to implicit moral judgements or an undifferentiated whole of desire because, on the contrary, it is solely concerned with the unconscious determinants of thought and action. Of course, it is always possible to substitute a representation for Deleuze's thought, but this is to separate an effect of reading Deleuze's thought from the act of thinking it. The frequent failure to comprehend Deleuze's philosophy on the part of readers and critics is a result of attempting to *represent* it, reinscribing it within a foreign semiotic regime – saying that really it is this or that, or using alien concepts to describe it, as opposed to *rethinking* it, repeating the act of thought, which will always be repeated differently. For the Deleuzean unconscious differs in principle from that which can be represented: it consists of real activities (creating, speaking, loving, etc.) which representation replaces with abstract relations that pretend to embrace them.[51] A thought of love is not a loving thought; a representation is unable to love.

Deleuze's Spinozism gives its own diagnosis of moral intuitions and values: these are effects within consciousness of unconscious acts. Now, the duration of a representation depends on the act of representing, the effort to make conscious, rather than the act that is represented. Once the inspiration for a feeling of love has withdrawn, the representation of love remains as an after-effect. Precisely because this representation is no longer an expression, memory attempts to recover the past, and the act of representing commends itself as an obligation: 'You must continue to love.' The illusion of values is inseparable from the illusions of consciousness, as given through the symbolic order.[52] Morality is born from the death of love. And if one has a moral obligation to be moral when love is not yet dead, then a little sacrifice of love will work wonders.[53] Death empowers morality. It matters little whether such moral obligations are grounded in universal laws or necessary intuitions, as for Kant, for whom the universal and the necessary were criteria in representation for distinguishing the transcendental[54] – universality and necessity are simply projections of death, inseparable from a linear conception of time that involves death in each passing moment.[55] It matters little whether such moral obligations are local and specific, as for Levinas, for whom a command is given by the face of the Other. Such an obligation derives from the death of the Other and her love.

Deleuzean ethics offer an escape route from this predicament. If Deleuze's thought can be described as a 'reversal of Platonism'[56], then it is a reversal that does not merely invert all oppositions of a moral origin,[57] so as to privilege the body over the mind, but reveals a plane of immanence as the unity of humanity and nature, subject and object, spirit and matter, society and individual,[58] so as to increase 'compassion for reality, for the world, and for time'.[59] Deleuze's thought is mapped on a practical surface that joins matter and meaning, a surface of signs, events and affects, a surface that is produced by each ethos, *habitus* or conduct as an effect of acts that happen, a surface where concepts name the produced connections, disjunctions and conjunctions, a surface where desire, in turn, is a product of relations and assemblages. 'Immanence is the unconscious itself, and the conquest of the unconscious.'[60] Deleuze remained a rationalist philosopher in an otherwise post-modern era, a friend of concepts,[61] because the creation of concepts in an intuition specific to them, making illocalizable relations in thought, involves desire. *Unconscious desire reasons: it performs ethical and political acts.*

Deleuze's plane of immanence replaces the mental space of representation. For the post-modern predicament is an effect of representing primordial social space as empty, as though a space of representation was not sketched out on and constituted by a living body, filled with forces that affect what happens there. Whereas morality operates through representation, substituting an impartial relation between signifier and signified for the relation between a thought and its cause, Deleuzean ethics are partial, correlating acts of thought with acts of the body. This is not a question of reducing thought to electrochemical signals in the brain, for such a move still has the effect of reducing acts of thought to represented opinions corresponding to brain-states.[62] For Deleuze's materialism, a body is a physiological and social institution, a relationship, an intense capacity that is sensed, rather than being seen or touched: it is a site where forces engage with each other.[63] Instead of attempting to isolate thought from economic, social, cultural and psychological determinants, an immanent thought is entirely culturally conditioned: it measures the way in which it is affected. What happened? For ethical theory that is based on a primal scene of an originary, unmediated encounter is as politically naïve as moral theory that is based on a primal scene of a free, rational agent: we are already immersed in fields of subjectivity, where thoughts and passions are shaped by dominant strategies of subjectification; we are immersed in fields of signification, where meanings are regulated by hegemonic discourses; and we are immersed in fields of organization, where segments of bodies and materials are distributed through machinic interactions with segments of discourse.[64] If the three ecologies of subjectivity, society and nature are polluted, then possibilities of ethical encounter are restricted: there is no unscripted or disembodied encounter. In short, all encounters are judged relative to a particular body, but each body is not enclosed by its own skin: a body is merely a skin that enfolds the whole of life, nature and history from its own perspective.[65] Each body is an organ, an eye or liver, contemplating the world and processing the flows of light or toxins that come its way. Each body is a social assemblage.

The ethical problem concerns the *way* in which this world[66] will be enfolded: the constitution of a mode of existence as an ethos or way of expressing the world. Now, instead of reducing thought to a strategic practice merely expressing economic, social and cultural determinations, Deleuze affirms the autonomy of philosophy, endowing thought with its own ethos of resistance. Immanent, philosophical thought is less concerned with the world in which we live than with the way in which this world will be thought and lived. Ethical evaluations, for Deleuze, are not entirely determined by a network of exterior relations operating in an instantaneous present, such as a socio-economic context. There is an unknown of the body, just as profound as the unconscious of thought: we do not know what a body can do.[67] For the body does not only sense: it evaluates – it expresses emotions of love or hatred. Emotions exist over a duration, a difference in time: an increase or diminution in the power of a body must be felt relative to some preceding state.[68] Evaluations are emotions of joy or sadness experienced over a duration, coexisting with but never reducible to an instantaneous present – they cannot be inscribed in networks of power or vectors of force.

> Evaluations, in essence, are not values but ways of being, modes of existence of those who judge and evaluate, serving as principles for the values on the basis of which they judge. This is why we always have the beliefs, feelings and thoughts that we deserve, given our way of being or style of life.[69]

Modes of existence are localized, temporal and relational, implicating that which they contemplate and evaluate within themselves: they express the ethos of a moment, an hour, a season, an epoch – an event or haecceity – but also the ethos of a place, a group, a multiplicity – defined by reciprocal implication. *The micropolitical unconscious of a society is constituted by its shared ethos*, its shared implications, its reciprocal inclusions.

One may then distinguish between two kinds of world: this actual world which affects us, which our bodies contemplate from a particular perspective – made up of a network of relations that only exist in a timeless present, even if it changes; and an intense, virtual world of reciprocal implications, a world that does not exist outside of its expression, a world that belongs to the ethos of a moment or a multiplicity, defining a mode of existence – a world of phantasms that has a duration, and is experienced as past, absent, withdrawn; a world experienced as a *territory* or dwelling, a place of evaluation and desire. These two worlds are incompossible, and the difference between them produces an affect of shame.[70] How will one convert shame into joy? This is the point at which ethical, social and political problems coincide: 'What is to be done?' One turns once more to the temporality of bodies, this time oriented towards the future.

'There are never any criteria other than the tenor of existence, the intensification of life.'[71] A first such criterion, as we have discussed, is a belief in this world as it is, a compassion for the body and for time. Reality, in the form of a body and its affects, is never encountered within representation, as the post-modern paroxysm of idealism has demonstrated. Escaping representation, the first criterion includes another, defining modern thought as such in its reversal of Platonism, the criterion of *novelty*:[72] creation, emergence, heterogeneity – 'thinking otherwise'.[73] For only the new is interesting and remarkable, producing wonder, capable of making a difference and resisting the present[74] – one only encounters and is affected by that which is new. By incorporating that which is new into a mode of existence, one expands one's range of possible affects. Nevertheless, many new products of capitalism are of little interest; the new is only of interest if it is capable of affecting us. A further criterion is implied within novelty:

> Of course it is not only a conquest or extension that matters, but an amplification, an intensification or an elevation of power, a growth in dimensions, and a gain in distinction.[75]

Here, the intensity of joy produced by an affect is a measure of an increase in power. Joy is the ethical test that measures degrees of virtualization or implication. In this respect, the new is not what we are, but what we are in the process of becoming in so far as it differs from what we are.[76]

There is, however, a certain sense in which joy does not answer the ethical problem of the future. Joy responds to a past encounter; it does not give a criterion for predicting encounters that will intensify life. An asymmetry characterizes the flow of time, differentiating the receptivity by which the past is preserved in itself from the spontaneity through which the future is created.[77] Deleuze described the paradoxical condition of spontaneity: one must welcome a heterogeneous future, accepting the full consequences of temporality, by 'affirming all chance'.[78] This marks a cessation of evaluation: one no longer reacts and evaluates simply according to emotions. One is no longer constrained to constitute the body as an organ expressing a particular point of view on the world. This is the occasion when Deleuze tempers Spinozism with a Stoic ethos: philosophy is a preparation for death, an acceptance of fate, so that the philosopher appears to be unaffected by whatever events occur. The temporality of a living, animate thought gives way to a model and experience of death in the unconscious: the thinking animal dies; thought encounters something unthinkable. This asceticism and sobriety is merely an elimination of superfluity,[79] so as to discover the plane of immanence as a power of pure affirmation. The future, or the unknowable difference that constitutes temporality, is not void or arbitrary: it is conditioned by exterior relations. This future is actualized in an encounter with the sensible, producing an effect of *deterritorialization* on one's implied territory. 'Thinking takes place in the relationship of territory and the earth.'[80] An appeal to temporality, discovering time as pure difference or disjunction, discovers within time a site of ethical differences,[81] a utopian social space in which bodies will communicate, the creation of new possible worlds.

Futurity and temporality, therefore, are essentially relational, social, utopian – a way of synthesizing modes of existence. Repetition gives us a further criterion of immanence: 'we are never judged except by ourselves and according to our states,'[82] that is, according to our ethos. This dictum resonates with that of a more notorious immoralist: 'Judge not, that you be not judged. For with the judgment you pronounce you will be judged, and the measure you give will be the measure you get.' It appeals to an alien figure of justice or equalization: an exchange between the actual and the virtual world, so that they express each other. This ethical criterion is an ethos or conduct of time which is also a *socius* or conduct of relations. One conducts oneself temporally and immanently within the asymmetry of time by applying the test of the eternal return: by the folding of a receptive affect into a spontaneous ethos, so that friendship is judged from the point of view of its friendliness, its own power to affirm itself and reproduce itself.[83] Whereas morality enacts injustice, giving steals obligation, and re-presentation brings absence, friendship may still be friendly. There is a redoubling of the receptive in the spontaneous, a repetition of an intensive difference, where friendship creates, posits and affirms itself. This is the properly Deleuzean sense of desire. Instead of time being judged in relation to the death of its contents, Deleuze conceived of time purely in terms of life: 'This is the powerful, non-organic Life which grips the world.'[84]

These criteria of immanence enable mutually affirmative encounters. Positive encounters have a property that is not shared with destructive ones: 'When an external state involves an increase in our power of acting, it is joined by another state that depends on this very power.'[85] When an encounter increases a power of acting, that power of acting or ethos is a new existent in the world, a spontaneous creation that coexists with its prior conditions. It is a local utopia, a self-creating society, a bond between people. This autopositing dynamism is always untimely, rather than present or historical – it is eternal (in the sense that its mode of existence is eternal recurrence), even if it only lasts as long as the material support that it synthesizes,[86] and the friendship it installs between people quickly gives way to division and betrayal.[87] An 'aesthetics of existence' should be understood precisely at this non-organic but social level: the creation of new bonds between people. In Spinozist terms,

> This eternal and singular essence is the intense part of ourselves that expresses itself relationally as an eternal truth; and existence is the set of extensive parts that belong to us under this durative relation.[88]

Its beauty is inseparable from the distinctive affect that it expresses: *active joy* is the supreme ethical test.[89] It is the antidote to all poisons: 'Perhaps one day we will know that there wasn't any art [or ethics] but only medicine.'[90] Even though such friendship is temporary, ending in the joy of flight, it manifests the eternal within time:

> The good or strong individual is the one who exists so fully or so intensely that he has gained eternity in his lifetime, so that death, always extensive, always external, is of little significance to him.[91]

Ethics of potency

The situation of the flesh

Let's hold the celebration right there: there is something at once pernicious and glorious in Spinoza's ethics of affirmation. Although each encounter produces both a composition and a decomposition of relations, sadness and joy, from the perspective of God, the whole of nature, there are only compositions of relations. This affirmation that does not know death, whereby death only comes from without, means that God is affected by our joyful modifications but not by our pains; God invests his substance in his modifications, so as to extract a surplus value of joy. It is not even the same kind of joy, for God causes this joy from his own essence. God, like capital, is immune to our pains of labour.

Spinoza reproduces Bergson's 'closed society' founded on exclusion, for the good is identified as 'whatever is conducive to the common society of men, or, whatever brings it about that men live together in agreement.'[92] When all men live under the guidance of reason, that is, according to common notions that express the essence of each of them, they do not harm each other, for what they do agrees with the nature of each.[93] This universal human nature can only prosper by sacrificing other natures, just as one decomposes the food one eats.[94] Here affirmation is incomplete, sacrificing other natures in order to protect itself: Spinoza's ethics are constructed on the assumption of an infinite plenitude of extension. The same is certainly not true for Deleuze, who replaces closed relations based on common notions with open relations of desire. The cost, however, is an inability to explain the occurrence and occasion of relations of desire. Desire may then be enabled by an ethos or spirituality of encounter that removes repressive obstacles to desire, but it does not become a political force which can transform the world.

For immanence generates its own contradictions. The most obvious of these is the elevation of a plane of immanence as a transcendent ideal of thought; a plane of immanence will always fail.[95] The presupposition of a plane of immanence as an image of thought and matter of being is an attempt to remove all transcendent perspectives from which life can be judged. For transcendent perspectives are formed in practice by elevating particular contents of thought and attributing to them a universal role, or elevating particular conceptual distinctions and making them fundamental. As such, immanence is the completion of critical theory. Yet, to the extent that the concept of 'immanence' is defined in opposition to transcendence, as that which 'does not hand itself over to the transcendent or restore any transcendent,'[96] and life is defined as resistance to death, then immanence and life are understood in opposition to a simulation. Immanence, the refusal of all borders, has as much reality as the borders that it resists. Then the plane of immanence remains a simulacrum, with all the powers to insinuate itself into every aspect of life that a simulacrum affords. The plane of immanence, as an absolutization of simulation, is the death of thought, the unthinkable within thought that thought is forced to think. It plays the role of the immobile motor, the model and experience of death in the unconscious that produces life and forces thought to take place. Its power, however, derives from its dissimulation: the plane is merely a product, an absolutization of the game of difference and repetition – it can never be attained, and remains unthinkable, because it simply does not exist.[97] The drive to attain it derives from the fact that it is unattainable. The full experience of death in philosophy is encountered when the plane itself is revealed as a simulacrum. This is a new conversion of philosophy:

> It is at this mobile and precise point, where all events gather together in one that transmutation happens: this is the point at which death turns against death; where dying is the negation of death, and the impersonality of dying no longer indicates the moment when I disappear outside of myself, but rather the moment when death loses itself in itself, and also the figure which the most singular life takes on in order to substitute itself for me.[98]

Such deliberate simulation is an attempt to constitute reality[99] through the pathos of humour: 'In truth, there are never any contradictions, apparent or real, but only degrees of humour.'[100] For the aim of Deleuze's work is not to subject reality to thought, but to produce reality through thinking. The reality produced is a mode of existence, an episode, a life, a mode of expression, an ethos or a style that cannot be encompassed within thought; it thinks. This contradiction between mode of expression and content, expressing itself as humour or as a contrary pathos, operates by dismantling the content it has produced. The very failures of thought constitute its own vitality, its own renewed wonder:

> And, actually functioning, it functions through and because of its own dismantling. It is born from this dismantling.[101]

The illusions of transcendence always threaten to re-emerge from contradictions locatable in the way in which thought is expressed. If all is simulated, however, then so are the contradictions; all that counts is the ethos of thinking expressed in the contradictions.

Deleuze remained caught in Spinozism, however, to the extent that he defined the plane of immanence as at once a presupposition about the nature of thought and the material of being. If, however, one transforms the meaning of philosophy so that it is no longer modelled primarily on the true – the unity of thought and nature, or the infinite movement between thought and being[102] – but conceived in ethical and temporal categories as an attempt to generate an ethos of thought that expresses an intensification of life, then the unity of thought and being is replaced by an aspiration for the unity of a living thought and the unthought which gives life to it. Freedom from illusion is no longer decisive; it is the value for life that counts. Here, the plane of concepts itself forms a barrier to thought, and thought requires a dimension beyond concepts in order to grasp the plane of immanence itself: *'philosophy needs a nonphilosophy that comprehends it.'*[103] One of the few attempts to describe this non-philosophical element was made by Deleuze in the final essay published in his lifetime:

> It will be said that pure immanence is A LIFE, and nothing else. It is not immanence to life, for the immanent which is in nothing is itself a life. A life is the immanence of immanence, absolute immanence: it is sheer power (puissance), utter beatitude.[104]

The accent, here, is placed on the indefinite article, in order to distinguish life from the individual who lives it. Deleuze cited an incident from *Our Mutual Friend* by Charles Dickens when there is an attempt to resuscitate the hated Rogue Riderhood, who is on the verge of death by drowning:

> All the best means are at once in action, and everybody present lends a hand, and a heart and soul. No one has the least regard for the man: with them all, he has been an object of avoidance, suspicion, and aversion; but the spark of life within him is curiously separable from himself now, and they have a deep interest in it, probably because it is life, and they are living and must die … .

See! A token of life! An indubitable token of life! The spark may smoulder and go out, or it may glow and expand, but see! The four rough fellows seeing, shed tears. Neither Riderhood in this world, nor Riderhood in the other, could draw tears from them; but a striving human soul between the two can do it easily.[105]

What, then, is the potency of thought? A life, a singular life, a life that dies in the event, a fragile life that does not live in time and cannot be evaluated in terms of money – a life that necessarily dies in its incarnations. The life of a persona – a rogue like Riderhood; the persona who comes to life. Throughout the history of philosophy, philosophers have elevated bizarre idols to obscure this transcendental field: concepts of God that lack divinity, concepts of the subject that lack selfhood, concepts of world, society, culture, communication that lack reality, concepts of desire that lack *jouissance*; the situation is hardly improved when one throws out the transcendent, allowing capital and time to become impersonal grounds of evaluation and thought. Life is controlled by that which does not live. All manner of tyrants and idols have been worshipped as supreme values, as dogmatic images of thought, or as transcendentals – philosophy is superstitious, all too superstitious.

All it requires is for thought to consider a transcendental persona, to show a little care for a dying rogue, to try resuscitation once more, to breathe a little life into 'this dank carcase,' 'this flabby lump of mortality', for thought to lend 'a hand, a heart, and a soul'. For, in modern life, this dying rogue is no one but ourselves, and the transcendental persona of thought is our doctor. Life is immanence, 'the most intimate within thought', yet it is also transcendence, 'an outside more distant than any external world because it is an inside deeper than any internal world.' So often the concepts of immanence and transcendence are opposed to each other, as if one could be thought without the other. Nevertheless, the criteria for absolute immanence and absolute transcendence are the same: they consist in removing all pretenders from the role of the absolute. Transcendence only has a relation to this world in immanence; immanence only constitutes this world in transcendence.

Once more, then, we are led to the problem of the reality and significance of death. Death is no longer external, coming from without; it is a potency or trauma which is perpetually present. Sigmund Freud, in *The Interpretation of Dreams*, recounted the dream of a man whose child had died, and whose corpse was lying in the next room in the care of an older man, while the father slept. In his dream, his dead child spoke to him, 'Father, can't you see I'm burning?' He awoke to find that an overturned candle had set light to the bed on which his child's body lay. Conventionally, one attributes reality to the material situation of the dead child and the burning bed. Jacques Lacan, however, used this example of a dream to point to the psychical reality of the dead child's message:

Is there not more reality in this message than in the noise by which the father also identifies the strange reality of what is happening in the room next door? Is not the missed reality that caused the death of the child expressed in these words? ... *Father, can't you see I'm burning?* This sentence is itself a firebrand – of itself it brings fire where it falls – and one cannot see what is burning, for the flames blind us to the fact that the fire bears on ... the real.[106]

For Lacan, the psychic, affective reality of the death of the child is its trauma, its significance.[107] This reality, however, is never encountered, and can only express itself in repetition in psychic life where it is forever concealed. The affective reality of trauma escapes symbolization and mastery. It can only be encountered, but it is encountered as *souffrance* – both as suffering, and 'in abeyance'.[108] The reality of trauma can drama- tize itself in dreams, where it is always repeated as absent, in chance encounters with a material reality which corresponds to it, such as the child's corpse burning which repeats the event of the child's death, and in transference. No one can know the reality of trauma, the reality of the real in itself: it is unconscious. Hence, according to Lacan, the true formula of atheism is not 'God is dead' but 'God is unconscious'.[109] The real event of death is encountered as trauma. Always absent from the symbolic order and simulation, always displaced in time, the real drama- tizes itself in material reality: 'man thinks with his object'.[110] Ultimately, however, Lacan identifies the real, the absolute Other of the subject, in a manner resembling Levinas and Derrida as the source of the ethics of psychoanalysis:

> my thesis is that the moral law, the moral command, the presence of the moral agency in our activity, insofar as it is structured by the symbolic, is that through which the real is actualized – the real as such, the weight of the real.[111]

Trauma constitutes what we are: there is no possibility of evasion of the command, neither is it merely contingent. Death simply matters. Nevertheless, the potency of trauma is 'repressed' or rendered unthinkable by the ethos of thought that constitutes our 'real world' by symbolization. Matter is that which is mastered, measured, or exchanged, rather than that which lives. Consensual reality is constructed from a neurotic evasion or flight from trauma, constructing self-positing island domains, allied with the self-positing power of exterior forces, which give a limited shelter from the perpetual storm. Freedom is not the capacity to choose whether or not death matters; freedom is merely a capacity to distance oneself from identi- fication with one's island shelter. Freedom is the ability to ride the potency of immanent powers.

The schizophrenic Antonin Artaud was one of the few who has been able to abandon the neurotic flight, so as to think beyond death:

> Who, in the heart of certain anxieties at the bottom of some dreams, has not known death as a shattering and miraculous sensation with which nothing in the order of mental experience could ever be confused? ... You are going to die ... just at that very moment some humidity, a moistness from iron or rock or wind, refreshes you unbelievably and consoles your thought, and you yourself liquefy as you flow to your death, to your new state of death. This running water is death; and from the moment you contemplate yourself serenely and record your new sensations, the great identification begins. You died, and yet here you are again, living – EXCEPT THIS TIME YOU ARE ALONE.[112]

Death, here, is a process within the mind – typical delusions encountered within schizophrenia are that the self or the world have been destroyed. Of less significance than death, therefore, is the cessation of processes of a mental order in order to allow a different level of awareness to be manifested, a level which was already present: 'Childhood knows sudden awakenings of the mind, intense prolongations of thought which ... were impregnated with perfect knowledge, impregnated all things, were crystallized, eternal.'[113] Deleuze cites the example of very small children, who have hardly any individuality, but a series of singularities – a smile, a gesture, a grimace – as being traversed by an immanent life that is 'pure power (*puissance*) and even beatitude through the suffering and weakness.'[114] Such a life, however, remains unconscious and unthinkable for Deleuze – for the schizophrenic and the child remain purely conceptual personae, without being actualized in a life.[115] But, in Artaud's work, awareness of such a life becomes possible:

> My reason will certainly one day have to receive these unformulated forces exteriorly shaped like a cry which are besieging me, and they may then supplant higher thought. There are intellectual cries, cries which stem from the marrow's delicacy. This is what I personally call the Flesh. I do not separate my thought from my life. With each of my tongue's vibrations I retrace all the paths of my thought through my flesh ... . In the course of this research buried in the limbo of my consciousness, I thought I felt explosions, like the shock of magic stones or the sudden petrifaction of fires. Fires like imperceptible truths, miraculously vitalised ... . It is this indescribable knowledge which explodes in gradual thrusts.... But I must look into this aspect of the flesh which is supposed to give me a metaphysics of Being and a positive understanding of Life.[116]

Conclusion

Does death merit our attention? This is, in Bergsonian terms, a false problem. For it posits death within a space of representation over which one has freedom of choice. Death, far from being external to attention, is internal to attention as such. Modern consensual reality knows nothing of this. For in modernity, attention is captured by production, distribution and consumption: that which demands attention is that which saves time, which wards off death, which makes a profit, which is useful, which produces pleasure. Such attention, such a 'pleasure principle', is driven by flight from the trauma that faces us all.

Trauma disrupts consensual reality. Those who have experienced trauma are often more sensitive to the trauma of others. For trauma exposes the lie that life is good, that everything is as it should be. Instead, events of the past attract interest and attention, or determine behaviour, that have no possible use or pleasure. Trauma disrupts the pleasure principle, and the consensual reality founded on it, by drawing attention to elements that do not fit. The past comes to dominate the present. This supposed 'death instinct' which so puzzled Freud expresses a potency within attention. For attention is attracted by that which does not fit, by that which provokes awe or wonder. Then attention may sacrifice its liberty, its pleasures, its present, for the sake of the interest of the past. Moreover, the interest of the past may form the basis of expectations of the future. True freedom is the ability to refuse consensual reality, conditioned by external interests, and attend to the significance of the past and the future. It is a synthesis of time.

If the present god is to be murdered once more – and nothing is more urgent – then this will only be possible when there is a new god, a new source of meaning which organizes our existence. The coming god is even older than Mammon: it is Death. Death, although perpetually present, will soon be in evidence all around us, threatening all of us, advancing from every side. Where capital gains its power from warding off death, its fundamental contradiction is to bring the death which it attempts to displace. The whole of humanity is now faced with the problem of subsistence. Death is the ultimate internal limit of capitalism. Consensual capitalist reality, the capitalist religion, will be shattered by appreciation of the magnitude of the crisis which affects us all. Death itself will murder the god of capital, who will die of lack of hope – the sooner the better, if a remnant is to be saved.

Notes

1 Given this context, complaints against the environmental discourse of limits and the need for survival which arise from religious, Marxist, multiculturalist and feminist sources simply refuse to engage with reality. See John S. Dryzek, *The Politics of the Earth: Environmental Discourses*, Oxford: Oxford University Press, 1997, p. 42.

2 See, for example, James P. Carse, *Death and Existence*, New York: Wiley, 1980, p. 9.
3 Jacques Derrida, *The Gift of Death*, Chicago: University of Chicago Press, 1995, p. 41.
4 In regard to the death of others, Heidegger writes: 'The dying of Others is not something we experience in a genuine sense.' *Being and Time*, Oxford: Blackwell, 1962, p. 282. In regard to the death of the self, see Maurice Blanchot, *L'Espace littéraire*, Paris: Gallimard, 1955, pp. 103–209.
5 Derrida, *Aporias*, Stanford: Stanford University Press, 1993, p. 22.
6 Martin Heidegger, *On Time and Being*, New York: Harper Colophon, 1977, p. 3.
7 Simmel, as cited by Graham Parkes, 'Death and Detachment', in Jeff Malpas and Robert C. Solomon (eds), *Death and Philosophy*, London: Routledge, 1998, p. 90.
8 Levinas noted how in Bergsonism the qualitative is a way of being, a how rather than a what, and in this respect Bergson anticipates Heidegger's *Being and Time*, Oxford: Blackwell, 1962. See Emmanuel Levinas, *Time and the Other*, Pittsburgh: Duquesne University Press, 1987, 130n.
9 See Heidegger, *On Time and Being*, p. 11; *Being and Time*, *passim*.
10 Heidegger, *On Time and Being*, pp. 14–15: 'futural approaching brings about what has been, what has been brings about futural approaching, and the reciprocal relation of both brings about the opening up of openness.'
11 Heidegger, *On Time and Being*, p. 16.
12 See Henri Bergson, *Time and Free Will*, London: Swan Sonnenschein, 1910, pp. 96–101.
13 Heidegger, *Being and Time*, pp. 279–311.
14 Levinas, 'Time and the Other', in Sean Hand (ed.), *The Levinas Reader*, Oxford: Blackwell, 1989, pp. 37–58.
15 Levinas, *Ethics and Infinity*, Pittsburgh: Duquesne University Press, 1985, p. 89.
16 Levinas, *ibid.*, pp. 89–90.
17 Derrida has gone the furthest in showing how death is the 'possibility of an impossibility', an aporia, an impossibility which cannot appear as such. Moreover, he has shown how any history or anthropology of death depends on metaphysical presuppositions about the nature of death, whereas an existential analysis of death depends on a theological anthropology. Derrida, *Aporias*, p. 80.
18 See Derrida, *The Gift of Death*.
19 Derrida, *Aporias*, 76.
20 Derrida, *ibid.*, pp. 73–4.
21 For a critique of the role of death in philosophy of religion, see Grace M. Jantzen, *Becoming Diving: towards a Feminist Philosophy of Religion*, Manchester: Manchester University Press, 1998, pp. 129–41.
22 Sigmund Freud, 'Totem and Taboo', in *The Origins of Religion*, Harmondsworth: Penguin, 1990, pp. 116–17.
23 A theology student cited by Stanislav Grof and Joan Halifax, via Albert Heim, in *The Human Encounter with Death*, London: Souvenir, 1978, p. 135.
24 Tem Horwitz, 'My Death', in Jeff Malpas and Robert C. Solomon (eds), *Death and Philosophy*, p. 9.
25 Horwitz, 'My Death', pp. 10–11.
26 See Heim's own personal report, recounted in Grof and Halifax, *The Human Encounter with Death*, p. 133.
27 The diversity of phenomena associated under the heading 'sacrifice' may raise doubts as to the existence of a unitary religious phenomenon at all. J. C. Heesterman defends the concept of sacrifice as a unitary phenomenon that has

developed from rites and customs of exorcism, divination, expiation, healing and scapegoating, but which has subsequently spread worldwide as a complex of three elements: killing – even of vegetables; destruction; and food distribution. J. C. Heesterman, *The Broken World of Sacrifice*, Chicago: University of Chicago Press, 1993, pp. 7–9. From our philosophical perspective, we are less concerned with whether a variety of phenomena, carried out for a variety of reasons, can be comprehended under a single heading of 'sacrifice', than to analyse what is involved in depth in the complex of killing, destruction and distribution.

28 See, for example, Henri Hubert and Marcel Mauss, *Sacrifice: its Nature and Functions*, Chicago: University of Chicago, 1981, p. 97.

29 See Wendy O'Flaherty, *Tales of Sex and Violence*, Delhi: Motilal Banarsidass, 1987, p. 20.

30 'In the beginning, Prajapati [the Lord of creation] was both mortal and immortal; his breaths were immortal, his body mortal. By the sacrifice properly performed, the sacrificer makes his body undecaying and immortal.' *Satapatha Brahmana* 10.1.4.1, cited in John Bowker, *The Meanings of Death*, Cambridge: Cambridge University Press, 1991, p. 155.

31 Hubert and Mauss, *Sacrifice*, p. 98.

32 Hubert and Mauss, *ibid.*, pp. 25–8. This element is not always present in religious sacrifice. Its absence, however, might indicate less the inadequacy of Hubert and Mauss' theory, than that a fundamentally different phenomenon is present. The term 'sacrifice' is broad enough to include a variety of different phenomena.

33 Hubert and Mauss, *ibid.*, pp. 35–43.

34 See Jean-Pierre Vernant, 'At Man's Table: Hesiod's Foundation Myth of Sacrifice', in Marcel Detienne and Jean-Pierre Vernant (eds), *The Cuisine of Sacrifice among the Greeks*, Chicago: University of Chicago Press, 1989.

35 For example, Lara Jefferson and William Leonard, in Bert Kaplan (ed.), *The Inner World of Mental Illness*, New York: Harper & Row, 1964, pp. 6, 312.

36 Grof and Halifax, *The Human Encounter with Death*, p. 9.

37 Grof and Halifax, *ibid.*, p. 125.

38 Grof and Halifax, *ibid.*, p. 51.

39 Grof, *Realms of the Human Unconscious*, London: Souvenir, 1979, 128; Skopzy was a religious sect whose members mutilated themselves by castration.

40 This is why Nietzsche's doctrine of the 'will to power' is often misunderstood; it only appears as a desire for the feeling of increase in power to a reactive consciousness, but it is not knowable in itself within consciousness. See Deleuze, *Nietzsche and Philosophy*, London: Athlone, 1983, pp. 172–3.

41 Bergson, *The Two Sources of Morality and Religion*, p. 40. The mystics named by Bergson are St Paul, St Teresa, St Catherine of Sienna, St Francis and Joan of Arc (p. 228).

42 Bergson, *ibid.*, p. 81.

43 Bergson, *ibid.*, p. 28; emphasis added.

44 Gilles Deleuze and Félix Guattari, *What is Philosophy?*, London: Verso, 1994, pp. 59–60.

45 Deleuze, *Spinoza: Practical Philosophy*, San Francisco: City Lights, 1988, p. 23.

46 Deleuze, *Spinoza: Practical Philosophy*, p. 18.

47 Deleuze, *ibid.*, p. 19.

48 Deleuze, *ibid.*

49 See Deleuze, *Negotiations*, New York: Columbia University Press, 1990, p. 3.

50 See Deleuze and Guattari, *Anti-Oedipus*, London: Athlone, 1984, pp. 78–9: 'the exclusive relation introduced by Oedipus comes into play not only between the various disjunctions conceived as differentiations, *but between the whole of the differentiations that it imposes and an undifferentiated that it presup-*

172   *The problem of ethics*

poses... .Oedipus creates both *the differentiations that it orders and the undifferentiated with which it threatens us.*'
51 Deleuze, *Nietzsche and Philosophy*, London: Athlone, 1983, p. 74.
52 Deleuze, *Spinoza: Practical Philosophy*, p. 23.
53 John Milbank, 'Can Morality be Christian?', *Studies in Christian Ethics*, 8(1), 1995, pp. 48–50.
54 Immanuel Kant, *Critique of Pure Reason*, Basingstoke: Macmillan, 1933, pp. 43–4.
55 Kant, *Critique of Pure Reason*, pp. 10, 77, 167–9, 183–4.
56 Deleuze, *The Logic of Sense*, London: Athlone, 1991, p. 253; Michel Foucault, 'Theatrum Philosophicum,' in *Language, Counter-Memory, Practice*, Ithaca: Cornell University Press, 1977, pp. 167–8.
57 Deleuze, *Nietzsche and Philosophy*, p. 96.
58 Deleuze, *Cinema 2: The Time-Image*, London: Athlone, 1989, p. 96.
59 Foucault, 'Theatrum Philosophicum', p. 168.
60 Deleuze, *Spinoza: Practical Philosophy*, p. 29.
61 Deleuze and Guattari, *What is Philosophy?*, p. 5.
62 Deleuze and Guattari, *ibid.*, p. 209.
63 Deleuze, *Nietzsche and Philosophy*, p. 40.
64 Deleuze and Guattari, *A Thousand Plateaus*, London: Athlone, 1988, p. 159.
65 Deleuze, *The Fold: Leibniz and the Baroque*, London: Athlone, 1993, p. 89.
66 Deleuze, *Cinema 2*, pp. 171–3.
67 Deleuze, *Spinoza: Practical Philosophy*, p. 19.
68 Deleuze, *ibid.*, p. 39.
69 Deleuze, *Nietzsche and Philosophy*, p. 1.
70 Deleuze and Guattari, *What is Philosophy?*, p. 107.
71 Deleuze and Guattari affirm Kierkegaard's knight of faith in this context: see *What is Philosophy?*, p. 74.
72 Deleuze, *Cinema 2*, pp. 146–7.
73 Deleuze and Guattari, *What is Philosophy?*, p. 51, 112.
74 Deleuze and Guattari, *ibid.*, pp. 108–10.
75 Deleuze, *The Fold*, p. 73.
76 Deleuze and Guattari, *What is Philosophy?*, p. 112.
77 Deleuze, *Foucault*, Minneapolis: University of Minnesota Press, 1988, p. 107.
78 Deleuze, *Difference and Repetition*, London: Athlone, 1994, p. 194.
79 Deleuze and Guattari, *A Thousand Plateaus*, p. 279.
80 Deleuze and Guattari, *What is Philosophy?*, p. 85.
81 François Zourabichvili, *Deleuze: une philosophie de l'événement*, Paris: Presses Universitaires de France, 1996, pp. 106–15.
82 Deleuze, *Spinoza: Practical Philosophy*, p. 40.
83 Deleuze, *Nietzsche and Philosophy*, pp. 68–72.
84 Deleuze, *Cinema 2*, p. 76.
85 Deleuze, *Spinoza: Practical Philosophy*, p. 40.
86 Deleuze and Guattari, *What is Philosophy?*, p. 166.
87 Deleuze and Guattari, *ibid.*, p. 177.
88 Deleuze, *Spinoza: Practical Philosophy*, p. 40.
89 Deleuze, *ibid.*, p. 29.
90 Jean-Marie Le Cléziot, in Deleuze and Guattari, *What is Philosophy?*, p. 173; my interpolation.
91 Deleuze, *Spinoza: Practical Philosophy*, p. 41.
92 Spinoza, *Ethics* Book IV, Prop. LX, London: J. M. Dent, 1989, p. 170. Here it seems to me that attempts to appeal to Spinoza for an affirmation of difference are too optimistic. See, for example, Moira Gatens and Genevieve Lloyd, *Collective Imaginings: Spinoza Past and Present*, London: Routledge, 1999.

93 Spinoza, *Ethics*, Book IV, Prop. XXXV, proof, 163–4.
94 Thus Spinoza will argue that Orestes' matricide can be differentiated from Nero's matricide as good from bad because of the idea associated with it, loyalty to or agreement with the murdered Agamemnon. Spinoza, 'Letter 23 to Blyenberg' in A. Wolf (ed.), *The Correspondence of Spinoza*, London: George Allen & Unwin, 1928, p. 190.
95 Deleuze and Guattari, *A Thousand Plateaus*, p. 269.
96 Deleuze and Guattari, *What is Philosophy?*, p. 60.
97 Deleuze and Guattari's piety in relation to the plane is revealed by their attitude to Spinoza. *What is Philosophy?*, p. 59.
98 Deleuze, *The Logic of Sense*, p. 153.
99 See Deleuze and Guattari, *Anti-Oedipus*, p. 87
100 Deleuze and Guattari, *ibid.*, p. 68.
101 Deleuze and Guattari, *Kafka: Towards a Minor Literature*, Minneapolis: University of Minnesota Press, 1986, p. 48.
102 Deleuze and Guattari, *What is Philosophy?*, p. 38.
103 Deleuze and Guattari, *ibid.*, 218.
104 Deleuze, 'Immanence: a life … ', *Theory, Culture and Society*, **14**(2), May 1997, p. 4.
105 Charles Dickens, *Our Mutual Friend*, London: Oxford University Press, 1953, pp. 443–4.
106 Jacques Lacan, *The Four Fundamental Concepts of Psychoanalysis*, London: Penguin, 1979, pp. 58–9.
107 For an extended discussion of the analysis of this dream, see Cathy Caruth, 'Traumatic Awakenings', in Hent de Vries and Samuel Weber (eds), *Violence, Identity and Self-Determination*, Stanford: Stanford University Press, 1997.
108 Lacan, *The Four Fundamental Concepts of Psychoanalysis*, p. 56.
109 Lacan, *ibid.*, p. 59.
110 Lacan, *ibid.*, p. 62.
111 Lacan, *The Ethics of Psychoanalysis 1959–1960: The Seminar of Jacques Lacan Book VII*, London: Routledge, 1991, p. 20.
112 Artaud, *Anthology*, San Francisco: City Lights, 1965, p. 49.
113 Artaud, *ibid.*, p. 50.
114 Deleuze, 'Immanence: a life …', p. 6.
115 For the schizophrenic as a conceptual persona manifesting the pathic features of thought alone, see Deleuze and Guattari, *What is Philosophy?*, p. 70
116 Artaud, 'The Situation of the Flesh', *Collected Works Vol. I*, London: Calder and Boyars, 1968, pp. 165–6.

Part III

The problem of piety

7   Piety

Given that reason is invested with an ethos and piety, what knid of piety is able to bring an ethical potency to reason?

Religion and violence

The rapid expansion of the global economy towards its ecological limits will produce an increasing scarcity of the means of subsistence. Shortages of clean water, fertile land, fish stocks, forests, oil, shelter from storm, flood, and fire, and sustainable ecosystems, will increase pressure at all levels of society, exacerbating mass migration, illegal immigration, social conflict and war. The result may resemble Hobbes' account of the 'state of nature', where conflict arises from competition and fear: anticipation of aggression from others produces pre-emptive aggression in an attempt to attain security. In such a condition, just as there is a scarcity of resources, there is also a scarcity of 'glory' – reputation of power being power – leading to competition for honour as a source of conflict.[1] Then anticipation of an apocalyptic future may be transformed into present violence, becoming a self-fulfilling prophecy. The fundamental determinant here is an orientation towards the future – a piety, a faith. Just as in the religion of capital where faith, manifested as expectation of a return on investment, determines the present, so it is in the religion of death where fear of the future, manifested as anxiety, may shape our conditions of existence.

The extent of the production of scarcity will demonstrate that the global market, together with the legal form of the modern nation state that supports it, have at least as damaging consequences, and no greater moral legitimacy, than the institutions of slavery and colonial domination which preceded them and made them possible. The price of our piety before these institutions is global devastation. The price of suspicion and critique is similarly threatening. For the modern nation state was created, to a significant extent, in reaction to religious conflict, inspired by the philosophers of early modernity and the Enlightenment who preached toleration as freedom of thought and religion. Following the tradition of Hobbes, the state was formed to provide security against conflict, whether caused by competition for material resources or religious prerogatives.[2] Although internal conflict was displaced into a conflict between nations and into imperial conquest, the nation state has had a modest degree of success in this role. More successful is the recent development of a global market, joining competing interests into cooperation for the sake of trade. Such success may break down when subsistence becomes a universal problem. Once the legitimacy of law, contract and power breaks down, there is no longer a moral constraint against conflict.

Strangely, the blatant injustice of the market and the poverty bred in overpopulated cities have not often led to violent revolution. If investors can find a better deal elsewhere, then resistance is futile. Poverty breeds despair, isolation and powerlessness. The multitude has little power of collective action and institutional self-organization, except in so far as it unites loosely around ideals of freedom against government – a move which, as illustrated in both 1968 and 1989, usually results in increasing fragmentation, making the population more fertile for market relations as the only means of uniting heterogeneity without reducing nominal liberty.[3] By contrast, scarcity may give rise to conflict when it is mediated by collective identity, when a group can fight for its collective interests. Similarly, conflict itself gives rise to the identification of an enemy, and the reactive creation of identities that will increase the conflict. Here, religious discourse and practice are among the most effective means of mobilization, as well as the most effective base for a sense of collective identity.[4] For religious discourses claim a legitimacy which is absolute, superior to that of any nation or law, as well as superior to passions and material interests. Already the signs are present that the vacuum of meaning left by the murder of capital as god may be filled by resurgent religion.

Mark Juergensmeyer, in a study based on interviews with six religious terrorist groups, has set out the preconditions for religious terrorism: the religious community is broadly in support of the aims desired by the terrorists; there is a moral presumption of the superiority of the cause over civil duties; the cause is accompanied by internal conviction as well as social acknowledgement, often being granted a stamp of approval from a legitimizing authority; and there is the belief that the world is already an inherently violent place. Moreover, given the prevalence of martial symbolism and imagery in religious traditions, the struggle can be understood as a cosmic war of good against evil when resistance is perceived as a defence of basic identity and dignity, when losing the struggle would be unthinkable, and when the struggle is blocked and cannot be won in real time and in real terms. Finally, such a cosmic war may be manifested as actual violence when the cosmic struggle is understood to be occurring in this world rather than in a mythical setting, when believers identify personally with the struggle, and when the struggle is at a point of crisis in which individual action can make all the difference.[5]

In a possible world where the ecological threat makes the illegitimacy of the current world order transparent, and religion provides the alternative source of meaning and legitimation, all these conditions become fulfilled – not merely for a few extremist groups, but globally. The prospects in the new century for unprecedented levels of violence – fuelled by drought and mass migration – are chilling. There is, of course, no simple and automatic relation between religion and violence; religion has often been the most powerful source for peace and social progress. Nevertheless, when religion posits an absolute of greater importance than human life itself, it ruptures an ethical bond that it may not succeed in reinstating. A critical theory of religion, separating religion from the violence it spawns, has an essential contribution to make in preserving the future of humanity.

Yet when our most urgent concern is survival, what time and money remains for a consideration of religion? Survival demands that we be rational and economical. Religion, like nature is lavish. The amount of time, energy and resources that humanity dedicates to religious activities such as offerings, prayer, meditation, worship and renunciation is inestimable. In each case, the product of human labour is withdrawn from circulation; all religion is sacrifice. Similarly, the amount of intellectual activity squandered in the repetition of dull and questionable beliefs, self-justifications, and clichés is also immense; it wastes the application of attention to the real conditions of existence.

Religion is excessive, not economic: attending to that which cannot be determined in terms of space, time, energy and information, it invokes excess. Moreover, religion as a phenomenon is excessive: in its pervasiveness, variety, complexity and irreducibility of forms, religion exceeds rational description and definition. Furthermore, religion is irrational in the ways in which it deploys and 'wastes' its excess. Few accounts of religion have investigated religion in its own proper element of excess. Alfred North Whitehead's philosophy of religion, for all its shortcomings, did approach what is essential here:

> Ritual is the primitive outcome of superfluous energy and leisure. It exemplifies the tendency of living bodies to repeat their own actions ... . Ritual may be defined as the habitual performance of definite actions which have no direct relevance to the preservation of the physical organisms of the actors.[6]

There is no necessity for religion. Religion is supererogatory; it is a pure gift. The only explanation for the variety of religion is that there is no sufficient reason.

Theories and descriptions of religion have been unable to grasp religion in its excess. For to the extent that religion can be explained, that reasons can be given for its occurrence, or to the extent that it can be described, that other concepts may be substituted for its own, it is brought back into the sphere of economy. Religion is then regarded from the perspective of its function, its utility, or else its dysfunction, as a necessary illusion. There is an obvious danger of distortion in the study of religion: to the extent that religion manifests itself in wastage, then there is an excess in religious repetition that cannot be encompassed within circulation and exchange. Rational thought necessarily excludes that which is excessive and exceptional.

For example, there are many theories of religion which link the origins of religion to violence, whether natural or human. For David Hume, religion arose out of the anthropomorphic projection of the causes of disastrous accidents.[7] For Nietzsche, religion is an attempt to give meaning to suffering.[8] For Mircea Eliade, religion is an attempt to call upon cosmic powers to restore meaning in the face of disorder.[9] For Walter Burkert, religion expresses the biological drive for the preservation of life, which, when faced with the great unknown of death, manifests itself in sacrifice.[10] For Leszek Kolakowski, religion seeks a future compensation to mask the pain of the present.[11] For René Girard, religion derives from the rationalization and concealing of scapegoating as a means of discharging mimetic, competitive violence.[12] Such theories have a double role: they both define and explain their object.[13] Religion may be identified as that which arises from violence in such a way. This very nomination of religion is both violent and exclusive. It depends on the self-evidence of tautology. Edmund Husserl has identified such self-evidence as follows:

> Self-evidence means nothing more than grasping an entity with the consciousness of its original being-itself-there. Successful realization of a project is, for the acting subject, self-evidence; in this self-evidence, what has been realized is there, *originaliter*, as itself.[14]

Tautology is founded on overcoming the difference between thinking and being, identifying the entity grasped and the original entity.[15] Only subsequent to such identification is the objective, *qua* objective, absolved from considerations of subjectivity. Yet tautology depends on postulating itself: the hypothesized, 'religion' that is thought, is identified with the conclusion, 'religion' that exists, on the basis of postulating 'religion'. Tautology, the foundation of logic and Western European reason, commits the fallacy of *petitio principii*. This tautological repetition is the paralogism of reason once more.

Such ideal objectivity is also dependent upon the possibility of naming the referent of 'religion' as religion, on itself as a proper name, and on the invariance and univocity of this name. As Husserl showed, such naming is dependent upon a common language,

> a community of those who can express themselves, normally, in a fully understandable fashion … The objective world is from the start the world for all, the world which 'everyone' has as world-horizon. Its objective being presupposes men, understood as men with a common language.[16]

It is precisely such a community of modern thinkers, including theorists of religion, that is founded on the exclusion of exceptions such as the religious *qua* religious. To the extent that religion is a way of facing the excessive and the exceptional, then it will exceed rational analysis and critique in its present form. Thus if truth is dependent on the social practice of the community in which it is constituted, including its practices of self-identification, exclusion, violence and sacrifice, then even the practice of reason itself has ethical (or unethical) and religious dimensions which are constitutive of its mode of truth. Moreover, such truth excludes the truth of the religious *qua* religious. Then the perspective from which religion may be explored, apart from its rational, critical distortions, is from the point of view of the excluded exception.

Modern critical reason has much in common with the superstitions which it denounces and explains. Instead of remaining with conflict, then, we must explore a more profound agreement – only as such can conflict, contradiction and violence be overcome as explanatory principles of the dialectic.[17] This agreement is to be found in the repetition which leads to absolution – repetition remains the principle of religion and modernity. Principles of repetition and difference, the ultimate principles of modernity, are accompanied by a social practice dependent on their mode of piety.

Ritual piety

Repetition

Piety is unproductive in so far as it is repetitious. Chants, mantras, drumming, invocations, liturgies, rituals, festivals, pilgrimages, dances, songs, storytelling, veneration of ancestors, preservation of traditions, doctrines and laws – repetition is to be found throughout religious phenomena. Ritual, the punctuation of time by repetitive actions, is a vibration between sacred gesture and profane time. It is often noted that in traditional societies ritual and economic activities are inseparable: one would not think of sowing seed without offering a prayer; one would not think of building a home without offering a sacrifice – both aspects are regarded as both ritual and economic.[18] From a modern perspective, however, one likes to distinguish between those uses of space, time, energy and information that enter into exchange in determinate ratios so that they may recirculate, and those which irrationally squander finite resources. Everywhere it appears, ritual repetition appears to be unproductive, 'irrational', conservative, or unprogressive. Repetition is a waste of time.

Such an economic perspective presupposes too much: it assumes that we have an ordered, secure and meaningful world which can be preserved or improved. It assumes that we have a determinate system of values, that we know what is worthy of attention. From a modern perspective, 'life', its duration and quality, becomes the objective measure of values: it is 'life' that demands attention.[19] Where money measures value in circulation, and labour-time measures value in production, life-time measures value in consumption. Indeed, this is a way of giving attention to time: on the one hand, labour-time is regarded as a countable stock, a linear quantity; on the other hand, life-time has a quality and duration. In ritual, however, attention is paid to that which lies outside of the experience of time. For alongside the sphere of the distribution of value, there is also a sphere of the distribution of attention.

Émile Durkheim grounded his distinction between the profane and the sacred on these two ways of symbolizing value: the ways of action which a society imposes upon its members 'are, by that very fact, marked with a distinctive sign provocative of *respect.*'[20] Such representations of collective influences distinguish the sacred from the profane.[21] Just as Durkheim distinguished two fundamental mental states, Bergson distinguished two fundamental functions of the intelligence of the human-species: tool-making and myth-making.[22] Where tools are used in the fashioning of material objects, myths are used in the fashioning of fantastic images. Such images escape the economic circuit. By giving attention to them, the myth-making function generates an idleness, a non-productivity, a detachment from present need in which recollection can occur. Such recollection is a spontaneous action of the memory in coming to the present which effectively determines the distribution of attention. Then our relation to life is mediated by our mode of distribution of attention – whether habitual, ritual, or driven by interest. There is no immediate, one-to-one, face-to-face encounter in the present which is not mediated by a host of memories, spirits and powers which function as a virtual past. For such memories, spirits and powers determine the flow of attention: they shape the very passage of time. Then modern attention to life is based on a disavowal of the very conditions of attention, and of life itself.

Ritual repetition places attention on the source of values, and thus renews an appropriate distribution of honour, value and attention within the community. According to Mircea Eliade, those who practise sacred repetition are threatened by a disordered and uninhabitable domain, filled with ghosts, demons or 'foreigners': chaos.[23] Sacred repetition ontologically founds the world as an ordered cosmos by repeating the primordial acts of the gods in creation. Chaos, the wilderness of an uninhabitable terrain governed by wild and disordered forces, threatens Eliade's *homo religiosus* with existential terror.

To the extent that ritual functions as a 'machine for the suppression of time,'[24] it opens itself up to irreversibility, to birth and death, only to reinscribe the ruptures of existence that threaten to overwhelm the world with meaninglessness within a precisely described symbolic time. Ritual repetition repeats that which it dare not encounter, but repeats it in a sanitized, sacred form, where it reproduces the current order of existence. All rituals are aversion rituals. Instead of denying the reality of that which exceeds circulation, aversion rituals acknowledge the powers which they attempt to ward off. On the one hand, the power of rupture is to be removed; on the other hand, it must be engaged in the ritual itself. According to Eliade, this dangerous gesture can only be validated if ritual opens up to more powerful supra-mundane powers: those of the sources of cycles, continuity and order.[25] At the same time as suppressing the 'historical' time of change, creation and destruction, ritual recreates an ideal past as the source of cycles.[26] Ritual involves an attempt to repeat, to make present, a perfect past as the source of power and order.

Nevertheless, one cannot simply assume that ritual is static.[27] There is an error of judgement here: it is assumed that ritual aims at the repetition of its chants, formulae, gestures, doctrines and laws, as though these material expressions of repetition were themselves the objects of veneration. Ritual is subsumed under an imposed category of 'fetishism'. Religion and magic, whatever degree of order, stability and preservation they aim at, and however regularly or occasionally engaged, invoke ways of coping with the accidental, the incomprehensible, the unfortunate and the calamitous in so far as these interrupt the stability of life in ways that matter. Even if the accidental intrusion is as natural as a birth, death, marriage, or maturation, it threatens the symbolic stability of society in so far as an element appears that no longer has a symbolic role or place. Rites of passage which set the life of the individual within the cyclical life of the people as a whole are ways of both acknowledging and managing the appearance of discontinuity. What is essential is not that the static order should be reproduced, but that an order should be produced. In Bergson's so-called 'static' religion, one has to adopt techniques to engage in recollection. Indeed, even Bergson admitted that it 'sometimes happens that well-nigh empty formulae, the veriest magical incantations, contrive to summon up here and there the spirit capable of imparting substance to them.'[28]

Ritual attends to crisis, upheaval, discontinuity, excess and uncertainty.[29] In divination, possession, shamanistic healing, and exorcism, the ancestors or spirits do not simply belong to an immortal past that must be repeated. Instead, they enter into direct transactions with their people. What counts here, is less the 'technological' solution that results from such a process, but that the search for a solution to the problem should be conducted religiously. What must be done, in cases where innovation is required, must be something worthy of honour, given on the authority of the ancestors or spirits. Just as market transactions without currency rely on a degree of trust and guarantees, so ritual conduct in times of uncertainty searches out a solution that can be honoured. What is essential, in ritual repetition, is not precision but piety. It is more important to die with honour than to live in breach of duty to ancestors and spirits.

Where a modern perspective sees repetition as wastage and inhibition, a cultic perspective sees commerce with the gods or ancestors. Expenditure of labour, time and attention is placed within a broader, more general economy. Such commerce is not purely material: it involves veneration. Rituals do not have to include material offerings to ancestors for them to be a gift of time. For even where material and social intercourse between individuals and ancestors no longer occurs, following death, there is still a transaction in operation. On the one hand, the ancestors give gifts of customary, ritual behaviour itself; they give order and shape to life. On the other hand, the living return honour to ancestors by repeating such rituals. To follow the ways of the ancestors is to pay them attention. Such an exchange between the living and the dead takes place in one and the same practice: the same ritual is that which is given as order, and returned as honour. In the same gesture, a gift is both received and returned. Indeed, such rituals only exist in so far as they are exchanged, received and returned. One gets what one gives and one gives what one gets. Tradition, in so far as it is repeated, is experienced as the gift of a cosmos. What is repeated is already there, *in illo tempore*, as itself. The result is a transfiguration of life, so that everything may be experienced as gift.

Ritual time is neither labour-time nor lived-time: it is given time. Such a time is not quantifiable; nor can it be said to pass. Instead, it can only be given. The gods watch the ritual. They have an interest, a share in the sacrifice. For watching is not purely passive: one gives time. While people glorify the gods by offering the sacrifice, the gods glorify people by taking an interest in them, attending to them, giving time to them. There is therefore a commerce with the gods, but it is not a commerce of commodities. It is a commerce of attention, interest, giving time. Of course, everything is uncertain here, even the very existence of the gods. What is given in ritual, however, is a way of attending to time, which, not passing, is immune to life and death: it is an eternity which coexists with a short duration. It is a collective memory which gives social cohesion. It is a distribution of values, dramatized in the sacrifice, whereby attending to that which is most important gives each value its proper place, its appropriate share or portion of the sacrifice.

In the heart of the sacred, however, a new danger arises from the hierophany itself, expressed in Rudolf Otto's formula *mysterium tremendum et fascinans*.[30] While the outcome of ritual may be a static social and cosmic order, this is merely its success, not its element. In spite of its repetitious nature, ritual is shrouded in uncertainty. For entering into commerce with beings who exceed the natural order implies that there is no guarantee that such commerce will be successful.[31] Since the blessings of the gods are uncertain and fortuitous, they cannot be subjected to scientific verification through repetition. The given time of ritual has either just been given, or it is yet to come. The gods, who abide in a virtual past, never become present. Each transaction is a venture into the unknown. Indeed, the assumption that a ritual transaction will be successful exposes the intention to manipulate the gods, to exert power over them, to put them in a position of obligation with regard to the worshipper. Ritual becomes a forlorn attempt to act on the supernatural world as one does on the social world. Collapsing the excess of the supernatural over the natural, such piety reveals its own impiety. Then ritual, in view of its own impiety, may bring down the wrath of the very objects of worship who are able to bring security.

Piety is extremely precarious. The danger is that ritual will be reinscribed within an economy, albeit a mythical one. For rituals may be repeated as stereotypical gestures, formulae, chants or objects apart from piety – that is, apart from a relation to the gods. In this case, the gesture is intended to oblige the gods to bless the community. Alternatively, ritual may be understood symbolically, according to its purpose or function. Here it is replaced by its meaning, which substitutes for a relation for the gods. In this case, the gods are obliged to explain themselves, to account for their conduct as the 'just measure' within a system of exchange of righteousness and reward. An abstract principle is substituted for the actual conduct of the gods. Both material repetition of gesture and symbolic repetition of meaning place ritual in the market-place, where it is no longer accompanied by guarantors. Piety, constitutive of ritual as ritual, cannot be exchanged in this way. Piety concerns the repetition of the ritual as a gift from the gods.

In order to preserve piety and its blessings, then, the divine origin of the ritual must be effectively encountered as an origin. One must wait for a hierophany. For if a hierophany came regularly on demand, then the divine would be subject to human manipulation, losing its transcendence over the human. The divine can only exist if it arrives late. Anxiety may attempt to short-circuit the interval by constituting the 'origin' as an origin, by absolving it from all economic relations of interdependence. This is itself a process of sacrifice: the sacred origin is granted an apotheosis, becoming an origin retrospectively, whereby the sacred reveals that it has emerged from above. Nevertheless, such an 'origin' derives from the symbolic practice of the community. Once taken as a fundamental point of orientation, however, then it does effectively function as the singularity that structures the socially constructed reality. It confirms itself retrospectively as an origin because it is made to function as an origin.

One suspects that there is a triple exclusion here: in the first place, there is an 'originary violence', a violence of the origin at the origin, by which the supposed origin both names and individuates itself as an origin. In the process, there is an exclusion of any supervenient hierophany. The gods become inaccessible. In the second place, there is an exclusion of all chaotic forces which do not fit into the symbolic order constructed around the origin. For when the origin belongs to a component within a symbolic order itself, anything which opposes that origin must be excluded. The symbol of the origin functions as a marker of identity.[32] In the third place, those who object to the symbolic practice of the community must themselves be excluded as a threat to that community. For example, if one attempts to rationalize worship with a principle such as, 'The gods bless those who perform worship correctly', then when blessing is not received, someone must be to blame for impiety. One who is impious, or who is marked out by misfortune, is not to be trusted: their place is forfeited in a sacred community of trust and attention. Thus originary violence gives birth to real violence.[33] Moreover, it is not sufficient to denounce this symbolic practice in the name of revelation as the true hierophany or in the name of secular truth: in both procedures, the same symbolic practice is repeated.[34]

Let us sum up the argument so far: scarcity brings anticipations of disaster, which in turn exacerbates conflict, scarcity of resources and scarcity of meaning. Human civilization, as a cosmos, is threatened by chaos – intensifying the need for religious sources of meaning which can restore meaning as collective identity and overcome death. Such religious sources of meaning, in so far as they are constructed around the sacred or the absolute, must defend the sacred at all costs, else they risk relapsing into chaos. The cost of mounting such a defence is the symbolic exclusion of incompatible perspectives, which may be intimately connected to the violent exclusion of others.

Now, meaning is produced in this way so as to cover or conceal future chaos. Whether, as in capitalist modernity, the future is constructed by extrapolation from the present, or whether, as in traditional societies, the future is constructed as a repetition of the past, the chaotic and spontaneous future is simply covered over. Piety forms a synthesis of time by which it joins past, present and future, but such a synthesis is precarious: it must be maintained through repetition by the force of will. If the force of chaos is too great, however, then such an effort of the will may not be maintained.

Historical piety

Difference

The emergence of a new kind of piety directed towards future historical events, faith, seems to be a rupture in the history of religion. On this occasion, it would seem that ritual repetition was not able to come to terms with the rupture in question. Eliade related history to crisis and suffering: where humans aim at ritual repetition, it is misfortune which brings change and history into human experience.[35] Of course, in traditional societies suffering has an all too apparent reality; suffering, by itself, does not make history. Eliade's account of 'archaic ontology', that objects or acts only acquire a value and become real when they repeat an archetype, seems improbable: unrepeatable, contingent suffering is all too real. Suffering feels significant, and therefore it bears a meaning within it. The first step in coping with suffering is to discover its meaning, the reason why it has happened: whether from the magical action of an enemy, possession by a spirit, the breaking of a taboo, or the anger of a god. Where in modern thought, suffering is the result of natural forces or human malice, and its meaning is entirely separate from its degree of pain or significance, in traditional thought no such separation need be made. Suffering is meaningful because it is painful; the 'supernatural' world expresses the objective reality of the fact that what happens matters. Far from being meaningless, suffering has an excess of meaning; its supernatural origin expresses this excess of significance.

Comparative mythology has shown a common pattern to myth in Afroasiatic cultures, at the root of Semitic religions. Its logic is dualistic and patriarchal: a vulnerable female sun deity is offered to a violent male storm-god, resulting in a destructive downpour; this storm-god is killed by a younger male deity, who then weds the goddess in a sacred marriage.[36] Such a mythological pattern anticipates some modern conceptions of history: progress occurs through overcoming and reconciliation. One of its earliest and influential manifestations is found in the ancient Babylonian New Year ceremony, which involved the recitation and re-enaction of the *Enuma elish*, the myth of the victory of Marduk over the chaos monster Tiamat. Eliade interpreted this as a regeneration of time: the past year is abolished in the annual expulsion of sins, diseases and demons.[37] Chaos is allowed to reign for a short period, before being expelled in a repetition of the mythical moment of the passage from chaos to cosmos. In ritual piety, historical change is abolished: or, more accurately, it is preserved within myth as the deed of the gods, or as cosmogenesis. Ritual piety is not ignorant of history; history is known as suffering, and subordinated to repetition so that its excess of meaning will not overwhelm. Nevertheless, here, within mythology itself, one finds the possibility of historical progress as a violent, mythical archetype, available for repetition: old gods may be replaced by new ones.

More than this is required for the introduction of history. For in order that history should itself find a determinate rather than excessive meaning, it must be reinscribed in economy:

> In general, it may be said that suffering is regarded as the consequence of a deviation in respect to the 'norm' ... there is nothing that does not, in one way or another, find its explanation and justification in the transcendent, in the divine economy.[38]

In order to give a determinate meaning to a degree of suffering, it must be measured against a 'divine economy', a metaphysical framework. It is no longer sufficient to repeat the sacred, or to signify transcendence; the transcendent must bring some form of recompense.[39] The Hebrew prophets interpreted historical events in terms of present debts and future reparations. Once history is inscribed within the divine economy of justice, historical faith concerns itself with the future, rather than the past.

In order to explore what the finite order of debts signifies, let us compare piety with economy. As Pierre Bourdieu described them, ancient economies, in the absence of coinage, functioned on the basis of trust or credit. The gift or good-faith economy functions by patronage: interactions are conducted on the basis of a web of interdependency, a network of relatives, guarantors, obligations and favours. Prestige, in such an economy, is not superior competence so much as superior integrity: the generous person, who has benefited others, will be called on as a guarantor or patron, will receive gifts of gratitude, and will be able to call on a large number of workers for major projects.[40] Indeed, in so far as economic interdependence is the natural condition of humanity, then integrity and generosity must be regarded as components of primordial human nature alongside the Hobbesian state of conflict.[41] As Bourdieu indicated, we must take account of the degree of uncertainty involved in such transactions. Given the interval of gift and counter-gift, it is not easy to analyse particular cycles and debts at the everyday level – it is rarely entirely clear which obligation one is repaying. In long-term relations of mutual interdependence, one no longer counts how many times one has done a deed for another, or has received a gift. While a community may function materially through such exchanges, in practice each person will only be known for their habitual conduct and their degree of wealth. The interval of gift and counter-gift obscures all the precise relations which connect quality of conduct to degree of wealth; moreover, many other factors will also affect the latter. Thus there is no obvious natural relation between integrity and wealth. Indeed, the obvious empirical relation is quite the reverse: one will gain a favourable, short-term outcome if one cheats, uses or manipulates others.

While the outcome of one's economic conduct in traditional societies may be ensured in practice by custom or morality, in each individual transaction success appears to be gratuitous. Moreover, if one is honest and becomes wealthy, this goes against rational expectations of the superior value of cheating. Against expectation, success appears to be guaranteed supernaturally. Piety may be regarded as an ideological reflex of an economic order that is dependent on the integrity of its participants in order to function. The highest principle of this worldly wisdom is the success of personal honour and integrity:[42] one only enters into transactions with those whom one trusts. The patent falsehood of this principle, so that short-term advantage can be gained by the mere appearance of honourable conduct, is belied by the fact that it is simply necessary to act as if one believes it in order to maintain one's honour and one's long-term prosperity. Believed without evidence, in contradiction to short-term interests, the principle appears to be supernatural: the deceitful or wicked may prosper for a short time, but will be punished by God.[43] Hence the principle of temporal retribution emerges from economic conduct. Its corollary, that the one who keeps most faithfully to the rules of the game, who fears supernatural retribution the most and is therefore publicly recognized as the most pious, will be the most successful, is expressed in the cardinal principle of Hebrew wisdom: 'The fear of the Lord is the beginning of wisdom'.

In such a context, misfortune can be regarded as a payment of a debt: a punishment for a failure to meet one's obligations. What is distinctive, here, is that supernatural meaning is now read off from the course of events: the righteous prosper and the wicked perish. Moreover, piety is no longer directed solely to the past, to the repetition of an archetype, but is directed towards an uncertain future, where one does not know the outcome. Abraham, in his journey from Ur of the Chaldeans and in his belief in the divine promise of descendants, is the type of such an economic piety: he makes a business venture, trusts in a promise. Value is now located in two forms: in the ethical quality of one's conduct, and in the material outcome of one's fate. Economy is a kind of conquest of mythology: value need no longer be embodied in ritual repetition of cosmogonic powers, but can be embodied in the material substance of one's possessions. Value becomes natural rather than supernatural: it is reified in the object of wealth. Just as the myths of Zeus and Adonai repeat elements of the Babylonian myth of the slaying of a monster of chaos, so ethical monotheism slays ritual piety in creating a new source of meaning and value.

Furthermore, it is possible for those with integrity to observe exceptions to this supernatural principle. Just as it is possible to gain wealth through integrity and patronage, it is also possible to gain wealth through exploitation of the poor. If the Hebrew prophets began to associate wealth with evil, such evil is judged in relation to the morality of economic integrity.[44] If the course of history is understood as a punishment for sin, such a punishment measures the debt of integrity owed to God. If punishment is expected to lead to restoration and reconciliation, such an eschatological justice is the restoration of economic integrity. Economic ideology may not merely explain the course of events; it may also produce the metaphysics of monotheism.

There is, of course, no necessary reason why such an ethical, future-oriented piety should be opposed to a ritual, past-directed piety; in practice, they rarely exist in a pure state, separate from each other. Indeed, the separation between them is purely conceptual, not phenomenological, based on their differing syntheses of time. These two clash, first of all in recorded history, in the message of the prophet Amos.[45] If there is to be a clash, it is a condition, not of necessity, but of the will: if economic piety is intensified, then, just as Abraham binds his son Isaac to the altar, everything else must be put at stake, ventured, given, sacrificed. The supreme gesture of economic piety is thus to sacrifice one's ritual piety, exposing oneself entirely to chance, to the course of events, to the flow of history. The message of Hebrew monotheism, in its rejection of idolatry, is simply the requirement that one puts one's faith in Adonai alone, that one ventures oneself, that one behaves with complete integrity before the God of history, of events, of economics. Sacrifice takes on an entirely different meaning. Such a piety works, not by abolishing or exorcising the past, but by sacrificing it, so that God alone will be the mediator between one's conduct and its outcome. The spirits of the virtual past are banished.

Ethical monotheism manifests its violence in the ban:

> If you hear it said ... that scoundrels from among you have gone out and led the inhabitants of the town astray, saying, 'Let us go and worship other gods,' whom you have not known, then you shall inquire and make a thorough investigation. If the charge is established that such an abhorrent thing has been done among you, you shall put the inhabitants of that town to the sword, utterly destroying it and everything in it – even putting its livestock to the sword. All of its spoil you shall gather into its public square: then burn the town and all its spoil with fire, as a whole burnt offering to the Lord your God. It shall remain a perpetual ruin, never to be rebuilt. Do not let anything devoted to destruction stick to your hand, so that the Lord may turn from his fierce anger and show you compassion.[46]

The ban on letting anything devoted to destruction 'stick to your hand' is necessary to ensure that such acts of ritual destruction are conducted out of piety alone, and not out of impure or mixed motives for the sake of gain. Mammon is already a potential rival for God. Destruction of another for the sake of personal gain is prohibited by economic integrity. Moreover, if all events are understood as judgements on integrity as a whole, then such judgements imply the existence of a single judge – destruction of a city demonstrates the existence of one God. Monotheism is inseparable from a legislation against other objects of worship. Furthermore, if the power of God is manifested in a future reward, according to a structure of promise and fulfilment, then such an eschatological consummation must restore the direct rule of God, at the same time as it eliminates all alternative powers. Monotheism necessarily implies a final judgement which enacts the ban. Then the ban also forms the structural precondition of Christian thought, not merely in so far as nearly all of the New Testament writers invoke a violent eschatology as the consummation of divine judgement, not merely in the universalism that eliminates other faiths, not merely in the belief in one truth, one faith and one church, but in the very concept of eschatological consummation itself.

Expectations of such future violence manifest themselves as violence in the present. Human community, in so far as it is founded upon mutual trust and its obligations of honesty and integrity, appeals to a supernatural or eschatological principle that belies the empirical expectation that advantage can be gained by deceiving others. Any threat to this order must be condemned so that the basis of trust upon which the community is built can survive. The corollary is that one who is not successful is not to be trusted: the unfortunate may fall outside of the privileged community when, deprived of trust, they fail to prosper. The virtuous circle of trust and prosperity in an interdependent community is doubled by a vicious circle of mistrust and exclusion. This victimage mechanism may become the foundation of the social order in so far as it demonstrates how the righteous prosper while the wicked are punished.

Apocalyptic piety

Singularity

Modes of piety are syntheses of time. Historical piety splits human existence into two dimensions: one's ethical conduct and the outcome of one's life. These dimensions are mediated by divine justice. This latter, a transcendent connection between action and reward, is a remnant of ritual piety. In historical piety, both ethos and history are temporal and historical; there is no need to posit a transcendent mediation. An immanent critique of historical piety leads to materialism: all relations between conduct and reward will be mediated by physical and temporal causes. Time itself, the unity of spontaneous action and receptive intuition, is that which is ultimately signified by historical piety.

Similarly, ritual piety splits human existence into two dimensions: the sacred and the profane. On the one hand, there are those portions of life marked out as belonging to ritual, which effect repetition and participate, albeit indirectly, in the life of the gods; on the other hand, there are those portions of life that are not incorporated into the framework of cosmic meaning generated by ritual. In both ritual and historical piety, existence itself is a vibration, an intercalation of one dimension with another, a synthesis.

In both cases, the meaning of temporality is actually given by the mode of piety involved: time is conceived as profane flux or sacred repetition, ethical freedom or historical necessity. Such modes of piety cannot be considered as eternal or temporal, for they constitute the very meaning of time and eternity. Since they are not subject to eternal necessity or historical conditioning, they exhibit a limited degree of freedom.

Kierkegaard was able to isolate what is essential here:

> The human being is spirit. But what is spirit? Spirit is the self. But what is the self? The self is a relation which relates to itself, or that in the

relation which is its relating to itself. A human being is a synthesis of the infinite and the finite, of the temporal and the eternal, of freedom and necessity. In short, a synthesis. A synthesis is a relation between two terms. Looked at in this way a human being is not yet a self.[47]

Immanent modes of piety are modes of relating oneself to oneself: constituting oneself in a relation of sacred to profane, of ethical to historical. Kierkegaard constructed an existential typology of modes of piety, such as despair, anxiety, resignation, interest and faith. With the synthesis, we are now able to find an immanent definition of modes of existence: the self is an ethos, no longer simply in relation to time or environment, but in relation to itself. This is an inward mode of piety. It would appear to be something that must be constructed. Yet as soon as an inward mode of piety is posited as possible, it becomes actual: to be unconscious of one's inward piety is itself a mode of relating to one's inward piety. Now, although inward piety appears on the stage of historical piety, in the form of one's ethical relation to oneself, it is indeed something different, for the relation itself is now substituted for one's concrete, historical experience. Kierkegaard applied the categories of ethical relation to this new self instead of the concrete; thus, to be religious is to break with all ethical obligations to concrete ends.[48] Inwardness is intensified by a renunciation of the historical, whether considered as duty or reward, so that one is suspended in faith: 'lying out on seventy thousand fathoms.'[49] Then the negative modes of piety, such as despair and anxiety, may be 'educative' because they consume all finite, historical ends.[50]

The intensity of piety, however, is not simply subject to an effort of will. For piety is conditioned and intensified by its encounter with potency. Chaos, disruption, discontinuity and meaninglessness impose themselves upon us with force; anticipation of the power of chaos is conditioned by exposure to prior states of disruption. Moreover, such destructive potency is mediated through social conditioning with its threats of violence and exclusion. In this respect, one can expect a very large degree of conformity in matters of religion, for dissenters are exposed to higher degrees of chaos, as well as losing the socially sanctioned legitimation which shelters one from chaos. Similarly, the conformists have a dual advantage: modes of piety are contagious, for they resolve social conflicts by symbolic reunification, thus sheltering their adherents from external chaos as well as internal social conflict.

There will always be exceptions; yet the voice of those who are excluded is rarely heard, for it constitutes a challenge to piety. Indeed, there is a particular privilege belonging to the perspective of the excluded: the ideological illusions of symbolic unity lose their luminous, salvific power, for they are not able to save the one who is already excluded from the community; at the same time, the actual violent practice of the community is impressed on the experience of the excluded with such emphasis

that it may begin to outweigh the attractive power of symbolic reunification. The excluded have a privileged access to empirical truth, even if
they do not enjoy a privileged revelation. Distinct within the history of
religions are communities formed of those who, for one reason or
another, have left the prevailing social order – Taoist sages, Vedic
renouncers, Buddhist monks and nuns, Islamic *sants*, Sikh gurus, Jewish
prophets, Christian monks and nuns, Cynic philosophers – even if their
innovative power forms the focus of symbolic reunification. Such movements are rarely founded on social criticism alone; the prime aim is
religious reform. Then their main message is not simply a denunciation of
the violence and exclusion practised by established religious communities,
and not simply an appeal to universal peace in opposition to violence; they
articulate distinctive modes of piety.

For if piety is precarious, if it provides shelter from chaos by effacing its
own 'origin' in constructing an origin, then reform proceeds by denouncing
the impiety of piety, and by recalling or revealing the 'origin'. Of course,
this practice may follow the logic of the sacred or the logic of faith, but
there is at least the possibility of an alternative. For just as piety attempts to
shelter from chaos without, it also encounters chaos within – as a loss of
meaning, a collapse of established modes of piety, as a 'murder of God'.
Anticipation – whether of death, of the apocalypse, of eschatological
consummation, of divine reward, or even of a return on investment – leaves
an interval of waiting in which the cosmos has not yet been completed or
sealed. Anticipated chaos may not yet have arrived, but there is a moment
of indeterminacy, of hesitancy, where the laws of the divine economy or the
laws of nature have not yet been fulfilled. Moreover, such a temporal delay
is essential for piety, for if there were no delay, then the divine will would
be identified entirely with the natural order, as for Spinoza.

The chaotic interval admits of no anticipation and no reinscription
within a symbolic order. Broadly speaking, the phenomenology of religion
is not complete until one adds to the categories of ritual, narrative, belief,
ethics, sacred and faith, the category of 'experience' – although this is
perhaps a misleading term. While far from being universal, anomalous
experience is widespread in the history of religion, and perhaps essential in
the emergence of religious traditions. The 'irrational' or extravagant dimension of religion, where it borders on the phenomenology of psychosis,
involves an immense diversity: sensing the presence of supernatural beings;
identification with the ultimate or divine; prophetic or messianic vocation;
revelations of the hidden, divine order of things; withdrawal from mundane
reality; a sense of guidance or providence; voices; dreams; hallucinations; a
sense of impending doom, including dissolution of the world or the self;
visions or experiences of heaven or hell; sectarian paranoia; shamanic initi-
ation and other-world journeys; and extraordinary feelings of benevolence.

Such experiences are scandalous for modern reason: it is not possible to
assess epistemic claims made on their basis by means of publicly agreed

criteria; they are élitist, in so far as they claim access to privileged blessings and insights not available to others; they are ethically dangerous, in so far as they lead to a self-absorbed quest for individual experience; they are politically dangerous, in so far as they detract attention from the concrete historical situation of humanity and the environment; and they lead to superstition, fanaticism, cults, abuse and even insanity. Such judgements are certainly reasonable; nevertheless, it would be rash to deny the importance of such experiences in the history of religion. Indeed, in major world religions, such experiences are often both desired and feared: ecstatic experience may form part of the metaphysical, mythological or eschatological framework of religion, even when it is not encountered in practice in concrete historical experience. A Christian may not expect the heavens to open and the Holy Spirit to descend like a dove, while still expecting to enter heaven filled with the Holy Spirit; a Muslim may not expect to hear the archangel dictating Koranic verses, while believing that they were so dictated; a Buddhist may not expect to suddenly enter nirvana, while meditating in order to reach nirvana. Nevertheless, the art of cultivating ecstatic states is so widespread in traditional cultures that it has been called a major world religion in itself: shamanism.

This 'apocalyptic' piety – an experience of the chaotic interval – seems to be a merging of the former two: the sacred no longer simply repeats itself, but comes to live a historical life. The religious ecstatic begins to live within a mythology. The subjective experience of history as a duration, changing through time, is now applied to the sacred itself: one intuits the sacred. Innovation occurs in the history of religion when the sacred itself acquires a history. In this way, one conceives this kind of piety under the category of 'religious experience'. What is questionable, however, is whether the former two categories can determine the third, or whether they are themselves incomplete without the third. The sacred, the eternal, and the concrete, the historical, become foci of piety in so far as they possess a spiritual power or significance. Such power is not constituted by frequency of repetition, or by degree of discontinuity or difference, or even by the degree of piety with which they are embraced. Then following Rudolf Otto and Gerardus van der Leeuw, it would be necessary to define the spiritual intensity of a focus of piety as itself a potency, as *sui generis*.[51]

Religious experience, like psychosis, is a break with consensus reality and a consensual state of consciousness; it is exceptional. Established ways of making sense of the world through ritual or economic rationality exclude the exceptional a priori. Singularities, in physics or history, are the limit of rational thought: they are what thought must think, the very punctuations which determine existence, yet what thought cannot think. The exceptional cannot be comprehended from the point of view of the regular. Thus a philosophy of religion, in so far as it appeals to public or economic standards of rationality, is doomed to exclude the religious *qua* religious. The phantasmagoria of religious experience appears to take one as far as possible from concrete, historical fact. This is not entirely true: religious experience is itself a historical fact, one that can be of enormous significance. For example, an alien abduction – even if it is a dream or hallucination arising from sleep paralysis, or even if it is a false memory implanted through suggestion under hypnosis – is itself an interruption in the course of one's life which can make an enormous difference to one's relation to oneself. It is therefore helpful to distinguish between religious experience as an immanent sign, an event, and the transcendent or supernatural feature signified by experience. Reason cannot easily test any truth claims based on the latter. Moreover, ethics cannot easily incorporate modes of existence revealed in religious experience. From a historical perspective, a religious experience is a sign, a disjunction, an event: something has happened. If the event is of significance, however, then there is a double disjunction: a change in external states of affairs, an anomalous event or experience, is combined with a change in one's ethos, and perhaps even a change in one's relation to oneself. A discontinuity in one's mode of existence is produced. Thus, from an immanent perspective, the intensity of an event of religious experience can be measured by its effects: the changes it produces in a life.

The essence of piety is neither ritual nor historical: it is problematic, speculative and interested. Piety, enquiring into the sacred, the spiritual, the eternal, the infinite or the singular, seeks a currency through which to trade. Indeed, piety itself is a currency, a medium of exchange: as a vibration, it mediates the relation between the separate poles which it embraces. Piety mediates between the potency of chaos and the potency of the chaotic interval. At the same time, it mediates between time and eternity, the profane and the sacred, giving and receiving. As a vibration, it joins such opposing poles in a synthesis; such a synthesis is only accomplished, however, because it is mediated by the relation between another pair of poles. In this respect, each vibration encompasses a further vibration. Each currency traded in piety is also an exchange. No currency takes privilege over the others; each is defined in relation to the others. Modes of piety may thus be considered on a plane of immanence. In immanence, each mode of piety is a vibration, a sign. Yet what is signified is not transcendent to the sign. Instead, the sign signifies the medium in which it vibrates, the currency through which it trades its selected poles; it signifies its own modality.

Piety may thus function as a strange kind of currency, a medium of exchange. Like money, it is inserted into the chaotic flux of existence as a general equivalent. Like money, it has no necessary force or value. Like money, it extracts a surplus value from existence. Like money, it produces interest. The interest of piety differs from that of money in a significant respect, however: money is both a measure of the value of commodities, and a value that can be measured. The surplus value extracted by money, the interest it makes, is capital, always expressed in the form of monetary value. Piety, by contrast, is not primarily interested in itself; its interest is usually displaced onto the successive poles between which it mediates. Piety is interested in a 'celestial capital', the gift of the gods. Even when it aims to take its mode of existence from the gift of the gods, its interest lies in the giving rather than the given. Even when it is most self-interested, piety retains humility: its value is not to be found in itself, but rather in the sacred source of piety which it can never possess, but only ever attempt to repeat. Piety does not aim to repeat itself as a sign, but to repeat what it signifies. Piety is a mode of distribution of attention.

Economism is the extreme limit of historical piety: each existent is reified and commodified; its value no longer derives from its intrinsic properties, but from the network of relations among those who trade in it. The value of the concrete, historical commodity is given by the 'inwardness' of capital: capital's relation of itself to itself, the relation which capital is. Capital is the parody of the inward self. Yet where capital constitutes a commodity by repeating the sign of its value as a sign, piety attempts to repeat what is signified by the sign. Where capital is the repetition of the same, piety is the repetition of difference. Where capital is an extreme monism, excluding all exceptions, piety is an extreme pluralism, embracing the singular and the exceptional as that which is signified. Even if the transcendental signified cannot be grasped in itself, piety may at least enter into certain transactions with it. The relation between piety and the singular may be mediated by a currency; but such a currency is itself a mode of piety.

Such transactions, however, are more than simple discontinuities, more than mere signs. Each has its own singular character, as though something from outside interposed itself between moments in the flow of time, at the same time as something from inside interposed itself in the self's relation to the self. In relation to immanent thought, that which emerges from outside and inside are both unthinkable in their essence. This, far from disempowering thought, makes experience into a condition of possibility of thinking as such. One asks, 'What has happened?' 'How did we get to this point?' Here, in immanence, philosophical enquiry rejoins spirituality. The aim is not to conquer the unthinkable by subjecting it to the categories of reason; the aim is to merge oneself with the mode of existence of the unthinkable, so that one acquires its power. Here, the problems of reason, ethics and piety may be reunited into a superior unity.

Notes

1 Thomas Hobbes, *Leviathan*, ch. 13 Cambridge: Cambridge University Press, 1996, pp. 87–8.
2 Thus John Locke distinguished a Commonwealth as a 'society of men constituted only for preserving and advancing their civil goods' – these being life, liberty, health, freedom from pain, and possession of lands, money, furniture and the like – from a Church as a free and voluntary society for the 'public

worship of God.' *Letter on Toleration*, Oxford: Clarendon Press, 1968, pp. 65, 67, 71.

3 In this regard, Michael Hardt and Antonio Negri's *Empire*, Cambridge, MA: Harvard University Press, 2000, although coming from the same philosophical tradition as myself, seems dogmatically tied to a metaphysics of production, while refusing to acknowledge the clear material limits to production.

4 Bruce Lincoln, 'Conflict', in Mark C. Taylor (ed.), *Critical Terms for Religious Studies*, Chicago: University of Chicago Press, 1998, p. 66.

5 See Mark Juergensmeyer, *Terror in the Mind of God: The Global Rise of Religious Violence*, Berkeley: University of California Press, 2000.

6 Alfred North Whitehead, *Religion in the Making*, Cambridge: Cambridge University Press, 1927, p. 10.

7 David Hume, *The Natural History of Religion*, Oxford: Clarendon Press, 1976, p. 36.

8 Friedrich Nietzsche, *On the Genealogy of Morals*, New York: Doubleday Anchor, 1956.

9 Mircea Eliade, *The Sacred and the Profane: the Nature of Religion*, San Diego: Harcourt Brace, 1959.

10 Walter Burkert, *Creation of the Sacred*, Cambridge, MA: Harvard University Press, 1996.

11 Leszek Kolakowski, *Religion*, Oxford: Oxford University Press, 1982, p. 36.

12 René Girard, *Violence and the Sacred*, Baltimore: Johns Hopkins University Press, 1977.

13 Maurice Bloch admits the dangers of begging the question in theories of religion. Bloch, unlike the preceding mentioned theorists, regards violence as originating in religion, rather than vice versa; the account that follows will be consonant with Bloch's approach. See Bloch, *Prey into Hunter: the Politics of Religious Experience*, Cambridge: Cambridge University Press, 1992, pp. 3–7.

14 Edmund Husserl, 'The Origin of Geometry', in Jacques Derrida, *Edmund Husserl's Origin of Geometry: an Introduction*, Brighton: Harvester, 1978, p. 160.

15 See Parmenides' fundamental insight into being: 'for the same thing is for thinking and being.' See also Martin Heidegger: 'To think the true means to experience the true in its essence and, in such essential experience, to know the truth of what is true.' Heidegger, *Parmenides*, Bloomington: Indiana University Press, 1992, p. 1.

16 Husserl, 'The Origin of Geometry', p. 162.

17 This, as we have seen, is the next stage of Schelling's dialectic.

18 Mircea Eliade, *The Myth of the Eternal Return*, Princeton: Princeton University Press, 1971, pp. 27–8.

19 Giorgio Agamben draws this point from Michel Foucault. See Agamben, *Homo Sacer: Sovereign Power and Bare Life*, Stanford: Stanford University Press, 1998, p. 3.

20 Émile Durkheim, *The Elementary Forms of the Religious Life*, London: George Allen & Unwin, 1915, p. 208.

21 Durkheim, *ibid.*, p. 212.

22 Henri Bergson, *The Two Sources of Morality and Religion*, Notre Dame: University of Notre Dame Press, 1977, 107–8.

23 Mircea Eliade, *The Sacred and the Profane: the Nature of Religion*, San Diego: Harcourt Brace, 1959, p. 31.

24 Edmund Leach, *Culture and Communication*, Cambridge: Cambridge University Press, 1976, p. 44.

25 Eliade, *The Myth of the Eternal Return*, p. 82.

26 Eliade, *ibid.*, p. 21

27 This point of view, attributable to Marx and Durkheim, is challenged by Robert M. Torrance, drawing on Van Gennep's theory of 'rites of passage', and its development by Victor Turner. See Torrance, *The Spiritual Quest: Transcendence in Myth, Religion and Science*, Berkeley: University of California Press, 1994.

28 Bergson, *The Two Sources of Morality and Religion*, p. 215.

29 Bronislaw Malinowski noted that magical and ritual practices are invoked in economic activities where the outcome is uncertain. See Malinowski, 'Myth in Primitive Psychology', in Robert A. Segal (ed.), *The Myth and Ritual Theory: an Anthology*, Oxford: Blackwell, 1998, p. 174.

30 Rudolf Otto, *The Idea of the Holy*, London: Oxford University Press, 1923.

31 It is possible that some traditional religions do not posit any strict distinction between the natural and supernatural orders, between the sacred and the profane (see Fiona Bowie, *The Anthropology of Religion*, Oxford: Blackwell, 2000, p. 26; such is the vision of an 'organic society' described by Murray Bookchin in *The Ecology of Freedom*, Palo Alto: Cheshire Books, 1982), obviating any uncertainty. Yet as Jonathan Z. Smith warns us, it is possible that traditional ritual dramatizes an ideal of social relations with the gods that may have no relation to the actual relations between people and the natural world (see Jonathan Z. Smith, *Imagining Religion*, Chicago: Chicago University Press, 1988)). The temporal nature of human existence is decisive here: anticipation brings a degree of uncertainty which is not overcome in this context by anthropomorphic promises.

32 For the relation between monotheism, identity and violence, see Regina M. Schwartz, *The Curse of Cain: the Violent Legacy of Monotheism*, Chicago: University of Chicago Press, 1997.

33 For an account of this tertiary structure of violence in Derrida's work, see Richard Beardsworth, *Derrida and the Political*, London: Routledge, 1996, pp. 20–5. The perspective outlined here, however, differs from Derrida in regarding the question of the origin itself as a product of contingent symbolic practice.

34 If, by contrast, one were to claim that God himself performs the repetition, that God gives himself for distribution by the cosmic order which he founds, then one would be able to claim access to supervenient grace. The origin of this supernatural order, however transparently revealed by God, would not be subject to verification outside of this order. The interval of piety is then filled by eschatological consummation. Nevertheless, the logic of exclusion remains. There is a test for such supernatural revelation: it concerns the consistency of the content of revelation with its determinate symbolic and material practices in relation to that which constitutes its outside. A discourse of love and peace which maintains its purity by a symbolic practice of violent exclusion cannot do what it says. Even supernatural repetition cannot overcome performative contradiction. The perspective from which the truth of the sacred may be discerned, then, is not that of the pious, but that of the excluded outsider.

35 Eliade, *The Myth of Eternal Return*, p. 95.

36 Julian Baldick, *Black God: the Afroasiatic Roots of the Jewish, Christian and Muslim Religions*, London: I. B. Tauris, 1997, p. 4.

37 Eliade, *The Myth of Eternal Return*, p. 54.

38 Eliade, *ibid.*, pp. 97, 100.

39 Émile Benveniste has argued that the earliest meaning of *credo* was both religious and economic: an 'act of confidence implying restitution' and 'to pledge something on faith in the certainty that it will be returned'. Benveniste is cited by Julia Kristeva, *In the Beginning was Love: Psychoanalysis and Faith*, New York: Columbia University Press, 1987, p. 30.

40 Job is precisely such a man: he is emphatic about the honour, esteem and grati-
    tude with which he had been regarded by young and old, princes and poor,
    needy and strangers, and alludes to the benefits which he derived from that. See
    Job 29:7–20.
41 It is mere romanticism to regard interdependence and trust as primordial to the
    exclusion of conflict, as Murray Bookchin does, for the possibility of separa-
    tion, isolation and encounter apart from interdependence was always present.
    See Bookchin, *The Social Ecology of Freedom*, Palo Alto: Cheshire Books,
    1982.
42 See, for example, Psalm 112, especially verses 5 and 9: 'It is well with those
    who deal generously and lend, who conduct their affairs with justice … . They
    have distributed freely, they have given to the poor; their righteousness endures
    for ever; *their horn is exalted in honor.*'
43 Job 20:5–7.
44 See Amos 2:6–7.
45 See Amos 5:21–4.
46 Deuteronomy 13:12–17.
47 Søren Kierkegaard, *The Sickness unto Death*, Harmondsworth: Penguin, 1989,
    p. 43.
48 See, for example Kierkegaard, *Stages on Life's Way*, Princeton: Princeton
    University Press, 1988, p. 162.
49 Kierkegaard, *ibid.*, pp. 351, 444–5.
50 Kierkegaard, *The Concept of Anxiety*, Princeton: Princeton University Press,
    1980, p. 155.
51 This is, of course, not to follow their definitions. Otto's idea of the numinous
    as *mysterium tremendum et fascinans* is an attempt to identify a core of reli-
    gion that can be universally repeated, as well as assimilating this to a concrete
    historical experience: it subordinates ecstatic piety to the former two kinds. See
    Otto, *The Idea of the Holy*; Gerardus van der Leeuw, *Religion in Essence and
    Manifestation*, London: George Allen & Unwin, 1938.

8   Experience

Universal psychosis

At the turn of the third millennium, the threat of global ecological catastrophe seems probable. At the same time, a mere two decades has seen the acceleration of a process of globalization where the freedom of governments, corporations, communities and individuals for self-determination is set within shrinking constraints generated by a global liberation of finance capital. Responding to the cataclysmic collision between such universal limits of experience and such organizing powers of universal relevance constitutes the contemporary demand laid on religion, morality and truth.

At the same time, the murder of God initiates a universal psychosis. Lacking awareness of the occupants of the structural roles of God, the subject and the world, there is no longer a universal religion, morality or truth – as we approach the universal, there is no viable consensus reality, consensus on value, or consensus on religion. With hindsight, from within the current state of fragmentation, any claim to an idea of universal significance appears to be a ruse of a particular tradition in its attempt to dominate others: the one who has the power to determine the conditions of a public and universal representation of reality, shapes that reality itself. Yet universal reality is shaped outside of representation.

Today we are immersed in a sea of inadequate ideas, not because such ideas do not correspond to local experience, but because all experience is enmeshed in networks of interdependence where unseen consequences are experienced elsewhere. Experiential and experimental verification, correspondence and coherence are no longer sufficient to establish truth, because the truth about our hypotheses is staged beyond the confines of the laboratory. Each hypothesis bears with it a secret surplus, concealing networks of interdependence through the past, across the present and into the future. A consumer's knowledge and experience of eating chocolate does not encompass the experience of a slave who tended the cocoa plantation from which it derives. The laws and practice of the internal combustion engine do not encompass the experience of those whose lives will be devastated by floods caused by climate change. Even our claims for truth, that it has an absolute or even merely a local significance, reproduce the strategy of fragmentation that is liable to cause a global disaster through ignorance of interdependence. We live in narrow states of consciousness, isolated from universal reality.

The experience which speaks the truth about our delusions is already available. It is experience at the end of networks of interdependence. It is an experience of which it is all too easy to hear and know nothing. It is an experience which rarely brings ecological recompense: shattered human lives and bodies do not contribute significantly to global pollution. No memory calls them to mind. In order to overcome the distance that stretches out networks of interdependence, some mediation of information is required. The media may draw attention to the consequences at the far end of networks of trade and finance; it may draw attention to the consequences of current uses of technology. The media is limited in the context of a market, however, in that it has to attract attention to itself in order to fulfil its role of communication. Attention is attracted by giving recognition to the needs, desires and impulses of the consumers of the media. Cases are reported if they are liable to attract interest – that is to say, media reports become a stage dramatizing collective fantasy. Once the external world has become a figure of desire, consumers are enclosed within a narcissistic circle where access to the real world is denied. There is a sleight of hand in this process, whereby the desires of the recipients are concealed. After all, recipients do indeed pay attention to others through the media. Networks of interdependence need not be revealed: instead, others are selected as figures to dramatize consumers' desires and fears. Under the guise of information, consumers are fed a diet of self-gratification and self-justification. The only indicators of any deception are sales and viewing figures themselves – the amount of attention given to the media, in comparison to those who immediately surround each other, is immense. Moreover, by this sleight of hand, the media launders the consciences of its recipients: they have exercised their responsibility, they are in touch with what is going on in the world, they fulfil their duties as citizens by taking an interest in the common good – even if they have done nothing.

When the common good degenerates into a mass of isolated individuals in narcissistic titillation of their similar individual interests and desires, then social cohesion becomes tenuous. Such is the basis of 'consensus reality'. This supposed bulwark against universal psychosis is simply the consensus of the majority in prioritizing its own interests and desires above any interests of minorities. For in so far as consensus involves the distribution of viewpoints available for exchange, knowledge is treated as a market. Just as in the market, where liberty and right are only given in practice to the wealthy who have the power to determine prices in relation to their own interests, so it is in the market where what counts as 'reality' is traded, where those who can combine to create a greater buying power, a consensus, are simply the majority acting in their own short-term interests.[1]

Hence the discussion of issues of religion, morality and truth, in so far as they demand commitment, judgement, or condemnation, must keep to the safe and neutral territory of describing or condemning minorities. Thus God disappears from public life. Similarly, in so far as individuals do not wish to infringe the liberties of others by speaking of commitment or judgement, God disappears from private conversation. In a free-market society, God can only be reborn as the ideological representation of the interests of a consensus, collectivity or community.

If God has been murdered, this does not mean the end of religion. Not only is there a resurgence of collective needs for social cohesion, but there also remain global and universal absolutes which in practice mediate our relations to ourselves: money, information, time and death. Even if we do not believe in these gods, we must still pray to them, for it is in our best interests. We remain pious. People form their daily liturgical practice around the demands of the market. People fear death. People believe in the ideological opinions which serve their own interests, or the interests of those who dominate them. People affirm ideals of truth, liberty and right, reproducing ancient pieties enshrined within these concepts. Religion becomes resurgent and ubiquitous.

The terror of universal psychosis is not the absence of God. On the contrary, there is too much God: the unconditioned may be located anywhere in experience. The crisis of modernity is neither nihilism, nor atheism, but religious delusion: starting from a condition of fragmentation, people construct and locate their absolutes in the most diverse of places. Through the mechanism of 'ideas of reference', anyone may construct their own partial clarities and immediate certainties. A useful example is given by Daniel Paul Schreber, in his *Memoirs of My Nervous Illness*: 'in daytime I thought I could notice the sun following my movements; when I moved to and fro in the single-windowed room I inhabited at the time, I saw the sunlight now on the right, now on the left wall (as seen from the door) depending on my movements ...'[2] One may decompose this narrative into four kinds of signs generated by four ways of composing experience. First, by associating different perceptions of light, Schreber generated the idea of the sun as the common light source. Second, by selecting his own movements to be associated with those of the light, Schreber generated the idea of a correlation between the movements of himself and the sun. Third, by fixing this correlation as a constant, Schreber generated an idea of purpose: the correlation, an effect of the play of light, is taken as a cause, so that the sun intends to follow his movements. Finally, by combining this fixed purpose with other delusions of reference, Schreber confirmed his own metaphysical status as the 'greatest seer of spirits of all millennia'.[3] One does not need to suffer delusions of grandeur, or to focus on oneself, to follow an analogous process: any fixing of attention on a point that resolves a series of signs may become a local absolute.

A new enlightenment, a new critique of religion, is required to liberate thought from captivation to its own hallucinations. Since the former Enlightenment is implicated in the piety which it condemns, its methods will not be sufficient here.

Kant's critical philosophy

Immanuel Kant attempted to liberate thought from the superstitions of 'spirit-seers' and metaphysicians in one and the same gesture – intimations of a universal psychosis were visible as early as 1766. In discussing the 'arch spirit-seer of all spirit-seers',[4] Emmanuel Swedenborg, he attempted to restore access to truth via consensual reality, for 'if different people have each of them their own world, then we may suppose that they are dreaming'.[5] Kant invented an imaginative explanation for madness: real perceptions may be distinguished from imaginary ones in that, although both involve some kind of brain activity, such activity results from a focus outside the brain in the case of real perception, and produces a focus inside the brain in the case of imaginary ones. If, by means of some disturbance, the focus of the imagination should be located outside the brain, then it would become indistinguishable from a real perception.[6] The only way to test the reality of perceptions, then, is by common consensus. Kant's illustration is revealing:

> Scales, intended by civil law to be a standard of measure in trade, may be shown to be inaccurate if the wares and weights are made to change pans. The bias of the scales of understanding is revealed by exactly the same stratagem, and in philosophical judgements, too, it would not be possible, unless one adopted this stratagem, to arrive at a unanimous result by composing the different weighings ... . I formerly used to regard the human understanding in general merely from the point of view of my own understanding. Now I put myself in the position of someone else's reason, which is independent of myself and external to me, and regard my judgements, along with their most secret causes, from the point of view of other people.[7]

Here, the truth of philosophy, now situated in the market-place as an exchange between strangers, can only be tested in relation to a general equivalent. Distinctive individual perceptions are disregarded. This text also contains the origins of Kant's Copernican revolution,[8] for his true target in this text is not the visionary – Kant does not even bother to refute or even properly investigate Swedenborg – but the metaphysician who sees something which no other normal person sees: 'there is a certain affinity between the dreamers of reason and the dreamers of sense.'[9]

For the mistake of the metaphysicians, like those of the spirit-seers and religious psychotics, is to attempt to locate the unconditioned in objective reality:

> For what necessarily forces us to transcend the limits of experience and of all appearances is the *unconditioned*, which reason, by necessity and by right, demands in things in themselves, as required to complete the series of conditions. If, then, on supposition that our empirical knowledge conforms to objects as things in themselves, we find that the unconditioned *cannot be thought without contradiction*, and that when, on the other hand, we suppose that our representation of things, as they are given to us, does not conform to these things as they are in themselves, but that these objects, as appearances, conform to our mode of representation, *the contradiction vanishes.*[10]

Kant's solution, then, is to find the unconditioned in the regulative ideals of reason, the transcendental ideas. This is Kant's reasoning in favour of a transcendental philosophy. Metaphysics, because it posits entities beyond the limits of consensual experience, makes not a transcendental but a *transcendent* use of principles which takes away these limits, 'or even incites us to tear down all those boundary-fences and to seize possession of an entirely new domain which recognizes no limits of demarcation.'[11] Metaphysics creates its own dream world when its focus on the unconditioned is located outside the mind in objective reality.

Kant did recognize, however, that the demand to pass the limits of experience so as to attain the unconditioned is a demand of reason: '*if the conditioned is given, the entire sum of conditions, and consequently the absolutely unconditioned (through which alone the conditioned has been possible) is also given.*'[12] Kant envisaged two ways in which such a movement beyond the limits of possible experience could be achieved: either every condition in a series is itself conditioned, but the series itself is unconditioned as an infinite series; or else there is a first condition in the series.[13] The unconditioned is synthesized as the Whole or the One, importing an organization into the series of conditions. Even if God is not encountered in experience, even if one can infer nothing about an object corresponding to the idea of God, the idea of God returns here as the primordial being, the highest being, and the being of all beings.[14]

God becomes a transcendental, regulative idea of reason; that is to say, reason regulates itself through its own piety. It is such piety which no longer seems necessary after the murder of God: one does not need to run through the whole series of conditions in order to determine a price. In spite of the best efforts of economists to determine the laws of the market, no such rational unity is in fact necessary. Prices are formed as local absolutes, which, once constructed, have all the appearance of necessity. Kant's critique of the ontological argument for the existence of God, that existence is not a predicate – 'my financial position is, however, affected very differently by a hundred real thalers than it is by the mere concept of them'[15] – no longer holds when banks and brokers can create money by mere postulation. Under certain conditions, existence can become a predicate.

Treating the unconditioned as a regulative ideal may avoid the contradiction of treating it as a metaphysical object, but leads to a further contradiction: the unconditioned, unknowable in itself, remains conditioned by the piety of reason, the very practice it is intended to constitute. For whether the unconditioned is conditioned by objects or by thought, it is still subject to conditioning.

Scotus and pure ontology

If, then, on supposition that our empirical knowledge conforms to our mode of representation, we find that the unconditioned still cannot be thought without contradiction, then we may, on the other hand, suppose that the plane of thought is not conformed to our representations, but constitutes an autonomous environment itself. There is an alternative to Kant's dilemma which derives from John Duns Scotus:[16] instead of finding the unconditioned on the side of the object or the subject, to locate it in a transcendental field, a metaphysical plane of being *qua* being. Scotus faced the same dilemma as Kant, located in theology rather than philosophy. For if the unconditioned, which unites a series of conditions, can be understood by the human intellect – and for Scotus the unconditioned is God – then God is subject to human understanding, and must act according to the dictates of reason. In short, the unconditioned is itself conditioned by the series that it is invoked to organize. The temporal series of conditions seems to produce the effect of the eternal God, in one and the same movement as the eternal God produces the temporal series of conditions. God becomes controlled by metaphysics.

In response, to safeguard the power of God, Scotus posited a purely univocal thought and being common to God and creatures. Being, said only in a single sense, does not distinguish between 'the knowledge of *whether a thing is* and *what it is*', for Scotus was concerned with *objectivum esse*, the objective structure of being, formally distinguished from knowledge of existences and essences.[17] The emancipation achieved for God by this move, that God's existence is no longer subordinate to God's essence, no longer subject to a series of conditions, is then also achieved for creatures as a fortunate by-product.[18] If God is no longer the condition of, yet conditioned by, a transcendent plane of organisation, then neither are creatures conditioned by it.

This move would seem to leave only an arbitrary relation between God and creatures, one which is only mediated by the liberty of the divine will.

Scotus did return to the series of conditions, however, in his argument for the existence of God: at first sight, Scotus appears to follow the Thomist strategy, for he claimed that one can prove the existence of the primacy of a first efficient cause, a final end, and a supreme eminence, on the grounds that an ascending infinite regression is impossible.[19] Subsequently, however, he argues that this primary cause, end and eminence is infinite.[20] This apparent contradiction between refusing infinite regression while positing the infinite is resolved by the way in which Scotus constructed the concept of the infinite:

> The more perfect and simple concept possible for us is the concept of unqualifiedly infinite being. This is simpler than the concept of good being or true being or others similar to these, since infinity is not, as it were, an attribute of being or of that of which it is said, but predicates an intrinsic mode of that being; so that when I say 'infinite being,' I do not have, as it were, an accidental concept from a subject and an attribute, but rather, a concept of the subject itself in a certain grade of perfection, namely infinity – just as 'intense white' does not predicate an accidental concept such as 'visible white.' Rather, intensity predicates an intrinsic degree of whiteness in itself.[21]

Scotus did not arrive at eminence via analogy here, even if an analogy is invoked. The infinite is constructed by removing all transcendent or comparative determinations or limitations. God is not the first in a series of discrete conditions, the origin or sum of a series; instead, God is the unlimited intensity of being itself. God is the eminent existence; the result appears similar to Thomas' *analogia entis*, but the logic is closer to Spinoza: God is an immanent cause.

In Scotus, then, there is no separation between the unconditioned and the series of conditions – thus the Kantian problem is overcome. Instead of the series being one of discrete conditions in infinite regress, each condition is an intensification of what it conditions: it is an immanent cause, to be discovered by immanent critique. This indicates an alternative to a psychotic world of inadequate ideas, in which ideas are confused with their objects or ideatum, as well as to critical theory, in which ideas are explained by their objective unconscious conditioning. The alternative is as follows: to comprehend an idea in relation to its immanent cause, without reference to its object or *ideatum*, as well as without reference to its historical preconditions in a series. An idea is then simply a mode of thinking, a modification of truth, and its truth may be discerned by the way that it modifies the plane of thought. It would seem, here, that thought is detached entirely from objective reality, in the most psychotic of conditions. Nevertheless, since every real thought actually exists, it is merely sufficient to extract its immanent cause as the truth of its existence, the prior identity of thinking and being.

This is the method pioneered by Spinoza. Now Spinoza defined an adequate idea as, 'an idea which, if considered in itself without relation to the object, has all the properties or intrinsic denominations of a true idea.'[22] Furthermore, someone who has a true idea, knows at the same time that he or she has a true idea, and is not able to doubt it.[23] Such certainty is rarely to be found in modern reason. Even in mathematical proofs, one may be convinced of the truth of a theorem by following the proof itself, but one cannot be entirely sure that one has not made an error in the derivation of the proof, unless such a proof is also confirmed and accepted by others. In practice, such certainty as described by Spinoza is only to be found in religion and psychosis, where it is attached to the most unexpected, diverse and contradictory ideas.

Spinoza pointed to the criterion of truth: 'All ideas, in so far as they have reference to the idea of God, are true.'[24] For the idea of God is substance: 'that which is in itself and conceived in itself.' There is an identity of thinking and being.[25] This identity is the goal of the enquiry, its primary cause, end and eminence, yet it is by no means attained. A true idea must be thought through its cause in order to generate certainty. Now, it is possible to have a true idea, without having any idea of this idea; that is to say, to have an idea, but without knowing how to generate it. Error arises from assimilating such an idea to imagination, attaching the certainty which comes with it to an image of that of which it is an idea. Every idea is therefore obscure until it is comprehended through its immanent cause. The critical problem, then, is that of distinguishing between an idea and an image, a mode of thinking and a thought. It is a question of determining that which gives or provokes thinking within a thought, that which is most thought-provoking. It is a question of determining that which inspires interest or wonder. The essence of an idea, then, is the power which it implicates, but which remains too great for it. The essence of an idea is its interest, its way of implicating, or thinking about that which remains unthinkable.

Spinoza, in his idea of God or concept of substance, gives us a formal criterion of truth; yet he does not give us an adequate idea. For, as we have seen, Spinoza's substance is set out as an eternal cause, conditioning all existence through necessity, while temporal fluctuations themselves remain unexplained. In order to develop Spinozism, then, truth must be encountered in experience, and built constructively from experience. One must begin with a 'true idea', but the truths of geometry utilized by Spinoza are no longer sufficient, for they do not contain the practice of sovereignty which they carry with them as a germ of a social order preserved in thought. Geometry is dependent for its meaning on both its *ideatum*, a plane of represented space which it signifies, as well as the conditions of the thinker. Furthermore, we should also give some credence to Schelling's critique of Spinoza, that Spinoza in practice leaves the subject, contingency and freedom out of his understanding of substance. This is not the case with Scotus, whose concept of God as the infinite intensity of being allows subjectivity for both God and creatures. Finally, we may note that Spinoza's concept of substance is ultimately to be conceived as the power of a mode – where each mode is a power of existing or a degree of intensity of being. To comprehend intensity as a quantity, here, is to assimilate thought to number and geometry once more. Then the fundamental problem to explore is the meaning of 'intensity', the way in which a mode implicates the thought that generates it.

Singularity and disjunction

Inadequate ideas are those which are unconscious of themselves – which do not have an idea of their own idea – which do not extend through the networks of interdependence in which they are conditioned. Inadequate ideas are propagated as signs which are unable to preserve their immanent cause; once such signs circulate in networks of exchange and substitution, then access to the immanent cause is lost. For the interests of distributors and consumers determine the circulation and exchange of ideas, not the immanent interests of the ideas themselves. Since the idea in circulation does not signify the interest that determines it, it has no access to its own immanent cause. All ideas formed by processes of substitution are therefore inadequate.

True ideas are necessarily singular – they remain embedded within their conditions, not subject to substitution. A paradigm of a singularity, as a limit to experience, is death. As Derrida has said:

> If death ... names the very irreplaceability of absolute singularity (no one can die in my place or in the place of the other), then all the *examples* in the world can precisely illustrate this singularity. Everyone's death, the death of all those who can say 'my death', is irreplaceable. So is 'my life'. Every other is completely other.[26]

In this respect, one always carries around 'within' one, contemporary with one, the singular experience of one's own death. Now, of course, one knows neither the meaning nor the referent of the word 'death';[27] death is insufficiently determined. Indeed, the concept of 'death' is formed from an attempt to generalize what is singular: everyone will die, yet no one knows what dying means. 'Death' itself is an inadequate idea; nevertheless, it is a symptom indicating the presence of a singularity. Although death itself cannot be regarded as an immanent cause, singularity does exist in the form of irreversible time. Recent developments in physics draw attention to the minimal exigencies which differentiate our world from a reversible circulation in space, time energy and information: these are the existence of irreversible time, of events which determine which of possible divergent paths are followed, and the coherence of the behaviour which results.[28]

For example, a process which tends towards an equilibrium state, whatever its initial conditions, cannot be reversed by imagining time to run backwards – it will simply remain in its equilibrium state, the information regarding its initial conditions having been annihilated. Alternatively, a process which is determined by equations of motion having multiple solutions requires the creation of information in its actual selection of a solution. Irreversibility, the creation or annihilation of information, is constituted as a relation of time to itself. It is enabled by the disjunction and inequality between time that passes and time that is measured. Disjunction is thus the condition for singularity and irreversibility. One is constituted as singular, as a concrete historical life, not by death, but by disjunction: even if one is like all the others, one is an exception, is singular, to the extent that one's existence is produced by disjunction.

Birth, therefore, provides a better image than death for the existence of singularity.[29] All life is embryogenesis, becoming, coming-into-being. Yet instead of each coming-into-being emerging from nothingness, it emerges from maternity through parturition. Instead of positing the primordiality of alterity, alterity is constructed through parturition, divergence. The key feature here is that there is an asymmetry between mother and child. Each event is a birth, a disjunction, a parturition. There exist events which, insufficiently determined by previous causes, create the character of the world. They choose one among a number of possible divergent lines; they constitute life as a narrative. They transform the range of the possible into the impossible. For it is not simply the new line that is added to the world. A new birth changes everything, especially the mother; it creates a new web of dependency at the same time as it closes off countless opportunities and possibilities. One cannot reverse the lines of divergence, so as to discover an 'original unity'; genealogical inquiry produces distortion. For divergence is precisely the introduction of history, of irreversibility; to attempt to reverse the process is to introduce a new divergence.

Birth, considered as change in the passage of irreversible time, is not reducible to chains of conditions, or to the action of pure spontaneity. It is neither conditioned entirely from without, nor unconditioned. Since it is unpredictable, it can only be encountered in experience. Yet birth sets limits to experience: in each event of coming-into-being, most of the possibilities inherent in the preconditions are left unrealized; in addition, the one who is born gains a relative degree of independence from the mother, so that there is a break in the chain of automatic conditioning – the conditions of the mother's life no longer entirely determine the conditions of the child's life; furthermore, the experience of mother and child as separate is enabled by their mutual attention to each other. Singularity is encountered in neither eternity nor time, in neither cause nor effect, in neither necessity nor spontaneity, in neither mother nor child, in neither the passage nor the measuring of time, but in the disjunction between the two. This disjunction may be called 'experience'.

The concept of experience, so frequently invoked as the basis of knowledge, may provide the basis of a new epistemology when understood in this precise sense. For we are unconscious of reality. The experience of our truth is staged outside of consciousness, outside the subject, elsewhere. We do not have possession of our being. To know oneself, therefore, is to know the experience of others. It is to trace one's networks of interdependence into the past, through the present and into the future. There are insuperable obstacles to progress in such an enterprise. This does not make it any less necessary. While a complete picture is impossible, a partial picture is sufficient to give a vague impression of the kind of beings we are. This vague impression may be sufficiently shocking to induce an affect; it is such an affect that brings with it a partial knowledge, freed from some of the snares of self-deception.

There is a further dimension to experience: we experience that to which we pay attention. To pay attention is to attribute value and significance. Attention can only be spent; it cannot be hoarded or saved. We define ourselves by the attention we distribute, in addition to being defined by the experiences which make us possible. To have to allocate attention is a difficult responsibility to bear. It is much easier to have one's attention attracted, or to be distracted. For attention is rarely given freely; it is subject to all manner of impulses. Experiences are normally given to us or imposed upon us; it is rare to have the liberty to choose one's own experience by paying attention.

The work of the philosopher, as described by Bergson, consists in the disciplining of attention.[30] Liberty consists in directing one's attention through discipline, rather than having one's attention captured. Experience can only be controlled through the disciplining of attention. When the experience of others is too distant to attract our attention, attention may be directed towards that experience. For the philosopher, attention is directed towards the conditions of experience. In so far as experience is shaped by the allocation of attention, then it is the mechanisms of attracting, distracting and disciplining attention that form the conditions of possible experience.

We shall call 'piety' any determinate practice of directing attention. A mode of experience, then, is defined in two separate ways: by the experiences and networks of interdependence which make it happen; and by the piety through which it is shaped. Change in one's mode of experience is made possible by having one's attention attracted by a conditioning experience, or by directing one's attention to experiences that will change it. Liberty, then, is only attained through piety.

There is also a third determination of one's mode of experience. For although the suffering of others that constitutes one's mode of experience may be inaccessible, especially if it lies in the past without record, or if it lies in the future, there are analogous voices which whisper in the ears of current experience. For when thought directs attention to the categories of objects or conditions which substitute for experience, the categories of essence and existence, then experience itself becomes inaccessible: as Bergson remarks, where metaphysics lies dead in theses, it is living in philosophers.[31] This is not without some cost. For essence is founded on the substitution for experience, and existence is founded on the sacrifice of experience. For the power by which the categories of objects and conditions gain their validity or currency is the life of experience itself. Thought, formed by categories of objects or conditions, cuts itself off from its own power; it remains haunted by a nostalgic desire to recover lost experience. For experience is not found in the concepts of experience, but in experience itself. This is the source of the antinomies of pure reason, and of countless debates in philosophy: if concepts are born from the sacrifice of experience, it is easy for an opponent to point out the absence of the referent in the concept.

Experience itself is made possible by the experience of others. To know oneself, therefore, is to know the experience of others. Experience may be initially identified by the symptom of the pain felt by a living thought on being sacrificed to a symbolic representation. For where representation directs attention away from experience, experience imposes itself on attention by means of the suffering which is undergone. All experience tends to impose itself on attention according to its degree of intensity or power. If such attention is denied, then the tendency remains as a condition of subsequent experience.

The power by which suffering imposes itself on attention is the *unconditioned within experience*. Suffering attracts attention. Moreover, suffering is always singular – no one can undergo my suffering for me, on my behalf. Thus there are no possible substitutions or sacrifices which can retain the power of attracting attention in suffering. No experience can substitute for it. Then this power itself is not conditioned by any other experience, for the relation of conditioning involves shifting attention from a result to a condition. To shift attention in this direction is contrary to the power which directs attention to itself.

The matter of suffering

It has been said that Plotinus gave the only complete definition of philosophy. To the question, 'What is philosophy?' he replied 'what matters most'.[32]

What matters most? What is infinite being? These questions are, or can be, identical. If being, reality, is that which matters, what matters most is its highest degree, the criterion of truth. Materialism may point us in unexpected directions to find the substance of reality. Adorno once remarked that the 'need to lend a voice to suffering is a condition of all truth.'[33] Sloterdijk comments:

I believe that Critical Theory has found a provisional ego for critique and a 'standpoint' that provides it with perspectives for a truly incisive critique – a standpoint that conventional epistemology does not consider. I am inclined to call it *a priori pain* ... . What we perceive of the world can be ordered in psychosomatic coordinates of pain and pleasure. Critique is possible inasmuch as pain tells us what is 'true' and what is 'false'.[34]

From the perspective of 'nature and history', pain is of little account: nature is prodigal in its production of suffering; history still more so. Only life protests against pain, and such a protest may become a basis for thought. In human thought, however, we are accustomed to assimilate thought on suffering to nature or history. In answer to the question, 'Why is there so much pain and misery in life', reason explains why suffering is in the nature of things, is part of the eternal order of the universe – suffering is naturalized. In short, one engages in theodicy or cosmodicy, explaining suffering by justifying the present order of existence. The moral weakness of this rationalization is that if suffering is made to appear natural, then it is excused, without heeding the demand to examine the specific causes of suffering in each case and whether they include artificial and preventable constructions, such as those of relations of class, race and gender. In short, such a defence of suffering becomes ideological, repairing the fabric of a meaningful world without attending to the fabric of the real world. Only the meaning of suffering counts; suffering itself may be ignored.

By contrast, if thought is assimilated to history, then the historical, social and cultural causes of suffering may be investigated, and definite action proposed to cut suffering off at the root. The point is not to interpret the world, but to change it. A future, liberated from present constraints, may be substituted for the present one. Yet without taking away from the importance of action, one may wonder whether this approach is sufficient to address what is experienced in suffering, rather than its proximate causes, quantity, degree and occasion.

For the apocalypse has already happened. A slave has been beaten to death. A child has died of diarrhoea. A lover has vanished without trace. A woman has been murdered by her husband. A child has been suffocated, sexually abused, and resuscitated by her own father. A people has been subjected to genocide. A city has suffered intensive fire bombing. A country has been destroyed by a hurricane. A region has been reduced to mud following a flood. An ocean has been depleted and poisoned. Let us not count occasions and figures, though the occasions are too numerous and the figures too immense to count. Each event, in its own significance, outweighs the counting of numbers. Unless one counts total destruction as qualitatively different, there is no evil which could happen on Earth which has not already happened. One may hope to diminish some of the tragedies of the future, but all action comes essentially too late. One may hope to judge such tragedies from the perspectives of God, morality or truth, but any such God, morality and truth profits from the existence of suffering, in relation to which it finds a role.

Both such responses are insufficient to address an apocalyptic degree of suffering. Suffering is that which is *unconditioned within experience.* Suffering exceeds in importance any meaning or any future which can be substituted for it. It is not that suffering lacks meaning or temporal duration. Suffering has an excess of meaning and significance which cannot be captured by substitution or superposition. Suffering is always singular; it marks itself out as a singular event. Suffering matters. It is the matter, and the revelation of mattering. Suffering is substance. Instead of positing the universal and the necessary as marks of the a priori, as Kant does, subordinating experience to the Whole or the One, suffering and singularity are marks of the transcendental – they are the unconditioned source of thought which actually provoke thinking.

Suffering is a sign which does not signify. There is nothing of sufficient importance which could substitute for it. Whatever is attempted by psychoanalysis, suffering cannot be encompassed within interpretative fields based on temporality or eternity, liberty or necessity, history or ritual. Suffering is apocalyptic. Yet suffering bears within it a power to generate thought and action, an urgency which is a demand of life. To treat suffering as mattering, as the unconditioned within experience, is to adopt a relation to the unconditioned: it is a mode of piety. In so far as suffering is irreducible to meaning or history, then such piety does not fall within the spheres of knowledge and ethics. Piety, unable to grasp the significance of its object, is exposed to the infinite, to an excess – not an unlimited series, but an infinite intensity of being.

There is a mode of piety which consists in paying attention to suffering.[35] Just as suffering has a power of imposing itself upon attention, attention has a power of meeting and 'fulfilling' – an inadequate word – suffering. Such 'fulfilment' does not give suffering a purpose; it does not remove suffering. It merely satisfies the demand for attention. For suffering expresses its import; this import is recognized when it is given due attention. Moreover, this is an entirely separate power – for suffering which imposes itself upon attention does not by this means attract recognition. Suffering can only be fulfilled when its demand is met from outside, as a gift. The two powers are not in competition, but in agreement, or conversation. This power of fulfilling suffering is the *unconditioned within attention.* While attention may be directed or distracted, while it may be disciplined by piety, its power of fulfilling suffering cannot be conditioned. For the power of distributing attention is singular; only attention distributed is subject to exchange and transfer. Thus each mode of experience is characterized by two powers: a power of imposing upon attention, and a power of distributing attention.

Once suffering receives sufficient attention, then its mode of experience is transformed. Although it remains otherwise unchanged, its power of imposing itself upon attention ceases. Suffering can then be left in the past – it becomes an event in a series which constitutes what we are. It becomes a part in the fabric of existence, without continuing to express itself as pain. There is no need to redeem the past. One can even come to love the past, to love one's pain, if at the same time one forgives one's pain. This is not possible within a philosophy of essence, whereby that which is evil in essence will remain so for all time, and so will not be forgivable. Neither is it possible within a philosophy of existence, which aims at negating the evil of the past. For to love and forgive a past experience of suffering does not imply that one affirms it in essence, that one wishes that it will recur, or that one would not try to end it if it were to happen again. For none of these responses is sufficient to face the demand of suffering, its demand for attention. Only when sufficient attention has been given, and suffering no longer imposes itself upon attention, can its demand be neutralized so as to form a part of the varied character of experience. Our bodies and lives are composed of our scars.

Politics

Potencies are manifested as the unconditioned within experience. The demand of suffering for attention and the power of attention to resolve suffering are always expressed in singularities. There is no temporal dialectic, no eternal meaning, which may relate such singularities to each other. Such relations between singular potencies are constructed within experience: they are political relations. A philosophy of experience proceeds through constructing a politics of thought; logical relations are replaced with political relations.

Spinoza found a theological argument for natural right. Since the existence of natural things is independent of their essence, then the power of existing and continuing to exist does not derive from the essence of things themselves; neither can it derive from another natural thing, for this in turn would require a power of existing independent of it. Thus 'the power whereby natural things exist and operate is the very power of God itself', and 'every natural thing has by nature as much right, as it has power to exist and operate.'[36] Natural right derives directly from the liberty of God. Spinoza proceeded directly to the idea of God as an immanent cause, without considering a chain of conditions.

This argument can be adapted for potencies. On a plane of pure experience, the power of suffering to impose itself upon attention is unconditioned within experience – while an experience itself is always conditioned, its intensity is not. As unconditioned, this power is a natural right. Nevertheless, suffering has a demand which exceeds its power, for attention is rarely adequate to the demands of suffering. Suffering does not abate simply through having imposed itself on attention; it has a second power, a power of recurrence, whereby it continues to impose itself until it has been granted sufficient attention. This second power of suffering, its demand, is the correlate of the capacity to give attention. There is an asymmetry here: suffering demands attention throughout the networks of interdependence which forms its condition, yet it does not have sufficient power to impose itself throughout the network. The power of suffering needs augmenting by attention. Even if experience does not have sufficient power to impose itself upon all the networks, it has a stake in such networks, a demand for recognition, equal to its own intensity of suffering, its immediate degree of power. One may therefore distinguish natural right as the power of experience to impose itself, its degree of intensity – whether of suffering or of joy, and a more fundamental natural right which is the demand that experience should receive attention throughout its network of interdependence. The latter is impossible to achieve. The attention demanded is in proportion not only to degree of intensity, but also in proportion to the degree to which a mode conditions or is conditioned by the experience. Fundamental natural right varies according to the relation in question; it is in proportion to responsibility.

Civil right derives from the power of attention to fulfil the demand of suffering. For this power of attention is a stock of value to be distributed. It is a stock that must necessarily be distributed; it cannot be saved or hoarded. Although natural right is coextensive with nature, being the power of existents to impinge upon each other, civil right is restricted to those beings which have the power to fulfil suffering by directing attention. It is found to some degree in the higher animals, and more extensively in humanity. There is no social contract, no origin of the civil state, for the power of distributing attention is unconditioned within experience. The power of giving attention cannot therefore be regarded as a property of humanity, or as the product of historical evolution. If, in physical nature, there is little evidence of an asymmetry between time that passes and time that is measured, as though time were reducible to number, this does not mean that such an asymmetry is not an ontological constituent of the universe. If historical evolution enables access to higher intensities of attention, it does not for all that create such attention. It is the same with piety: if disciplinary practices of attention enable access to enhanced powers of attention, they do not for all that create such powers.

The distinction between nature and culture, between natural right and civil right, is thus not contractual but ontological. To confuse the two is to confuse two fundamental potencies or singularities: the power to impose on attention, and the power to give attention. To interpret civil right through the categories of necessity is to deny the possibility of the gift, to reduce spirituality to economy. For example, joy, although as important as suffering, differs from suffering in that it does not impose itself upon attention. Joy does not have a natural right. All joy is excessive, a bonus or gift.

For the essence of joy is that it is surprising; it is not subject to management and manipulation. Joy is always a singularity belonging to civil right.

Nevertheless, there are illusions internal to attention by which civil right can become confused with natural right. One should distinguish between civil right, the power to distribute attention, and civil honour, the expectation of attention. The difference between power and expectation may become expressed in the fundamental class difference between householders and speculators, for speculators, who trade in the medium of expectation, benefit from the accrual of civil honour, the accumulation of expectation. Civil honour may be expressed in a sign or token, which, once expressed, may substitute for the experience of attention. This substitution is convenient, since it saves expenditure of attention while pledging to make it available when required. Signs are objectifications of one's power of attention; such alienated attention, however, only has as much power to command attention as the degree of intensity invested within it. Every time one is asked to act on a pledge, the claim of the pledge must be weighed against other claims and impositions.

Pledges are not easily redeemed. On the one hand, the pledge is a recognition of a certain claim of experience for attention; once the attention is granted, then the claim is fulfilled and the pledge redeemed. On the other hand, every gift of attention is a pledge, for it is preserved in memory as a sign, an expectation of a future gift. Expectation of attention, on the basis of pledges, is a force promoting cohesion. Expectations, however, are not rights – they may often be disappointed, and rightly so. For the intensity of expectation is by no means identical to the claim of experience for attention, or identical to the power of attention to match expectations. Expectation, therefore, differs in relation to natural and civil right.

To treat a pledge as a right – and to use it as a basis for a claim – is to interpret culture through the categories of nature. It is to treat time as an abstract medium in which no further experience takes place, as though conditions will be unchanged when one comes to redeem a pledge. The liberty of the civil state becomes constrained by the necessity of the natural order. Law is a conventional system of constraint, simulating the necessity of the natural order, which treats public pledges, expectations and honours as rights, on the basis of which claims can be made. In so far as law functions as a basis for trust and social cohesion, it is the indispensable condition for the extension of trade. The sacrifice of fundamental natural rights to the claims of law would seem to be a justifiable expense for the sake of greater cohesion and cooperation.

Property, for example, is a non-reciprocal relation of expectation. I expect that my property will be available, will attend to me, when I so require. In this sense, the essence of appropriation is marking with a sign. It is not necessary, however, for such property to receive a public mark of identification. It is merely sufficient that it is marked in memory and expectation for it to be appropriated. The result of this, however, is that property may be held in common. A conflict of expectations may arise over property held in common. Such conflicts may be adjudicated on the basis of the relative strengths of any claim to property. The initial basis for adjudicating such claims is the degree of expectation, measured by custom and usage.

The adjudication of property claims produces a judgement. This judgement is a further sign, indicating a collective expectation: we may call it a title. Once one is entitled to property, then the title is a stronger degree of expectation because it is collective. In most cases of subsequent adjudication of property, title takes precedence over other claims. Nevertheless, title is not possessed in the way that property is possessed; to appropriate entitlement is to steal. Title remains the property of the collective body adjudicating; thus the collective body retains the right to transfer title and property elsewhere, in line with fundamental natural right.

The adjudication of claims is an exercise of authority. Such authority consists in the expectations of those who recognize the right of authority. Thus authority is granted through the investment of attention in the claims of an authority. Authority is therefore a sign of attention. There is no transfer of sovereign right from an individual to an authority; instead, there is an alienation of the power to grant attention in so far as it is invested in a sign. Authority has a claim to be recognized which depends on its status as a condition of peace. The potential suffering incurred by the removal of an authority constitutes the claim to recognition that an authority has as a condition of peace.

Collective expectation, as invested in authority, is a force of social cohesion. It results in the recognition of titles, and consequent coexistence in peace. Moreover, those who have claims for attention that is not yet given, may turn to the adjudicating authority for redress and entitlement. The adjudicating authority, invested with the power of granting titles, has the responsibility for distributing collective attention. In fact, it is not attention itself that the authority is able to adjudicate, although attention will be given in the process of adjudication, but simply titles as claims to attention, when the occasion requires. Thus a successful plea for adjudication may result in property sufficient to satisfy instincts, but does not in itself satisfy the claim to attention.

Just as it is essential in a civilized society to have an adjudicating body which deals with claims regarding property, it is also essential to have an adjudicating body which handles claims regarding attention. A society which recognizes the claims of property, contract and debt, but does not recognize the claims of need and distress, is fundamentally unjust and immoral. The responsible distribution of attention is particularly difficult in a democracy. For democracy is founded on the assumption that the commonwealth is composed of a collection of individual rational subjects, unities of thought and existence, whose interests may be served by representation, giving due attention. This adaptation of civil right to natural right is only apparent. For in the first place, democracy is the rule of the consensus. If the consensus is formed as the lowest common denominator of collective, conscious interests – those interests that attract attention because they motivate the buying of self-gratification and self-justification – then it may fail to represent the true interests of the majority. Moreover, the weakness of democracy is the disenfranchisement of many of the 'stakeholders', especially those of the past and the future, as well as those who participate in circuits of trade without participating in the benefits of the state because they dwell elsewhere. For a polity is much larger than the citizens it encompasses. A polity also includes the claims of 'land' as that which has no say in the property relation, of children, of past and future members, and of those outside in networks of interdependence through trade and ecology. In an age of the global market and mass media, democracy inevitably degenerates into populism which, intent on short-term interests, has brutally destructive consequences elsewhere, and is incapable of prudent government.

In the second place, democracy cedes its sovereignty to forces from without. Since all democratic relations are mediated through signs, then the self-positing logic of signs may come to take precedence over the wishes of those represented. Such external forces are evident above all in capital investment. A nation can become enslaved in a form of debt bondage: while opening a nation to capital investment may be in the short-term interest of the people, the long-term consequence is that economic policy, and any additional policy which may have an impact on the economy, is ultimately controlled by the needs of capital to maximize return on investment. In a global market, the threat of capital flight resulting in economic meltdown is sufficient to direct national policy on the basis of the needs of capital. Such a political reality is not a democracy, neither is it even an oligarchy of transnational companies, financial speculators and capital investors; it is direct rule by the impersonal forces of the market itself. Capital, as an abstraction from experience, does not express the needs of experience.

In the third place, democracy is subverted by its own logic of representation. For the interests of the representatives, who may be motivated by ambition, financial interest, desire for fame or dogmatic attachment to certain policy objectives, may not correspond with the interests of the people. Moreover, the capacities which lead to political advancement, including appearance, personality, rhetoric, wealth and debating skills, do not correspond to the capacities which contribute to prudent government, including a thorough knowledge of international history, politics, economics, law, sociology and philosophy, as well as a powerful ethical sensibility. Ideological commitment to the views of a dominant party does not make for prudent government. Furthermore, the representation of representatives to the people is mediated by the interests of the media, where misinformation, caricature and simplification appeal more directly to the emotions and sell more effectively than faithful representation or intelligent analysis. Representation, being mediated, is overtaken by external interests.

Democracy has no adequate defence against the sacrifice of responsibilities in favour of opportunities, the sacrifice of present demands in favour of future expectations. Alongside the vast amounts of significant need, there are also vast resources of human creativity and human labour which are wasted in a market economy. The problem lies in bringing them together. The mediation of the market is irrational, leading to the creation of artificial needs alongside ignoring many important needs; it leads to many working in pointless occupations which contribute little if any good directly to human society. By contrast, the mediation of reason is unproductive, for planned economies can make gross errors and lead to a fundamental problem in motivation for production.

The reformulation of concepts of right, liberty and piety may lead to a reconception of politics. For piety – any determinate practice of directing attention – belongs to the business of politics as much as right and liberty. An ethical society cannot rely on individuals, pressure groups, the media and politicians to effect a responsible distribution of attention. In addition to an independent judiciary charged with administering right, and a government charged with directing liberty, it is necessary to have an independent global religion, charged with directing attention, and redistributing civil honour in its alienated form as wealth. In order to prevent such an institution being dominated by extrinsic interests, it would have to be self-regulating, not accountable to any external powers – the dangers of self-regulation being outweighed by the dangers of external regulation. For accountability implies subordination; an institution charged with discerning what matters most must not be subordinated. Such an institution would be composed of members who combine the roles of spiritual leaders, religious ascetics, intelligentsia and investigative journalists. Its priorities would include wealth redistribution, sustainable development, regenerating local community, bringing creativity and labour together to meet significant need, education for citizenship, and the cultivation of spiritual awareness. Such a secular religion, concerned with experience, would not replace existing religions or institutions, but merely supplement them, so as to bring together their demands, and unite their aims.

Could such a public religion be possible? While its broad outlines may be common, its critical piety is singular.

Notes

1 This process is not absolute, however, for it is skewed by the extent to which the production and dissemination of knowledge is dependent on financial investment, adapting knowledge to the commodity market, in order to serve the interests of investors and the careers of researchers or journalists. These

interests must collaborate with the consensus, however, for any publication wishing to sell will not include much material of merely particular interest; it will always appeal to the consensus, the lowest common denominator of collective interest – the interests of investors and consumers are interdependent. Such is the 'real world' in which we live.

2 Excerpt taken from Bert Kaplan (ed.), *The Inner World of Mental Illness*, New York: Harper & Row, 1964, p. 127.

3 Kaplan (ed.), *ibid.*, p. 127.

4 Immanuel Kant, 'Dreams of a spirit-seer elucidated by dreams of metaphysics', *Theoretical Philosophy 1755–70*, Cambridge: Cambridge University Press, 1992, p. 341.

5 Kant, 'Dreams of a spirit-seer', p. 329.

6 Kant, *ibid.*, p. 333. It should be noted that in Kant's epistemology the object of perception is only known in so far as it is represented; thus real and imaginary perceptions become indistinguishable, and the reality of the object of perception has to be assured by the consensus of the faculties.

7 Kant, *ibid.*, p. 336.

8 See Gernot Böhme, 'Beyond the Radical Critique of Reason', in Dieter Freundlieb and Wayne Hudson (eds), *Reason and Its Other: Rationality in Modern German Philosophy and Culture*, Providence: Berg, 1993, p. 88.

9 Kant, *ibid.*, p. 329.

10 Kant, *Critique of Pure Reason*, Basingstoke: Macmillan, 1933, p. 24.

11 Kant, *ibid.*, p. 299.

12 Kant, *ibid.*, p. 386.

13 Kant, *ibid.*, p. 391.

14 Kant, *ibid*, p. 492.

15 Kant, *ibid.*, p. 505.

16 Scotus has been described as the 'founding father of modern philosophy'. See Éric Alliez, *Les Temps Capitaux 2/1: Les état des choses*, Paris: Cerf, 1999, p. 88.

17 André de Muralt, *L'enjeu de la philosophie médiévale*, Leiden: E. J. Brill, 1991, pp. 112–17

18 See John Duns Scotus, *Contingency and Freedom: Lectura I 39*, Dordrecht: Kluwer, 1994.

19 Scotus, *Opus Oxoniense*, Bk 1, d.3, q.1, in Arthur Hyman and James J. Walsh (eds), *Philosophy in the Middle Ages*, Indianapolis, IN: Hackett, 1973, p. 607.

20 Scotus, *ibid.*, Bk 1, d. 3, q.1, 611.

21 Scotus, *ibid.*, Bk 1, d. 3, q. 1, 605–6.

22 Spinoza, *Ethics*, II, Def. IV, London: J. M. Dent, 1989), pp. 38–9.

23 Spinoza, *ibid.*, II, Prop. XLIII, p. 70.

24 Spinoza, *ibid.*, II, Prop. XXXII, p. 64.

25 The quest for this identity determines each stage in the progress of the thought of Schelling. Negative and positive philosophy result, celebrating reason and liberty, necessity and freedom. Lacking a proper concept of an intensive infinite, Schelling was not able to solve the problem.

26 Jacques Derrida, *Aporias*, Stanford: Stanford University Press, 1993, p. 22.

27 Derrida, *ibid.*, p. 22.

28 See Ilya Prigogine and Isabelle Stengers, *Entre le temps et l'éternité*, Paris: Flammarion, 1992.

29 On the importance of natality as defining the human condition, in contrast mortality, see Adriana Cavarero, *In Spite of Plato*, Cambridge: Polity, 1995, Grace Jantzen, *Becoming Divine: Towards a Feminist Philosophy of Religion*, Manchester: Manchester University Press, 1998, and Jantzen (ed.) 'Beginning with Birth?', *The Scottish Journal of Religious Studies*, **19**(1), Spring 1998: 3–122.

30 See Henri Bergson, *Introduction to Metaphysics*, London: Macmillan, 1913. Bergson had difficulty elaborating his notion of intuition. While following the path he indicated, we shall be constructing it with different concepts.

31 See Bergson, *ibid.*, p. 75.

32 See Leo Chestov, *In Job's Balances: on the Sources of the Eternal Truths*, London: J. M. Dent, 1932, p. 32. No reference to Plotinus supplied.

33 Theodor W. Adorno, *Negative Dialectics*, London: Routledge, 1990, pp. 17–18.

34 Peter Sloterdijk, *Critique of Cynical Reason*, London: Verso, 1988, pp. xxxiii.

35 The psychoanalytic relation would appear to be one of attention to suffering, as Julia Kristeva has emphasized, in, for example, *In the Beginning was Love*, New York: Columbia University Press, 1987. Nevertheless, in psychoanalysis and counselling there are numerous dangers that may disrupt attention to suffering: attention may be motivated by the payment of money, rather than the potency of attention; the hidden trauma may lie undiscovered and incommunicable; or suffering may be overlaid with an interpretation. In short, the demand of suffering may not be felt in the body of the listener.

36 Spinoza, *Political Treatise*, ch. 2, New York: Dover, 1951, pp. 291–2.

9   Awakening

The unthinkable

The potency of thought

Does God exist? Yes or no?

Can any reasons be found to support an answer?

The search for reasons is not the same as finding them. For the stately progress of argument from reasons to conclusions is performed on the neutral stage of the public sphere, where an argument carries by its force, its persuasiveness, its necessity; but the search for reasons is a practice, a rehearsal conducted in private, away from the interrogatory glare of public examination. Such a search may draw on all available resources: customs, techniques, traditions, inventiveness, discipline, morality. It may express material interests, or the interests of class, gender, race and 'creed'. It may even be conducted with piety or impiety.

Can God be brought before the interrogatory glare of public examination? If the neutral stage of the public sphere is constructed by the logical outworking of forces of delusion, greed and hatred, then can God expect a fair trial? What piety might be required to think God today? For example, what is signified by the word 'God'? If, in contradistinction to human failings, one attributes to God the traditional perfections – unity, eternity, immutability, omnipotence, omniscience, benevolence, necessary being – such concepts are the products of human thought. One encounters the problem of projection: the unconditioned is thought on the basis of the conditioned. Before deciding whether such a practice of thought is adequate for God, it is important to enquire into which perfections are appropriate for God, and thus into the essence of divinity as such.[1]

Awareness of the political nature of reason gives rise to a more fundamental question: in what way may such an essence be *given* to us? According to what social practice or economy?[2] How can God, the unconditioned, be conditioned or given in temporal thought? Can God be given as a phenomenon?[3] Does God give Godself?

No answer to these questions can be given within the public spheres of reason and history. For if the unconditioned is encountered in reason or history, then it will be unthinkable or invisible. How, then, may it be possible today to indicate God, to perform the existence of God within thought, to individuate a divine essence? Must one construct one's reasoning in regard to God from eternity or temporality, through ritual or historical piety, so excluding God in advance from thought? Or is it possible to reconstruct reason from experience through experience? Philosophy of religion may leave aside questions of the essence and existence of God in order to explore the possibility of an unconditioned experience. For that which presents no form may still affect the distribution of attention.

Such a radical thought may begin with an elimination of all that has previously been presupposed in regard to the essence and existence of God, for such presuppositions already delimit what is thinkable. This elimination is, quite simply, the 'murder of God'. Life is no longer brought before the categories of thought; thought must be plunged into the categories of life. Liberated from its piety, its focus on the sacred or absolute, as well as liberated from its impiety, its focus on concrete historical experience, thought becomes determined by 'life, nature and history'. Thinking is no longer united with the being that is thought according to the Parmenidean model of truth: there is an abyss beneath all grounds, an unthinkable, unconscious source of thought which escapes thought. More fundamental than the difference between beings and Being, and more fundamental than the difference between the given and the gift of Being and time, is the difference between thought itself and the potency that affects it. That which remains unthinkable – the wonder, awe, passion or interest that drives thought – is that which philosophy must think.[4]

Philosophers have therefore attempted to think the impossible. For Spinoza, thought was determined by nature on a geometric plane of sovereign powers; yet Spinoza could not fully account for the temporal conditioning of thoughts in experience. For Schelling, thought was determined by history in a narrative of free will; yet Schelling could not fully explain how one identifies the ways of God revealed in history. For Deleuze, inspired by Nietzsche and Bergson, thought was determined by life on an immanent plane of intensive quantities; yet Deleuze could not fully account for the occasions on which life creates thought. Then let us raise once more the question of philosophy, leaving aside Spinoza's geometric plane, Schelling's historical narrative, and Deleuze's immanent plane, each of which is insufficient to think the unconditioned within experience.

Awareness as potency

The unconditioned may be encountered in experience. That which cannot be thought under the image of eternity or under the image of temporality remains unthinkable precisely because it is excluded from thought by the ritual and historical pieties that construct thought under the image of eternity or temporality. The unconditioned, in so far as it shapes thought, may be thought according to an apocalyptic piety which is entirely determined by the unconditioned. The first potency, the unconditioned within experience, is the demand of suffering which imposes upon attention. The second potency, again unconditioned within experience, is the power of attention to fulfil suffering. Each of these appears in experience as a singularity: suffering and attention are not subject to substitution, exchange or comparison. They cannot be subjected to rational thought; they cannot be explained, predicted or measured. If a relation is to form between them in experience, then such a relation must be constructed. Modes of piety are ways of conjoining such singularities: they distribute attention in response to chaotic rupture. Modes of piety express the politics of thought.

Nevertheless, the two manifestations of the unconditioned would remain incommensurable if there were not an anticipation of their conjunction in a mode of piety, and this very anticipation empowers the construction of a mode of piety. The anticipation is neither suffering, nor attention, but a *dim awareness* of suffering by attention. Beside the two potencies, then, there is a third: each radical disjunction is based on a more profound conjunction. The third potency is an awareness which escapes attention. Attention is a focusing or selection imposed on experience. While experience is determined by a network of interdependent conditions, it cannot focus on the entire network. Instead, it constitutes a signified object, treating this focus as if it were the cause or object of experience. In reality, one does not experience the products of imagination, but experiences a synthesis of real conditions of experience. Thus there is an awareness of these conditions, an experience of them, even if this experience converts itself into an imaginary focus of attention.

Indeed, experience escapes attention. For experience is not that which can be measured in the passage of time, neither is it the passing of time itself; it is a chaotic interval which syntheses time. A mode of experience is determined on the one hand by the networks of conditioning which make it possible; it is determined on the other hand by the mode of attention through which it shapes itself. In addition to these, however, a third determination is the intensity of the dim awareness that joins the two and conditions experience. Such dim awareness escapes attention, however, for we are not conscious of the way we are affected by networks of conditioning: we are only conscious of what is signified by the signs we construct. One may thus depict the semiotic square by Figure 9.1

The resolution of a signified from a sign is always an illusion: it is an imaginary focus of the mind. In fact, the signified has no location, either inside or outside the mind; it is a pure phantasm, outside of any space of representation, until a space of representation is added to constitute the

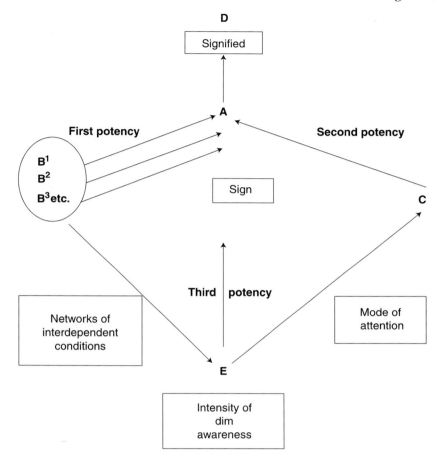

Figure 9.1 Semiotic square

signified as part of a meaningful world. At this point, the product of a human mind enters into relations with other products, a set of relations which are themselves constituted by the mode of piety of the mind itself. All representation is commodity fetishism. By means of this conjunction of sign and signified, a signified object substitutes for an intensity. It seems as if the signified object will then determine the sign, which in turn determines the mode of attention to represent the signified object. In practice, however, a network of interdependent conditions produces an intensity demanding recognition. In so far as one attends to the signified object, instead of the intensity, then the demand of experience is not fulfilled, and this demand continues to express itself in the production of signs. Thus desire becomes captured by the signified, without the possibility of it ever being fulfilled by attending to experience.[5]

A sign is merely a trace of an intensity: it cannot bring that intensity to attention, if attention is not attuned to that intensity. Then each intensity is obscured by its own representation in a signified. Dim awareness comprises both the demand of experience for attention, and the pain that a living experience feels when it is obscured by a representation. There is then a fundamental asymmetry, for attention is insufficient to meet the demands of experience. Whereas inorganic nature is largely determined symmetrically by its network of preconditions, organic life is characterized by asymmetry: in Bergson's classic analysis, vital perception is the capacity to limit automatic response, to select and filter out one's stimuli, to withhold attention.[6] The demand of experience for attention then becomes a drive to reconstitute a mode of experience so that it becomes adequate to attention. Biological drives for growth, reproduction and preservation, and human drives for sex, power, wealth and fame may all be regarded as expressions of the unconditioned tendency of experience to seek attention.

Alongside the delusions, attention does sense the demand of experience, even if it 'projects' this demand on to a signified object; in practice, this demand constructs the signified object. We are accustomed to imagining that all sensation must be mediated through matter, composed of discrete objects in a space of representation. Such a space of representation, however, is constructed from the substitution and superposition of exchangeable elements. As Bergson argued, by this substitution we eliminate what is essential in time and motion: duration and mobility.[7] Bergson thus attacked the doctrine, common to materialism and idealism, that perception is formed miraculously in the brain: as though consciousness is inexplicably added to physical movement here.[8] Bergson explained how this requires a 'transformation scene from fairyland':

> The material world which surrounds the body, the body which shelters the brain, the brain in which we distinguish centres, he [the materialist or idealist] abruptly dismisses; and, as by a magician's wand, he conjures up, as a thing entirely new the representation of what he began by postulating. This representation he drives out of space, so that it may have nothing in common with the matter from which he started.[9]

Instead, the perceived object, the rays of light it reflects, the retina, the nerves affected and the brain all form a single whole. The radical force of Bergson's theory derives from his insight 'that it is really in [the perceived point] P, and not elsewhere, that the image of P is formed and perceived'.[10] Perception overflows the material boundaries of the body in space. For if existence in space is defined by mutual separation, rendering action at a distance inexplicable for Newtonian dynamics, existence in time implies some degree of 'mutual penetration, an interconnexion and organization of elements'.[11] That an object endures in time, and does not merely exist in space, allows at once that it may be conditioned by perception and recol-

lection – by a mode of attention, a mode of piety.[12] This insight is sufficient to overturn the heritage of modern philosophy.

For modern secular thought is essentially Cartesian: it denies the possibility of awareness beyond the clear and distinct ideas subject to attention.
Religions, by contrast, are characterized by the claim that there are potencies of awareness in experience which exceed human attention. Indeed, this
characteristic is so universal among those phenomena normally classified
as religions that it may be useful for constituting a working definition of
religion which specifically excludes the false religions of capital and death:
*religion may be defined as attention to a potency of awareness in experi-
ence which exceeds all possible objects of thought.* Religion attends to that
which escapes its attention. Then the condition for a public religion,
however difficult to achieve, is simply as *awakening* of this potency.

To suggest that there are potencies of awareness in experience which
exceed attention may seem like an improbable claim. Yet experience lacks
clear principles of individuation and identification for attention, unless it
combines a material sensation with a constructed sign. The experience of
dim awareness, by contrast, is singular: it is only felt as a becoming, as an
affect and as indeterminate. Since one cannot trace the limits and bounds
of experience, experience escapes attention.

Moreover, experience imposes itself upon attention. The human subject
is not a master of its experience. Events happen to us. In so far as we are
conditioned by experience, we constitute an object of experience together
with a corresponding impulse or drive. Since the drive endures for a period
of time, then it is not satisfied by the object of experience which it constitutes. The drive, therefore, is the symptom of a lack of resolution of the
imposition of experience upon attention. The drive is evidence that there is
something in experience which has not been attended to.

Furthermore, attention has the power to give itself over time. Such
power demonstrates that attention is not completely determined by the
objects of experience. Attention, in its power of self-determination, has a
measure of self-awareness – attention to attention – necessarily brought
into play when it determines itself. This self-awareness is not attended to
when attention is turned towards the object of experience. Thus self-
awareness is not yet constituted.

The most powerful argument for awareness beyond attention is to be
found in the experienced fact that, on rare occasions in abreaction, in
communication, and in meditation or worship, attention resolves suffering.
This resolution cannot be comprehended through categories of essence and
existence. Suffering, when resolved, still remains as suffering. It does not
change in essence or existence; suffering does not 'cease' in temporal
terms. The 'cessation of suffering', an experience of the unconditioned,[13] is
only encountered in experience: that is to say, the experience of suffering
may be transformed when it is met by attention. This extraordinary fact
does not admit of easy explanation.

What happens, then, when attention resolves suffering? Suffering is substance or matter. To attend to suffering is to unite thinking and being. Attention to suffering is Truth, the unity of thinking and being. Moreover, since suffering matters most, attention to suffering is the highest form of value, or the Good. Nevertheless, the Truth cannot admit of becoming a signified object – Truth is the potency of experience, the mode of experience itself. In so far as attention can only focus on a signified object, just as one can only pray to representations of the gods, it is not capable by itself of attaining Truth. If Truth occurs – and it does indeed occur when suffering is resolved by attention – then it manifests itself by means of its own potency through which it imposes itself upon attention and experience. The awareness of Truth, then, does not come from directing attention appropriately, for attention cannot be directed to the Truth. If Truth is discovered, then it gives its own certainty, its own idea of its idea, as the awareness of Truth. Such awareness of Truth lies outside the subject. Then the experience of resolution brings to us an awareness which is an unconditioned potency alongside those of experience and attention.

A final argument for awareness beyond the bounds of attention builds on experiences of resolution. There is a direct experience of higher potencies of awareness. Such experiences reveal their own potency through their own self-awareness. They are self-certifying; yet, since it is impossible to draw attention to them, they remain secret – even to the memories of those who have experienced them. They may only have evidential value as testimony, both to those who have experienced them as well as to those who do not. Nevertheless, one may remember that they are given with absolute certainty, and this memory may constitute grounds for believing that we are dealing with a reliable witness.

A mode of awareness is nothing other than a mode of awareness. It is not a subject's awareness of an object, which could be subject to falsification. It is not awareness of prior conditions, or of its current mode of attention, which could be subject to distortion and self-deception. It is simply the mutual transparency and identity of Truth, Good and Awareness. Each of these are attributes of one and the same substance. Moreover, awareness is not set apart from experience, but is itself a mode of experience.

Dialectic

Truth is a potency which bears down upon us. Lacking the mode of attention that would reveal it, our dim awareness compels us to construct a signified object as a manifestation of the sacred. Since the sacred fails to bring Truth to attention, construction of the object must be repeated in an obsessive–compulsive cycle. The situation changes when the inadequacy of the signified object may come to attention, displacing attention on to the sign itself. Then the sign constitutes a promise for faith of the coming of the Truth. History may receive a paranoid interpretation as a series of signs which promise to explain the dim awareness of Truth. Finally, the apocalyptic moment may arrive: Truth is no longer subjected to the categories of thought, but thought is plunged into the categories of Truth. The result is a psychotic and free-floating construction of objects and signs of immense significance. Interpretation of such objects and signs begins the cycle of delusion once more. For in order to gain awareness of Truth, one would have to abandon all habits and patterns of thought, all attachment to the 'reality' constituted by the consensus.

There are experiences powerful enough to transfigure thought. In so far as they produce a breakdown in established patterns of the constitution of reality, and in so far as they break with consensus reality, they appear as madness. Indeed, all creation of philosophical ideas, in so far as they constitute the bases for new ways of thinking, is the work of madness. They can only be tested by their own internal criteria. An anonymous account of a psychotic breakdown reports:

> At the onset of panic, I was suddenly confronted with an overwhelming conviction that I had discovered the secrets of the universe, which were being rapidly made plain with incredible lucidity. The truths discovered seemed to be known immediately and directly, with absolute certainty. I had no sense of doubt or awareness of the possibility of doubt. In spite of former atheism and strong antireligious sentiments, I was suddenly convinced that it was possible to prove rationally the existence of God.[14]

If such accounts have been frequent, effective philosophies resulting from them have been extremely rare. For the danger lies in attaching certainty to inadequate ideas by locating the unconditioned within external reality. Such revelations can only become meaningful when they are accompanied by an extreme philosophical rigour which dismantles illusions internal to reason. As Schelling has said, although theosophy has an advantage of depth, richness and vivacity of content over philosophy, all science must pass through the dialectic: there is no understanding in intuition, in and of itself.[15]

Yet Schelling's first two potencies – the withdrawal and self-preservation of the sacred, the expansion and self-giving of history – would seem to be products of modes of piety which are overwhelmed by potencies. Schelling's error is the paralogism of reason once more: to take the mode of conduct of the potencies as the essence of the potencies. His thought is caught between the signified and the sign, without attaining the theosophical level of awareness. In order to escape from the necessary illusions of the eternal and the temporal, the sacred and the historical, the modes of piety by which they are constructed must be raised to the point of their own auto-critique. Repetition and difference, applied reflexively to themselves, will explode. A dialectic of potencies must describe the construction of modes of piety and their dissolution.

Unconditioned within experience I

Eternal return

There exists a famous account of an apocalyptic experience through which a philosopher may undermine repetition and transfigure thought. Nietzsche constructed a strange synthesis of philosophical reason and psychotic insight:

> A philosopher: a man who constantly experiences, sees, hears, suspects, hopes, dreams extraordinary things; who is struck by his own thoughts as if from without, as if from above and below, as if by *his* kind of events and thunder-claps.[16]

According to Pierre Klossowski, for Nietzsche the 'act of thinking became identical with suffering, and suffering with thinking'.[17] Nietzsche's most intense experience, the eternal return,[18] attempted to address the problem of suffering:

> To redeem the past and to transform every 'It was' into an 'I wanted it thus!' – that alone do I call redemption! ...
>   Willing liberates: but what is it that fastens in fetters even the liberator?
>   'It was': that is what the will's teeth-gnashing and most lonely affliction is called. Powerless against that which has been done, the will is an angry spectator of the past.[19]

All suffering seems to be a longing for release, for change, for a different future – not for any future in particular, but one that abolishes the past. To have done with the past: this is what all suffering seems to require. The past has too great a weight of suffering for us to endure. To completely affirm the innocence of existence, one would have to abolish or affirm the past.

Being a kind of psychotic phantasm, Nietzsche's 'most valuable insight' was first presented as the temptation of a creeping demon, before being privately entertained as a cosmological hypothesis:[20]

> What if some day or night a demon were to steal after you in your loneliest loneliness and say to you: 'This life as you now live it and have lived it, you will have to live once more and innumerable times more; and there will be nothing new in it, but every pain and every joy and every thought and everything unutterably small and great in your life will return to you, all in the same succession and sequence ... .' Would you not throw yourself down and gnash your teeth and curse the demon who spoke thus? Or have you once experienced a tremen-

dous moment when you would have answered him: 'You are a god and never have I heard anything more divine.'[21]

This particular experience is significant for the way in which it disciplines attention on experience itself, leaving aside questions of essence and existence. As Nietzsche wrote in his notebook, 'In place of "metaphysics" and religion, the *doctrine of Eternal Return* (this as a means of training and selection).'[22] This doctrine may be instructive, but only if we leave aside commentary and interpretation in order to unleash the potencies active in the thought itself – by thinking it again, even if one thinks it differently.

Nietzsche's doctrine of eternal return suggests a formula for the unconditioned, apart from the Whole or the One. For the doctrine leads one to exceed a discrete chain of individuals: 'We are *more* than the individuals: we are the whole chain as well, with the tasks of all the futures of that chain.'[23] If posed as a cosmological hypothesis, so that the world recurs as a finite series of states in infinite time, then at first one might assume that each cycle conditions the next in a succession of linear time. It is a specific denial of any purpose, creation, end or goal to existence: it is the ultimate formula of atheism, the expression of the murder of God. Moreover, eternity seems to be produced as a surface effect of repetition in time. Eternal return dissolves any unconditioned perspective outside the cycles from which one could assess the value of existence. Yet this also dissolves any perspective from which one could judge orders of succession of the cycles: if there is no unconditioned, then there is no longer a transcendent flow of linear time. Thus, it becomes impossible to count the cycles as separate: return collapses all recurrence. As a cosmological hypothesis, however doubtful, the formula unmakes even itself. This is the secret of its power.

The abolition of linear time collapses causality into immanent causality. Kant was already aware of the dangers of omitting this flow of linear time:

> If I omit from the concept of cause the time in which something follows upon something else in conformity with a rule, I should find in the pure category nothing further than that there is something from which we can conclude to the existence of something else. In that case [we would] be unable to distinguish cause and effect from one another.[24]

Nietzsche thus regarded the eternal return as the abolition of cause and effect, the abolition of the concept of necessity, and the abolition of the will.[25] Neither causality, nor logical necessity, nor the will are required to pass from one condition to another in a series; instead, the series exists in all its contingency. Here, the passage of time is not separate from the existence of the series; it simply is the existence of the series itself. Thus Deleuze regarded the eternal return as constituting the passage of time: he treated it as an answer to the problem of passage.

The passing moment could never pass if it were not already past and yet to come – at the same time as being present. If the present did not pass of its own accord, if it had to wait for a new present in order to become past, the past in general would never be constituted in time, and this particular present would not pass. We cannot wait, the moment must be simultaneously present and past, present and yet to come, in order for it to pass (and to pass for the sake of other moments).[26]

In order for the temporal sequence to constitute a passing series, each term is only a passage, a moment, a becoming, and that becoming must recur as past, present and future. This raises the further question of the meaning of 'simultaneous' and 'return' in these passages: in what time is time itself expected to pass? Just as eternal return generates eternity as a surface effect, it also appears to generate 'the pure and empty form of time', time as an abstract straight line. Time itself is a synthesis, an effect of return.

Deleuze also interpreted the eternal return as a transcendental idea: it is a solution to the Kantian problem of moving beyond experience by synthesizing a series of conditions, so as to contain the unconditioned. The cosmological hypothesis leads directly to the transcendental idea: for if the series of conditions is subject to return, then there is no place for any first term or any need for a complete series, for the One or the Whole. The series returns on itself, conditions itself – it is both the conditioned and the unconditioned. Eternal return is the fullest affirmation of a pure ontology, where being is no longer subject to transcendent terms such as the Whole or the One. Eternal return is the modality of an immanent cause. Just as in Scotus, where creatures attain their liberty because God has complete liberty, the series of conditions merely exists as a set of contingent facts. We have a universe of 'crowned anarchy', where there is no causality, reason and order, and each existent conditions itself immanently. This is the greatest extreme of psychotic fragmentation.

One may question whether Deleuze's interpretation of the eternal return is sufficiently radical. For if the passage of time is conditioned by a broader envelope of time in relation to which it passes, just as accented bars of music are inscribed within accented 'hyperbars', then we again have an ascending series of conditions, which may also be subject to return. Time always passes in relation to a broader envelope which marks its passage, a more intense time. Now, even this series of conditions returns to condition itself. There is no longer any up or down, more or less intense. Each moment itself is the unconditioned condition of the whole series. Each moment is implicated in all the others. There is no absolute distinction between analysis and synthesis. Each moment is cause and effect, fate and chance, freedom and necessity, transcendental and empirical. The very thought of eternal return, should it be true, is then both an empirical event of thinking, and the transcendental condition of existence.

What, now, could it mean to say that this one thought, a sign extracted from experience, should be true? The condition of truth, here, as in the thought of Spinoza's substance, is that it should be a cause of itself: thinking it should be sufficient to make it happen. Eternal return becomes the unconditioned condition of itself. It is this internal demand of return, rarely noticed by commentators,[27] that on the one hand constitutes its power – if it is actually thought, it will actually bring itself about –, while on the other hand constitutes its extreme difficulty – it can only be thought when it has the power to bring itself about.[28] Alongside the cosmological hypothesis and transcendental idea, then, we have eternal return as a categorical imperative.

Nietzsche's initial presentation of the doctrine is as a categorical imperative: a transcendental idea, whose objectivity as a cosmological hypothesis can for the moment be suspended. The question, 'Do you desire this once more and innumerable times more?' is presented as the greatest possible weight upon one's actions:[29] it is the acceptance of finitude, the renunciation of all ideals and goals, the abandonment of any hope for an end or a beyond to existence. It is a question of affirming the whole series of life, including its highs and lows, pleasures and pains, intensities and banalities, good and evil. Such an affirmation would at first seem to be in opposition to all morality: even the most evil is part of the series. Moral judgement is replaced by an infinite desire – desire, not merely for repetition, but for infinite repetition, even of the worst. The thought does, however, act as an ethical imperative: one must select only those actions that one wishes to perform eternally, just as one desires all the circumstances that one suffers to recur eternally. Moreover, the action that one selects and affirms is the one that will lead to the return of the entire series. This is a crucial point: if it is implicit in the eternal return as a transcendental idea that there is no unconditioned point outside of the series, then the cycle is not imposed upon the series from without. The cycle must make itself circular. This affects the ethical requirement of recurrence: it is not sufficient to attempt to will the eternal return of peak experiences – one must attempt to will those experiences which will lead to the whole eternal return. It is not merely rejoicing in solitude; it affects the entire conditions of existence, the whole network of relations. As a fateful predicament, as the greatest weight, the eternal return is a condition laid upon one's will or existence. But the eternal return, in its very status as a transcendental idea, is conditioned by an empirical will: it is divine, because it transfigures the one who wills it into a god who brings about the eternal return of the same:

> 'God' as the moment of culmination: existence an eternal deifying and un-deifying. But in that not a high point of value, but a high point of power.
>
> Absolute exclusion of mechanism and matter: both are only expressions of lower stages, the most despiritualized form of affect (of 'will to power').[30]

God is the being, the member of existence, who wills eternal return, the being of the series.

Nevertheless, to bring about the eternal return does not require an absolute control over the history of the cosmos, an absolute, sovereign, divine power sufficient to turn the doctrine into a cosmological blueprint. For if the cosmological hypothesis dissolves itself, then the categorical imperative lacks a sense. To function as a categorical imperative, the will is presumed to be unconditioned, in a state of absolute liberty. Yet if it regulates itself by this thought, then the thought is unconditioned, while the will conditions itself through this thought. The will remains a Kantian mode of piety, a power of self-determination. In the eternal return, however, just as the moment brings about the return of the whole series, the series brings about the return of the moment. There is thus no free, unconditioned will. There is no 'crowned anarchy', no nomadic distribution. Moreover, as both condition and conditioned, it abolishes the distinction between active and passive. One cannot try to will the eternal return, for the doctrine abolishes the will; one can only affirm the eternal return, in so far as it affirms itself in and through oneself. It is not an ideal to be attained, but a hypothesis which realizes itself. In the thought of eternal return, the thought itself is the unconditioned condition that generates its own existence. It posits itself through its own power, and not through the effort of any extraneous will. 'If this thought gained hold of you, it would change you as you are, or perhaps crush you.'

Could the doctrine of eternal recurrence be true? That is, could it be made true, or could it make itself true, affirming itself? Ridiculous as it may seem as a cosmological hypothesis, it demolishes the concepts of past and future outside of a single cycle upon which the succession of cycles is based. There is only existence, the innocence of becoming. Then the question is not one of finding some infinitely ingenious way of reproducing the history of the universe in its every detail; it is simply a matter of reproducing the detail of the universe in its every moment, just as time itself reproduces that detail anyway. To align one's will to eternal recurrence is to align one's will to the actual production of existence. To think eternal recurrence is thus to affirm existence to the full; one affirms life as it is. In this respect, eternal recurrence is the will of 'life, nature and history': it is true, in so far as it is actually affirmed by being. Recurrence is the affirmation and realization of being by being.[31] This conformity to existence gives the thought of eternal recurrence its shocking power, its truth, its reality.

At this point, one is inclined to protest, with Giorgio Agamben:

'Do you want Auschwitz to return again and again, innumerable times, do you want every instant, every single detail of the camp to repeat itself for eternity, returning eternally in the same precise sequence in which they took place? Do you want this to happen again, again, and again for eternity?' This simple reformulation of the experiment suffices to refute it beyond all doubt, excluding the possibility of its even being proposed.[32]

Yet even Agamben admits that while eternal recurrence is ridiculous as an ethical imperative, it still happens: *'in truth it has never ceased to take place; it is always already repeating itself.'* Agamben cites the recurring dream of Primo Levi:

> And in fact, as the dream continues, bit by bit or all of a sudden – each time it's different – everything falls apart around me, the setting, the walls, the people. The anguish becomes more intense and pronounced. Everything is now in chaos. I'm alone at the center of a gray, cloudy emptiness, and at once I *know* what it means, I know that I've always known it: I am once again in the camp, and nothing outside the camp was true. The rest – family, flowering nature, home – was a brief respite, a trick of the senses.[33]

Auschwitz may have been a singular experience; so are the estates, sweatshops and homes where an estimated 27 million slaves – more than twice the total number deported from Africa – are today confined. Moreover, the inner anguish of Levi's dream may be no more intense than the fantasies experienced by schizophrenics. Whatever the intensity, the 'camp' recurs. The eternal return reveals that at the heart of existence, eternal horror coexists with any eternal joy gained by affirmation.

Lou Salomé observed that Nietzsche himself suffered so much that the prospect of an eternal return was horrifying to him.[34] The doctrine puts aside ethical questions of training the will, just as it puts aside the imaginations of metaphysics, to fix attention firmly on experience: what are your experiences of suffering and joy? Far from escaping reality in a peak experience, the eternal return confronts us with reality. In an age of universal psychosis, nothing is more needful than redemption from the delusions that go beyond reality. Eternal recurrence is a 'negative philosophy', having a purely restorative role. It is a psychotic fantasy which, in an age of psychotic fantasy, can restore us to reality, however unpalatable that reality may be.

One cannot simply regard the eternal return as a bland affirmation of all that happens because it happens.[35] This is not Stoic resignation: one affirms that which brings about its own return, which affirms itself. For example, violence is a relation which tends to negate itself by destroying one of its constituents. Similarly, sovereign power is a relation which tends to negate itself by increasing the inequality of distribution of value. All ideas which are constructed with reference to the mediation of the passage of time, therefore, do not meet the test of eternal return. Only the unconditioned in experience, the 'will to power' – neither a will nor a power, but a potency – meets the test of the eternal return. As a selective thought, then, the thought of eternal recurrence distances its thinker from destructive actions, just as it negates metaphysical concepts. One does not will the return of cruelty, for such an affirmation is not itself affirmed by cruelty. It is ridiculous to will the eternal recurrence of Auschwitz, for the perpetrators of Auschwitz, however much they enjoyed their cruelty, could not will the eternal recurrence themselves, could not will the eternal return of those they despised and destroyed. Since the literal, cosmological hypothesis undermines itself, there is no need to affirm each event in world history if one affirms eternal recurrence; instead, one affirms an ethical principle which judges the events of world history.

Here we come to a further paradox of eternal recurrence: unrestricted affirmation is merely a mask, a stage one has to think through and put aside. Each attempt we make to think through the eternal recurrence is itself in error, is a mask that must be thrown aside as the thought intensifies and deepens itself. The eternal recurrence is one of a few singular thoughts which have the power to perpetually transform themselves, never resting in a proposition about being, but always becoming. Moreover, at the same time as transforming itself, it transforms the thinker and transforms existence. Affirming transformation, then, it affirms becoming. Indeed, if transformation is that which is affirmed, which recurs, then being itself is replaced by becoming. Moreover, this is not a bland affirmation of change as such; it is an affirmation of this singular becoming. Nothing seems true; the most deeply ingrained habits, and the most well-concealed of beliefs, in so far as they consist in a repetition of the same, are exposed as illusions by the thought of the eternal recurrence. For every conventional thought and action is unable to join thought and being, is unable to attain that infinite movement which is returning: 'the world unrestrained and abandoned and fleeing back to itself – as many gods blissfully eternally fleeing and re-seeking one another.'[36]

The final test of the eternal return is the test of its own doctrine. If we posit the eternal return as the unconditioned which conditions all existence, then we place this thought once more outside the cycle.[37] The thought itself is an illusion which contradicts and negates itself. Yet before dismissing it summarily as nonsense, let us pause to ask: what has done the negating here? The power in the thought, negating all metaphysics and values before returning to negate the thought itself, has not yet been thought. The force of the thought of eternal return is an intensive power of the thought itself, but it is not identical to that thought. Indeed, the thought is compromised by a conceptual limitation: it relies on a concept of repetition which, although it is able to complicate itself, ultimately remains abstract. 'Repetition' becomes an unconditioned principle, separable from the conditions it repeats. The thought of eternal return remains too abstract; there is no pure repetition as such, but only determinate modes of repetition.

We should therefore conclude that the doctrine is not 'true' – in the sense that it is not the highest thought, it is not adequate to experience. There remains something in experience that escapes Nietzsche's formulation of his own experience as a thought, just as there remains much in the doctrine of eternal return which Nietzsche himself did not manage to express in his thought. The doctrine is not adequate to suffering. Yet it is a useful principle of 'training and selection', drawing attention to suffering. For thinking through the possibility of the doctrine strips away all ritual piety, all repetition, from which one shelters from the potencies.

Unconditioned within experience II

Absolute faith

A second apocalyptic experience is necessary to attend to singularity. Instead of being repeated in itself, like the eternal return, this experience is extended through time. It begins with the insight that there is a potency in thought exceeding attention. Piety now attends to a mode of awareness in experience which escapes attention, even though such awareness presents no form in existence. One no longer believes in the signified object; each sign is recognized as a sign of an intensity – an intensity not contained within the sign. The intensity is the unthinkable source of thought which actually determines thought. Each thought is now merely a sign of its own immanent cause.

This mode of attention may be called absolute faith: it is not faith in any signified object of thought, neither is it faith in the repetition of any sign within thought, nor is it faith in faith itself. For the potency differs from any of these: absolute faith affirms absolute difference, not repetition. Such a faith does not earn grace; it risks failure. It is merely faith in a potency of which it knows nothing. There is no question of the truth of this experience of faith, for it is merely a mode of piety; one may only question the value of its distribution of attention. This is a question which absolute faith has no hesitation in raising, and no ability to answer. Exposed to extreme anxiety, absolute faith grasps nothing, but relinquishes all means of self-determination. This very relinquishing allows the possibility of discontinuity in time, for instead of expecting or determining the future on the basis of the present, absolute faith allows the future to be constituted as a gift of the potencies. Absolute faith waits.

As such, absolute faith functions as a condition of possibility for improbable and singular events. For networks of interdependent conditions are not always entirely conditioned by their elements. Interdependency is like eternal return: just as a whole conditions a part, a part conditions a whole. Each element is thus conditioned by all the other members in the network, while each conditioning member is also conditioned by each conditioned element. Purely physical networks, operating according to determinate laws, are the exception here. In practice, physical, chemical, biological, ecological, economic, sociological, linguistic, cultural and psychological networks all interact to condition events. In historical experience, multiple conditioning is the general rule. Moreover, in historical experience, the individuation of networks of conditions may be insufficiently determined, allowing multiple outcomes. Multiple conditioning produces effects similar to quantum physics: the individuation of determinate outcomes may itself be shaped by relevant modes of attention. While this happens synchronically in respect of objective manifestation, it may also happen diachronically in respect of significance: the sense and value of events may change through time according to their outcome.

To the extent that our modes of distribution of attention are determined by habit or ritual, then they produce consistent individuations of networks of interdependence. Once a determinate mode of attention is relinquished, then habit may still come into play by default, but there is the opportunity for one and the same potency to individuate networks of interdependence as well as a mode of distribution of attention. Such a singular event will escape comprehension by empirical analysis, for there is no instance of repetition through which it can be compared or judged.

Absolute faith leads a singular historical life. Even though, as Kierkegaard said, there are no outward distinguishing marks to separate the knight of faith from the bourgeois[38] – for faith presents no sign, no outer form for comprehension – such a singular historical life is not composed through repetition. This history is double: on the one hand, the life of absolute faith is composed of signs of the potency which impinges upon it; on the other hand, the life of absolute faith is composed of attention to the unthinkable potency. The culmination of these two histories is an overwhelming insight into their unity. A history of events, constituted by networks of interdependence, and a history of attention, constituted by a mode of piety, are one and the same historical experience. The potency of attention expresses itself in the history of signs, while the potency of the signs expresses itself in the history of attention. Each expressing and recognizing itself in the other, they may come to awareness in a revelation of identity: 'I am'. One achieves direct awareness of suchness, the individuation of a network of signs, and of thisness, the lived experience of the network. This direct awareness does not appeal to any Cartesian *cogito* or any metaphysics of presence, for it is the unconditioned awareness of a potency mediated by its own singular, lived history. Moreover, in attending to the history, one also attends to a direct awareness of that which can never be the object of attention, direct awareness itself. This awareness is the source, not the object, of thought.

Absolute faith gains the gift of itself as a direct awareness of singularity. Relinquishing its grasp on the sign, it returns to actual lived experience. I am an awareness, an act of attention. I am the thisness of this experience. I express my values by paying attention to the intensity instead of the sign or the signified. Yet the intensity of my experience is conditioned by the intensity of the experiences which impinge upon my dim awareness. Absolute faith interprets each encounter with another as a sign of an intensity; it directs its attention towards the singularity of another in order to extract the intensity from other interpretations imposed on signs. Others only emit signs of intensity in so far as they do not conform to habit or expectations. Intensity is encountered as becoming, as affect, as indeterminacy: it is when life no longer works, when everything breaks down, it is through our pathologies that we become knowable and lovable.

An ethical relation, extended over time, is composed of two pairs of histories: each partner has a history of signs, expressing intensities, and a history of attention, constituted by a mode of piety. Any relation between these histories is manifested first of all as a dim awareness. Such dim awareness forms a bond which may subsequently shape the histories. Expressing itself in both a history of signs and a history of attention, it may come to awareness as the identity of a singular relation. Direct awareness of this bond constitutes a reality of greater significance than the suffering expressed in the history of signs, for while suffering is temporal, an ethical bond, although expressed through time, is a relation that 'endures' outside of time. It shapes time. The experience of suffering and the experience of the ethical bond are incommensurable; they do not exist 'at the same time'. While suffering brings pain and meaninglessness, the ethical bond brings joy and significance.

An ethical relation between singularities may be contrasted with relations based on collective histories, collective fantasies, common notions, or even reciprocal exchange. For a relation between singularities is only possible in so far as there is an exchange of signs which indicate difference. Where an economistic perspective reduces an exchange of difference to a trade, constructing value from a postulate of equality in exchange, the exchange of attention requires non-reciprocity and inequality: it is not the same attention which is given and returned. Attention is never wholly 'given' – alienated in space and as property – for it remains a singular attention which is directed to a singular experience.

Yet even ethical relations of encounter between singularities do not have an absolute value. For such relations, based on singularity, novelty and difference, focus attention on historical experience without giving due regard to the powers which connect experience to attention. In order to complete a critique of value in the dialectic of potencies, it will be necessary to turn to a third apocalyptic experience.

Unconditioned within experience III

Awareness of potency

Awareness is normally dim because, although it can direct attention, there is nothing which can reveal it as a focus of attention. The unthinkable, even though it is thought by right, does not normally come into thought. Piety cannot choose to indicate a potency. Yet potency may indicate itself.

Whether in global catastrophe or in minor domestic cruelty, suffering is a sign that indicates an absolute: there is something that matters, something that motivates and empowers us. The very demand of suffering for attention is the sign of the unconditioned, but it is a sign which cannot reveal or individuate the potency that lies immanent within it. Such a sign does function as an *indication*, even if it indicates nothing other than itself. For to treat suffering as substance is merely to institute a measure of values; it does not tell us anything of the value of this scale of measure. To raise the question of the value of values institutes the dialectic of philosophical reflection; it is to supplement the theosophical revelation of substance and the practical imperative of action with thought. Philosophy begins in freedom: its distribution of thought and values is not compelled by prior thoughts and values. Yet philosophy does not perform an arbitrary choice, for its attention is attracted by a potency expressed in interest or wonder. Attention has its own immanent cause. The experience of suffering, by indicating itself as unconditioned, draws attention away from external expressions of value, whether economic or religious. It institutes the 'murder of God', whereby credibility is withdrawn from all other expressions of value. Instead, it simply signifies its own terrible significance. Thus the potency of suffering, expressing the measure of values, and the potency of attention, expressing the value of measures, become united in a singular, unthinkable point.

The experience of attention resolving suffering is a second sign of the unconditioned. This inexplicable and unpredictable phenomenon gives sense and value to ethical relations. It *dramatizes* the unconditioned, demonstrating its existence through experience. For the unconditioned will remain concealed in dim awareness until an experience arises capable of giving it expression. In this respect, all experience is abreaction, even if the abreacted events happen to someone else, or do not even happen at all until they are abreacted. For in abreaction, a potency comes to expression: it determines the construction within imagination of a memory, an episode or a life. Such images function as a sign of the intensity which is abreacted. Of less significance than the sign, here, is the accompanying emotion. This again is dual: on the one hand, there is the emotion of the experience itself that is abreacted, its specific feeling, tone, quality and intensity; on the other hand, there is the emotion of release, discharge, or joy specific to the event of abreaction itself. While abreaction constructs an image associated with a corresponding emotion, it also performs an event which discharges the potency into experience. A potency will thus be dramatized indirectly via abreaction, for when a 'complex' – a tightly knotted network of interdependent conditions – achieves representation along with its intensity, the potency which drives it is expressed as an active joy. Such joy of fulfilment is the demonstration of the existence of unthinkable potencies.

A third element is the individuation of a potency. Individuation of a network of interdependent conditions may have many possible solutions.

A solution will only be selected as available for attention when it can be dramatized or expressed in an experience. Individuation of a potency, however, is distinctive, for it concerns the unconditioned source of thought. Following the murder of God, following the test of the eternal return, following the experience of absolute faith, a potency is individuated by its own power, and through its own awareness. Self-individuation is already common in experience. Raymond Ruyer, a successor to Bergson, invented the concept of 'self-survey' to describe such processes of individuation: he distinguished between multiplicities which have exterior parts like a chessboard – *partes extra partes* – and multiplicities as networks of interdependence.[39] He pointed out that while one needs an eye to observe a chessboard, one does not need a third eye to observe one's own perceptions. The brain does not observe the image on the retina; instead, the retinal image is in a state of self-survey.[40] Where the chessboard is observed from without, the retinal image composes itself in the brain through a process of individuation or embryogenesis, the simultaneous formation of the mind and the 'informing' of the mind.[41] This is how a potency may individuate itself, without coming to awareness. Similarly, Gilbert Simondon created a philosophy of individuation or ontogenesis based on the paradigm of transduction, whereby a crystal forms by structuring an amenable exterior milieu. A living individual, then, is a 'theatre of individuation'.[42] Thus a potency may only individuate itself within a milieu of thought which may be subject to its forces. A potency cannot come to awareness without appropriate attention.

Such a milieu may be given by a list of categories appropriate for potency. Potency may crystallize within the categories of experience, rather than those of essence and existence. A potency is unconditioned, although preparation of an amenable milieu may be enabled by piety. A potency expresses its power on the occasion of suffering, although it brings joy. A potency dramatizes itself in a singular experience, although such dramatizations may be repeated differently. A potency is infinite, in that its intrinsic degree of power does not exist within a common space of representation where it could be limited by other powers. A potency may express infinite intensity, bringing adequacy and fulfilment; it may be infinitely compelling, imposing itself upon attention; it may be infinitely attentive, and thus compassionate; it may be 'limited' from without, however, not in itself in dim awareness, but in so far as it does not find an appropriate milieu in which to crystallize. Finally, a potency may 'prepare' its milieu by destabilizing existing orders of sense and value in so far as it draws attention away from them. Such an operation, which we have called the 'murder of God', does not proceed by a dialectical operation of critique in the sense of contradiction: its method of critique is constructive, drawing attention to that which has been excluded and overlooked in established operations of power. It prepares and constitutes its own milieu from the elements that are excluded.

Philosophy of religion may find these intrinsic modes of experience – the experienced, the unconditioned, the matter, the singular, the infinite, the intense, the compelling, the attentive, and the unthinkable – dramatized in a singular experience of awakening to God. Such an experience of God is composed by processes of indication, dramatization, and individuation: it is God for us. This is not to deny that there is a God in Godself, for the third potency is the potency of awareness – which is aware of itself by right, even if we are not normally aware of it. Experience of God in Godself, however, is so rare and strange as to afford little benefit, and indeed, much danger in its discussion. The experience of God for us, however, is common, while limited by the availability of appropriate categories of experience.

Conclusion

The most urgent and fundamental political problem is to restore to people an insight into the power and freedom of their attention. For in a world of excessive mediation, attention is captured by image, spectacle and glamour; it is demanded by economic necessity; it is seduced by flattery of greed, lust and ambition; it is compelled by fear. Mediation substitutes for singular experience, leaving segmented, isolated and fragmented individuals enclosed by the walls of their own thoughts and desires. All too often, escape from isolation builds collectivity out of violence against difference and singularity. In such a condition, nothing is more needful than the redemption of attention: the discovery of the possibility of turning towards that which matters.

To restore attention requires piety, not mediation. Piety is not awareness. Piety is attention to the signs left by higher potencies of awareness. Critical piety is an attention which does not mistake these signs for anything other than inadequate ideas of a withdrawn revelation. Such piety is without superstition or credulity. It is an immanent mode of experience. Ritual piety attends to signs left behind by higher potencies in order to recover a little of their potency. Historical piety attends to an ongoing series of signs in order to see evidence of the continuing work of that potency. Apocalyptic piety attends to the signs of experience in order to expose itself to the higher potencies of awareness that coexist with experience. Where ritual piety tends to explain suffering, and historical piety tends to remove suffering, apocalyptic piety leads to the possibility of a transfigured experience of suffering. In the transfigured experience, suffering remains, but it remains alongside a joyful self-awareness which has been added to it. Suffering and awareness remain incommensurable – there are no possible considerations of gain or loss, of whether the end justifies the means, or whether the pain was worth it. Experience has no price. Hell exists in experience alongside heaven.

Apocalyptic piety has no name for the God it experiences, no identity on which to cling. It is merely an experience after the death of God, the subject and the world. It follows the dissolution of reality and the dissolution of the will. If it awakens to God as Truth, Goodness and Awareness, this is not a God it can condition, possess or will. It is merely an experience. Apocalyptic piety stands outside itself: it is a capacity to laugh at, relinquish and forgive oneself; it is a capacity to attend to suffering; it is a capacity to bear within oneself little fragments of heaven and hell. It is compassion.

Piety alone, as a disciplining of attention, does not have sufficient power to direct attention. Instead, attention must be placed in contact with its own immanent power through an experience of 'awe' or 'wonder' that attracts attention. This is a progressive process, beginning slowly, but accelerating as the milieu of thought is progressively refashioned. There may be plateaux and blockages on the way, for each of our established ways of making sense of life excludes the potency that bears down upon us. Its energy may be harnessed to preserve unstable beliefs and practices that secure themselves by passing on the dissolving force of the potency to others. The more one becomes exposed to potency, the more powerful the forces in motion, and the more dangerous it may become. To raise the question of philosophy, to begin thinking, to expose oneself to the forces of the outside, is a perilous act – not only for oneself, but also for others. Only when complacency becomes even more dangerous is it worth the risk of thinking.

Awakening to the experience of God – a conceiving of God, rather than a mere concept of God – is a gift of potency. As a foundation for thought and existence, it directs attention not to itself but to that which matters: suffering and singularity. It liberates us from the dissolving force of potency by restoring an absolute. The dissolving force of potency may even tend to dissolve this individuation, dramatization and indication of itself, yet such dissolution results in giving us the experience of God once more. The internal dialectic of God – the presence of hell in Godself – , whereby potency shields us from its own *opus alienum*, may be of little direct concern to us. Yet piety feels a little of this terror in the suffering which comes from without and the internal dissolution which comes from within. Such suffering, such dissolution, such violence, when borne within to shield others from their force, are merely the true price of piety.

Notes

1 Martin Heidegger drew attention to the basic concepts which determine the way that we acquire an understanding of our subject matter. The most fundamental enquiry explores structures of existence as such; it explores the meaning of the Being of beings:

> Only from the truth of Being can the essence of the holy be thought. Only from the essence of the holy is the essence of divinity to be thought. Only in the light of the essence of divinity can it be thought or said what the word 'God' is to signify.

Heidegger, 'Letter on Humanism', Basic Writings, London: Routledge, 1993, p. 253.

Of course, few theologians would accept the priority of the 'holy' or 'divinity' over God. The meaning of God can only be revealed as the truth of the true God that happens to exist. Nevertheless, Heidegger's influence over subsequent Christian theology has been immense, because he indicates fundamental questions that belong to theology as such: theology can only comprehend itself appropriately when it adapts its reasoning to the essence of divinity. In shifting attention from metaphysics to ontology, from God to divinity, from the content of knowledge, beings, to the nature of knowledge, the meaning of Being, Heidegger recapitulates the Trinitarian move from Father to Son, from the true to the truth, from the source of the Godhead to the logos.

2 In Heidegger's later work he raised a more radical question: if Being and time are given phenomena – determining each other reciprocally but in such a way that Being is not temporal and time is not a being – then what is the meaning of '*Es gibt Sein* [There is, it gives Being]' and '*Es gibt Zeit* [There is, it gives time]'? Heidegger, *On Time and Being*, New York: Harper Colophon, 1977, pp. 3 – 6. This move from Being to *das Ereignis*, the event of the gift of Being and Time, may be regarded as a recapitulation of the trinitarian move from the Son to the Spirit, from God as truth to God as donation.

3 Jean-Luc Marion has expanded on this indication:

> 'God' defines himself as the being-as-given – *par excellence* – and *not* as the donor-being. This supremacy denotes neither sufficiency nor efficient causality nor primacy, but the fact that he (God) gives himself and allows a giving that is being, more than any other being-as-given. In short, with 'God', we are dealing with the being-as-given *par excellence*, the being who is completely given (*l'étant abandonné*).
>
> Jean-Luc Marion, 'Metaphysics and Phenomenology', in Graham Ward (ed.), *The Postmodern God*, Oxford: Blackwell, 1997), p. 291.

   In the gift of love, the giver gives himself completely, without restriction or reservation. The gift is the giver himself or herself, who is given unreservedly, with nothing withheld. The result is that existence is saturated with the presence of God. As such, God presents no form and is thus invisible: ' "God" becomes invisible not *in spite of* his donation, but *by virtue of* this donation' (p. 292). If God is invisible and presents no form, then there is no adequate concept of God. God is without Being; one cannot speak of God's existence.

4 See Philip Goodchild, *Gilles Deleuze and the Question of Philosophy*, Madison: Fairleigh Dickinson University Press, 1996.

5 This discussion is a revision of the concept of 'conjunctive synthesis' developed in Deleuze's *The Logic of Sense*, London: Athlone, 1990, and in Deleuze and Guattari's *Anti-Oedipus*, London: Athlone, 1984. Because they regard conjunction as a relation between otherwise equivalent series of intensities, in a monism of desiring-production, they are unable to explain the energy, fascination and certainty which accompanies conjunction. The difference here is that we are operating with three, not one, fundamental potencies; moreover, instead of identifying desiring-production with the connection of a series of conditions, we are here treating potencies on a plane of experience, independent of conditions.

6 See Bergson, *Matter and Memory*, London: George Allen & Unwin, 1911, pp. 21–29. Bergson's argument itself is not strong here; nevertheless, his prior distinction of kinds of time in *Time and Free Will* is sufficient to establish an 'interval' of indetermination between action and recollection.

7 Bergson, *Time and Free Will*, London: Swan Sonnenschein, 1910, p. 115.

8 Bergson, *Matter and Memory*, pp. 79–80.

9 Bergson, *ibid.*, pp. 32–3.
10 Bergson, *ibid.*, pp. 37–8.
11 Bergson, *Time and Free Will*, p. 101.
12 Bergson's discovery that the object takes place in the object itself grounds his method of intuition, by which one may turn directly to experience. Bergson's difficulty in elaborating his method of intuition arises from lacking the conceptual distinction between the object, the network of conditions and the intensity of experience. Experience, which is a relation between conditions and attention, is indeed outside the mind. It is an objective plane of being. In this respect, Bergson's insight points the way for an overcoming of modern epistemology based on the representational power of the subject, but it does not effectively attain that overcoming.
13 See the Buddha's classic description of nirvana in the Pali Canon: *Udana*, p. 80.
14 Bert Kaplan, *The Inner World of Mental Illness*, New York: Harper & Row, 1964, p. 94.
15 F. W. J. von Schelling, *The Ages of the World* (second draft, 1813), Ann Arbor: University of Michigan Press, 1997, p. 118.
16 Friedrich Nietzsche, *Beyond Good and Evil*, 292, Harmondsworth: Penguin, 1973, p. 198.
17 Pierre Klossowski, *Nietzsche and the Vicious Circle*, London: Athlone, 1997, p. 23.
18 Nietzsche's experience can be dated to August 1881, in Sils-Maria, from a letter of 14 August to Peter Gast. See Christopher Middleton (ed.), *Selected Letters of Friedrich Nietzsche*, Chicago: University of Chicago Press, 1969, p. 178.
19 Nietzsche, *Thus Spoke Zarathustra* II, 'Of Redemption', Harmondsworth: Penguin, 1969, p. 161.
20 Nietzsche, *The Will to Power*, 1062, 1066, New York: Vintage, 1968, pp. 546, 548–9.
21 Nietzsche, *The Gay Science*, 241, New York: Vintage, 1974, pp. 273–4.
22 Nietzsche, *The Will to Power*, 462, translation modified following Daniel Smith in Klossowski, *Nietzsche and the Vicious Circle*, p. 106.
23 Nietzsche, *The Will to Power* 687, p. 366.
24 Kant, *Critique of Pure Reason*, Basingstoke: Macmillan, 1933, p. 262.
25 Nietzsche, *The Will to Power*, 1059–60, pp. 545–6.
26 Deleuze, *Nietzsche and Philosophy*, p. 48.
27 This possibility is noted by Klossowski, *Nietzsche and the Vicious Circle*, pp. 124–5.
28 This accounts for the way in which the doctrine is presented in *Thus Spoke Zarathustra*. It is normally assumed that the difficulty lies in affirming the recurrence of the lowest, the dwarf. Zarathustra breaks through this obstacle, he realizes the significance of the doctrine, but he does not become the Ubermensch. If Zarathustra's realization is the great noontide of world history, it is not yet the great midnight, the point at which the day can constitute itself over and over again. The relation between the doctrine of eternal recurrence and the Ubermensch – that the Ubermensch is the one who will bring recurrence about – is rarely appreciated by commentators. Yet we should note that to 'bring it about' does not require an absolute control over the history of the cosmos, absolute, sovereign, divine power sufficient to turn the doctrine into a cosmological blueprint. For the cosmological hypothesis, as we have noted, dissolves itself. Similarly, then, the meaning of 'power' in the will to power that effects the eternal recurrence is no longer sovereign power, but an intensive mode of power.
29 Nietzsche, *The Gay Science*, 241.
30 Nietzsche, *The Will to Power*, 712, p. 379.

31 See Deleuze, *Difference and Repetition*, p. 42.
32 Giorgio Agamben, *Remnants of Auschwitz: the Witness and the Archive*, New York: Zone, 1999, p. 99.
33 Levi is quoted by Agamben, *Remnants of Auschwitz*, p. 101.
34 Salomé is cited in Klossowski, *Nietzsche and the Vicious Circle*, p. 95.
35 See Nietzsche, *Thus Spoke Zarathustra* IV, 'The Awakening', pp. 321–2; the ass, here, recalls the depiction of Jesus by Nietzsche in *The Anti-Christ*.
36 Nietzsche, *Thus Spoke Zarathustra*, III 'Of Old and New Law-Tables', p. 215.
37 This I take to be the objection raised by Deleuze and Guattari to the 'cyclic unity of the eternal return, present as the nonknown in thought.' *A Thousand Plateaus*, p. 6.
38 Søren Kierkegaard, *Fear and Trembling*, Princeton: Princeton University Press, 1983, p. 39; the missing element in this depiction of the knight of faith is, of course, a sensibility that directs attention to suffering.
39 Raymond Ruyer, *Néo-finalisme*, Paris: Presses Universitaires de France, 1952, p. 64, 95.
40 Ruyer, *ibid.*, p. 97.
41 Ruyer, *ibid.*, p. 40.
42 Gilbert Simondon, *L'individuation psychique et collective*, Paris: Aubier, 1981, p. 16.

Conclusion

The 'murder of God' is the symbol of a fundamental shift in human history which at once unites that history and globalizes the world. This shift is the emergence of the global role of finance capital, which progressively expands its despotic sovereignty into a concealed, global neocolonial empire that is inserted into, straddles and mediates an ever-increasing quantity of human relations. Undemocratic and ideologically driven institutions such as the International Monetary Fund, the World Bank, the World Trade Organization, and the G8 Summit effectively govern the world in line with the demands of capital. Three fundamental limits to human experience have eventually become manifest as a result of this shift: an ecological limit, beyond which environmental conditions are no longer capable of sustaining human life; a socio-economic limit, whereby the ultimate encompassing determinant of the viability of relations mediated through production is the interest of finance capital; and a psychic limit, whereby suffering can no longer be understood as subordinated to some higher end such as human progress by an ascetic ideal, but comes to take on an ultimate significance in its own right. We have at last arrived in the age of the universal.

In this context, local alternatives aimed at regeneration may certainly coexist with global capital, but will have no power or defences against its direct interventions. They cannot become significant in their own right until the power of finance capital evaporates – either by being recaptured by sovereign states, or by imploding under its own mechanism. Until a global power can guarantee freedom for local initiatives, no substantial progress can be made. In the meantime, the despotic power of global capital is supported by ideology, commercial practice, law and piety. The foundations of this nexus were laid in the studies of early modern philosophers through the concepts of piety, liberty and right which they created. Where piety became invisible through the mechanisms of ideology, liberty and right became self-certifying values that shaped human relations for the market, and thus for the advent of capitalism. Indeed, it should be noted that such concepts themselves were created within the episteme of European rationalism which was constructed in Athens as a reflection of its commercial society.

The advent of global finance capital brings a new development to this history. The spheres of piety, liberty and right, the provinces of institutions of religion, government and the judiciary respectively, have been increasingly appropriated by finance capital itself. Religions adapt to make themselves more appealing in a competitive market; government policies are controlled by balancing the needs of their people against the controlling needs of finance capital which alone is able to offer prosperity; laws are enforced only when they conform to the interests of global finance. The system of global finance – not the financiers themselves who are merely constrained to act as its servants – gains an increasingly despotic and destructive power, arrogating to itself the prerogatives of piety, liberty and right.

The coming catastrophes of the next few decades – ecological catastrophes of storm, flood, poisoning and shortage of essential resources such as water and oil; socio-economic catastrophes of global and local depressions, political turmoil, populism and war; personal catastrophes whereby few people remain untouched by the above – gather visibly like clouds on the horizon. They are unlikely to be addressed effectively until they have wreaked considerable havoc. Only when the crisis comes will there be an opportunity for significant change. At this stage, it will be vital that there is viable alternative – and that the capitalist system is not simply reborn through lack of imagination of an alternative. It will also be vital that this alternative is both global in scope and local in sensibilities, so that it can address disorders which are external in origin to any scale of locality. To avoid the dangers of despotism, we may require global institutions of government, judiciary and religion, functioning according to new concepts of liberty, right and piety.

A step towards constructing this alternative may take place once more in the studies of philosophers: the reconstruction of concepts of liberty, right and piety which are not based on inadequate ideas, and which do not lend themselves to usurpation by despotic powers. Here we have attempted to sketch out foundational concepts of piety, liberty and right which are formed within a mode of thinking sensitive to the fast encroaching limits of human experience. Liberty, far from being a given value, becomes a state that may be achieved through the disciplining of attention: it is the power to condition experience by directing attention, mediating experience by constructing a due regard for the past, present and future. Right becomes the demand of suffering for attention throughout its network of interdependence. Piety becomes a determinate practice of directing attention towards that which matters. Such liberty, right and piety require new global institutions for their administration. For the essence of the contemporary predicament lies in misdirected attention, a mismanagement of piety.

How we are still pious

Modern reason was founded on a critique of piety: for it was through complicity in shared beliefs that people were subjected to hierarchical domination by powers and authorities. Denouncing the pieties of tradition, daring to speak of what is different or new, modern reason does not turn attention to its own determinate practices of directing attention. It disavows its own piety, and this very disavowal constitutes its piety. By means of this refusal, the determining principles of contemporary experience remain unacknowledged.

For people still believe in modern European economics, culture, reason and values. Its senses and values are enshrined within the dominant global discourses and practices. Rejecting 'supernatural' causes, modern reason believes in the principle of sufficient reason, that effects do not exceed their causes. In doing so, it disavows the 'miracle' which takes place every time a reason, an order of ideas, produces an effect, an order of things. For reason cannot explain the transcendent pivot between cause and effect, reason and action. Instead, every rational explanation involves a circular reasoning, for it cannot explain rational explanation as such. The relation between the eternal order of reasons and the temporal order of existence cannot be easily bridged. Ignoring the fundamental problem of the eternal and the temporal, modern thought still produces a relation between the eternal and the temporal within temporal existence. Modern thought relates to the eternal through its strategies of repetition and exchange; it relates to temporal existence by subordinating it to these strategies. These determinate strategies of directing attention give honour to the eternal objects of belief, as well as attending to the outcome of events where the effect precedes knowledge of the cause. In these very strategies, modern thought manifests its own ritual and historical pieties. For to be temporal and free is to be pious.

The practice of repetition within the constitution of knowledge expresses an implicit piety before the sovereignty of truth. This repetition, found pre-eminently in the paralogism of pure reason by which the mode of representation is taken as the form of truth, absolves the 'truths' that it discovers into isolated unities. Through a process of commodity fetishism, these abstract 'truths' and 'values', prepared for exchange, seem to take on a life of their own, becoming imaginary causes that shape human existence. Abstract symbols such as 'right' and 'liberty', substituting themselves within attention for experience, and for other symbols, become general equivalents, absolutes, or organizing principles which centralize themselves and capitalize on thought. Their dynamics of expansion, encompassment, and capitalization derive from their own self-positing structure, and not from experience, in relation to which they are linked by the slenderest of threads. Human thought becomes dominated by the dynamics of thought itself, external to human experience. Absolute symbols, which mediate all exchanges, become transcendental signifiers, for their degree of exchangeability exceeds their degree of meaning. They signify transcendence. Capitalism becomes a religion in thought itself, embedded in the liturgical performance of symbols: we no longer believe, but the symbols believe for us. Such is the dominant modern piety.

This piety arises from a disavowal of the determinate practices of directing attention, and of the social and ethical relations enacted within all events of thought. Then to alter the currency, to change piety, it is necessary to direct attention to freedom of thought as possibilities of expressing honour, spontaneity, ethical relations, and piety within and alongside all determinate acts of thinking and living.

An ethics of thinking

Modern thought has an ethos: through its practices of repetition, it expresses obedience before the sovereign model of truth, against which all thought may be judged; through its practices of exchange, thought is constructed as a market, where sovereignty is distributed to all who possess symbolic capital so that they can make their thought appear to be publicly valid. In such a market, validity is constituted by exchangeability. Those thoughts which offer themselves for general consumption, which satisfy base interests, which flatter the complacency of the consumer, which gratify desires, which devalue alternatives, are those which can circulate the most freely. Thus, in a sovereign market of thought, consensus reality is built upon delusion, greed and hatred.

It is essential to change this ethos of thinking. For to think is to honour: it is to think about something, to pay attention. Thinking is essentially social and temporal. To expend oneself in thinking is to perform an act of giving which honours the recipient. Now, where thought is largely conditioned by distractions, habit and customs, thought may be disciplined into acquiring freedom by splitting the moment of exchange into abstract flows of objectivity, subjectivity, sense and value. For when the subjective experience of thinking is detached from the habitual objects of thought, there is the possibility of thinking otherwise. Such freedom of thinking is not expressed as domination, as mastery over an objective domain of thought, but as an ethos, a synthesis of time, a way of relating past, present and future. Freedom of thought is expressed in hopes and expectations about the future; it is expressed in the recollection of memories and traditions; it is expressed in the preservation of the past. Freedom, far from requiring a contradiction and overcoming of the past, involves the way in which the past will be selected, synthesized and preserved. Then the freedom of thought is social in a second sense, in that the association of the past into a synthesis as an ethos is a work of freedom.

Freedom is thus necessarily mediated, both by the objects of thought, and by the synthesis that determines the ethos of thought. Such mediations offer the opportunity for thought to expend itself, to create senses, values and ethical bonds. They also offer the opportunity for thought to be captured by its media of exchange. The clearest example of this process is the capture of value by the self-positing logic of money. Such economic capture effects a process of successive centralization and capitalization that creates a transcendent source of sense and value, a god. In economic terms, the divinity of a medium of exchange results in a fundamental social separation between speculators and householders, between those who exercise apparent freedom, and those who are bound by the practical necessity of the need for subsistence. Indeed, a similar class difference is manifested in thought itself between professional thinkers, who have access to the means of production of valid thought, and amateur thinkers, who simply think from their own experience of life. Such economic capture also includes a capture of subjectivity in the form of the constitution of a synthesis of time: time must be spent in being saved, warding off death.

This economic capture can be defeated by the courage to face and experience death. Once the thought of death appears as a simulation, then an immanent ethics of thought can be constructed which no longer treats death as the absolute source of meaning and value in ethics. Value is withdrawn from objects of evaluation, such as death, so as to return to acts of evaluation immanent in thinking. Thinking has an ethos, a way of enfolding life, nature and history, which is expressed in its accompanying emotions. Such emotions are potential relations: thought becomes a possible world, a utopian social space, a society constituted by ethical bonds and differences, by exchanges of honour and attention.

Nevertheless, for such an ethos of thinking to acquire power to displace other modes of thinking from attention, it must itself express the potency of its life, a power immanent within attention. Here, it is not sufficient that an ethos of thinking is constituted by memory alone, for memories can be selective, violent and exclusive. Neither can such an ethos be simply creative, for novelty may detract attention from elsewhere by focusing it upon a fantasy of the future. Instead, thinking must acquire its own potency.

Critical piety

Modern thought fails because of its misdirected attention. Modern constructions of knowledge and value are shaped through the capture of attention by external powers. It is not the case that modern knowledge is not true and modern values are not valuable; the weakness lies in their piety. Such truths and values do not direct attention to the fundamental natural right of suffering to receive attention throughout its networks of interdependence.

If power is mediated through attention, then we live in a world dominated by pieties, whether or not these are called 'religions'. Each piety has its own internal criteria, its own 'theological' practice of self-articulation and self-critique. Each piety may use such criteria to evaluate the others. The supposedly neutral stage of the public sphere of reason, where pieties may meet for dialogue and debate on democratic terms, or which may evaluate the claims of pieties, proves simply to express the piety of the market-place.

Yet if universalization and globalization have been thrust upon us by a local tradition, it cannot for all that dissipate once its pretensions are exposed. For it has led to a global and shared problem, the true universal of ecological limits. In order to survive, we require a new universal form of reason – simply in order to protect local pieties and modes of experience.

Just as the time has come for pieties to stop meeting as enemies on a battlefield where they defend their property rights over the Truth, the Good and God, the time has also come for pieties to stop meeting in a market-place as strangers for the purpose of exchange. Instead, there is a new encompassing framework for the meeting of traditions, a new common notion, a new 'human nature' for a rational commonwealth. Where pieties may be divided over the eternal essence of reality and where pieties may shape their temporal existence through exchange, they may be united in a common experience. For to be rational today is to pay attention to the universal limits of human experience. The truth of common experience is the ecological limit, the suffering of the planet. The truth of the cause of this suffering is the socio-economic limit, the capture of piety by uncontrolled global free-market capitalism. The absolute truth common to the great traditions of piety is the psychic limit, that suffering matters. These may easily be recognized by all. It only takes a small further step to recognize that the path to the cessation of suffering begins with attention to suffering.

In this respect, there is potential for the development of a universal piety. Such a piety would not be in competition with existing forms of piety, seeking to supplant them. Neither would it simply affirm them all, giving them democratic rights to speak and exchange. A universal piety is a basis for critique – but this need no longer be understood in the dialectical terms of negation and overcoming. Instead, a critical, universal piety draws our attention to that which matters. The 'murder of God', although expressed as a most extreme dialectical symbol, becomes merely a displacement of attention. To criticize a mode of piety it is sufficient to draw attention to its role in networks of interdependence, and in particular in relation to universal limits.

The 'murder of God', as has been evident to most theological commentators, is merely the death of an idol. Even today, the dominant focus of attention for piety is an imaginary construct. The piety expressed in contemporary capitalism and market speculation is an orientation of attention to an anticipated future at the expense of the past and the present. Such a projection is measured in relation to the onward march of linear time, the time experienced by clocks and inanimate objects. This dead time is the norm against which the future is judged; it becomes a screen which excludes experience of the present and recollection of the past. It deflects attention from experience, isolating and fragmenting consciousness, where networks of interdependence are obscured by imaginary futures.

Such an economic piety, expressing scarcity, may be contrasted with religious piety, expressing excess. Nevertheless, even in the most economic thought, there is still an unnoticed excess: attention is directed and spent. It is necessary to determine whether such attention is spent wisely. For any distribution of attention may be affected by a host of memories, spirits and powers. Any mode of attention which disavows its conditions of experience risks being overwhelmed by external powers. In this respect, traditional rituals at least acknowledge the powers which they attempt to ward off. Nevertheless, the ritual act of repetition – whether found in modern thought or traditional religion – tends to constitute its own image of the sacred through repetition. It directs attention to an image of its own creation. Then the practice of constituting the sacred may efface the sacred – hence the need for a 'murder of God'.

Similarly, faith or credit gives meaning to concrete historical experience by regarding future outcomes as a return on current investments. Attention becomes directed to present conduct and future outcome, ignoring all other demands. Such a focus for attention, as a principle of conduct, thus affirms the same conduct in others where honourable conduct leads to mutual benefit. It creates a closed order of society, however, where those who do not prosper are not to be trusted. Both ritual and historical piety, which constitute eternal essence and temporal existence respectively, may practice a violent exclusion, and may be changed by drawing attention to the suffering of the victim. While ritual piety pays insufficient attention to present experience, historical piety pays insufficient attention to the casualties of an eschatological limit.

Networks of interdependence, then, are experienced in the chaotic interval between a perfect past and a final future. Such networks are experienced outside the realm of order based on an eternal sacred, and outside the realm of justice instituted by temporal judgement. Reason, constructed from repetition and difference, order and justice, is unable to comprehend singular experience. Singular experience may give rise to thought of the absolute, however, in the revelation of its own potencies: the demand of suffering for attention, the power of attention to fulfil suffering, and awareness of potency. Critical piety finds its completion in potency, for the demand of suffering is that which produces repetition, while the fulfilment by attention is that which grants difference as a reward. Then awareness of potency may proceed through an immanent critique of repetition from the perspective of the demand of suffering, drawing attention to what is concealed within repetition. It may also proceed through an immanent critique of difference from the perspective of absolute faith, which grants attention to difference apart from reward. The consummation of critical piety comes in the form of awareness of potency, when a potency indicates, dramatizes and individuates itself. Such an awareness, such a rare experience, empowers attention no longer to focus simply on itself but to grant attention to what lies outside, to that which matters.

Such is the aim of philosophy.

Index

Abraham 189
absolute faith 13, 237–9
absolute, the 12, 202
abyss of freedom 111
accidental, the 90, 182
adequate idea 207–8
Adorno, Theodor 8, 10, 45, 108, 124n27, 211
affect 20–21, 78
affirmation 156, 162
Agamben, Giorgio 197n19, 234–5
Ages of the World, The 109, 112, 124n47
Alliez, Éric 128, 146n11, 146n5, 146n18
Althusser, Louis 96n12
Amos 189
ancestors 184
apocalyptic piety 193–5, 242
Arianism 54
Aristotle 30, 35, 90, 128, 136
Arius 67n50
Artaud, Antonin 168
ascetic ideal 25
Athanasius, Saint 54–5, 67n50, 67n51, 68n55
atheism 18–19, 26–7, 40n52, 231
attention 12, 123, 143–4, 210, 213–4
Augustine, Saint 68n55
Auschwitz 234–6
authority 217
awakening 242–3
awareness 13, 227–8, 238–42, 253

Bacon, Francis 45
Bank of England 31
Bataille, Georges 87–9, 121
becoming 20–21, 25, 78, 129
Being 20–1, 64, 117, 197n15, 243n1

belief 52–3, 85
Benoist, Jean-Marie 66
Benveniste, Émile 198n39
Bergson, Henri 11, 105–9, 124n43, 149, 156–7, 163, 170n8, 182, 183, 210, 211, 221n30, 223, 226, 244n6, 245n12
birth 209, 220n29
Bloch, Maurice 197n13
Bookchin, Murray 199n41
Bourdieu, Pierre 89–93, 188
Braudel, Fernand 41n67
Buber, Martin 38n5
Buddha 245n12
Burkert, Walter 180

Cantor, Gregor 147n21
capital 36, 43–4, 65, 104, 128–9; and time 133, 145; contrasted with piety 196; power of 144–5; religion of 83, 85, 249; self-propagation of 86
capitalism 81, 83–7, 247–8
capitalization 11, 80–1, 249, 250
chaos 182, 187, 192
chaotic interval 193–4
Christian doctrine 52–3, 64
Christianity 10, 19, 52–3, 74; critique of 25–6
Church, the 55–6
circular reasoning 2
class division 81–2, 136, 140, 143, 145
Climacus, Johannes 14n10, 119–20
coinage 30, 63, 85, 89
commerce 29
commodification 10, 107, 129
commodity abstraction 61–3, 94
commodity exchange 58–9, 61–2, 116
commodity fetishism 82–3, 118, 225, 249

commodity fiction 35
commodity form 11, 80–7
common emotions 78, 97n46, 251
common experience 252
common good 201
common notions 78, 97n46
commons, enclosure of 28
commonwealth 78–9, 196n2
conjunctive synthesis 244n5
conscience 26
consciousness 22
consensus reality 194, 200–1, 203, 229, 250
Constantine 53–4
Constantinople, Council of 55
contracts 139–40
contradiction 111–12, 125n70
creed 54, 56
critical theory 2, 6, 8, 44, 84
Cynic materialism 72
cynicism 48, 70

death 12, 148–55, 169, 251; and affirmation 121–2; as potency 166; as simulacrum 153–4; as singularity 208; beyond 168; experience of 152–5; postponement of 142; promise of 34; religion of 169, 177; screen of 145
death-wish 152, 169
debt 47, 103, 119
Deleuze, Gilles 12, 22, 86, 96n5, 98n66, 129, 130, 132, 146n12, 146n17, 147n21, 156–65, 168, 223, 231–2, 246n37
Delphic Oracle 51, 71
democracy 43, 217–19
Derrida, Jacques 11, 50, 67n37, 114–19, 121, 148–9, 150–1, 167, 170n17, 198n33
Descartes, René 40n38
desire 162, 164
despotism 10, 38, 43, 74
destiny 20
determination, insufficient 104
dialectic 112, 228–9
Dialectic of Enlightenment 8
Dickens, Charles 165
différance 116–7
difference 12, 13, 253; absolute 237
dim awareness 224, 226, 227
Diogenes Laertius 71, 96n5
Diogenes the Cynic 17, 71, 96n5
disjunctive synthesis 112, 209

domination 8, 69n79
Donatist schism 53
dramatization 240
Duns Scotus 124n27, 205–6, 208, 220n16, 232
Durkheim, Émile 182

economic crisis xi
economic growth 138
economic piety 189
economic reductionism xiv
economic rationality 28
economics 11, 46–7
economy: divine 187; good-faith 89, 188; of différance 116; tribute 139
Eliade, Mircea 180, 182–3, 186–7
emotion 77, 251
Empire 197n3
enclosure of the commons 28
England 28–9, 41n73
Enlightenment xiii, 8, 19, 25, 44–8, 51–2, 177; new 203
Enuma elish 187
environmental crisis ix-x, xiii, 148, 177
epistemology 210
eschatology 190
essence 12
eternal return 13, 230–7
eternal, the 12, 103, 110, 118, 163, 191–2, 249
ethical relation 162, 164, 239, 250
ethics 5–7, 11, 104; immanent 12, 156–65; of time 133; of transcendence 148–55
Ethics 77, 157
evaluation 23, 160, 251
evolution 18
exception 192, 209
exchange 10, 49–50, 65, 85, 115, 249, 250; logic of 11; power in 135–6
exchange-value 61–3, 80
exclusion 191, 192–3, 253
existence 12
existence of God 1, 5, 204–6, 222
expenditure 87–8, 95
experience 209–11, 223–4; categories of 241; common 252; limits of 247; mode of 210; of excluded 201; of God xii; religious 193–5; singular 12
exploitation 137, 138, 145
exteriority 128, 135, 218
extraction of surplus value 142–5

faith 186
faith, absolute 13
fantasy 143–4, 201
feminist theory 146n5
Feuerbach, Ludwig 68n55
financial management 141
finance capital 35–8, 136, 139–40, 247–8
final causes 75
flesh 12
Foucault, Michel 146n5, 197n19
Frank, Manfred 8
Frankfurt school 2, 8
free market 10
free will 10, 22–3, 77; as false problem 106
freedom 11, 104, 107, 124n27, 144, 167, 250; and time 108–13; and association 113
Freud, Sigmund 23, 151, 166
fulfilment of suffering 213
future profit 37–8, 142, 252

Gay Science, The 17
Gauchet, Marcel 4
gender 136
general economy 87, 99n96
geometry 60–1, 207
Gift, The 49
gift 49–50, 87, 92, 114–15, 184
gift, logic of 11, 114–15, 118–19
gift-exchange 90
Gilson, Étienne 67n52
Girard, René 180
global ecology xiii
global history xiii
global warming ix-x, 148
globalization x-xi, 177, 200, 247–8, 252
God 242–3; and faith 119; and public life 202; and thought 43; as unconditioned 205; Christian 19; concept of 13, 26–7, 222–3, 244n1; excess of 202; existence of 1, 204–5, 222; idea of 204; in eternal return 233–4; metaphysical 23; murder of xii, 3, 10, 17–18, 26–7, 29, 31, 73, 87, 103–4, 200, 223; sovereignty of 10, 52, 75; Spinoza's concept of 73, 75, 76, 77–8, 163
good-faith economy 89
Gorz, André 28
Gospel, the 52–3,

Goux, Jean-Joseph 66n28, 80–2, 98n66
government: reduction of xi
Greece, ancient 10, 58–60
Grof, Stanislav 155
Guattari, Félix 86, 147n21, 246n37

Haar, Michel 39n14
Hardt, Michael 197n3
Hayter, Teresa 147n25
Hebrew prophets 188–9
Heesterman, J. C. 126n120, 170n27
Hegel, Georg 26, 68n55
Heidegger, Martin 39n17, 61, 146n12, 149–50, 170n4, 170n8, 197n15, 243n1
Heim, Albert 153
Heraclitus 59
Hesiod 59
hierophany 185
historical materialism 66n28
historical piety 186–91, 242, 253
history 187–8
history of ideas 27
Hobbes, Thomas 32, 36, 37, 48, 107, 124n27, 177
Holy Spirit 55
honour 5–6, 87, 89, 92–4, 115, 177, 182, 188, 216
Hooker, Richard 32, 107
hoplites 60
Horkheimer, Max 8, 10, 45
Horwitz, Tem 152
householder 136–8, 142, 145, 251
Hubert, Henri 171n32
human nature 78
Hume, David 180
Husserl, Edmund 180

identity 178, 186
ideological circle 5
ideological strategies, 5–6
ideology 44, 54, 56, 57, 144; and philosophy 58; as foundation of economy 94
ideology critique 47–8, 74
illusions: of attention 216; transcendental 96n7, 166
imaginary causes 21–6, 33, 105
immanence 157, 159, 164–6
immanent cause 206, 231
immanent critique 9, 11, 13, 73, 76, 156
immanent ethics 12, 156–65; criteria of 161–2

indication 240
individuation 241
Industrial Revolution 32
Interpretation of Dreams, The 166
infinite, the 37, 206
information 45
insufficient determination 104
Intellectual and Manual Labour 61–4
integrity 188
intensity 208, 224–6
interest 120
interiority 130, 132, 134–5
interpellation 129
intuition 110, 229, 245n12
inward piety 192
inwardness 120
Irigaray, Luce 116–7
irreversibility 208–9

Job 14n9, 198n40
joy 161, 215–16
Juergensmeyer, Mark 178

Kant, Immanuel 3, 44–5, 65n4, 96n7,
    131–3, 146n11, 146n12, 158,
    203–5, 220n6, 231
Kierkegaard, Søren 11, 14n10, 103,
    119, 172n71, 191–2, 238
kingdom of God 53, 67n38
Klossowski, Pierre 230
knight of faith 172n71, 238, 246n38
knowledge: commodification of 10,
    44–5; morality of 22
Kolakowski, Leszek 1, 180
Kristeva, Julia 221n35

labour theory of value 83–4, 98n73
Lacan, Jacques 117, 126n99, 166–7
Law's system 41n69
laws of the market 137
Leibniz, Gottfried 4
Leeuw, Gerardus van der 194
Levi, Primo 235
Lévi-Strauss, Claude 48–51, 66n35, 90
Levinas, Emmanuel 38n5, 105, 109,
    150, 159, 167, 170n8
liberalism xiii
liberty 29, 32–3, 107, 210, 232, 248
life 165–6, 168, 182
life, nature and history 10, 18, 32–3,
    73, 156
Lindbeck, George 40n43
Locke, John 10, 30, 31, 32–7, 42n90,
    105, 107, 196n2

Logic of Practice, The 89, 93
Logos, the 55, 57
logos, philosophical 117
Lukács, Georg 44, 65n4, 68n63
Lyotard, Jean-François 38n11

Malebranche, Nicolas 40n38
Malinowski, Bronislaw 198n29
Mammon 27–8, 64, 169, 190
Mander, Jerry xiii
Manent, Pierre 29
marginal utility 136–7
market 11–12; and reason 10; laws of
    137; power in 36; self-regulating
    10, 29–30, 32, 36
market economy 30
market value 135–45
marks of the Church 55–6
Marion, Jean-Luc 244n3
Marx, Karl 11, 23, 41n70, 61, 64, 70,
    80–7, 94, 116, 118, 135
mason in Kabylia 93
material relations 10–11
materialism 12, 145, 159, 191, 211
Mauss, Marcel 48–9, 87, 89, 171n32
media 201
Memoirs of My Nervous Illness 202
mercantilism 40n66
metaphysics 24–5, 107, 118; critique of
    203–5; of production 84
Milbank, John 126n102
Mill, John Stuart 13n2
mode of experience 210
money 11, 30, 63–4, 79, 81, 116,
    146n15, 195; as measure of values
    xii; as virulent simulacrum 134;
    invention of 30, 35, 63, 128; logic
    of 127–8; 250–1; paper 10, 31–2;
    religion of 84–5
money fetishism 84
money form 80
monotheism 54, 190, 198n32
Montesquieu, Baron de 28–9
morality 8, 10, 18, 21–4, 158
murder of God xii, 3, 17–18, 26–7, 29,
    31, 38, 52, 73, 87, 95, 103–4,
    118, 200, 231, 241, 247, 252
myth 95, 182, 187
mythical thinking 8, 10, 45–6

nation state 177
necessity 151
networks of interdependence 73, 200,
    237–8, 253

Negri, Antonio 76, 79, 197n3
Nicea, Council of 53–4, 57
Nietzsche, Friedrich 3–4, 10, 17–27,
    33, 37, 44, 76, 103, 105, 106,
    156, 171n40, 180, 223, 230–7,
    245n18
nihilism 70, 82, 95
Nye, Andrea 68n59

Oedipus 158, 171n50
onto-theology 118
Otto, Rudolf 184, 194, 199n51
Our Mutual Friend 165
Pannenberg, Wolfhart 124n49
pantheism 77–8
paradox 103, 120
paralogism of pure reason 44–5, 49,
    180, 249
paralogisms of psychoanalysis 98n66
Parmenides 58, 61, 64, 197n15
Peirce, Charles Sanders 72
perception 226
philosophy 50–1; and commodity
    exchange 60–4; and death 161,
    164; and strangers 93; as disci-
    plining of attention 210; as
    ideology 58; contemporary chal-
    lenge for 65; emergence of 58;
    Greek 58–64, 90–1, 103; modern
    70–1; question of 9, 20, 50, 243
*Philosophy of Mythology and
    Revelation* 110
philosophy of religion 2–3, 7, 26, 64
Piaget, Jean 66n34
piety 1, 3–5, 12–13, 242–3, 248,
    251–2; and time 6; and material
    interests 74–5; and ritual 183,
    185; and suffering 213; and
    syntheses of time 191; apocalyptic
    193–5, 242; as condition of truth
    57; as foundation of economy and
    reason 94; defined 210; disinter-
    ested 3–4; economic 189; essence
    of 195–6; historical 186–91, 242;
    in language 22; inward 192;
    modern 249–50; of metaphysics
    19; price of 243; resurgent 202;
    ritual 181–6, 191, 242; tempo-
    rality of 7
Pitt, William 41n67
plane of immanence 159, 162, 164–5,
    195
Plato 13n3, 71, 99n108, 117
Platonic idealism 71–2

Platonism, reversal of 159
pleasure principle 169
pledge 216
Plotinus 131–3, 146n7, 146n11,
    147n18, 211
Plumwood, Val 69n79
Polanyi, Karl 35
politics 13, 214–19
Political Treatise 79
Politics 30
post-modernism 38n11, 119
Postone, Moishe 98n73
poststructuralism xiii
postulate of equality in exchange 62–3
potencies of time 111–2, 123
potency 12, 13, 166, 169, 192, 224,
    229, 251; as unconditioned 214;
    awareness of 239–42, 253; of
    awareness 227; of religious expe-
    rience 194; of thought 13, 166,
    243
potlatch 87
power 65, 107, 144; divine 77
price 11, 62–4, 79; of piety 243; of
    thought 70–1, 73
production, as metaphysics 84
property 32, 34, 139–40, 216–7
Pseudo-Dionysius 14n12
psychoanalysis 221n35
psychosis 193, 202
public sphere 9, 14n19, 251

quantitative simulation, triangle of 141

reason: and market 10, 106, 250; as
    domination 8, 45, 69n79; as sacri-
    fice 95; circular 2, 5, 249; critique
    of 14n16, 17–21, 25–6; economy
    of 114–19; eternity of 1–2;
    European 8–9, 11, 94, 118–19;
    historical conditioning of 2;
    history of 110; honour of 95;
    modern 248–9, 251; piety of 204,
    249; search for 1; secular 2
reform 193
Reformation 27, 88
reification 44, 46
religion 4, 10, 133, 178–81; as excess
    179; as sacrifice 179; critique of
    19, 21–6; defined 227; institu-
    tional 219; of money 84–5;
    resurgent 178; static 183; struc-
    turalist theory of 50; theories of
    179–80

repetition 2, 6, 10, 12, 13, 46, 181, 236, 249, 250, 253; and immanence 162; and sacrifice 154; and truth 51–2, 65
representation 45, 106, 118, 129, 158, 218, 225
responsibility 11, 43, 104, 114
revelation 6–7, 14n12, 55, 198n34
revenge 22
revolution 178
reward 3–4, 23–4, 76, 189
right 32–3, 43, 214–16, 248
ritual 95, 181–6
ritual piety 191, 242, 253
Ruyer, Raymond 123n2, 241

sacred 154–5, 182–6, 253
sacrifice 88–9, 91, 95, 121–2, 154, 170n27, 179, 184, 190
Salomé, Lou 235
Schelling, Friedrich 11, 109–14, 132, 197n17, 207, 220n25, 223, 229
Schreber, Daniel Paul 202
science, faith in 18
self-survey 241
semiotic square 224–5
semiotic triangle 72–3
Sextus Empiricus 13n2
shares 140
signifier 50, 116; transcendental 249
Simmel, Georg 93, 149
Simondon, Gilbert 241
simulacrum 127, 129, 164
singularity 194, 208–9, 213, 238
slave trade 31
slavery 33–4, 36, 37
Sloterdijk, Peter 48, 211
Smith, Jonathan Z. 198n31
Socrates 99n108
Sohn-Rethel, Alfred 61–4
Solon 91
Sophist, The 99n108
sovereignty 34, 37, 57, 86, 107, 155; ancient Greek 59; and land 60; Spinoza's critique of 74
sovereignty, of God 10, 54–5
speculation 12
speculator 136–8, 142, 145, 251
Spinoza, Benedict de 11, 13, 73–9, 96n7, 109, 155, 156–7, 163, 172, 173n94, 193, 206–8, 214, 223, 233
spirit 24, 112–3, 191–2
Spirit of Laws 28–9
State, the 31–2

state of nature 34, 48, 177
structuralism 48–51, 66n25, 66n28, 66n35
subsistence 36, 136, 177
suchness 238
suffering 186–7, 211–14, 230, 239–40
suffering, truth of xii
supernatural 188
superposition 106
surplus value 86, 142–5
suspicion 4, 7, 93–4, 119
Swedenborg, Emmanuel 203
symbolic capital 91
symbolic order 115–6
symbolization 50; logic of 80, 116–18

tautology 180
Taylor, Mark C. 68n55
temporal, the 12, 191–2, 249
tendency 124n43
terrorism 178
theodicy 4–5, 212
Theognis 60
thinking 7, 19–20; as mechanical process 28, 46; ethics of 11, 105, 109, 119–20, 165, 250–1; temporal 11
thisness 238
Thomas Aquinas, Saint 5, 206
Thomson, George 58–9
Thus Spoke Zarathustra 19
Timaeus 13n3
time 11, 105; and death 150; and evaluation 130–1; and money 134–5; and piety 6; concept of 130–3, 146n12, 149–50; 191; ethics of 133; homogeneous 63; logic of 122; synthesis of 108, 112–13, 122, 149, 232
title 217
Torrance, Robert M. 197n27
traditional religions 198n31
transcendence 5–6, 10, 37, 50, 166, 249; in reason 23; loss of 9; new 133
transcendent pivot 4, 24–5, 249
transcendental illusion 96n7, 166
transcendental method 96n7, 204
trauma 12, 166, 169
tribute economy 139
Trinitarian theology 58, 244n1, 244n2
Trinity, the 55
trust 94
truth 10, 44–5, 47–8, 51, 249; and repetition 51–2; as paradox

120–1; as surplus 200; credal
    model of 56; Spinoza's concept of
    76–7
Truth 228
Two Treatises of Government 32,
    41n74

Ubermensch 245n28
unconditioned within experience 211,
    213, 223–4
unconscious 159, 160; of freedom 111;
    of thought 157; structural 49, 51
underdevelopment 139
unthinkable, the 21, 23, 162, 164, 196,
    207, 223
use-value 62

value 11, 62–3, 117, 142, 144, 249
value of values 19, 127–8, 156

Vernant, Jean-Pierre 59–61
violence 12; and religion 179–80, 253;
    and monotheism 190–1; originary
    117; 185–6
virulent simulacra 11, 134–5

wealth 30, 35, 139, 142–4
Western thought: questioning of xii,
    7–9
Whitehead, Alfred North 179
will 109–10, 124n47; critique of 22–4
will to power 19, 171n40
will to truth 18–19, 103
Williams, Rowan 67n50, 67n41
wisdom 71–2

Zarathustra 19, 245n28
Zeno's tortoise 153
Žižek, Slavoj 58, 85, 110, 125n69